D1571248

CAREER DEVELOPMENT AND VOCATIONAL BEHAVIOR OF RACIAL AND ETHNIC MINORITIES

VOCATIONAL PSYCHOLOGY

Samuel H. Osipow, Series Editor

CAREER DEVELOPMENT AND VOCATIONAL BEHAVIOR OF RACIAL AND ETHNIC MINORITIES

Frederick T. L. Leong, Editor
The Ohio State University

LEA , LAWRENCE ERLBAUM ASSOCIATES, PUBLISHERS
1995   Mahwah, New Jersey   Hove, UK

Lawrence Erlbaum Associates, Inc., Publishers
10 Industrial Avenue
Mahwah, New Jersey 07430

Library of Congress Cataloging-in-Publication Data

Career development and vocational behavior of racial and ethnic
  minorities / Frederick T. L. Leong, editor.
     p.   cm.
  Includes bibliographical references and indexes.
  ISBN 0-8058-1303-9 (alk. paper)
    1. Career development—Social aspects—United States.
  2. Minorities—Employment—United States.   3. Social values—United
States.   4. Needs assessment—United States.   5. Psychology,
Industrial—United States.   I. Leong, Frederick T. L.
  HF5549.5.C35C363   1995
  331.7′02′089—dc20   95-21576
                                                             CIP

Books published by Lawrence Erlbaum Associates are printed on acid-free
paper, and their bindings are chosen for strength and durability.

Printed in the United States of America
10 9 8 7 6 5 4 3 2 1

To Sandy, Kate, and Sarah
For all the Love, Support and Joy.

Contents

PART II: ASSESSMENT AND INTERVENTION

PART III: FUTURE DIRECTIONS

Foreword

You are probably wondering how much time you should invest in reading this book. Good question. You are asking the right person because I have read the entire book and can give you some frank advice about how to proceed.

One advantage of this book is that each chapter is self-contained. No chapter is a prerequisite to any other. You can start anywhere in this book and get some meaty information on a topic of your choice.

Where you begin depends on what you want to know. If you have just a short time and need a snapshot of the multicultural issues to which counselors should be sensitive, read Chapter 11 by Betz and Fitzgerald. They summarized the key findings beautifully. You might even want to read that chapter twice to make sure you did not miss something.

Now your curiosity will be aroused. On what basis can they justify the generalizations about ethnic groups? What is the source of that information? You may now want to delve more deeply into the information about specific cultural groups. The organization of the book makes it easy to do so. If you are primarily interested in the counseling of African Americans, then Chapter 2 by Brown and Chapter 6 by Bowman will inform you. Chapters 3 and 7 by Arbona and Fouad, respectively, will provide some insights about the Hispanic-American cultures. If your special interest is Asian Americans, concentrate on Chapter 4 by Leong and Serafica and Chapter 8 by Leong and Gim. You will be enlightened in Chapter 5 by Johnson, Swartz, and Martin and Chapter 9 by Martin if you read their accounts of career counseling with American-Indian populations.

Perhaps you are a researcher wondering what urgent research questions need attention. Chapters 2, 3, 4, and 5 will be particularly helpful. Many unanswered questions are posed in these chapters. Researchers will find a wealth of ideas to inspire future research proposals.

Practicing counselors work with a variety of populations. Chapters 6, 7, 8, and 9 focus on assessment tools and interventions that address individual needs within the four cultural groups. Perhaps the most complex dilemma facing practicing counselors is how to be sensitive to the cultural heritage of various groups while responding to each individual's unique perspective. Teaching counselors about group differences introduces the risk of stereotyping. Each of the authors addressed the issue of within-group variability. Some of this variability is due to the fact that each of these four major groups consists of numerous subgroups. And, of course, each person within each subgroup has a somewhat different view of the world than each other person.

In counseling we usually deal with just one individual at a time. Does that one person now sitting in my office share the stereotypical view of the world characteristic of his or her ethnic group and/or gender? There is no way to know at first. Asking outright would be patronizing and insulting. The best course of action is to honor each individual's uniqueness. You may ask, however, "Why then do we need to know anything about group characteristics?" There are some enlightening answers suggested in this book. Knowing about cultural norms and values sensitizes us to potential client perspectives and helps us to appreciate the complexities that exist for each individual. For example, an Asian-American male who is contemplating a career choice that will displease his parents may be experiencing different stressors than a white Anglo male with the same problem, although we cannot be sure. Our sensitivity to the potential etiology of these stressors keeps us in better tune with the client.

The theoretical chapters look at how traditional career development theories apply to minority populations. The authors criticize these theories for ignoring cultural differences. However, Martin in Chapter 9 states that social learning theory is probably the least biased in this regard. I would agree (of course) because social learning theory incorporates cultural, political, economic, and environmental variables to explain why certain kinds of learning are either facilitated or inhibited. It also specifically recognizes genetic determinants such as race and gender. Theories of career counseling need strengthening, as Osipow and Littlejohn point out in Chapter 10. One major need is to identify facilitative interventions that accommodate different cultural styles of communication and behavior. One suggestion, for example, is that group counseling may be better suited to African-American than to Asian-American clients.

Differences in cultural values and behavior pose major problems for clients who were raised in one tradition but must work in another. Assertiveness, for example, is demanded for success in the dominant American culture, but it is often deemed inappropriate in many Asian and Native-American groups. What is the resolution of this for, say, an Asian-American client who wants to succeed in American business? The solution suggested by several authors in this book (and others referenced in this book) is bicultural competence. In essence, help the client to recognize that a person may apply one set of norms and behaviors in one setting (business, for example) and another set of norms and behaviors at home. There is nothing inherently unethical or schizophrenic about applying different standards. Bicultural competence involves learning how to "work within the system" to make the existing structure serve the client's needs.

Excellent writing and Frederick Leong's fine editing have produced a book that is easy to read and packed full of information. I enjoyed reading it. I learned from it. I invite you to learn from it too.

John D. Krumboltz
Stanford University

Introduction and Overview

Frederick T. L. Leong
The Ohio State University

During the last decade, there has been growing recognition of the increasing cultural diversity of the population and the workforce in the United States. With this recognition of the changing U.S. demography has come an increasing number of publications devoted to improving our understanding of racial and ethnic minorities in the workforce (see Jackson & Associates, 1992; and Triandis, Kurowski, & Gelfand, 1994, for two recent examples). The current book is an addition to this burgeoning collection, but from a perspective embedded in the field of counseling psychology. In 1991, I served as the Guest Editor of a special issue of the *Career Development Quarterly*, which focused on the Career Development of Racial and Ethnic Minorities. An excerpt from my Guest Editorial (Leong, 1991) for that special issue provides a context for the need of the current book:

> As we begin the last decade of the twentieth century, there has been much discussion about major changes in the composition of the workforce in this country. One of these changes involve the increasing cultural diversity of the human resources that underlie our organizational systems. The often quoted Hudson Institute report on *Workforce 2000* has identified several major trends for the United States workforce in the year 2000 (Johnson, 1987). First, growth in the population and the workforce will proceed more slowly than in the past half century. Second, the population and the workforce will both be older, while the pool of young workers will become smaller. Actually, there will be more middle-aged workers in the workforce

1

in the year 2000. Third, women will continue to enter the workforce in significant numbers. For example, the female share of the workforce will increase from 42.5% in 1980 to 47.5% in 2000, while the number of females working will grow from 51.5% in 1980 to 61.1% in 2000. The increase in the number of women participating in the workforce from 1986 to 2000 will be 25% while the increase for men will be only 11.8%. Fourth, there will be more minority persons in the workforce with an increase of 13.6% in 1980 to 15.5% in 2000. From 1986 to 2000, the number of White workers will increase 14.6%, while the number of Black workers will increase 28.8%, Hispanic workers 74%, and Asian workers 11.6%. Finally, there will also be more immigrants in our workforce. All of these changes will result in a significantly more diverse workforce in the United States; only 15% of the new entrants into the workforce between 1985–2000 being native White males, and 42% being native White female, 20% native minorities, and 22% immigrants.

As researchers and organizational leaders have begun to discuss the strategic implications of these changes (e.g., Morrison & Von Glinow, 1990), more and more career counselors and vocational psychologists are also considering the manner in which they need to prepare themselves to meet the upcoming challenges of increasing cultural diversity (e.g., McDaniels, 1989). This special issue of the *Quarterly* has been produced as one step in the process of preparing career counselors for working with culturally different clients, particularly racial and ethnic minority persons.

The special issue of the *Career Development Quarterly* was only able to capture a small slice of the knowledge base that has been accumulated on the career development of ethnic minorities. As a second step, the current book was proposed and readily accepted for publication by Lawrence Erlbaum Associates in their Vocational Psychology series. I was fortunate to be able to assemble a team of leading scholars and researchers to contribute to this project, and this book is the product of their expertise. More detailed information about the background of the contributors are presented elsewhere in this volume.

The primary purpose of the book is to serve as a resource to (a) graduate students, who are learning about career development and career counseling; (b) counselors and psychologists, who provide career counseling to racial and ethnic minorities; and (c) psychologists and counselors who do research on the career development of these diverse groups. At present, it serves as a single most comprehensive source of the knowledge on the career development of racial and ethnic minorities.

In recognition of the value of both culture-specific and culture-general information about the vocational psychology of racial and ethnic minorities in the United States, the book has been given a dual focus. After the Introduction, the first eight chapters are devoted to culture-specific information about the career development and vocational behavior of racial and ethnic minorities. The last two chapters are devoted to a synthesis and integration of the materials presented in the eight culture-specific chapters. In addition, given the focus of the book on both theory and practice, the text has been divided into three sections. The first section, which focuses on "Career Theory and Research with Racial and Ethnic Minorities," consists of a review of the relevance and utility of various career theories and models from mainstream vocational psychology to our understanding of the vocational behavior and career development of racial and ethnic minorities. These chapters also summarize other theories from ethnic minority psychology that add to our understanding of the career development of racial and ethnic minoriries (e.g., the role of African-American racial identity on career development of African Americans).

Finally, the chapters also review the existing empirical literature on the career development of these groups and provide a critique of this literature with recommendations for future research. In this section, a separate chapter covers each of the major racial and ethnic group in the United States, namely, African Americans (Brown), Hispanic Americans (Arbona), Asian Americans (Leong and Serafica), and Native Americans (Johnson, Swartz, and Martin). Although these chapters are targeted primarily at researchers, we also believe that the reviews of the theories, research, and conceptual frameworks will be of interest to practitioners and will serve as a valuable foundation for guiding their interventions.

The second section also consists of four chapters, one on each of the same racial and ethnic groups, namely, African Americans (Bowman), Hispanic Americans (Fouad), Asian Americans (Leong and Gin) and Native Americans (Martin). This section focuses on "Assessment and Interventions with Racial and Ethnic Minorities." The authors discuss the problems and issues involved in career assessment with these groups. The inclusion of the assessment dimension is very important because assessment is such a large and significant component of the career counseling process. The authors also present guidelines and recommendations in providing career interventions with the racial and ethnic minorities. In providing these guidelines, the authors also discuss some of the cultural factors unique to each group that may serve as either facilitators or inhibitors in the career counseling process.

The third and final section consists of commentaries, suggestions, reactions, and syntheses of the previous sections from scholars in the field of vocational psychology. These authors identify and discuss the common principles, problems, and themes running across the chapters as well as provide suggestions for advancing the field of racial and ethnic minority vocational psychology. A discussion of the theory and research chapters in the first section is provided by Samuel Osipow and Eugia Littlejohn. A discussion of the assessment and intervention chapters in the second section is provided by Nancy Betz and Louise Fitzgerald.

It is the hope of the editor and contributors of this volume that this book will become both a valuable source of current information about the vocational psychology of racial and ethnic minorities as well as an inspiration for future research into the career development and vocational behavior of these culturally different individuals.

REFERENCES

Leong, F. T. L. (1991). Guest Editor's Introduction. Career development of racial and ethnic minorities [Special issue]. *Career Development Quarterly, 39,* 196–198.

Jackson, S. E., & Associates. (1992). *Diversity in the workplace: Human resources initiatives.* New York: Guilford Press.

Triandis, H. C., Kurowski, L. L., & Gelfand, M. J. (1994). Workplace diversity. In H. C. Triandis, M. D. Dunnette, & L. M. Hough (Eds.), *Handbook of industrial and organizational psychology* (Vol. 4, 2nd ed., pp. 769–827). Palo Alto: Consulting Psychologists Press.

I

THEORY AND RESEARCH

The Career Development of African Americans: Theoretical and Empirical Issues

Michael T. Brown
The University of California, Santa Barbara

The career development of the country's almost 30 million African Americans needs urgent attention. They are the largest ethnic group in the United States after Whites, representing 12.1% of the population, but 1990 census data indicate that their poverty rate is about 31.9% and has fluctuated between 30% and 36% since 1970; in contrast, the rate for the nation is about 13.5%, fluctuating from only 8.7% to 12% during the same period (cf. Swinton, 1992). Census data also show that the average family income for African Americans has been about 58% of White family income in recent years.

The unemployment rate for African Americans has been above 11% each year since 1978 and has run about 2.5 times the rate for Whites for the last two decades (Swinton, 1992). Among teenagers, African Americans had an unemployment rate above 36% in 1990, whereas Whites had a rate less than half of this.

Swinton (1992) concluded that African Americans are disadvantaged not only economically, but also occupationally. Swinton observed that only 36.9% of African-American men, but 61.8% of White men were employed in the "good" jobs (i.e., executives, administrators, managers, and sales occupations) in 1990, whereas 45.2% of African-American men and only 23.9% of White men were employed in the "bad" jobs (i.e., administrative support, laborers, other service workers, and transportation and material movers occupations). Similarly, African-American women were less likely to be employed in "good" jobs than were White women; the relative percentages were 28.1 versus 40.8, respectively. Furthermore, African-American women were more likely to be employed in "bad" jobs than were White women; the respective percentages were 37.3 and 22.9.

Education has historically been viewed as the ticket to a better life, especially for African Americans. But McBay (1992) pointed out that most African-American children remain in de facto separated and unequal schools. Further, due to the insidious nature of poverty, McBay estimated that as many as half of all African-American children may not be prepared for the academic environment when they enter school. African-American educational attainment also continues to lag behind that of almost all other racial and ethnic groups, as reported in the 10th annual status report of *Minorities in Higher Education* (Carter & Wilson, 1992), published annually by the American Council on Education. Data show that African Americans have made some gains in college participation since 1985, but have not reduced the margin of difference between their rate and that of Whites (Carter & Wilson, 1992). Especially noteworthy is that the ratio of African-American earnings to White earnings, given comparable levels of education, is 87.9% for men and 92.53% for females, with the racial gap decreasing with increasing educational levels.

Importantly, the proportion of men in total African-American enrollment has consistently declined over the decade. In addition, Carter and Wilson (1992) reported that those few gains made in the number of African Americans awarded bachelor's and master's degrees in 1991 were made by African-American women. Given the economic and social status of African Americans, Jaynes and Williams (1989), of the National Research Council, concluded that, by almost all aggregate statistical measures, African Americans remain substantially behind Whites. Those data also caused Hacker (1992) to observe that two nations exist in the United States: one African American, the other White. He further observed that these nations were separate, unequal, and hostile to one another. Clearly there is a need to direct the attention of psychologists to the economic and social needs of African Americans.

Facilitating the career development of African Americans may be one key to their economic, social, and psychological emancipation. John E. Jacob (1992), President and Chief Executive Officer of the National Urban League, reported that because African Americans are plagued by various forms of discrimination, opportunities for upward mobility, currently reduced for all persons, are even more limited for them. Citing Gallup survey results, Wilson and Brown (1992) reported that African Americans were three times as likely as Whites to express a need for career development assistance. Yet, as others (e.g., Brooks, 1990; Greenhaus & Parasuraman, 1986; London & Greller, 1991) indicated, little is known about the career behavior of African Americans, and meaningful research in the area has essentially halted since the late 1970s.

The purpose of this chapter is to review the current theoretical and empirical state of affairs as it pertains to the career development of African Americans and, if possible, to stimulate and advance such scholarship. Initially, an attempt was made to provide readers with an exhaustive review of the empirical literature appearing since Smith's (1975, 1983) reviews of the literature. However, it became clear that the large and disorganized nature of literature warranted the sacrifice of breadth to gain parsimony and clarity; the intent being to focus current understanding and to best direct future scholarly endeavors.

What follows is a review of some of the major and most influential theories of career development including an articulation of its relevance or lack thereof with African-American populations. Also included in the review are relevant empirical findings supporting or disconfirming the applicability of the various theories to African Americans. A general review of the extant empirical literature concerning the career development of African Americans is then presented followed by a summary to the most clear, striking, or relevant findings. Finally, a discussion of future theoretical and empirical directions is presented. It should be noted that, due to space limitations, the career choice literature is the main focus of this chapter.

THEORIES OF CAREER CHOICE

Theories of career choice have been frequently criticized for their lack of relevance to the career behavior of ethnic minorities, particularly African Americans (Brooks, 1990; Carter & Cook, 1992; Cheatham, 1990; Leonard, 1985; LoCascio, 1967; Osipow, 1983; Smith, 1975, 1983; Warnath, 1975). These criticisms center on three main points (cf. Brooks, 1990): They are based on erroneous assumptions, the theoretical concepts are not applicable to the various ethnic groups, and important determinants of career behavior are not addressed in the theories.

As many of the critics have stated (see Leonard, 1985; Smith, 1983), most theories of career choice assume that there is dignity in all work, that work is central to the lives of all individuals, that there exists a free and open labor market, and that most career choices flow essentially from the character of one's personality. Some of these assumptions are questionable, in general, but particularly so when considered from the perspective of most ethnic minorities. For example, a cursory examination of occupational prestige data reveals that some jobs are more prized than others (e.g., see Featherman & Hauser, 1976). Also, the assumption of a free and open labor market discounts or ignores the fact of various forms of unjust discrimination, including colorism and ethnic bias.

As acknowledged by various theorists, most theories of career development were developed from research on primarily White, middle-class males; for example, one may wish to consider Super's (1953) Middletown study or Roe's (1951a, 1951b) studies of eminent scientists. The observation has led some (e.g., Carter & Cook, 1992; Cheatham, 1990; Smith, 1975, 1983; Warnath, 1975) to conclude that existing theoretical concepts lack applicability to ethnic minorities. However, later I show that such a conclusion may be premature given the paucity and inadequacy of research putting those concepts drawn from the theories to empirical tests using ethnic minority populations. It is more reasonable to assert that many concepts that have or may have relevance to the career development of ethnic minorities have been excluded from the most common or frequently cited theories, such as racial/ethnic discrimination or colorism.

What follows is a review of the most major and influential theories or models of career choice currently available as well as a review of relevant research on African Americans that supports or refutes theoretical claims. Also presented is an analysis of what might be missing from those theories that could render them more useful for understanding the career behavior of African Americans. An attempt is made to present alternative models or conceptions that may have particular impact on our understanding of African-American career development. For the purposes of this discussion, the following theories were selected: trait and factor theory (as reviewed by Brown, 1990), Roe's theory (as revised in Roe & Lunneborg, 1990), Holland's (1985) theory, and Super's (1990) theory. Also included is Hackett and Betz's (1981) career self-efficacy theory, Cheatham's (1990) model of Africentricity and career development, and discussions of the concepts of colorism and racial/cultural identity, as these appear to be rich sources of new career development constructs.

Trait and Factor Theory

According to Brown (1990), the essence of the trait and factor theory lies in the following four propositions: Each individual has a unique set of traits that can be reliably and validly measured; occupations require that individuals possess specific traits to be successful; it is possible and desirable to match a person's unique set of traits to those required by occupations; the closer the match between personal characteristics and those required by an occupation, the greater the likelihood of satisfaction with and productivity and tenure in the occupation. Brown stated that the theory is as applicable to minorities as it is to White males. However, no specific test of these propositions, using African-American populations, were uncovered in this review.

Several problems are associated with the propositions that appear to limit the extent to which the theory may be useful in understanding African-American career development. For example, given the general controversy regarding the psychological testing of African Americans and other ethnic minorities (cf. Anastasi, 1982), particularly as it pertains to ability testing (cf. Franklin, 1991; Guthrie, 1976; Helms, 1992; White, 1984), the trait–factor proposition concerning reliable and valid measurement of traits remains a prominent issue as pertains to these persons. But perhaps a greater problem with the measurement proposition is that, because of an inadequate understanding of the diverse life experiences of African Americans, an untapped domain of potential factors salient to the career behavior of these persons has been inadequately defined, operationalized, and investigated.

Regarding the proposition that occupations require a person to possess certain traits in order to be successful in it, the assumption may hold for both African Americans and Whites, but research has not addressed whether both groups are required by occupations to have the same or different sets of traits. Recently, however, Edwards and Polite (1992) developed a profile of successful African Americans based on their research that includes elements likely to be similar to Whites, like faith and personal responsibility, and others that are likely to be different, like transcendence of a racial-victim perspective and managing others' racial perceptions and reactions; however, this work is in need of cross-validation and extension.

The trait–factor assertion that it is possible and desirable to match individual characteristics to those required by an occupation assumes that the most important or relevant traits or factors regarding African-American career success are reliably and validly measured. But if the requirements for success are different for African Americans, a question arises as to whether that difference is justifiable, legal, and measurable.

The last trait–factor proposition is that, the closer the match between individual traits and those traits required by the occupation, the greater the likelihood of individual success. This issue has yet to be explored with African Americans. The characteristics most relevant to African-American career success, aside from the pioneering work of Edwards and Polite (1992), have yet to be identified, measured, and cross-validated. It is well known, however, that psychological measures account for 36% of the variance in performance ratings, at best (Brown, 1990); consequently, 64% of that variance must be accountable by other factors. A number of important questions arise: Might factors like those identified by Edwards and Polite account for the unexplained portion of performance rating variance? Are there racial/ethnic differences in those success factors? If so, what are the implications of those differences, particularly for African Americans?

The preceding discussion notwithstanding, it may be premature to dismiss the trait and factor theory as irrelevant to the career behavior of

African Americans, given the paucity of well-controlled, well-designed research testing the validity of trait–factor notions to the career behavior of African Americans. However, given that many of the propositions appear untenable, Brown's (1990) conclusion that the theory is likely to apply equally well to African Americans and other ethnic minorities seems premature at best, most likely misleading, and unwarranted, at worst.

Roe's Theory

There are two major contributions Roe (1956; Roe & Lunneborg, 1990) made to the career development literature: a psychologically based classification system of occupations and a theory of how personality development affects occupational choice. Regarding the classification system, Roe proposed that occupations can be ordered both along a continuum based on the intensity and nature of the interpersonal relationships involved in them and hierarchically on the basis of the degree of responsibility, capacity, and skill involved in each occupation. No specific test of Roe's structure of occupations with African-American populations could be located. Roe and Lunneborg (1990) indicated, however, that the classification system does not address "minority issues" (p. 80). Those minority issues were not specified, but it is clear that Roe's occupational categories, as well as other currently available classification systems, fail to consider the overrepresentation of African Americans in low-level service and laborer fields (Gottfredson, 1978a; Swinton, 1992; U.S. Department of Labor, 1991), and that the structure of occupations, not unlike the structure of occupational opportunity, may be very different for African Americans.

As pertains to the theory of personality and occupational choice, Roe proposed that genetic endowments combine with family background and childrearing experiences to shape individual need structures that, in turn, affect the level and kind of occupation chosen and pursued. In discussing the impact of race on occupational choice and opportunity, Roe suggested social, and not physical, differences might account for ethnic differences in career choice behavior (see June & Pringle, 1977; Roe, 1956). More recently (see Roe & Lunneborg, 1990), Roe articulated a formula that includes race within the constellation of factors classified as background factors. She (Roe & Lunenborg, 1990) stated that: "belonging to a minority group may be a heavily weighted aspect" (p. 88), with the determining issue being the extent to which a minority group member's background differs from the majority. Nonetheless, no specific test of Roe's formula with African-American populations could be located. Some questions need to be answered before it is known to what extent Roe's propositions have relevance to understanding the career behavior of African Americans. For example, can the experience of racial/ethnic discrimination be measured and related to vocational needs and career choice behavior? If so, what is the relationship between the experience of racial/ethnic discrimination and occupational need structure?

After examining available findings, Roe and Lunneborg (1990) concluded that there appears to be no direct link between parent–child relations and occupational choice, although Roe never postulated such a relationship. Nonetheless, it is generally concluded that occupations are distinguishable on the basis of their need-satisfying properties (cf. Dawis & Lofquist, 1984; Osipow, 1983), just as Roe posited, but no extensive study of the relationship between needs and occupational choice for African Americans exists.

There are some other conceptual issues concerning Roe's theory that also need exploration. Roe has stated that genetic inheritance sets limits on all characteristics but, especially, intellectual abilities and temperament. The long controversy surrounding ability testing (cf. Anastasi, 1982; Gottfredson & Scharf, 1988; Helms, 1992) shows that it remains unclear as to what extent racial differences are prevalent in measured abilities, particularly given the confounding of socioeconomic status in racial/ethnic comparison studies. It is also unclear as to what degree other abilities such as those identified by Edwards and Polite (1992) affect occupational choice and advancement, particularly for African Americans. Future studies could examine the extent to which these skills, relative to "intelligence," might be as important or more so to the occupational behavior of African Americans.

Super's Theory

Super (1990) proposed that the self-concept determines occupational choices and that both the self-concept and the manner in which it is implemented vary as a function of stage of development. However, many scholars contend that discrimination and poverty are more important determinants of African-American career choices than the self-concept, but offer little more than anecdotal data to support their assertions (cf. Carter & Cook, 1992; Osipow, 1975; Smith, 1983). Countering their criticism, Super (1990) cited the research of Kidd (1984) and Salomone and Slaney (1978) supporting the role of the self-concept in the occupational choices of the economically disadvantaged. Notwithstanding, the relationship between the self-concept and career behavior has yet to be systematically investigated with African-American populations.

Super (1990) argued that socioeconomic status (SES) probably has a twofold effect on career development: opening/closing career opportunities and shaping occupational and self-concepts (p. 229). Similarly, it may be that the experience of racial/ethnic discrimination may not just restrict ranges and types of opportunity, as most authors commonly assert, but also shape occupational and self-concepts. However, the role of SES and discrimination on occupational/self-concepts have yet to be investigated. In addition, Super observed (Super & Bohn, 1970) that racial discrimination appears to operate the same way as do SES handicaps by motivating some people to overcome them, deterring others from trying, and preventing others who try from achieving (cf. June & Pringle, 1977). However, he failed to articulate the developmental antecedents that might account for these three patterns of occupational behavior.

Super's assertions that definable stages of career development exist and that how the self-concept is implemented varies as a function of stage of development are ideas that have not been validated with African-American populations. Previous research, whereas confounding race and SES, generally indicates that lower socioeconomic African-American youth, relative to Whites, evidence lower vocational maturity, which is the degree to which the developmental tasks of various stages of career development are accomplished (see Smith, 1975, for a review). But it is unclear as to what accounts for the observed differences in measured vocational maturity. Taking a step in this direction, Smith (1976) reported that African-American career maturity scores were positively related to their views of the opportunity structure in America.

The career maturity concept has also been criticized because it is correlated with SES, and, because most African Americans occupy the lower socioeconomic strata, the concept may also be racially/ethnically biased (cf. Smith, 1975, 1983). Smith (1983) maintained further that current career maturity research erroneously assumes that career maturity inventories measure vocational tasks common to all races or ethnic groups. Smith proposed that a person's minority status may add additional tasks not currently taken into account, such as coming to terms with how race may affect their career development and developing appropriate coping strategies (see also the work of Edwards & Polite, 1992). The concept of career maturity, then, may need to be revised for African Americans.

It is unknown whether differences in the nature of the African-American self-concept and in the manner of its vocational implementation occur over time in the manner posited by Super. This is a much needed area of research. It should be noted that as early as 1975, Osipow argued that Super's stages do not appear to fit the career reality of poor African-American males (e.g., early labor force entry, series of unrelated jobs, sporadic periods of unemployment), suggesting that occupational entry appears to be a reactive rather than a proactive process as Super assumed (Osipow, 1975).

Holland's Theory

Holland (1985) proposed that personalities and work environments can be characterized by their resemblance to six types: realistic, investigative, artistic, social, enterprising, and conventional. Central to his theory is the assertion that people seek work environments that allow them to express the character of their personalities. Holland posited that a range of "isms" (i.e., ageism, classism, racism, sexism) restrict the range of career options available to people and that if persons are blocked from pursuing the expression of the most dominant aspects of their personalities, they will pursue the next most dominant feature. However, Holland failed to articulate what the long-term implications of experiencing restricted options might have on the development of work personalities; such is the historic experience of many African Americans.

One of the major predictions from Holland's theory is that people in different occupations, classified according to Holland's typological system, should also evidence different patterns of interests. A number of studies have demonstrated support for this assertion for African Americans (see Bingham & Walsh, 1978; O'Brien & Walsh, 1976; Sheffey, Bingham, & Walsh, 1986; Walsh, Hildebrand, Ward, & Matthews, 1983; Ward & Walsh, 1981).

Regarding personality orientation research, Miller, Springer, and Wells (1988) found that most of their African-American respondents recorded Holland Social type as their highest or next highest personality type. Relatedly, Gottfredson (1978a) reported that realistic and social jobs surfaced as the most frequent source of jobs for African Americans, the latter being a particular source of high-level jobs. The findings of Miller et al. and Gottfredson are also mirrored in the findings of Arbona (1989). But, whereas a large proportion of all workers engage in enterprising work, African Americans were most poorly represented in this work category at all levels according to Gottfredson (1978b). Osipow (1975) suggested that the occupational environments described by Holland may not be equally available to ethnic minorities with many poor African Americans becoming channeled into lower level realistic jobs. Gottfredson's data support Osipow's assertion.

Another major aspect of Holland's theory is the notion of person–environmental fit or congruence, that persons of a particular Holland code should be found in occupations classified with similar codes. Empirical support for the congruence concept with respect to African Americans is plentiful (Henry & Bardo, 1987; O'Brien & Walsh, 1976; Sheffey et al., 1986; Walsh et al., 1983; Ward & Walsh, 1981). Notwithstanding, Greenlee, Damarin, and Walsh (1988) found support for the hypothesis that the

interest profiles of African-American workers would reveal less congruence with their occupation, relative to Whites, because of the greater
employment barriers African Americans face. Somewhat contradictorily,
however, the authors reported no race differences in Self-Directed Search
scores among persons in similar occupations, a finding echoed by others
(see Hecht, 1980; Henry, 1988a; Walsh, Bingham, Horton, & Spokane,
1979; Walsh, Bingham, & Sheffey, 1986; Walsh, Woods, & Ward, 1986).
Further, Mazen's (1989) findings supported that author's contention that
ethnic minorities may evidence congruence between their interest profiles
and their occupational preferences but less congruence between interest
profiles and actual occupational choices because of real and perceived
employment barriers.

The Holland concepts of differentiation and consistency have not been
well investigated for validity with African Americans. However, Greenlee
et al. (1988) found limited support for the reasoning that because of employment barriers African Americans would evidence lesser differentiation than Anglos.

Since 1974, two studies (Henry, 1988b; Wakefield, Yom, Doughtie,
Chang, & Alston, 1975) appeared in the literature that bear directly on the
relevance of the hexagonal model to depict the responses of African
Americans to measures of the Holland types and have offered supportive
findings.

Although more study is needed, many of Holland's propositions have
been found to generalize to African-American populations. However,
more research with African Americans is needed that addresses the concepts of congruence, consistency, differentiation, and identity.

Career Self-Efficacy

The career self-efficacy construct (cf. Betz & Hackett, 1986) offers substantial promise in furthering our understanding of the career development of African Americans. Based on the work of Bandura (1977, 1986),
career self-efficacy expectations are beliefs about one's own ability to
successfully perform an occupationally relevant behavior and that these
expectations determine one's actions, effort, and persistence in regard to
vocational behavior. As Bandura initially proposed, outcome expectations, personal beliefs about the results of performance, are viewed as
operating independently from efficacy expectations and are dependent
on actual performance, which in turn stem from efficacy expectations.

Recently, Lent and Hackett (1987) asserted that the construct of self-
efficacy might also be useful in explaining the career behavior of ethnic
minorities. Two studies have recently tested this assertion. Confidence
levels were found by Post-Kammer and Smith (1986) to be related to

consideration of math courses only for women who expressed lower consideration of math/science career choices relative to men. Somewhat to the contrary, Post, Stewart, and Smith (1991) found that self-efficacy and confidence played more of a role in the career considerations of African-American men relative to women, for whom interests played the most dominant role.

Although the role of efficacy expectations have been implicated in the career behavior of African Americans, much more research is needed. We need to know, for example, to what extent do efficacy expectations effect the perceived range of academic and occupational options, the effectiveness of career decision making, and academic achievement? If self-efficacy is found to play a major role in the career behavior of African Americans, then another set of important questions concerns whether and to what extent the self-efficacy expectations of African Americans are modifiable through career intervention.

Some theoretical refinement of the self-efficacy construct may also be in order in applying it to the career behavior of ethnic minorities like African Americans. Bandura proposed that the outcomes one can expect to receive for a given behavior are determined solely by the adequacy of that behavior that, in turn, is dependent on one's efficacy expectations. But for ethnic minorities, discrimination and other forms of systematic bias determine outcomes and/or one's expectations of outcomes, independent of the adequacy of one's behavior. Consequently, both efficacy and outcomes expectations may have joint and independent effects on career behavior for ethnic minorities.

Cheatham's Africentricity-Based Model

According to Cheatham (1990), African Americans share a sociocultural history and experience based on negative attributions of both race/ethnicity and color. In addition, the author maintained that the enforced isolation and disenfranchisement that was the legacy of slavery engendered systems and relations specific to the needs of African Americans. Further, these systems and relations evolved in the United States from African and Western European forms and traditions (see also Blassingame, 1979; Boykin, 1983; Nobles, 1991). Indeed, the dominant feature of the psychology of any African American is the product of the interplay of these two cultural traditions and is defined along the following oppositional dimensions, some of which explicitly were addressed by Cheatham (see also Carter, 1990; Kluckhohn & Strodtbeck, 1961; Nobles, 1991; White, Parham, & Parham, 1980): harmony with versus mastery of nature, experiential versus metric time, cooperation versus competition, community versus individual survival and achievement, oral–auditory versus visual–written information production and processing, and the equality versus the superiority of rational and affective experiences.

Cheatham, ignoring the confounding of race and SES, argued that the large body of literature indicating that African Americans differ from Whites on a number of career and career-related variables suggests that their psychological processes may be different and that some of these differences are culturally determined. The author also argued that existing theories of career development and life-span development suggest that cultural differences, such as those aforementioned, may be influential but fail to delineate and explicate them. Cheatham proposed that if one could measure these cultural attitudes, it would be possible to empirically document vocational correlates. For example, the overrepresentation of African Americans in social and behavioral science occupations may be a manifestation of the Africentric value of cooperation and community survival/achievement in operation. Cheatham's model likely overstates the presence of ethnic differences but appears to offer new and measurable variables for vocational research and theory building. Whereas no test of his model appears in the empirical literature, it is testable and interesting.

Colorism

It has long been observed in the African-American community that one's shade of blackness affected not only how one viewed one's self, but also how one was perceived and responded to by members of that community and the wider "White" society (for example, see Boyd-Franklin, 1991; Gatewood, 1990; Neal & Wilson, 1989; Ransford, 1970; Russell, Wilson, & Hall, 1992). Research conducted before and during the civil rights movement indicated that light-skinned African Americans evidenced higher educational attainment levels than darker African Americans, and that higher status African Americans tended to have lighter skins than those of lower status (e.g., Keith & Herring, 1991; Myrdal, 1944; Ransford, 1970). Recently, however, Hughes and Hertel (1990) and Keith and Herring analyzed data from the National Survey of Black Americans (Jackson & Gurin, 1987) and found that African Americans with lighter skin tones evidenced higher SES, as well as greater educational and occupational attainment, than those with dark skin, with the effect being as great as Black–White differences. In addition, skin tone was found to be a stronger predictor of occupation and income than background characteristics such as socioeconomic status. Further, these affects were much more significant for women than men.

The findings reviewed previously clearly underscore the importance of skin tone and implicate other characteristics of racial or ethnic physiognomy (e.g., hair texture, size of nose and lips, etc.) in the study of African-American career development, but many questions remain to be answered. For example, does skin color affect how people interact with the person in providing educational and occupational opportunity? Or does skin tone affect how one sees oneself or what one expects out of and for oneself (viz., self- and outcome expectations)?

Racial/Cultural Identity

Carter and Cook (1992) recently suggested that racial/cultural identity models (cf. Atkinson, Morten, & Sue, 1993; Cross, 1978; Helms, 1990; Sue, 1982) offer much promise for examining within racial/ethnic group psychological differences. They suggested that these models might help account for within-group differences in career paths. Although such may prove to be the case, there is reason to be skeptical of this latter assertion. As currently defined, racial/cultural identity is based on one's attitudes towards: one's self as a member of a racial/cultural group, one's racial group/cultural group, and the majority race/culture. Although racial/cultural identity likely influences career adjustment, it is difficult to discern how such attitudes might explain career choice differences or be related to correlates of career choice (e.g., self-efficacy, interests, skills, lifestyle aspirations, etc.). The psychological dimensions proposed in the discussion of Cheatham's model and discussed earlier address broader psychological issues and have more potential for contributing toward an understanding of African-American career choice behavior.

RESEARCH REVIEW

Ethnic Differences and Aspirations, Interests, Choices, and Preferences

The findings to date indicate that African Americans either prefer or select primarily social and low-level occupations (e.g., Bowman, 1986; Gottfredson, 1978a, 1978b; Miller et al., 1988; Sewell & Martin, 1976; Swinton, 1992), with some indication of gender differences (Arbona & Novy, 1991; Sewell & Martin, 1976). Some findings indicate that there may be a tendency among African-American women to avoid occupations in which discrimination is perceived (Evans & Herr, 1991), but accounting for gender differences in African-American career choices appears to be a needed area of future research.

Expectations

The expectations literature indicates that expectations play an important role in the career considerations of African Americans (see Picou, Cosby, Lemke, & Azuma, 1974) and that this role needs to be further examined. The findings also show that in many cases African Americans hold lower expectations than Whites (i.e., Farley, Brewer, & Fine, 1977; Gurin, 1981; Hughes & Demo, 1989; Turner & McCaffrey, 1974), although not always (i.e., Pelham & Fretz, 1982; Torrance & Allen, 1980), and that the causes and treatment of these lower expectations may be an important thrust of future research. For example, empirical literature reveals that the relative standing of African Americans and Whites with respect to career expectations varies as a function of type of expectations, gender (see Farley et al., 1977), epogenic influences, and educational and labor market experiences (e.g., Dawkins, 1982; Felson, 1981; Gurin, 1981; Lee, 1983; Moerk, 1974), although such findings are in need of further examination and cross-validation. The higher expectations of African Americans relative to European Americans with regard to athletic activities is troubling given that, according to Lee (1983), only 2% of high school athletes ever reach the professional level; such expectations need further study.

Levels of Aspirations and Expectations

Several investigators have studied the aspiration and expectation levels of African Americans, comparing these levels to those of Whites. Kelly and Wingrove (1975) reported that the educational aspirations of their sample of African-American males were lower than those of a comparable group of Whites or African American females, who did not differ. But Dillard and Perrin (1980) found that their sample of African Americans held higher career aspirations than the Anglo male students, with no differences found among females nor racial differences found in levels of career expectations. Adding to this seemingly discordant set of findings, J. Thomas (1976) and Gibbs (1985) observed no such racial/ethnic differences in occupational and educational aspirations, respectively, whereas Kelley, Good, and Walters (1974) found that the African-American girls had higher occupational aspirations than did the White girls.

The research literature yields a clearer picture concerning the relationship between SES and levels of educational and occupational expectations with the relationship uniformly found to be positive (cf. Dillard & Perrin, 1980; Gibbs, 1985; Gregory, Wells, & Leake, 1986).

The confusion of findings concerning racial/ethnic differences in levels of expectations and aspirations appears to be due to the influence of a number of mediating factors: geographic origin of the research population (i.e., urban vs. rural populations, northern vs. southern populations), gender, SES, and type of expectation/aspiration studied (i.e., educational vs. occupational). These research population variables will need to be systematically studied or controlled before clearer conclusions can be reached regarding the presence of racial/ethnic differences in aspirations and expectations.

The Relationship of Aspirations to Expectations

The literature regarding the relationship of expectations and aspirations is hard to characterize. In general, it appears that the occupational expectations of African Americans are lower than their aspirations (cf. Berman & Haug, 1975; Cosby & Thomas, 1976; J. Thomas, 1976; Thomas, Kravas, & Low, 1979). However, the gap between expectations and aspirations was sometimes found to be greater for African Americans than Whites (Kelly & Wingrove, 1975; Pelham & Fretz, 1982; M. Thomas, 1976), and in other cases, either the opposite was true or no racial/ethnic difference was observed (Berman & Haug, 1975). Gender, SES, and geographic origin play as yet unspecified roles in mediating the relationship.

Gender Differences

The contemporary research findings show that gender differences exist in the educational and occupational aspirations of African Americans (cf. Kelly & Wingrove, 1975; Smith & Allen, 1984), as well as on some work-related (Farley et al., 1977; Gurin, 1981) and self-efficacy expectations (Post, Stewart, & Smith, 1991). Sex/gender role socialization also operates in the career choice behavior of African Americans, particularly those who are males (see Bowman, 1986; Chester, 1983; Gottfredson, 1978b; Grevious, 1985; Teahan, 1974). Yet, further exploration is needed to determine whether gender differences may be found in variables that predict occupational aspirations (cf. Dawkins, 1981; Maple & Stage, 1991), relate to the vocational self-concept (cf. Brown, Fulkerson, Vedder, & Ware, 1983; Chester, 1983) and academic performance (cf. Smith & Allen, 1984), and relate to the perception of occupational barriers (cf., Miller & Wells, 1988). Other differences among African-American men and women are impossible to specify given the need for additional study controlling for the influences of SES and geography (cf. Lee, 1985).

Race and SES

A few studies have uncovered no relationship of race and SES to career goals (cf. Littig, 1975; Rotberg, Brown, & Ware, 1987; Teahan, 1974), but a number of other investigations have shown the importance of controlling for SES in studies of racial/ethnic differences in career choice variables (e.g., Rodman & Voydanoff, 1978; Slaney, 1980; Slaney & Brown, 1983). When one considers that the majority of African Americans are poor (cf. Hacker, 1992; Jaynes & Williams, 1989; Swinton, 1992), racial comparisons will confound race and social status unless the latter variable is controlled.

DETERMINANTS OF VOCATIONAL CHOICE

Interpersonal Influences (Family, Peers, Acquaintances)

A long line of investigations have focused on the role of parents in influencing vocational choice aspirations. The research literature indicates that, in some circumstances, parents, particularly mothers, influence the career development of their children, especially their daughters (Brook, Whiteman, Peisach, & Deutsch, 1974; Burlew, 1982; Dawkins, 1989; June & Fooks, 1980; Lee, 1984a, 1984b; V. Thomas, 1986). The influence of parents on their children's career development has been found in some circumstances to be greater among African-American than White families (cf. Dillard & Campbell, 1981; Fields, 1981; Lee, 1984a, 1984b), but further study is warranted. The impact of other interpersonal influencers (i.e., student peers, church and political leaders, exposure to role models) also needs greater study (see Hill, Pettus, & Hedin, 1990; Oliver & Etcheverry, 1987) as does the impact of encouragement and academic preparation.

Gender-Role Socialization

A few studies have examined the relationship between gender-role attitudes and the career aspirations of African Americans. Among the many but disparate findings, African Americans have been observed to hold more traditional views of women's family roles than Whites (Gackenback, 1978; Lyson, 1986), although Crovitz and Steinmann (1980) found them to be more liberalized. Gender differences have also been reported in the gender-role attitudes of African Americans (cf. Gackenback, 1978), but the differences in their attitudes appear to be smaller than that of Whites (Crovitz & Steinmann, 1980). Interestingly, some research findings indicate that African Americans place a minimum value on gender roles in making career decisions, relative to Whites (Gackenback, 1978; Lyson, 1986; Milham & Smith, 1981). Nonetheless, Thomas's (1985) findings indicated that gender-role socialization influenced college major choices of their sample of African Americans.

Somewhat in contrast to the studies cited earlier, Murrell, Frieze, and Frost (1991) found no differences were reported on attitudes toward non-traditional roles for men and women and that, regardless of ethnicity, college women choosing traditional occupations had more traditional attitudes.

Future investigations may clarify whether African Americans hold more liberal or traditional gender-role attitudes than Whites in regard to family roles. Yet, whatever the nature of these attitudes, they appear to affect the career decisions of African Americans differently than those of Whites.

Gender Type of Occupational Aspirations

The available research literature suggests that racial differences exist in occupational gender-typed aspirations, particularly among women (e.g., Dawkins, 1981; George, 1981; Jacobowitz, 1983; Kenkel & Gage, 1983; Littig, 1975, 1979; Miller & Stanford, 1986, 1987), but more research is needed to substantiate the observations that African Americans hold more gender-typed aspirations. More study is also needed comparing African-American women aspiring to traditionally closed occupations to those aspiring to traditionally open occupations in terms of occupational gender-typing behavior (see Littig, 1975; Murriel et al., 1991; Thomas, 1983). Some factors have been found to mediate the gender typing of educational and occupational aspirations in African Americans but are in need of additional study such as economic needs (Murriel et al., 1991), gender, social class, and confidence in one's ability (Dawkins, 1981).

Self-Concept and Related Dimensions

The research literature indicates that African Americans may differ from Whites on some self-concept dimensions (Brown et al., 1983; Burke & Hoelter, 1988), but the career development impact of these differences has yet to be demonstrated (see Dillard, 1976; Lawrence & Brown, 1976; McNair & Brown, 1983; Pound, 1978; Zuckerman, 1980).

Color consciousness (cf. Hughes & Hertel, 1990; Keith & Herring, 1991), a possible dimension of the self-concept of African Americans, has important implications for the career development of African Americans.

Career Maturity

The status of ethnic differences on career maturity measures remains unclear. Some investigators have observed that African Americans score lower than their White counterparts on career maturity measures (Loesch, Shub, & Rucker, 1979; Westbrook, Cutts, Madison, & Arcia, 1980; Westbrook & Sanford, 1991). However, that finding was not replicated by Westbrook, Sanford, and Donnelly (1990) and LoCascio, Nesselroth, and Thomas (1976).

Available data indicate that career maturity is not correlated with self-concept but is correlated with SES in African-American populations (e.g., Dillard, 1976; Lawrence & Brown, 1976; McNair & Brown, 1983; Pound, 1978; Smith, 1976).

Regarding the validity of the Career Maturity Inventory (CMI) for African-American samples, a number of investigators have failed to demonstrate whether any of the CMI subscales were related to appropriateness of career choices (Westbrook & Sanford, 1991; Westbrook et al., 1990; Westbrook, Sanford, Merwin, Fleenor, & Gilleland, 1988).

Career Decision Making

Only a few studies since 1976 focused on the career decision-making (CDM) process of African Americans, and these concerned the perception of CDM barriers. Although research on CDM processes of African Americans is sparse, it is suggestive of ethnic and sex/gender differences in the perception of occupational barriers (cf. Simons & Gray, 1980; Slaney, 1980; Slaney & Brown, 1983). Also, available findings indicate that African Americans hold positive attitudes toward career counseling activities (Piotrowski & Keller, 1990) and have expressed a need for career services to a greater extent than other ethnic groups (Brown, Minor, & Jepsen, 1991).

Work Values

Ethnic and sex/gender differences appear indicated with regards to many work values (cf. Bartol, Anderson, & Schneier, 1981; Bassoff & Ortiz, 1984; Dillard & Campbell, 1982; Lee, 1984b; Malpass & Symonds, 1974; Thomas & Neal, 1978; Thomas & Shields, 1987; Wagoner & Bridwell, 1989), but it is unclear how to characterize such studies or how much confidence one can put in the findings because they are so few. In addition, future research may determine more conclusively that the long-term unemployment that characterizes the plight of many African Americans affects their work values (see Isralowitz & Singer, 1987).

Career Interventions

One of the more striking features of the career intervention literature concerns its sparseness with respect to African Americans. We know very little about what forms of career intervention are most effective in bettering the employment and SES of African Americans, particularly of

African-American men. The use of the Vocational Exploration Group with economically disadvantaged African-American students was evaluated by Johnson, Johnson, Johnson, and Yates (1982), and the findings indicated that participants gained self- and occupational knowledge. Danford and Parker (1984) found no differences in the effectiveness of experiential and didactic group counseling techniques for improving personal and vocational development of African-American evening students. Obleton (1984) reported that a group of African-American women participants in a workshop using mentor-model relations expressed that it changed their personal behavior in career development, stress maintenance, and health improvement. Dunn and Veltman (1989) discovered that a summer high school program designed to increase minority participation in math, science, and engineering increased CMI scores, particularly in the areas of decisiveness and attitudes toward work.

There have been two studies found that aimed to increase the employability of unemployed persons. Freeman and McRoy (1986) described a group treatment for unemployed African-American teenagers based on developmental theory that increased the group's awareness of various ways of giving support and their functional independence from their parents. In the second study, Ekstrom, Freeberg, and Rock (1987) found that, at a 3-year follow-up, participants in a youth employment program evidenced more months of employment and greater satisfaction in program participants relative to nonparticipants.

Clearly, studies are needed that evaluate the effectiveness of career intervention programs for African Americans that increases their employability and employment and that successfully orients them toward nontraditional career fields.

ASSESSMENT

The assessment literature since the mid-1970s, as it pertains to African Americans, has focused on the use abilities tests and Holland tests like the Self-Directed Search (SDS) and the Vocational Preference Inventory (VPI). There was one review study of the Strong Interest Inventory (SII) for use with African Americans.

Ability Tests

Sung and Davis (1981) and Kass, Mitchell, Grafton, and Wing (1983) discovered that the factor structure of various ability tests replicated across gender and racial categories, but numerous gender and race differences in ability levels were evident (Sung & Davis, 1981). Jones (1984) reported evidence that the gap in achievement test scores between Anglo Americans and African Americans was narrowing with the levels for African Americans approaching that for the Anglo Americans.

Current data indicate that, whereas gender and ethnic differences exist in levels of various abilities, the qualitative nature of those abilities is invariant across those factors. The causes of the level differences and their career development implications for African Americans, however, have yet to be empirically determined.

Holland Instrumentation

Since 1974, there have been a number of studies conducted to determine the validity of the VPI and the SDS for use with African Americans. Wakefield, Alston, Yom, Doughtie, and Chang (1975) and Yom, Doughtie, Wei, Alston, and Wakefield (1975) discovered that the factor structures of the VPI and the SDS for African Americans and Whites were similar.

Scholars (i.e., Bingham & Walsh, 1978; O'Brien & Walsh, 1976; Sheffey et al., 1986) have demonstrated that both the VPI and the SDS discriminated among various occupational groups of African Americans in a manner consistent with Holland's theory. Further, no race or gender differences in the SDS scores have been uncovered for samples of African Americans and Whites (i.e., Hecht, 1980; Henry, 1988a; Henry, Bardo, Mouw, & Bryson, 1987; Walsh, Bingham, Horton, & Spokane, 1979).

The reviewed literature indicates that the VPI and the SDS have concurrent and discriminant validity among African-American populations and yield no race or gender differences.

Strong Interest Inventory

Carter and Swanson (1990) recently reviewed the psychometric literature and concluded that there was little evidence to support the adequacy of the SII for African Americans given the methodological flaws to which the studies fell victim: small sample size and reliance on male samples.

FUTURE THEORETICAL
AND EMPIRICAL DIRECTIONS

Almost every indice of social and economic adjustment supports the conclusion that the career development of African Americans needs urgent attention. However, little is known about African-American career development, and research data have been growing at a glacial pace since the late 1970s. Many of the current theories of career development have not been empirically tested using African Americans. Nonetheless, it may be that existing theoretical concepts are not as relevant to African-American career development as other untapped concepts, like colorism and Africentricity.

An important reason for the slow growth of career development information on African Americans involves research methodology. The need to control for factors such as skin tone, gender, geographic region, and SES, whereas also obtaining a large enough sample size to make the research results meaningful, renders African-American career development research a challenging enterprise. However, several new directions are indicated as a result of this review of the extant theoretical and research literature and a few of these are highlighted.

The trait–factor notion that it is possible and desirable to match individual characteristics to those required by an occupation assumes that the most important and relevant factors regarding African-American career behavior have been identified and have been reliably measured. The work of Edwards and Polite (1992) and Cheatham (1990) and others (e.g., Nobles, 1991; White et al., 1980) present some new theoretical concepts that are in need of measurement and investigation within and without current theoretical paradigms, including the trait–factor theory. With respect to Roe's theory, research is needed that offers measures of social distance between African Americans and Whites and relates such measures to needs structures and, ultimately, to vocational choice. Concerning Super's theory, there has been no systematic investigation of the relationship between self-concept variables and career choice behavior with African-American populations. Just as importantly, the role of SES and discrimination on the development of occupational and self-concepts has yet to be documented. Holland's theory has generated the most career research on African Americans, but more research is needed that addresses concepts like differentiation and identity. Career self-efficacy theory has just begun to generate African-American career development research, but basic issues like to what extent efficacy and outcome expectations affect educational and occupational choices have yet to be explored.

New research directions to be pursued include documenting additional vocational correlates of skin tone. Expectations research appears to be a particularly bountiful area of African-American career research, but gender differences in these expectations and their vocational correlates require more study. Sex/gender role socialization and occupational gender typing appear to be pervasive phenomena among African Americans, but current research is sparse, particularly that which addresses gender and ethnic differences. African-American parents appear to be stronger influences on their offsprings' career choices than White parents, but existing designs have not been well controlled, and the impact of other persons, like church leaders, has not been well documented. Clarifying the picture concerning ethnic differences on career maturity and work values measures, perhaps by controlling for gender, SES, and geographic origin, is also a research need. The career decision-making processes of African Americans is essentially virgin research territory, as is career intervention research.

Finally, a number of substantive areas of career choice research, identified by Fitzgerald and Rounds (1989) and Tinsley and Heesacker (1984), have not yet been investigated with respect to African Americans. Key areas to be targeted are correlates of vocational interests and choices, life-span developmental processes, leisure behavior, vocational identity, and job search behavior. These research directions represent the tip of the iceberg in terms of research possibilities and, hopefully, will serve to initiate a new era of growth in theory and research in African-American career development.

REFERENCES

Anastasi, A. (1982). *Psychological testing* (5th ed.). New York: Macmillan.

Arbona, C. (1989). Hispanic employment and the Holland typology of work. *Career Development Quarterly, 37,* 257–268.

Arbona, C., & Novy, D. M. (1991). Career aspirations and expectations of Black, Mexican American, and White students. *Career Development Quarterly, 39,* 231–239.

Atkinson, D. R., Morten, G., & Sue, D. W. (1993). *Counseling American minorities: A cross-cultural perspective* (4th ed.). Madison, WI: Brown & Benchmark.

Bandura, A. (1977). Self-efficacy: Toward a unifying theory of behavioral change. *Psychological Review, 84,* 191–215.

Bandura, A. (1986). *Social foundations of thought and action: A social cognitive theory.* Englewood Cliffs, NJ: Prentice-Hall.

Bartol, K. M., Anderson, C. R., & Schneier, C. E. (1981). Sex and ethnic effects on motivation to manage among college business students. *Journal of Applied Psychology, 66,* 40–44.

Bassoff, B. Z., & Ortiz, E. T. (1984). Teen women: Disparity between cognitive values and anticipated life events. *Child Welfare, 63,* 125–138.

Berman, G. S., & Haug, M. R. (1975). Occupational and educational goals and expectations: The effects of race and sex. *Social Problems, 23,* 166–181.

Betz, N. E., & Hackett, G. (1986). Applications of self-efficacy theory to understanding career choice behavior. *Journal of Social and Clinical Psychology, 4,* 279–289.

Bingham, R. P., & Walsh, W. B. (1978). Concurrent validity of Holland's theory for college-degreed Black women. *Journal of Vocational Behavior, 13,* 242–250.

Blassingame, J. (1979). *The slave community: Plantation life in the antebellum south.* New York: Oxford University Press.

Bowman, M. A. (1986). Specialty choice of Black physicians. *Journal of the National Medical Association, 78,* 13–15.

Boyd-Franklin, W. (1991). Recurrent themes in the treatment of African-American women in group psychotherapy. *Women and Therapy, 11,* 25–40.

Boykin, A. W. (1983). The academic performance of Afro-American children. In J. T. Spence (Ed.), *Achievement and achievement motives: Psychological and sociological approaches* (pp. 321–371). San Francisco: Freeman.

Brook, J. S., Whiteman, M., Peisach, E., & Deutsch, M. (1974). Aspiration levels of and for children: Age, sex, race, and socioeconomic correlates. *Journal of Genetic Psychology, 124,* 3–16.

Brooks, L. (1990). Recent developments in theory building. In D. Brown & L. Brooks (Eds.), *Career choice and development* (2nd ed., pp. 364–394). San Francisco: Jossey-Bass.

Brown, D. (1990). Trait and factor theory. In D. Brown & L. Brooks (Eds.), *Career choice and development: Applying contemporary theories to practice* (2nd ed., pp. 13–36). San Francisco: Jossey-Bass.

Brown, D., Fulkerson, K. F., Vedder, M., & Ware, W. B. (1983). Self-estimate ability in Black and White 8th-, 10th-, and 12th-grade males and females. *Vocational Guidance Quarterly, 32,* 21–28.

Brown, D., Minor, C. W., & Jepsen, D. A. (1991). The opinions of minorities about preparing for work: Report of the second NCDA national survey. *Career Development Quarterly, 40,* 5–19.

Burke, P. J., & Hoelter, J. W. (1988). Identity and sex-race differences in educational and occupational aspirations formation. *Social Science Research, 17,* 29–47.

Burlew, A. K. (1982). The experience of Black females in traditional and nontraditional professions. *Psychology of Women Quarterly, 6,* 312–326.

Carter, D. J., & Wilson, R. (1992). *Minorities in higher education.* Washington, DC: American Council on Education.

Carter, R. T. (1990). Cultural value differences between African-Americans and White Americans. *Journal of College Student Development, 31,* 71–79.

Carter, R. T., & Cook, D. A. (1992). A culturally relevant perspective for understanding the career paths of visible racial/ethnic group people. In H. D. Lea & Z. B. Leibowitz (Eds.), *Adult career development: Concepts, issues, and practices* (pp. 192–217). Alexandria, VA: The National Career Development Association.

Carter, R. T., & Swanson, J. L. (1990). The validity of the Strong Interest Inventory with Black Americans: A review of the literature. *Journal of Vocational Behavior, 36,* 195–209.

Cheatham, H. E. (1990). Africentricity and career development of African Americans. *Career Development Quarterly, 38,* 334–346.

Chester, N. L. (1983). Sex differentiation in two high school environments: Implications for career development among Black adolescent females. *Journal of Social Issues, 39,* 29–40.

Cosby, A. G., & Thomas, J. K. (1976). Patterns of early adult status attainment and attitudes in the non-metropolitan South. *Sociology of Work and Occupations, 3,* 411–428.

Cross, W. E., Jr. (1978). The Cross and Thomas models of psychological nigresence. *Journal of Black Psychology, 5,* 13–19.

Crovitz, E., & Steinmann, A. (1980). A decade later: Black–White attitudes toward women's familial role. *Psychology of Women Quarterly, 5,* 170–176.

Danford, R., & Parker, W. M. (1984). A comparison of experiential and didactic group counseling techniques with Black evening students. *Journal of Non-White Concerns in Personnel and Guidance, 12,* 34–39.

Dawis, R. V., & Lofquist, L. H. (1984). *A psychological theory of work adjustment.* Minneapolis: University of Minnesota Press.

Dawkins, M. P. (1981). Mobility aspirations of Black adolescents: A comparison of males and females. *Adolescence, 16,* 701–710.

Dawkins, M. P. (1982). Occupational prestige expectation among Black and White college students: A multivariate analysis. *Journal of College Student Personnel, 16,* 233–242.

Dawkins, M. P. (1989). The persistence of plans for professional careers among Blacks in early adulthood. *Journal of Negro Education, 58,* 220–231.

Dillard, J. M. (1976). Relationship between career maturity and self-concepts of suburban and urban middle- and urban lower-class preadolescent black males. *Journal of Vocational Behavior, 9,* 311–320.

Dillard, J. M., & Campbell, N. J. (1981). Influences of Puerto Rican, Black, and Anglo parents' career behavior on their adolescent children's career development. *Vocational Guidance Quarterly, 30,* 139–148.

Dillard, J. M., & Campbell, N. J. (1982). Career values and aspirations of adult female and male Puerto Ricans, Blacks, and Anglos. *Journal of Employment Counseling, 19,* 163–170.

Dillard, J. M., & Perrin, D. W. (1980). Puerto Rican, Black, and Anglo adolescents' career aspirations, expectations, and maturity. *Vocational Guidance Quarterly, 28,* 313–321.

Dunn, C. W., & Veltman, G. C. (1989). Addressing the restrictive career maturity patterns of minority youth: A program evaluation. *Journal of Multicultural Counseling and Development, 17,* 156–164.

Edwards, A., & Polite, C. (1992). *Children of the dream: The psychology of Black success.* New York: Bantam.

Ekstrom, R. B., Freeberg, N. E., & Rock, D. A. (1987). The effects of youth employment program participation on later employment. *Evaluation Review, 11,* 84–101.

Evans, K. M., & Herr, E. L. (1991). The influence of racism and sexism in the career development of African American women. *Journal of Multicultural Counseling and Development, 19,* 130–135.

Farley, J., Brewer, J. H., & Fine, S. W. (1977). Black women's career aspirations. *Journal of Employment Counseling, 14,* 116–119.

Featherman, D. L., & Hauser, R. M. (1976). Prestige or socioeconomic scales in the study of occupational achievement. *Sociological Methods and Research, 4,* 403–422.

Felson, R. B. (1981). Self- and reflected appraisal among football players: A test of the Meadian hypothesis. *Social Psychology Quarterly, 44,* 116–126.

Fields, A. B. (1981). Some influences upon the occupational aspirations of three white-collar ethnic groups. *Adolescence, 16,* 663–684.

Fitzgerald, L. F., & Rounds, J. B. (1989). Vocational behavior, 1988: A critical analysis. *Journal of Vocational Behavior, 35,* 105–163.

Franklin, V. (1991). Black social scientists and the mental testing movement. In R. Jones (Ed.), *Black psychology* (3rd ed., pp. 207–224). Berkeley, CA: Cobb & Henry.

Freeman, E. M., & McRoy, R. G. (1986). Group counseling program for unemployed Black teenagers. *Social Work with Groups, 9,* 73–89.

Gackenback, J. (1978). The effect of race, sex, and career goal differences on sex role attitudes at home and at work. *Journal of Vocational Behavior, 12,* 93–101.

Gatewood, W. B. (1990). *Aristocrats of color: The Black elite, 1880–1920.* Bloomington and Indianapolis: Indiana University Press.

George, V. D. (1981). Occupational aspirations of talented black and white adolescent females. *Journal of Non-White Concerns, 9,* 137–145.

Gibbs, J. T. (1985). City girls: Psychosocial adjustment of urban Black adolescent females. *Sage—A Scholarly Journal on Black Women, 2,* 28–36.

Gottfredson, L. S. (1978a). An analytical description of employment according to race, sex, prestige, and Holland type of work. *Journal of Vocational Behavior, 13,* 210–221.

Gottfredson, L. S. (1978b). Providing Black youth more access to enterprising work. *Vocational Guidance Quarterly, 27,* 114–123.

Gottfredson, L. S., & Sharf, J. C. (Eds.). (1988). Fairness in employment testing. *Journal of Vocational Behavior, 33,* 225–230.

Greenhaus, J. H., & Parasuraman, S. (1986). Vocational and organizational behavior: A review. *Journal of Vocational Behavior, 24,* 115–176.

Greenlee, S. P., Damarin, F. L., & Walsh, W. B. (1988). Congruence and differentiation among Black and White males in two non-college-degreed occupations. *Journal of Vocational Behavior, 32,* 298–306.

Gregory, K., Wells, K. B., & Leake, B. (1986). Which first-year medical students expect to practice in an inner-city or ghetto setting. *Journal of the National Medical Association, 78,* 501–504.

Grevious, C. (1985). A comparison of occupational aspirations of urban Black college students. *Journal of Negro Education, 54,* 35–42.

Gurin, P. (1981). Labor market experiences and expectancies. *Sex-Roles, 7,* 1079–1092.

Guthrie, R. (1976). *Even the rat was white: A historical view of psychology.* New York: Harper & Row.

Hacker, A. (1992). *Two nations.* New York: Scribner's.

Hackett, G., & Betz, N. E. (1981). A self-efficacy approach to the career development of women. *Journal of Vocational Behavior, 18,* 326–339.

Hecht, A. B. (1980). Nursing career choice and Holland's theory: Are men and blacks different? *Journal of Vocational Behavior, 16,* 208–211.

Helms, J. E. (1990). *Black and White racial identity: Theory, research, and practice.* Westport, CT: Greenwood Press.

Helms, J. E. (1992). Why is there no study of cultural equivalence in standardized cognitive ability testing. *American Psychologist, 47,* 1083–1101.

Henry, P. (1988a). Applying the Holland's self-directed search to nontraditional investigative-type students. *Journal of College Student Development, 29,* 473–475.

Henry, P. (1988b). Holland's hexagonal model applied to nontraditional premedical students. *Psychological Reports, 62,* 399–404.

Henry, P., & Bardo, H. R. (1987). Expressed occupational choice of nontraditional premedical students as measured by the self-directed search: An investigation of Holland's theory. *Psychological Reports, 60,* 575–581.

Henry, P., Bardo, H. R., Mouw, J. T., & Bryson, S. (1987). Medicine as a career choice and Holland's theory: Do race and sex make a difference? *Journal of Multicultural Counseling and Development, 15,* 161–170.

Hill, O. W., Pettus, W. C., & Hedin, B. A. (1990). Three studies of factors affecting the attitudes of Blacks and females toward the pursuit of science and science-related careers. *Journal of Research in Science Teaching, 27,* 289–314.

Holland, J. L. (1985). *Making vocational choices: A theory of vocational personalities and work environments* (2nd ed.). Englewood Cliffs, NJ: Prentice-Hall.

Hughes, M., & Demo, D. H. (1989). Self-perceptions of Black Americans: Self-esteem and personal efficacy. *American Journal of Sociology, 95,* 132–157.

Hughes, M., & Hertel, B. R. (1990). The significance of color remains: A study of life choices, mate selection, and ethnic consciousness among Black Americans. *Social Forces, 68,* 1105–1120.

Isralowitz, R. E., & Singer, M. (1987). Long-term unemployment and its impact on Black adolescent work values. *Journal of Social Psychology, 127,* 227–229.

Jackson, J. S., & Gurin, G. (1987). *National survey of Black Americans, 1979–1980.* Ann Arbor: University of Michigan Institute for Social Research.

Jacob, J. E. (1992). Black America, 1991: An overview. In B. J. Tidwell (Ed.), *The state of Black America 1992* (pp. 1–9). New York: National Urban League.

Jacobowitz, T. (1983). Relationship of sex, achievement, and science self-concept to the science career preferences of Black students. *Journal of Research in Science Teaching, 20,* 621–628.

Jaynes, G. D., & Williams, R. M. (Eds.). (1989). *A common destiny: Blacks in American society.* Washington, DC: National Academy Press.

Johnson, N., Johnson, S. C., Johnson, J., & Yates, C. (1982). Use of the Vocational Exploration Group with economically disadvantaged Black students. *Journal for Specialists in Group Work, 7,* 96–101.

Jones, L. V. (1984). White–black achievement: The narrowing gap. *American Psychologist, 39,* 1207–1213.

June, L. N., & Fooks, G. M. (1980). Key influences on the career directions and choices of Black university professionals. *Journal of Non-White Concerns in Personnel and Guidance, 8,* 157–166.

June, L. N., & Pringle, G. D. (1977). The concept of race in the career development theories of Roe, Super, & Holland. *Journal of Non-White Concerns in Personnel and Guidance, 6,* 17–24.

Kass, R. A., Mitchell, K. J., Grafton, F. C., & Wing, H. (1983). Factorial validity of the Armed Services Vocational Aptitude Battery (ASVAB), Forms 8, 9, and 10: 1981 Army applicant sample. *Educational and Psychological Measurement, 43,* 1077–1087.

Keith, V. M., & Herring, C. (1991). Skin tone and stratification in the Black community. *American Journal of Sociology, 97,* 760–778.

Kelley, E., Good, E., & Walters, S. (1974). Working-class adolescents' perceptions of the role of clothing in occupational life. *Adolescence, 9,* 185–198.

Kelly, P. K., & Wingrove, C. R. (1975). Educational and occupational choices of Black and White, male and female students in a rural Georgia community. *Journal of Research and Development in Education, 9,* 45–56.

Kenkel, W. F., & Gage, B. A. (1983). The restricted and gender-typed occupational aspirations of young women: Can they be modified? *Family Relations Journal of Applied Family and Child Studies, 32,* 129–138.

Kidd, J. M. (1984). The relationship of self- and occupational concepts to the occupational preferences of adolescents. *Journal of Vocational Behavior, 24,* 48–65.

Kluckhohn, F. R., & Strodtbeck, F. L. (1961). *Variations in value-orientations.* Evanston, IL: Row, Peterson.

Lawrence, W., & Brown, D. (1976). An investigation of intelligence, self-concept, socioeconomic status, race, and sex as predictors of career maturity. *Journal of Vocational Behavior, 9,* 43–52.

Lee, C. C. (1983). An investigation of the athletic career expectations of high school athletes. *Personnel and Guidance Journal, 61,* 544–547.

Lee, C. C. (1984a). An investigation of the psychosocial variable in the occupational aspirations and expectations of rural Black and White adolescents: Implications for vocational education. *Journal of Research and Development in Education, 17,* 28–34.

Lee, C. C. (1984b). Predicting the career choice attitudes of rural Black, White, and Native American high school students. *Vocational Guidance Quarterly, 32,* 177–184.

Lee, C. C. (1985). An ethnic group gender comparison of occupational choice among rural adolescents. *Journal of Non-White Concerns in Personnel and Guidance, 13,* 28–37.

Lent, R. W., & Hackett, G. (1987). Career self-efficacy: Empirical status and future directions. *Journal of Vocational Behavior, 30,* 347–382.

Leonard, P. Y. (1985). Vocational theory and the vocational behavior of Black males: An analysis [Special Issue: The Black male: Critical counseling, developmental, and therapeutic issues: II]. *Journal of Multicultural Development and Counseling, 13,* 91–105.

Littig, L. W. (1975). Personality, race, and social class determinants of occupational goals. *International Mental Health Research Newsletter, 17,* 2–6.

Littig, L. W. (1979). Motivational correlates of real to ideal occupational aspiration shifts among Black and White men and women. *Bulletin of the Psychonomic Society, 13,* 227–229.

LoCascio, R. (1967). Continuity and discontinuity in vocational development theory. *Personnel and Guidance Journal, 46,* 32–46.

LoCascio, R., Nesselroth, J., & Thomas, M. (1976). The career development inventory: Use and findings with inner city drop outs. *Journal of Vocational Behavior, 8,* 285–292.

Loesch, L. C., Shub, P. A., & Rucker, B. B. (1979). Vocational maturity among community college students. *Journal of College Student Personnel, 20,* 140–144.

London, M., & Greller, M. M. (1991). Demographic trends and vocational behavior: A twenty year retrospective and agenda for the 1990s. *Journal of Vocational Behavior, 38,* 125–164.

Lyson, T. A. (1986). Race and sex differences in sex role attitudes of southern college students. *Psychology of Women Quarterly, 10,* 421–428.

Malpass, R. S., & Symonds, J. D. (1974). Value preferences associated with social class, sex, and race. *Journal of Cross-Cultural Psychology, 5,* 282–300.

Maple, S. A., & Stage, F. K. (1991). Influences on choice of math/science major by gender and ethnicity. *American Educational Research Journal, 28,* 37–60.

Mazen, A. M. (1989). Testing an integration of Vroom's instrumentality theory and Holland's typology on working women. *Journal of Vocational Behavior, 35,* 327–341.

McBay, S. M. (1992). The condition of African American education: Changes and challenges. In B. J. Tidwell (Ed.), *The state of Black America 1992* (pp. 141–156). New York: National Urban League.

McNair, D., & Brown, D. (1983). Predicting the occupational aspirations, occupational expectations, and career maturity of Black and White male and female 10th graders. *Vocational Guidance Quarterly, 32,* 29–36.

Milham, J., & Smith, L. E. (1981). Sex-role differentiation among Black and White Americans: A comparative study. *Journal of Black Psychology, 7,* 77–90.

Miller, M. J., Springer, T., & Wells, D. (1988). Which occupational environments do Black youths prefer? Extending Holland's typology. *School Counselor, 36,* 103–106.

Miller, M. J., & Stanford, J. T. (1986). Sex differences in occupational choices of second-grade black children. *Psychological Reports, 59,* 273–274.

Miller, M. J., & Stanford, J. T. (1987). Early occupational restriction: An examination of elementary school children's expression of vocational preferences. *Journal of Employment Counseling, 24,* 115–121.

Miller, M. J., & Wells, D. (1988). Learning more about the vocational "barriers" of Black youths. *Psychological Reports, 62,* 405–406.

Moerk, E. L. (1974). Age and epogenic influences on aspirations of minority and majority group children. *Journal of Counseling Psychology, 21,* 294–298.

Murrell, A. J., Frieze, I. H., & Frost, J. L. (1991). Aspirations to careers in male- and female-dominated professions: A study of Black and White college women. *Psychology of Women Quarterly, 15,* 103–126.

Myrdal, G. (1944). *An American dilemma.* New York: Harper & Row.

Neal, A. M., & Wilson, M. L. (1989). The role of skin color and features in the Black community: Implications for Black women and therapy. *Clinical Psychology Review, 9,* 323–333.

Nobles, W. W. (1991). African philosophy: Foundations for Black psychology. In R. L. Jones (Ed.), *Black psychology* (3rd ed., pp. 47–63). Berkeley, CA: Cobb & Henry.

O'Brien, W. F., & Walsh, W. B. (1976). Concurrent validity of Holland's theory for non-college-degreed black working men. *Journal of Vocational Behavior, 8,* 239–246.

Obleton, N. B. (1984). Career counseling Black women in a predominantly White coeducational university. *Personnel and Guidance Journal, 62,* 365–368.

Oliver, J., & Etcheverry, R. (1987). Factors influencing the decisions of academically talented Black students to attend college. *Journal of Negro Education, 56,* 152–161.

Osipow, S. H. (1975). The relevance of theories of career development to special groups: Problems, needed data, and implications. In J. S. Picou & R. E. Campbell (Eds.), *Career behavior of special groups: Theory, research, and practice* (pp. 9–22). Columbus, OH: Merrill.

Osipow, S. H. (1983). *Theories of career development* (3rd ed.). Englewood Cliffs, NJ: Prentice-Hall.

Pelham, J. P., & Fretz, B. R. (1982). Racial differences and attributes of career choice unrealism. *Vocational Guidance Quarterly, 30*, 36–42.

Picou, J. S., Cosby, A. G., Lemke, J. W., & Azuma, H. T. (1974). Occupational choice and perception of attainment blockage: A study of lower-class delinquent and non-delinquent black males. *Adolescence, 9*, 289–298.

Piotrowski, C., & Keller, J. W. (1990). Black students' perspectives on career planning. *Psychology—A Journal of Human Behavior, 27*, 30–32.

Post, P., Stewart, M. A., & Smith, P. L. (1991). Self-efficacy, interest, and consideration of math/science and non-math/science occupations among Black freshmen. *Journal of Vocational Behavior, 38*, 179–186.

Post-Kammer, P., & Smith, P. L. (1986). Sex differences in math and science career self-efficacy among disadvantaged students. *Journal of Vocational Behavior, 29*, 89–101.

Pound, R. E. (1978). Using self-concept subscales in predicting career maturity for race and sex subgroups. *Vocational Guidance Quarterly, 27*, 61–70.

Ransford, E. H. (1970). Skin color, life chances, and anti-white attitudes. *Social Problems, 18*, 164–178.

Rodman, H., & Voydanoff, P. (1978). Social class and parents' range of aspirations for their children. *Social Problems, 25*, 333–344.

Roe, A. (1951a). A psychological study of eminent biologists. *Psychological Monographs, 65*(14, Whole No. 331).

Roe, A. (1951b). A psychological study of eminent physical scientists. *Genetic Psychology Monograph, 43*, 121–239.

Roe, A. (1956). *The psychology of occupations.* New York: Wiley.

Roe, A., & Lunneborg, P. W. (1990). Personality development and career choice. In D. Brown & L. Brooks (Eds.), *Career choice and development: Applying theories to practice* (2nd ed., pp. 68–101). San Francisco: Jossey-Bass.

Rotberg, H. L., Brown, D., & Ware, W. B. (1987). Career self-efficacy expectations and perceived range of career options in community college students. *Journal of Counseling Psychology, 34*, 164–170.

Russell, K., Wilson, M., & Hall, R. (1992). *The color complex: The politics of skin color among African Americans.* New York: Harcourt Brace Jovanovich.

Salomone, P. R., & Slaney, R. B. (1978). The applicability of Holland's theory to nonprofessional workers. *Journal of Vocational Behavior, 13*, 63–74.

Sewell, T. E., & Martin, R. P. (1976). Racial differences in patterns of occupational choice in adolescents. *Psychology in the Schools, 13*, 326–333.

Sheffey, M. A., Bingham, R. P., & Walsh, W. B. (1986). Concurrent validity of Holland's theory for college educated black men. *Journal of Multicultural Counseling and Development, 14*, 149–156.

Simons, R. L., & Gray, P. A. (1989). Perceived blocked opportunity as an explanation of delinquency among lower-class Black males: A research note. *Journal of Research in Crime and Delinquency, 26*, 90–101.

Slaney, R. B. (1980). An investigation of racial differences on vocational variables among college women. *Journal of Vocational Behavior, 16*, 197–204.

Slaney, R. B., & Brown, M. T. (1983). Effects of race and socioeconomic status on career choice variables among college men. *Journal of Vocational Behavior, 23*, 257–269.

Smith, A. W., & Allen, W. R. (1984). Modeling Black student academic performance in higher education. *Research in Higher Education, 21*, 210–225.

Smith, E. J. (1975). Profile of the Black individual in vocational literature. *Journal of Vocational Behavior, 6*, 41–59.

Smith, E. J. (1976). Reference group perspectives and the vocational maturity of lower socioeconomic Black youth. *Journal of Vocational Behavior, 8*, 321–336.

Smith, E. J. (1983). Issues in racial minorities' career behavior. In W. B. Walsh & S. A. Osipow (Eds.), *Handbook of vocational psychology Vol. 1. Foundations* (pp. 161–222). Hillsdale, NJ: Lawrence Erlbaum Associates.

Sue, D. W. (1982). *Counseling the culturally different: Theory and practice.* New York: Wiley.

Sung, Y. H., & Davis, R. V. (1981). Level and factor structure differences in selected abilities across race and sex groups. *Journal of Applied Psychology, 66*, 613–624.

Super, D. E. (1953). A theory of vocational development. *American Psychologist, 8*, 185–190.

Super, D. E. (1990). A life-span, life-space approach to career development. In D. Brown & L. Brooks (Eds.), *Career choice and development: Applying contemporary theories to practice* (2nd ed., pp. 197–261). San Francisco: Jossey-Bass.

Super, D. E., & Bohn, M. J., Jr. (1970). *Occupational psychology.* Belmont, CA: Wadsworth.

Swinton, D. H. (1992). The economic status of African Americans: Limited ownership and persistent in equality. In B. J. Tidwell (Ed.), *The state of Black America 1992* (pp. 61–117). New York: National Urban League.

Teahan, J. E. (1974). The effect of sex and predominant socioeconomic class school climate on expectations of success among black students. *Journal of Negro Education, 43*, 245–255.

Thomas, G. E. (1985). College major and career in equality: Implications for Black students. *Journal of Negro Education, 54*, 537–547.

Thomas, J. J. (1976). Realism and socioeconomic status (SES) of occupational plans of low SES black and white male adolescents. *Journal of Counseling Psychology, 23*, 46–49.

Thomas, L. C., Kravas, K. J., & Low, H. L. (1979). A current examination of vocational aspirations and actual vocational plans of Black students. *Journal of Non-White Concerns in Personnel and Guidance, 7*, 67–73.

Thomas, M. B., & Neal, P. A. (1978). Collaborating careers: The differential effects of race. *Journal of Vocational Behavior, 12*, 33–42.

Thomas, M. J. (1976). Realism and socioeconomic status of occupational plans of low socioeconomic status Black and White male adolescents. *Journal of Counseling Psychology, 23*, 46–49.

Thomas, V. G. (1983). Perceived traditionality and nontraditionality of career aspirations of Black college women. *Perceptual and Motor Skills, 57*, 979–982.

Thomas, V. G. (1986). Career aspirations, parental support, and work values among black female adolescents. *Journal of Multicultural Counseling and Development, 14*, 177–185.

Thomas, V. G., & Shields, L. C. (1987). Gender influencers on work values of black adolescents. *Adolescence, 22*, 37–43.

Tinsley, H. E. A., & Heesacker, M. (1984). Vocational behavior and career development, 1983: A review. *Journal of Vocational Behavior, 25*, 139–190.

Torrance, E. P., & Allen, W. R. (1980). Racial and sex differences in "Images of the Future." *Perceptual and Motor Skills, 50*, 285–286.

Turner, B. F., & McCaffrey, J. H. (1974). Socialization and career orientation among black and white college women. *Journal of Vocational Behavior, 5*, 307–319.

U.S. Department of Labor, Bureau of Labor Statistics. (1991, January). *Employment and earnings.* Washington, DC: U.S. Government Printing Office.

Wagoner, N. E., & Bridwell, S. D. (1989). High school students' motivations for a career as a physician. *Academic Medicine, 64*, 325–327.

Wakefield, J. A., Jr., Alston, H. L., Yom, B. L., Doughtie, E. B., & Chang, W. C. (1975). Personality types and traits in the Vocational Preference Inventory. *Journal of Vocational Behavior, 22*, 58–60.

Wakefield, J. A., Jr., Yom, B. L., Doughtie, E. B., Chang, W. C., & Alston, H. L. (1975). The geometric relationship between Holland's personality typology and the Vocational Preference Inventory for Blacks. *Journal of Counseling Psychology, 22*, 58–60.

Walsh, W. B., Bingham, R. P., Horton, J. A., & Spokane, A. (1979). Holland's theory and college-degreed working black-white women. *Journal of Vocational Behavior, 15,* 217–223.

Walsh, W. B., Bingham, R. P., & Sheffey, M. A. (1986). Holland's theory and college educated working black men and women. *Journal of Vocational Behavior, 29,* 194–200.

Walsh, W. B., Hildebrand, J. O., Ward, C. M., & Matthews, D. F. (1983). Holland's theory and non-college degreed working Black and White women. *Journal of Vocational Behavior, 22,* 182–190.

Walsh, W. B., Woods, W. J., & Ward, C. M. (1986). Holland's theory and working black and white women. *Journal of Multicultural Counseling and Development, 14,* 116–123.

Ward, C. M., & Walsh, W. B. (1981). Concurrent validity of Holland's theory for non-college-degreed black women. *Journal of Vocational Behavior, 18,* 356–361.

Warnath, C. F. (1975). Vocational theories: Direction to nowhere. *Personnel and Guidance Journal, 53,* 422–428.

Westbrook, B. W., Cutts, C. C., Madison, S. S., & Arcia, M. A. (1980). The validity of the Crites model of career maturity. *Journal of Vocational Behavior, 16,* 249–281.

Westbrook, B. W., & Sanford, E. E. (1991). The validity of career maturity attitude measures among Black and White high school students. *Career Development Quarterly, 39,* 199–208.

Westbrook, B. W., Sanford, E. E., & Donnelly, M. H. (1990). The relationship between career maturity test scores and appropriateness of career choices: A replication. *Journal of Vocational Behavior, 36,* 20–32.

Westbrook, B. W., Sanford, E. E., Merwin, G., Fleenor, J., & Gilleland, K. (1988). Career maturity in Grade 9: Can students who make appropriate career choices for others also make appropriate career choices for themselves? *Measurement and Evaluation in Counseling and Development, 21,* 64–71.

White, J. L. (1984). *The psychology of Blacks: An Afro-American perspective.* Englewood Cliffs, NJ: Prentice-Hall.

White, J. L., Parham, W. D., & Parham, T. A. (1980). Black psychology: The Afro-American tradition as a unifying force for traditional psychology. In R. L. Jones (Ed.), *Black psychology* (2nd ed., pp. 56–66). New York: Harper & Row.

Wilson, R., & Brown, D. (1992). African Americans and career development: Focus on education. In D. Brown & C. W. Minor (Eds.), *Career needs in a diverse workforce: Implications of the NCDA Gallup survey* (pp. 11–26). Alexandria, VA: National Career Development Association.

Yom, B. L., Doughtie, E. B., Wei, N. C., Alston, H. L., & Wakefield, J. A., Jr. (1975). The factor structure of the Vocational Preference Inventory for black and white college students. *Journal of Vocational Behavior, 6,* 15–18.

Zuckerman, D. M. (1980). Self-esteem, self-concept, and the life goals and sex-role attitudes of college students. *Journal of Personality, 48,* 149–162.

Theory and Research on Racial and Ethnic Minorities: Hispanic Americans

Consuelo Arbona
University of Houston

The term *Hispanic* is widely used by social scientists to refer to a very diverse group of people who share a history of Spanish colonialism in the American continent. Hispanics in the United States include people whose national origin is Mexico, Puerto Rico, Cuba, as well as countries in Central and South America (Tienda & Ortiz, 1986). The term *Hispanic* is also used to refer to people with links to Spain or Mexico who have been in the United States for many generations (mainly in Arizona, New Mexico, and Colorado), and who consider themselves of Hispanic origin even though they do not identify with any specific country in Latin America. This last group is commonly referred to as "Other Hispanics" (Bean & Tienda, 1987). The label *Hispanic*, however, is not universally accepted by the population of Latin American origin in the United States. Currently its use is debated among social scientists, many of whom would prefer a wider use of the term *Latino* to refer to this multiethnic group (Calderon, 1992; Gomez, 1992).

As of March 1991, the estimate of the Hispanic origin civilian, noninstitutional population in the United States was 21,437 million, or about 8.6% of the total population. Hispanics of Mexican origin accounted for approximately 62.6% of all Hispanics in the mainland United States, Puerto Ricans accounted for 11.1%, Cubans for 4.9%, Central and South Americans for 13.8%, and "Other Hispanics," for 7.6% (U.S. Bureau of the Census, 1991). During the decade of the 1980s, the Hispanic origin population increased by 48.3% compared to an 11.9% increase for the total population and a 9.3% increase for the non-Hispanic population (U.S. Bureau of the Census, 1991; Valdivieso & Davis, 1988).

As a group, Hispanics are one of the fastest growing minority groups, as well as the nation's youngest subpopulation. Because of their relative youth, high fertility rates, and continued immigration, it is expected that in the decades to come Hispanics will constitute a growing share of U.S. schoolchildren and young job seekers (Valdivieso & Davis, 1988). The Bureau of Labor Statistics (Fullerton, 1991) projects that Hispanics will constitute approximately 11.1% of the total labor force in 2005, up from 7.7% in 1990, which represents the largest increase in share of any other demographic group.

Besides the existence of a zeitgeist emphasizing diversity, the career development of Hispanics has become a salient issue in the social sciences literature because it is believed that the quality of the future U.S. labor market will depend, to a great extent, on this group's education and job skills. Economists from the Bureau of Labor Statistics noted that the United States needs a highly trained and skilled labor force to bolster production and maintain its competitiveness in international markets (Carey & Franklin, 1991; Kustcher, 1989). However, compared to other industrialized nations, U.S. youth rank among the lowest in terms of literacy and math and science proficiency (Kustcher, 1991). Although this lack of educational achievement is true of all groups, it is particularly pronounced among African-American and Hispanic youth. Because Hispanics are the fastest growing sector of the U.S. labor market, their lack of educational and occupational attainment raises considerable concern. In contrast to these demographic and economic trends, the career development of Hispanics has received very little attention in the theoretical and empirical literature (Arbona, 1990; Hackett, Lent, & Greenhaus, 1991).

The purpose of this chapter is threefold: (a) to review the relevance and utility of various career theories and models from mainstream vocational psychology to the understanding of the vocational behavior and career development of Hispanics; (b) to review theories from ethnic minority psychology that will add to our understanding of career issues related to Hispanics; and (c) to review research related to the theories discussed and suggest directions for future research. Because the empirical literature on the career development of Hispanics was reviewed recently by Arbona (1990), this chapter emphasizes recent research and research that is directly related to the theoretical approaches discussed. In the first section of the chapter characteristics of Hispanic subgroups are briefly discussed. Following, a framework for identifying and examining characteristics of Hispanic subgroups relevant for career development is offered. Finally, the areas of theory and research related to vocational psychology and career counseling with Hispanics is addressed.

WITHIN-GROUP VARIABILITY
AND THE CAREER DEVELOPMENT OF HISPANICS

In general, Hispanics have difficulty obtaining good jobs and earning a decent income even in prosperous times (Valdivieso & Davis, 1988). However, because of their location, education, and immigration histories, the various subgroups suffer in the labor market in different ways and to different degrees. Hispanics have immigrated to the United States at different times and for different reasons. The two largest groups, Mexicans and Puerto Ricans, have immigrated for mainly economic reasons. Cubans, for the most part, came to the United States as political refugees, whereas Central and South Americans have migrated for both political and economic reasons.

To understand the various Hispanic groups' position in the labor force, it is necessary to examine several indicators such as labor force participation rate (percentage of the population that is either employed or seeking employment), unemployment rate, distribution among occupations, education, and income. Lack of space precludes a detailed presentation and discussion of these demographic characteristics of the various Hispanic subgroups. Statistics provided by the Current Population Survey (U.S. Bureau of the Census, 1991), however, show that as a group Hispanics have similar rates of labor force participation than non-Hispanics, but considerable lower educational and occupational attainment. As it may be expected, Hispanics as a group also count with less economic resources and have a larger proportion of families living below poverty level than non-Hispanics (25.4% vs. 19.5%). Furthermore, all Hispanic groups have a considerably larger proportion of children living below poverty level (ranging from 31% among Cubans to 56.7% among Puerto Ricans) than non-Hispanics (18.3%). Puerto Ricans and Mexican Americans are in a more disadvantaged position in terms of all the socioeconomic descriptors than the other Hispanic groups, whereas Cubans seem to be the most advantaged group. Among the population 25 years and older, Mexican Americans have the largest proportion of people with less than 5 years of schooling (15.9% vs. 1.6% for non-Hispanics) and the smallest proportion with 4 years or more of college (7.4% vs. 25.2% for non-Hispanics). In contrast, Cubans and Central and South Americans have the highest proportion with college degrees (18.55% and 15.1%, respectively). Given the high school dropout rates among Hispanics, particularly among Mexican American and Puerto Rican youth (U.S. Bureau of the Census, 1988), it does not seem that the academic achievement of Hispanics will improve substantially in the near future.

Various authors have noted that prevalent career theories and their related research are most relevant for individuals who are or will become high-level, career-committed workers (Harmon, 1991; Osipow, 1975). Furthermore, most of these theories are based on the assumptions that individuals have a wide variety of career options to choose from as well as the resources (financial and educational) needed to successfully pursue the choice they identify as most desirable (Osipow, 1975, 1983). In light of their demographic characteristics, it seems quite clear that these assumptions are not true for the majority of Hispanic Americans, and that, therefore, these theories might not be useful in explaining the career development of many members of this group. The question then arises: Are new theories needed to account for the career development of this particular group, or may it be possible to expand current theories so that they will be relevant to special groups, including Hispanics (Astin, 1984; Betz & Fitzgerald, 1987; Osipow, 1983)?

Before these questions may be addressed, it is necessary first to define what it is about being Hispanic that merits special attention from career development theory and research. As Osipow (1975) observed, because individuals usually belong to several groups (e.g., gender, social class, ethnicity), it is important to examine under which conditions which group membership may be salient, as well as to consider the impact on career development of simultaneous membership in various groups. Factors that have been identified as meaningful in distinguishing among Hispanic subgroups include demographic characteristics, such as gender, socioeconomic background, and level of education, as well as culturally related variables such as country of origin, migration status (documented vs. undocumented), migration history (U.S. born vs. immigrant), and acculturation level (Castro & Baezconde-Garbanati, 1987, cited in Marin & Marin, 1991). In the following section a framework for identifying and examining the characteristics of Hispanic subgroups that may be relevant to career development is described.

FRAMEWORK FOR IDENTIFYING HISPANIC SUBGROUPS' CHARACTERISTICS RELEVANT FOR CAREER DEVELOPMENT THEORY AND RESEARCH

In examining the applicability of career theories to Hispanic populations, it is important to separate ethnicity from socio-economic background, characteristics that have been widely confounded in the career-related research (Arbona, 1990; Osipow, 1975). It is likely that the experiences and needs of middle-class Hispanics may be very different from the experiences and needs of Hispanics from low-socioeconomic background. And, it is possible that the patterns of similarities and differences in career development between White Americans and Hispanics of various social classes and generational levels may be distinct as well. At the same time, issues related to ethnic and racial identity and dealing with discrimination are likely to become salient regardless of one's social class because of the negative value attached to Hispanic ethnicity by the majority culture (Cervantes, Padilla, & Salgado de Snyder, 1991; Locci & Carranza, 1990; Penley, Gould, De la Vina, & Murphy, 1989; Ramirez, 1988). However, none of the existing theories in vocational psychology has examined the influence of race and ethnicity in the career development process (Thomas & Alderfer, 1989).

As Thomas and Alderfer (1989) noted, a unique experience of minority members is that often they need to become bicultural to function effectively in their families and communities and in mainstream institutions such as school and work. Migration history and socioeconomic background (economic resources and educational attainment) are two factors that are expected to influence significantly the Hispanic's ability to juggle these two worlds, because they are predictive of the resources the individual will have in meeting educational and occupational tasks. In reviewing the literature on family factors that influence vocational development, Schulenberg, Vondracek, and Crouter (1984) noted that family socioeconomic status (SES) is probably the best predictor of an individual's occupational status. In addition, various researchers have found that the type of psychosocial stress experienced by Hispanics in the United States is related to recency of immigration (Cervantes et al., 1991; Mena, Padilla, & Maldonado, 1987).

To understand the experience of Hispanic Americans, both sociodemographic characteristics and culturally related psychological processes need to be considered. Culturally related factors that are expected to impact the career development and occupational behavior of Hispanics include acculturation level, ethnic identity, race, and the experience of discrimination. Although these factors are expected to impact the life experience of most Hispanics, their specific effect on the life of individuals is believed to be moderated by the person's socioeconomic background and recency of immigration. Therefore, in the framework described here socioeconomic background and migration history are used as overarching dimensions to classify Hispanic Americans.

Socioeconomic background refers to the occupational standing and educational level of parents among children and adolescents, and of the individual (and spouse if applicable) among adults. For purposes of this discussion three levels of SES are identified: low, middle and high. However, it is recognized that for empirical purposes SES may be measured as a continuous variable (Duncan, 1961), or it may be categorized in terms of more levels (Hollingshed & Redlich, 1958). It is important to note that because recent immigrants from Latin American countries tend to experience a decline in occupational status due to language and credentialing issues, educational attainment is usually a more accurate indicator of SES among Hispanic immigrants than income or present occupation (Laosa, 1982).

Migration history refers to recency of immigration of the person and his or her family of origin and it is operationalized in terms of generation in the United States. For the purpose of this discussion three generational levels are identified: first, second, and third or later. First-generation immigrants are those who were born in a Latin American country, second generation refers to Hispanics who were born in the United States with parents (one or both) who were born elsewhere, whereas third and later generation refers to individuals of Hispanic descent who themselves and their parents were born in the United States (Keefe & Padilla, 1987; Marin & Marin, 1991).

In the framework proposed here, the three levels of SES (or educational level) and generational status are treated as separate axes forming a nine-cell matrix (see Fig. 2.1) that allows to categorize members of a particular Hispanic group in terms of both socioeconomic background and recency of immigration. For example, cell I would include first-generation immigrants of low SES, whereas cell IX would include third-generation (or later) immigrants of high SES. In general terms, this classification is relevant for all Hispanic national groups; however, the implications of the categories will differ somewhat among the groups. For example, first-generation immigrants from Mexico and South and Central Latin America may face problems with immigration and naturalization services not encountered by Puerto Ricans or many Cubans. Also, some national groups will be more represented in some cells than in others. For example, compared to the other groups, Cubans are likely to have a larger proportion of people in Cells II and III, whereas Puerto Ricans are likely to be concentrated in Cells I and IV. However, it is expected that all national groups are represented in all cells.

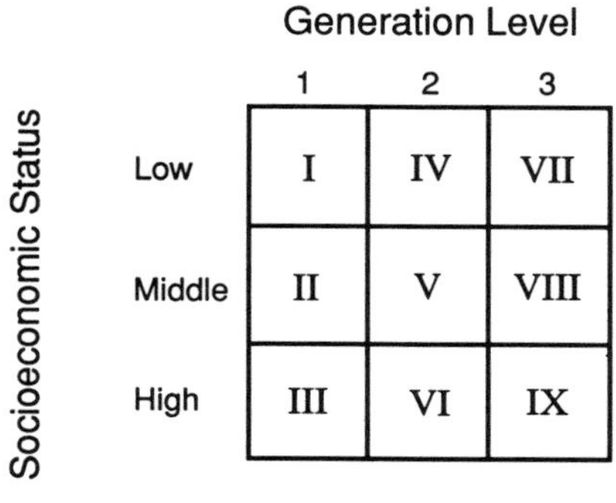

Generation Level

Socioeconomic Status		1	2	3
	Low	I	IV	VII
	Middle	II	V	VIII
	High	III	VI	IX

FIG. 2.1. Framework to classify Hispanic Americans.

As was indicated earlier, in examining the career development of Hispanics it is also important to consider the impact of culturally related variables such as acculturation, ethnic identity, race, and the experience of discrimination. Of these variables, acculturation has received the most attention among social and behavioral scientists. The term *acculturation* first appeared in the anthropological literature in the 1920s and referred to the process of cultural change fostered by the experience of continuous, firsthand contact between two culturally different groups (Olmedo, 1979; Keefe & Padilla, 1987). Theoretically, the process of acculturation may result in cultural changes in one or both groups. However, in the case of groups who differ in power, like Hispanic immigrants in the United States, the dominated group is the one who tends to experience the greatest change as a result of the contact (Hazuda, Stern, & Haffner, 1988). Consequently, *acculturation* is most often used to refer to the process by which immigrants adapt to the sociocultural and psychological characteristics of the host society (Olmedo, 1979), and level of acculturation is often interpreted as a measure of the person's capacity to function and interact in the larger society (Keefe & Padilla, 1987).

Given this definition, it is expected that higher levels of acculturation will facilitate the process of career development among Hispanic Americans. Results of the acculturation research have consistently shown that English language proficiency is one of the best indicators of degree of acculturation (Marin & Marin, 1991), and that among recent immigrants acculturation level is directly and positively related to socioeconomic status and level of education (Neggy & Woods, 1992). In terms of the framework described earlier, then, it is expected that Hispanics from the second and later generations (Cells IV to IX) will be more acculturated than first-generation Hispanics (Cells I to III), and that among first-generation Hispanics, those of higher socioeconomic classes and educational levels (Cells II and III) will be more acculturated than their more disadvantaged counterparts (Cell I).

Although acculturation and generational status are often positively correlated (Keefe & Padilla, 1987), some research suggests that the impact of acculturation among Hispanic adolescents may be mediated by generational level. For example, Wall, Power, and Arbona (1993) found that among first-, second-, and third-generation Mexican-American high school students acculturation was related to susceptibility to peer pressure among only the first-generation group. Therefore, in examining the relation between acculturation and career variables, both generational status and acculturation level should be taken into account.

It is beyond the scope of this chapter to discuss in detail the various acculturation models in the literature; however, it is important to mention that most recent models conceptualize acculturation as a complex, multidimensional process (Keefe & Padilla, 1987) that may include both an accommodation to the host culture as well as the retention of traditional cultural traits. Therefore, becoming proficient in the Anglo culture does not necessarily imply giving up Hispanic cultural traits; a Hispanic person may have developed a bicultural orientation that implies socialization and active participation in two or more cultures (Ramirez, 1984). Furthermore, the loss or adoption of cultural traits may vary from trait to trait and may be related to contextual factors (Keefe & Padilla, 1987). For example, a Hispanic person may prefer to use English and display highly acculturated behaviors in certain contexts such as work but prefer Spanish language and ascribe to Hispanic values in family situations. Therefore, in exploring the impact of acculturation in career development, it will be important to take into account the complexity of this process.

Ethnic identity refers to a person's feelings and attitudes toward affiliation with one's socially ascribed ethnic group versus the dominant or majority group (Keefe & Padilla, 1987; Phinney, 1990). The importance of ethnic (and/or racial) identity formation in the personality development of ethnic minorities has been recently recognized by various researchers (Helms, 1990; Phinney, 1990; Smith, 1991). Although in the acculturation research literature the terms ethnic identity and acculturation have often been used interchangeably (Phinney, 1990), these two constructs refer to related but distinct processes (Keefe & Padilla, 1987; Phinney, 1990). In acculturation the main focus is on how individuals relate to the dominant society, whereas in the process of ethnic identity formation the focus is on how individuals relate to themselves and their own group as a subgroup of the dominant society (Phinney, 1990). It is proposed here that ethnic identity formation is an important aspect of the career development process of Hispanic Americans that should be examined in the context of these developmental theories. This topic is discussed further later in the chapter.

The experience of discrimination based on ethnic, racial, and linguistic characteristics has been widely recognized as an important aspect of the life experience of most minority group members in the United States (Ramirez, 1988; Smith, 1991). A special study conducted by the National Commission for Employment Policy (NCEP; 1982) concluded that, besides lack of language proficiency and low levels of education, discrimination against Hispanics on the basis of their ethnic and linguistic characteristics has contributed significantly to their disadvantaged position in the labor market. Results of the NCEP (1982) study showed that Puerto Rican and Mexican-American men were in lower paying occupations than non-Hispanic Whites even when factors such as language proficiency and education were taken into account. Also, among men with similar language problems, Hispanics were in lower paying occupations than non-Hispanics.

There is some evidence to suggest that racial differences are also related to occupational attainment and discrimination among Hispanics. Hispanics vary widely in terms of racial characteristics, ranging from dark to light skin tone and from African- or Native-American to European physiognomy (Montalvo, 1991). Various researchers have found that Puerto Ricans and Mexican Americans of light skin color and European appearance are likely to report higher SES and educational levels and fewer experiences of discrimination than their darker, non-White-looking counterparts (Arce, Murgia, & Frisbie, 1987; Bullington & Arbona,1994; Denton & Massey, 1989; Relethford, Stern, Gaskill, and Hazuda, 1983). These findings suggest that in the process of career development the impact of ethnic and language discrimination may be moderated by the person's racial characteristics. Applying these findings to the framework outlined earlier, we may hypothesize that Hispanics included in Cells VI and IX, which are likely to include a large proportion of light-skinned and White-looking individuals with high levels of acculturation and English proficiency, will probably experience less discrimination than Hispanics included in the other cells. At the same time, the difficulties encountered by poor and uneducated Hispanics (Cells I, IV, and VII) may be augmented by the discrimination they may experience due to their racial characteristics. Therefore, it is crucial that vocational psychology theory and research examine the impact of discrimination in the career development of Hispanics.

In this section of the chapter a framework has been offered to distinguish among Hispanic populations based on two characteristics, SES and generational level, which are considered to significantly impact the career development process. Also, cultural and ethnic issues that are likely to be salient for Hispanics, regardless of social class, are discussed in relation to their impact on career development.

THEORIES OF CAREER DEVELOPMENT:
AN APPLICATION TO HISPANIC GROUPS

The theoretical and empirical literature related to careers is vast and complex. Reviewers of this literature have identified two major traditions in the study of careers, the counseling psychology and the organizational behavioral perspectives (Fitzgerald & Rounds, 1989; Hackett et al., 1991). The counseling psychology tradition has emphasized the process by which people make and implement career decisions focusing on vocational outcomes from the perspective of the individual (Borgen, 1991; Hackett et al., 1991). The organizational behavior perspective, on the other hand, has emphasized the study of the interaction between the person and the work situation, focusing on outcomes that are of more interest to the organization than to the individual such as working climate, productivity, absenteeism, and turnover (Hackett et al., 1991).

Researchers in the career development field (Borow, 1982; Collin & Young, 1986; Super, 1990) have concluded that a comprehensive theory of career development does not yet exist but that, instead, we have a series of "segmental" (Super, 1990) theories that address different aspects of the career development process that may be useful for different populations and different problems. In this section, I review some of these "segmental" theories within the counseling psychology perspective (dominant as well as emergent theories) and discuss how some of their constructs may be applied or expanded to examine career-related processes among Hispanic-American groups.

The theoretical approaches that are emphasized in this chapter are: (a) Super's (1957, 1990) developmental theory; (b) Vondracek, Lerner, and Schulenberg's (1986) contextual-developmental approach; and (c) social learning approaches, specifically self-efficacy theory (Hackett & Betz, 1981). These approaches are emphasized because of their possible applicability to the career development of Hispanic subgroups and also because they were identified as major general theoretical perspectives by recent reviewers of the career psychology research literature (Borgen, 1991; Hackett & Lent, 1992). Holland's (1985) theory of vocational choice, which is considered one of the most influential person–environment (P–E) approaches in the career literature, is covered only briefly because it is discussed in depth in chapter 6 of this book.

Holland's Theory

Holland's (1985) theory proposed that work environments and people may be classified in terms of six types based on their predominant areas of interests—realistic, investigative, artistic, social, enterprising, and conventional (RIASEC). According to the theory, individuals tend to choose educational paths and careers that match their most salient interests. Research related to Holland's theory has focused mainly on three areas: (a) the correspondence between personality and environmental types in different occupations; (b) the study of the definition and predictive validity of the constructs of congruency, consistency, and differentiation; and (c) the research on assessment instruments, mainly of career interests, based on the theory (Weinrach & Srebalus, 1990).

Of these three areas, only the last one has received substantial research attention among Hispanic populations. In summary, the findings of studies using different instruments with diverse Hispanic subgroups suggest that Hispanic high school and college students' view of the world of work is similar to the view held by the majority culture, and that the Holland scales are appropriate for assessing the career interests of these students (Arbona, 1990). Research with other minority groups and blue collar workers suggest that there is a general fit between personality and environment type among these populations which is consistent with related findings with Whites and college graduates. It is possible that this aspect of the theory will apply to Hispanic populations as well, however, this has not been tested empirically.

Super's Developmental Theory

In contrast to P–E fit approaches, which have focused on the content and predictability of career choices, developmental approaches have attempted to explain changes in career-related behaviors and attitudes across the life span, emphasizing the process (vs. the content) of career decision making. Of all the developmental perspectives, Super's theory (1957, 1990) is the most comprehensive and widely researched (Brown, 1990; Hackett & Lent, 1992).

Like development in general, career development has been conceptualized as a continuous, dynamic process that involves the interaction of many psychological and social factors. Super (1990) described this process as a series of vocational stages (growth, exploration, establishment, maintenance, and decline) that provide the framework for specific career-related tasks (behaviors and attitudes) to be mastered or accomplished. Other major aspects of Super's theory include: (a) the concept of career maturity, which refers to a person's ability to meet the demands of vocational tasks appropriate to one's age or life situation; (b) the implementation of the self-concept in the development of a vocational identity; (c) career patterns, or the occupational level and sequencing of jobs; and (d) role saliency, that is, the relative importance of the worker, student, leisurite, and homemaker roles for the individual.

In his early and recent writings, Super (1957, 1990) has acknowledged the possible impact of race, ethnicity, and SES in the process of career development. However, neither theoretical formulations nor empirical research to date have elucidated which specific aspects of SES or ethnicity impact which aspects of career development for specific populations. Most of the research related to Super's work concentrated on the development of instruments to assess major constructs such as career maturity (Super, Thompson, Lindeman, Jordaan, & Myers, 1981), adult career concerns (Super, Thompson, & Lindeman, 1988), and role saliency (Super & Neville, 1986). With the exception of the Career Pattern Study (Super, 1957), most of this research in the United States has been conducted with White college students, and therefore there is very little empirical information related to the validity of the instruments and the theory among people of low-socioeconomic resources (White and non-White) and among ethnic minorities.

As was suggested earlier, because of the great variability among Hispanic subgroups in socioeconomic background, racial characteristics, and acculturation, it is possible that many of the tenets of Super's career development theory are relevant to some Hispanic subgroups. It is suggested here that most aspects of Super's theory are likely to be relevant for middle- and upper-class Hispanics (Cells II, III, V, VI VIII, and IX) and, regardless of social class, for adolescents for whom the student and worker role is salient as well as for highly educated adults. The findings of a few studies provide some support for this proposition.

Research reviewed by Arbona (1990) suggests that middle-class and college-educated Mexican Americans and Anglos are similar in their attitudes toward work (Isonio & Garza, 1987; Raines, 1988) as well as characteristics related to need for achievement and career progression behaviors in white-collar occupations (Gould, 1980, 1982). Similarly, Penley et al. (1989) found very few differences in the reported career strategies or career expectations of Hispanic and non-Hispanic White college graduates in business. Arbona and Novy (1991) found more gender than ethnic differences in the career aspirations and expectations among African-American, Hispanic, and White college students. More directly related to Super's theory, Luzzo (1992) found that Hispanic college students did not differ from their White-American peers in career decision-making attitudes (Crites, 1978), career decision-making skills (Super et al., 1981), or vocational congruence (between assessed interests and occupational aspirations). And, finally, one study was found that suggested that Super's stage theory is relevant for Hispanic adolescents for whom school and career plans are salient issues. (Bullington & Arbona, 1994).

Bullington and Arbona (1994) utilized semistructured interviews with four Mexican-American high school students (two males and two females) from working-class backgrounds, who were participating in a summer academic enrichment program, to explore to what extent these youngsters were engaged in vocational-appropriate tasks according to Super's theory. Their findings suggested that these students were immersed in tasks that mark the exploratory stage of career development that, according to theory, are expected of those in their age group. Furthermore, these students showed clear indications of planfulness, exploration, and realism, which are important dimensions of Super's career maturity construct.

The study by Bullington and Arbona (1994) also suggested that issues related to ethnicity are salient among Mexican-American students. As they talked about their current lives and reflected upon their plans for the future, the four students showed an awareness of the negative ways in which Hispanics are often characterized. However, the feelings these students expressed regarding their ethnicity ranged from pride to ambivalence to detachment. In light of these findings and the theoretical and empirical literature on ethnic identity (Phinney, 1990; Smith, 1991), it is very likely that developing a sense of ethnic identity constitutes an additional developmental task that Hispanics need to contend with in the process of implementing their self-concept in a vocational identity. Research with African-American adults lends support for this proposition. For example, it has been found that (Gooden, 1980, and Herbert, 1986, cited in Thomas & Alderfer, 1989) although Levinson's model of adult development fit the experiences of African-American males from various professions and social classes, it did not account for the impact of race in their lives. For these men, coming to terms with their sense of self as African-American individuals (ethnic/racial identity) and dealing with the implications of race in their lives became a task in itself.

One way to expand Super's stage theory, then, to make it more relevant to Hispanics is to examine to what extent the process of ethnic identity formation becomes a developmental task in itself that affects the process of resolving more directly related vocational tasks. According to Erikson (1968), one of the central aspects of identity development among late adolescents is the selection of an occupational identity. Similarly, career development theory proposes that the crystallization of vocational plans, that is, the development of a vocational identity, is facilitated by the achievement of a clear and integrated sense of self (Holland, 1985; Super, 1957, 1990). Therefore, to the extent that issues related to ethnicity and race are salient aspects of minority adolescents' sense of self, such issues are likely to impact the development of a vocational identity.

Phinney and her colleagues found that exploration of ethnic identity issues is much more salient among minority adolescents and young adults (particularly African Americans and Mexican Americans) than among their majority counterparts (Phinney, 1989; Phinney & Alipuria, 1990; Phinney & Tarver, 1989). Ethnic or racial identity among members of minority groups is conceptualized as one domain of the overall ego identity of the person that, because of societal discrimination and oppression, often becomes a salient and overruling aspect of the personality (Phinney, 1990; Smith, 1991). Smith (1991), furthermore, argued that ethnic identity often becomes a "superordinate identity" (p. 183) that serves to limit the roles the minority individual may pursue. Smith's (1991) views are consistent with Ogbu (1992), who proposed that the lack of achievement among ethnic minorities may be explained in part by the way they define their ethnic identity. Ogbu's research (e.g., Fordham & Ogbu, 1986; Ogbu & Matute-Bianchi 1986, cited in Ogbu, 1992) with African-American adolescents suggested that these students often construe a sense of ethnic identity in opposition to the values and beliefs embodied by the school, which leads them to reject attitudes and behaviors conducive to school achievement, because they equate them with acting "White." Matute-Bianchi's (1986) observational study with Mexican-American high school students suggested that a similar process may take place among Hispanic adolescents. She found that academically successful Mexican-American students were pejoratively called "Wannabes," that is, wanting to become white, by their less school-oriented peers.

These propositions regarding ethnic identity formation among minority individuals have important implications regarding the career development of Hispanic Americans. To what extent, we may ask, do difficulties and successes in negotiating a sense of ethnic identity relate to Hispanic adolescents' behaviors related to career-related tasks? To what extent is progress in meeting vocational development tasks, such as personal and career exploration and commitment to career plans, related to the process of ego identity in general and ethnic identity specifically? What is the relationship between the process of ethnic identity formation and the development of a vocational identity among Hispanics?

Addressing these questions requires a conceptualization and an operationalization of ethnic and vocational identity in the context of overall ego identity development. Unfortunately, much work still needs to be completed on both fronts. Vondracek (1992) recently reviewed the attempts to incorporate Erikson's identity theory to vocational theory and concluded that the field still needs to develop an adequate construct of vocational identity and to explicate how this construct relates to ego identity in general. Similarly, various conceptualizations of ethnic and racial identity have been proposed (Helms, 1990; Phinney, 1990); however, further work is needed in defining this construct for Hispanic populations, devising methods to assess it, and examining how ethnic identity relates to overall ego identity development (Arbona, Flores, & Novy, in press).

Recent studies investigating the relation between general ego identity development and career development variables have utilized Erikson's (1968) model of ego identity development as operationalized by Marcia (1966, 1980). Marcia suggested that individuals may be described in terms of four distinct ego identity status characterized by exploratory and commitment activities related to establishing a sense of personal identity in areas such as occupation, ideology, and religion. These identity status are labeled *identity diffusion* (lack of exploration or commitment), *foreclosure* (commitment without exploration), *moratorium* (engaged in exploration without a commitment being made), and *achieved identity* (exploring and resolving ethnic identity issues). Results of studies with White college students suggest that level of ego identity development is related to career exploration and occupational commitment (Bluestein, Devenis, & Kidney, 1989), to career decision-making styles (Bluestein & Phillips, 1990), and to clarity of vocational goals, abilities, and talents (Savickas, 1985).

Concurrent with this work, and also based on Marcia's ego identity status, Phinney (1991) has proposed a model and a measure of ethnic identity development, which taps ethnic identity achievement (including both exploration and commitment), positive attitudes and sense of belonging, and ethnic behaviors. Phinney's model and instrument are applicable across ethnic groups including White Americans. In research with minority adolescents (including Hispanics), Phinney and her colleagues have found that higher levels of exploration and commitment related to ethnicity is positively related to psychological adjustment, ego development (Phiney, 1989), and self-esteem (Chavira & Phinney, 1991; Phinney & Alipuria, 1990).

In summary, research stemming from Marcia's and Phinney's models suggests that ego identity is related to career variables among White college students and that ethnic identity is related to psychological well-being among minority adolescents. These findings suggest that Marcia's model provides a useful framework from which to examine the relationship between ethnic identity and career development processes in the context of overall ego identity development. Research efforts designed to explore the relation between ego identity, ethnic identity, and career development variables among Hispanic adolescents and young adults are clearly indicated.

In summary, the literature reviewed suggests that many of the tenets of Super's career theory may apply to some segments of the Hispanic population, and that research efforts are sorely needed to explore the applicability of the theory to specific Hispanic subgroups. Also, it has been proposed that Super's stage theory needs to be expanded to examine the impact of ethnic identity formation in the career development process of Hispanics.

Developmental-Contextual Approach

Most of the research stemming from Super's theory has emphasized the relationship between intraindividual factors and vocational variables in isolation of the context or the environment. Very little attention has been paid in this research to the possibility that the context may mediate the intraindividual associations found (Vondracek et al., 1986). Sociological approaches, on the other hand, have widely documented that aspects of the context, such as SES and ethnicity, are strong predictors of academic and occupational attainment (Hotchkiss & Borow, 1990). However, this research has not examined the process by which specific factors associated with SES and ethnicity are translated into actual behaviors regarding schooling and career attainment.

Based on ecological models of human development, Vondracek and his colleagues (Vondracek, 1990; Vondracek et al., 1986) have proposed a framework for a developmental-contextual approach to career development that attempts to conceptualize the interaction between a changing person acting in and reacting to a changing context. This perspective describes the development process in terms of relationships within the person (intrapsychic approach) and relationships between people and their different contexts. Borrowing from Bronfenbrenner (1979), Vondracek et al. (1986) described the structure of the environment as nested, interconnected systems that vary in the degree of proximity to the individual person. These systems include the microsystem, which contains the developing person directly such as the family or the school; the mesosystem, which refers to the links between various microsytems (e.g., parents and teachers); the exosystem, which refers to aspects of the context that are indirectly related to the person like parents place of employment; and the macrosystem, which refers to the larger society including (but not limited to) public policy, laws, and cultural values.

According to the developmental-contextual model, several microsystems are relevant to adolescents' career development: family, school, peer group and job setting (Vondracek et al., 1986). Of these, the family and the school are considered to be most salient. These authors suggest that, to discover the causal link in the relation between characteristics of the family (such as SES and ethnicity) and academic and career development, one must investigate the impact of these factors on three mechanisms of occupational socialization: (a) the activities children and adolescents may engage in; (b) the quality of the interpersonal relationships within the family and other social contexts such as school and work; and (c) the roles the youngster has the opportunity to observe and engage in (Vondracek, 1991; Vondracek et al., 1986; Young, Friesen, & Pearson, 1988). Given the importance of the family in Hispanic culture, it seems relevant to examine the process by which the characteristics of the family influence the educational and career-related behaviors of Hispanic children and adolescents. By examining families who vary in SES and generational level (according to the framework suggested earlier), it may be possible to tease out socioeconomic- from culturally related influences in behavior.

Conducting research from the perspective of the developmental-contextual model is a very complex enterprise that requires approaches different from the quantitative psychologically based methodologies traditionally used in career-counseling research. Because the individual and the context affect each other in complex and reciprocal ways, it is not always possible to predict or to manipulate such interactions. What is needed, then, are longitudinal and qualitative studies that will allow for the observation and description of people's experiences as they interact with the various aspects of their environment (Vondracek et al., 1986). Exploratory and descriptive studies, however, are very scarce in the career literature in general (Vondracek, 1990) and practically nonexistent in the literature specific to Hispanics (Arbona, 1990). Young and his colleagues initiated an interview-based research program to uncover the activities and types of interpersonal relationships middle-class White parents use intentionally to influence their children's career development (Young & Friesen, 1990; Young et al., 1988). Their research has resulted in the identification of 10 categories of behavior used by parents for this purpose (Young & Friesen, 1992). In the study by Bullington and Arbona (1994) described earlier, the authors used semistructured interviews to examine to what extent four Mexican-American adolescents were engaged in appropriate career development tasks or activities as outlined by Super's theory. More extensive studies of this type are needed to explore what differentiates the Hispanic families and adolescents who are and who are not committed to schooling as a means to career achievement.

To illustrate the application of the ecological approach described earlier, I review a few qualitative studies (Delgado-Gaitan, 1992; Goldenberg, 1987, 1989, 1992) that have examined the processes by which activities and interpersonal relations between Hispanic parents and children affect both the children's academic attainment and the teacher's behaviors toward the child in school. Delgado-Gaitan (1992) examined the parent–child interactions regarding school tasks in the homes of six, low-income Mexican-American immigrant parents and their American-born second graders. Three children were classified as novice readers and three as advanced readers. Findings showed that both sets of parents provided emotional and physical support for their children's school activities by setting out a time and space for them to do their homework and either supervising that the task was completed or attempting to help them with it. However, because of their lack of educational experience in the United States and their low levels of educational attainment in Mexico, both groups of parents often experienced great difficulty in understanding the homework requirements. Compared to the other group, parents of the advanced readers contacted the teachers more often, which helped them better understand how to help the children at home.

In a series of case studies with nine low-income Hispanic first graders from immigrant families who were having difficulty in learning to read, Goldenberg (1987, 1989) found that the parents' help at home resulted in higher levels of skill acquisition and motivation in the child, which in turn influenced the teachers' decisions regarding reading-group level in the school. Goldenberg (1992) also found that the teacher's actions in enlisting the mother's help in reading-related tasks appeared to be a crucial intervention in enhancing the reading skills of one student for whom the teacher had low expectations of success at the beginning of the year. Lack of similar attention, on the other hand, negatively affected another student for whom the teacher initially had high expectations of success.

These studies illustrate how the reciprocal influence between parents' and teachers' behaviors affect the learning process among young Hispanic children. At the microsystem level, parent–child interactions were characterized by both support for educational attainment and inability to provide help with specific homework tasks (Delgado-Gaitan, 1992), which illustrates one way parental education impacts children's academic achievement. At the mesosystem level, results suggest that parents' interactions with teachers enhanced the parents' ability to help the children learn and also influenced the children's learning environment within the classroom (in terms of reading-group assignment).

Similar studies are needed to discover how parents and teachers influence the achievement and school persistence of Hispanic adolescents. It is possible that among low-SES Hispanics, parents' lack of ability to help their older children with school-related tasks influences both the adolescents and the teachers in ways that result in low-academic achievement and dropping out of school. As proposed by the ecological approach, longitudinal and case studies of parent–teacher–student interactions with Hispanic families of various social classes and immigration histories are needed to discover the processes by which these factors impact Hispanic's adolescents' activities, interpersonal relations, and roles, which in turn influence their decisions regarding schooling and career choice.

Self-Efficacy Theories

Self-efficacy beliefs refers to expectations about one's ability to initiate and successfully execute courses of action. Bandura (1986) proposed that these beliefs determine, to a great extent, individuals' willingness to initiate specific behaviors as well as their persistence in the face of obstacles or barriers. Because there is evidence to suggest that Hispanics are likely to encounter multiple barriers in the pursuit of their educational and occupational aspirations (Arbona, 1990), it seems that the self-efficacy construct could facilitate understanding the career development process of members of this ethnic group.

Hackett and Betz (1981) first utilized self-efficacy theory to explain gender differences in career choice. More recently, this construct has been examined in relation to other career-related variables such as academic achievement and persistence in college majors, career decision making, and educational and career choices of high school students. Because various reviews of the self-efficacy literature have been published recently (Hackett & Lent, 1992; Lent & Hackett, 1987), this section of the chapter focuses on the few studies that have examined academic and occupational self-efficacy with Hispanic populations (Bores-Rangel, Church, Szendre, & Reeves, 1990; Church, Teresa, Rosebrook, & Szendre, 1992; Hackett, Betz, Casas, & Roca-Singh, 1992; Lauver & Jones, 1991; Solberg, O'Brien, K. Villareal, Kennel, & Davis, 1993).

In general, studies examining the relation of self-efficacy expectations to career choice have found that both interests and self-efficacy beliefs predict extent of consideration of occupations and that males and females tend to express higher self-efficacy for same-gender-dominated occupations, than cross-gender-dominated occupations (Hackett & Lent, 1992; Lent & Hackett, 1987). Similar findings were reported in three studies with Hispanic students (Bores-Rangel et al., 1990; Church et al., 1992; Lauver & Jones, 1991).

In two separate studies with Hispanic seasonal farm workers (predominantly Mexican American) who were participating in a high school equivalency program, Bores-Rangel et al. (1990) and Church et al. (1992) found that students' willingness to consider specific occupations was related to their self-efficacy, interests, and perceived incentive satisfaction (defined as the extent to which student's most salient need or value was met) for those occupations. Regarding gender effects, the Church et al. (1992) results suggested that, whereas both Hispanic men and women reported greater self-efficacy for and willingness to consider occupations dominated by their own gender, women were less willing than men to consider occupations that were not gender consistent.

Lauver and Jones (1991) examined factors related to perceived career options among Native-American, White, and Hispanic (subgroup not specified) rural high school students (grades 9 and 11) and also found that students reported greater self-efficacy for gender-consistent occupations. The women in this study, however, reported higher self-efficacy for cross-gender occupations than the men, which is consistent with previous research with non-Hispanics (e.g., Hannah & Kahn, 1989). In terms of ethnic differences, Native-American students reported the lowest overall self-efficacy rankings, whereas White students reported the highest.

The application of self-efficacy theory to the content of career choice seems most relevant for students with relatively high academic achievement who are able to pursue a postsecondary education. Given the intimate relationship between Holland type of occupation and educational level (Arbona, 1989), the career choices available to students with a high school degree or less are, in reality, very limited. Therefore, it may be most relevant for the career development of Hispanic students who are at risk academically to examine the contribution of self-efficacy beliefs to their academic achievement.

Various studies have found that academic self-efficacy is related to academic performance among students of various educational levels (Bores-Rangel et al., 1990; Hackett et al., 1992; Lent, Brown, & Larkin, 1984, 1986, 1987), and that the relation between self-efficacy beliefs and academic outcomes is stronger among low-achieving than among average- or high-achieving students (Brown, Lent, & Larkin, 1989; Multon, Brown, & Lent, 1991). Two studies were found that examined these issues with Hispanics. In a study with Mexican-American and Anglo engineering students, Hackett et al. (1992) found that in regression equations gender nor ethnicity predicted academic achievement, whereas academic self-efficacy emerged as the strongest predictor. Furthermore, past performance was related to college grades only after the influence of academic self-efficacy was removed. Similarly, among a small sample of Hispanic students (31 out of 35 were Hispanic) enrolled in a high school equivalency program, students' self-efficacy ratings for subject matter at the beginning of the course were significantly related to posttest scores in the General Equivalence Development test (GED) even after controlling for GED pretest scores (Bores-Rangel et al., 1990).

These findings suggest that Hispanic students' academic achievement may be improved by helping them gain more confidence in their abilities. However, it is important to recognize that self-efficacy beliefs will enhance the probability of people engaging in specific behaviors only if they count with the required skills and the appropriate environmental support (Bandura, 1986). If self-efficacy and skill levels are low, remedial activities will be needed to enhance both self-efficacy and academic achievement (Lent et al., 1984). Therefore, the enhancement of self-efficacy may be most appropriate for Hispanic students that, because of their low socioeconomic background or minority status, tend to underestimate their abilities for desired educational and vocational goals.

There is some evidence to suggest that social class may have a powerful impact in the formation of career-related self-efficacy. Hannah and Kahn (1989), for example, found that, whereas male and female high school students in Canada did not differ in their overall level of self-efficacy, low-SES students consistently reported lower self-efficacy expectations than high-SES students, regardless of the prestige of the occupation being considered. Findings from two studies described earlier (Hackett et al., 1992; Lauver & Jones, 1991) suggest that SES may be related to self-efficacy among Hispanic students as well. In the Lauver and Jones (1991) study SES emerged as one of the predictors of occupational self-efficacy among Hispanic high school students. Hackett et al. (1992) found that Mexican-American college students reported significantly lower levels of academic and occupational self-efficacy than their White counterparts. Because research has consistently shown that, as a group, Hispanic college students come from lower SES backgrounds than their White peers (Olivas, 1986), it is likely that differences in self-efficacy are related to SES and not to just ethnicity.

In the studies reviewed thus far, scales constructed following procedures used by Hackett and Betz (1981) were developed to assess strength and degree of self-efficacy regarding occupational tasks (e.g., expectations of successfully completing training or performing job duties for specific occupations) or academic tasks (e.g., expectations of successfully completing math courses). Recently, Solberg and his associates (Solberg et al., 1993) developed the College Self-Efficacy instrument and validated it with Mexican-American students. No relation was found between any of the instrument's three scales (course efficacy, roommate efficacy, and social efficacy) and acculturation, gender, or class level. As the authors suggested, this instrument may be useful in exploring the relation between college self-efficacy and academic achievement and persistence among Hispanic and non-Hispanic college students.

Bandura (1982) recognized that factors such as beliefs about the consequences of performance (outcome expectations), performance incentives, and environmental support, interact with self-efficacy beliefs in influencing behavior. These factors, however, have received very little empirical attention. Because of their minority status and lack of economic resources, it is likely that many Hispanics (particularly those in Cells I, IV, and VII) have not had sufficient experiences conducive to the development of career self-efficacy such as performance accomplishment regarding vocational and academic pursuits and exposure to successful role models. As Lent and Hackett (1987) noted, if the impact of environmental and social forces in the career development of minorities is not taken into account, self-efficacy theory may result in "blaming the victim" research.

Bandura also proposed that often groups share a sense of collective self-efficacy, which refers to their beliefs regarding to what extent their specific actions may lead to desired goals. Lent and Hackett (1987) suggested that this sense of collective self-efficacy may help explain how sociopolitical forces such as discrimination become internalized and affect the educational achievement and the career development of ethnic minorities. Consistent with this view, Ogbu (1992) proposed that immigrants who have been incorporated into a dominant society involuntarily, through slavery, conquest, or colonization, tend not to do well in school in part because they do not believe that educational attainment will result in occupational and social mobility, that is, they lack positive outcome expectations for their educational efforts.

It is likely that among Hispanic subgroups a sense of collective self-efficacy will be influenced by SES as well as by country of origin. Velez (1989), for example, suggested that Puerto Ricans and Mexicans may be classified as involuntary minorities because they were annexed or incorporated to the United States by force and their migration is motivated mainly by economic reasons. The early Cuban immigrants, on the other hand, were for the most part White, middle-class, political refugees who were provided with major educational and work-related support programs. Because of these differences in immigration histories and their socioeconomic and political consequences, it is likely that, as a group, Cuban immigrants will have a higher sense of collective self-efficacy as well as higher expectations of improving their lives through educational attainment than the other two groups. However, because personal history of immigration may also have a powerful impact on an individual's sense of collective and personal self-efficacy, it is likely that Puerto Rican and Mexican immigrants from higher social classes will be more similar to middle-class Cuban immigrants than to low-SES immigrants from their own countries. These subgroup and individual differences should be taken into account when applying self-efficacy theory to Hispanic populations.

In summary, results of the few existing studies suggest that self-efficacy theory may be a fruitful construct to explore in relation to the career development of Hispanics. The existing evidence suggests that among both Hispanic and White students occupational and academic self-efficacy expectations are predictive of career choice and academic achievement, respectively. The construct of collective self-efficacy seems promising in understanding the relation between career-related behaviors of Hispanics and sociocultural forces such as socioeconomic background, minority status, and acculturation level. Given the educational difficulties faced by many Hispanics, exploring the contributions of self-efficacy beliefs to academic achievement may be most relevant to the career development of members of this ethnic group.

RECOMMENDATIONS FOR RESEARCH

In this last section some general recommendations for career-related research with Hispanics are offered. Because of space limitations, this section is brief and readers are encouraged to consult recent publications where research issues with Hispanics (Marin & Marin, 1991) and other minority groups (Ponterotto & Casas, 1991) are discussed more in depth. Recommendations for research cover issues related to sampling, instrumentation, and data gathering and analysis.

Marin and Marin (1991) noted that, in general, Hispanics tend to cooperate in research projects that promise some social good as an outcome.

They offered the following suggestions to enhance the completion of research protocols including survey and interview procedures:

1. Give participants the opportunity to select their preferred language for the survey or interview. They have found that in community-wide surveys approximately 20% of highly acculturated Hispanics prefer to answer questionnaires in Spanish rather than English. Detailed guidelines have been offered in the literature regarding the proper translation of research instruments (Brislin, 1986; Marin & Marin, 1991).

2. The linguistic and educational characteristics of the participants needs to be taken into account in designing the instruments' format. It is likely that individuals with little formal education will have difficulty in completing instruments with complex response scales and multiple-choice questions. Also, Spanish versions of instruments should use standard Spanish (the type of Spanish used in radio and television networks) rather than colloquial versions.

3. Interviewers and data gatherers should be bilingual and Hispanic, especially when gathering sensitive information (Bloom & Padilla, 1979). Marin and Marin (1991) reported that face-to-face interviews seem to be as effective as phone interviews in collecting information related to sensitive topics (e.g., sexual behaviors, drug use).

4. Because of the high mobility rate of recent immigrants and the fact that a large proportion of Hispanics rent rather than own homes, it is relatively difficult to maintain contact with Hispanic participants in longitudinal studies. In their research with community samples in California, Marin and Marin (1991) have reported attrition rates that vary from 23% within 1 month of the initial interview to 45% 1 year after the initial contact. Marin and Marin (1991) provide a series of strategies that may be useful in maintaining contact with research participants throughout longitudinal studies.

As was discussed earlier, it is imperative that in conducting research with Hispanics within-group differences are taken into consideration. Four areas merit special attention: country of origin, SES, generational history, and acculturation. To tease out the influence of these variables in the questions of interest, one of two approaches may be followed (Marin & Marin, 1991). Preliminary analyses may be conducted to examine to what extent there is similarity in the career variables of interest across Hispanic subgroups who differ in these cultural and demographic characteristics. Another approach is to use some of these variables to define meaningful homogeneous subgroups and to sample respondents based on combinations of these variables. The framework described ear-

lier in the chapter yields nine subgroups based on three levels of both
SES and generational level, and the number of cells may be increased to
27 if acculturation level (high, low, and bicultural) is added to the framework. Of course, a single study does not need to include participants
from all cells, but could focus on some specific subgroups (e.g., second
generation or later, middle SES, bicultural, Mexican-American college
students). It is also possible to combine both approaches. For example,
in a study related to the career maturity of low-SES Mexican-American
adolescents, we would concentrate on Cells I, IV, and VII of the framework proposed earlier (low-SES participants from three generational levels) and conduct preliminary analyses to examine the relation between
acculturation and the variables of interest within participants in each cell.
In a study related to ethnic differences in parenting style and adolescents'
academic achievement, Steinberg, Dornsbusch, and Brown (1992) parti-
tioned their sample in what they called "16 ecological niches" (p. 725)
defined by ethnicity (4 ethnic categories), SES (2 categories), and family
structure (2 categories). In the analyses of the data, they first examined
the reliability of the parenting scales in every subgroup and then proceeded to examine the relationship between parenting style and academic
achievement within each subgroup and across groups. This research strategy allowed them to discover that, not only parenting styles differed
across groups, but that the impact of parenting style on academic achievement was also different for the various ethnic groups.

   In examining the relevance of existing theories of career development
among Hispanics, researchers need to attend to two issues: the meaning
of constructs developed in the context of mainstream theories among
Hispanic subgroups, and the psychometric adequacy of existing research
instruments for Hispanic populations. Marin and Marin (1991) described
in detail a procedure, first suggested by Triandis (1972, cited in Marin &
Marin, 1991), for discovering the subjective meaning of specific constructs
within different cultural groups. This procedure involves the use of qualitative research strategies to identify meaningful response categories
related to the constructs of interest followed by the development of closed-
end questionnaires that would allow examination of the data quantita-
tively. For example, factor analysis could be used to examine to what
extent the latent structure of the items is similar across groups. Cervantes
et al. (1991) used this approach to develop a stress inventory for Hispanics
and found that the factor structure of the items was not the same for
first-generation as for second- or later generation Hispanic adults. This
process is also useful in defining and operationalizing culture-specific
constructs such as ethnic identity (Phinney, 1991).

   In using an instrument developed for mainstream populations, in either
its original or translated version, researchers need to examine the internal

structure (e.g., factor structure) of the instruments as well as their internal consistency (e.g., alpha coefficient) with the specific Hispanic population of interest. Other psychometric characteristics of importance are validity, distribution of scores in the population of interest, and norms. With the exception of scales measuring vocational interests, the psychometric properties of instruments currently used in career-related research have not been examined with Hispanic populations.

Finally, as Ponterotto and Casas (1991) noted, the use of qualitative research methods would likely enrich our knowledge regarding the influence of culture in behavior. As was mentioned earlier in the chapter, to discover the impact of the environment in career-related behaviors, we must use research methods, such as case studies, participant observation, and in-depth interviews, that allow for the observation and discovery of complex relationships between people and their surroundings. For a more detailed discussion of these issues the reader may consult Young and Borgen's (1990) book related to methodological approaches in the study of careers.

CONCLUSIONS

The purpose of this chapter was to examine the areas of theory and research in careers as they apply to Hispanic Americans. In doing this, two questions were posed: What is it about Hispanics that merits special attention from career development theory and research? and Do we need new theories to explain the career development of Hispanic groups, or is it possible to adequately incorporate ethnic issues into existing theories and models? In addressing the first question, a framework for conceptualizing and categorizing Hispanic subgroups based on SES, immigration history, and other cultural variables was offered. In addressing the second question, the later stance was adopted; that is, current theoretical approaches and models were examined in terms of their applicability to Hispanics, and suggestions were made regarding how some of these models may be expanded to explain aspects related to the experience of Hispanics as an ethnic minority group in the United States.

It is hoped that the issues discussed in this chapter will serve as a guide for future research and theorizing related to Hispanics career development that will allow us to provide definitive answers to the questions posed. As Hackett and Lent (1992) noted regarding the career development of women, in these efforts it is important to be sensitive to the commonalities in career development among Hispanics and non-Hispanics groups as well as to the heterogeneity among individuals of Hispanic origin due to SES and cultural factors.

REFERENCES

Arbona, C. (1989). Hispanic employment and the Holland typology of work. *Career Development Quarterly, 37,* 257–268.

Arbona, C. (1990). Career counseling research with Hispanics: A review of the literature. *The Counseling Psychologist, 18,* 300–323.

Arbona, C., Flores, C. L., & Novy D. M. (in press). Cultural awareness and ethnic loyalty: Dimensions of cultural variability among Mexican American college students. *Journal of Counseling and Development.*

Arbona, C., & Novy, D. M. (1991). Career aspirations and expectations among Black, Mexican American, and White college students. *Career Development Quarterly, 39,* 231–239.

Arce, C. E., Murgia, E., & Frisbie, W. P. (1987). Phenotype and life chances among chicanos. *Hispanic Journal of Behavioral Sciences, 9,* 19–32.

Astin, H. S. (1984). The meaning of work in women's lives: A sociopsychological model of career choice and work behavior. *The Counseling Psychologist, 12,* 117–126.

Bandura, A. (1982). Self-efficacy mechanisms in human agency. *American Psychologist, 37,* 122–147.

Bandura, A. (1986). *Social foundations of thought and action: A social cognitive theory.* Englewood Cliffs, NJ: Prentice-Hall.

Bean, F. D., & Tienda, M. (1987). *The Hispanic population in the United States.* New York: Russell Sage.

Betz, N. E., & Fitzgerald, L. F. (1987). *The career psychology of women.* San Diego: Academic Press.

Bloom, D., & Padilla, A. M. (1979). A peer interview model in conducting surveys among Mexican American youth. *Journal of Community Psychology, 7,* 129–136.

Blustein, D. L., Devenis, L. E., & Kidney, B. (1989). Relationship between the identity formation process and career development. *Journal of Career Counseling, 36,* 196–202.

Blustein, D. L., & Phillips, S. D. (1990). Relation between ego identity statuses and decision-making styles. *Journal of Counseling Psychology, 37,* 160–168.

Bores-Rangel, E., Church, T., Szendre, D., & Reeves, C. (1990). Self-efficacy in relation to occupational consideration and academic performance in high school equivalency students. *Journal of Counseling Psychology, 37,* 407–418.

Borgen, F. H. (1991). Megatrends and milestones in vocational behavior: A 20-year counseling psychology retrospective. *Journal of Vocational Behavior, 39,* 263–290.

Brislin, R. W. (1986). The wording and translation of research instruments. In W. J. Lonner & J. W. Berry (Eds.), *Handbook of cross-cultural psychology* (pp. 297–318). Boston: Allyn & Bacon.

Bronfenbrenner, U. (1979). *The ecology of human development.* Cambridge, MA: Harvard University Press.

Brown, D. (1990). Summary, comparison, and critique of major theories. In D. Brown & L. Brooks (Eds.), *Career choice and development* (2nd ed., pp. 338–363). San Francisco: Jossey-Bass.

Brown, S. D., Lent, R. W., & Larkin, K. C. (1989). Self-efficacy as a moderator of scholastic aptitude-academic performance relationships. *Journal of Vocational Behavior, 18,* 326–339.

Bullington, R. L., & Arbona, C. (1994). *An exploration of the career development tasks of Mexican American youth.* Manuscript submitted for publication.

Calderon, J. (1992). "Hispanic" and "Latino"; the visibility of categories for panethnic unity. *Latin American Perspectives, 19,* 37–44.

Carey, M. L., & Franklin, J. C. (1991). Industry output and job growth continues slow into next century. *Monthly Labor Review, 114,* 45–84.

Cervantes, R. C., Padilla, A. M., & Salgado de Snyder, N. (1991). The Hispanic Stress Inventory: A culturally relevant approach to psychosocial assessment. *Psychological Assessment, 3*, 438–447.

Chavira, V., & Phinney, J. S. (1991). Adolescent's ethnic self-esteem, and strategies for dealing with ethnicity and minority status. *Hispanic Journal of Behavioral Sciences, 13*, 226.

Church, T., Teresa, J. S., Rosebrook, R., & Szendre, D. (1992). Self-efficacy for careers and occupational consideration in minority high school equivalency students. *Journal of Counseling Psychology, 39*, 498–508.

Collin, A., & Young, R. A. (1986). New directions for theories of career. *Human Relations, 39*, 837–853.

Crites, J. O. (1978). *The Career Maturity Inventory.* Monterey, CA: McGraw-Hill.

Delgado-Gaitan, C. (1992). School matters in the Mexican-American home: Socializing children to education. *American Education Research Journal, 29*, 495–516.

Denton, N. A., & Massey, D. S. (1989). Racial identity among Caribbean Hispanics: The effect of double minority status on residential segregation. *American Sociological Review, 54*, 790–808.

Duncan, O. D. (1961). A socioeconomic index for all occupations. In A. J. Reiss, Jr. (Ed.), *Occupations and social status* (pp. 109–137). New York: Free Press.

Erikson, E. H. (1968). *Identity: Youth and crisis.* New York: Norton.

Fitzgerald, L. F., & Rounds, J. B. (1989). Vocational behavior 1988: A critical analysis. *Journal of Vocational Behavior, 36*, 225–248.

Fordham, S., & Ogbu, J. U. (1986). Black students' school success: Coping with the burden of "acting white." *Urban Review, 18*, 176–206.

Fullerton, H. N. (1991). Labor force projections: The baby boom moves on. *Monthly Labor Review, 114*, 31–44.

Goldenberg, C. (1987). Low-income Hispanic parents' contributions to their first-grade children's word recognition skills. *Anthropology and Education Quarterly, 18*, 149–179.

Goldenberg, C. (1989). Parents' effects on academic grouping for reading: Three case studies. *American Educational Research Journal, 26*, 329–352.

Goldenberg, C. (1992). The limits of expectations: A case for case knowledge about teacher expectancy effects. *American Education Research Journal, 29*, 517–544.

Gomez, L. (1992). The birth of the "Hispanic" generation: Attitudes of Mexican-American political elites toward the Hispanic label. *Latin American Perspectives, 19*, 45–58.

Gould, S. (1980). Need for achievement, career mobility, and the Mexican-American college graduate. *Journal of Vocational Behavior, 16*, 73–82.

Gould, S. (1982). Correlates of career progression among Mexican American college graduates. *Journal of Vocational Behavior, 20*, 93–110.

Hackett, G., & Betz, N. (1981). A self-efficacy approach to the career development of women. *Journal of Vocational Behavior, 18*, 326–339.

Hackett, G., Betz, N., Casas, M. J., & Roca-Singh, I. A. (1992). Gender, ethnicity, and social cognitive factors predicting the academic achievement of students in engineering. *Journal of Counseling Psychology, 39*, 527–538.

Hackett, G., & Lent, R. W. (1992). Theoretical advances and current inquiry in career psychology. In S. D. Brown & R. W. Lent (Eds.), *Handbook of counseling psychology* (2nd ed., pp. 419–421). New York: Wiley.

Hackett, G., Lent, R. W., & Greenhaus, J. H. (1991). Advances in vocational theory and research: A 20 year retrospective. *Journal of Vocational Behavior, 38*, 3–38.

Hannah, J. S., & Kahn, S. E. (1989). The relationship between socioeconomic status and gender to the occupational choices of grade 12 students. *Journal of Vocational Behavior, 38*, 3–38.

Harmon, L. W. (1991). Twenty years of the Journal of Vocational Behavior. *Journal of Vocational Behavior, 39*, 297–304.

Hazuda, H. P., Stern, M. P., & Haffner, S. M. (1988). Acculturation and assimilation among Mexican Americans: Scales and population-based data. *Social Sciences Quarterly, 69,* 687–706.

Helms, J. (1990). *Black and white racial identity: Theory, research, and practice.* New York: Greenwood Press.

Holland, J. L. (1985). *Making vocational choices: A theory of vocational personalities and work environments* (2nd ed.). Englewoods Cliffs, NJ: Prentice-Hall.

Hollingshed, A. B., & Redlich, F. C. (1958). *Social class and mental illness.* New York: Wiley.

Hotchkiss, L., & Borow, H. (1990). Sociological perspectives on work and career development. In D. Brown & L. Brooks (Eds.), *Career choice and development* (pp. 262–307). San Francisco: Jossey-Bass.

Isonio, S. A., & Garza, R. T. (1987). Protestant work ethic endorsement among Anglo Americans, Chicanos, and Mexicans: A comparison of factor structures. *Hispanic Journal of Behavioral Sciences, 9,* 413–425.

Keefe, S. E., & Padilla, A. M. (1987). *Chicano ethnicity.* Albuquerque: University of New Mexico Press.

Kustcher, R. E. (1989). Projections summary and emerging issues. *Monthly Labor Review, 112,* 66–74.

Laosa, L. M. (1982). School, occupation, culture, and the family: The impact of parental schooling to the parent–child relationship. *Journal of Educational Psychology, 74,* 791–827.

Lauver, P. J., & Jones, R. M. (1991). Factors associated with perceived career options in American Indian, White, and Hispanic rural high school students. *Journal of Counseling Psychology, 38,* 159–166.

Lent, R. W., Brown, S. D., & Larkin, K. C. (1984). Relation of self-efficacy expectations to academic achievement and persistence. *Journal of Counseling Psychology, 31,* 356–362.

Lent, R. W., Brown, S. D., & Larkin, K. C. (1986). Self-efficacy in the prediction of academic performance and perceived career options. *Journal of Counseling Psychology, 33,* 265–269.

Lent, R. W., Brown, S. D., & Larkin, K. C. (1987). Comparison of three theoretically derived variables in predicting career and academic behavior: Self-efficacy, interest congruence, and consequence thinking. *Journal of Counseling Psychology, 34,* 293–298.

Lent, R. W., & Hackett, G. (1987). Career self-efficacy: Empirical status and future directions [Monograph]. *Journal of Vocational Behavior, 30,* 347–382.

Locci, S. G., & Carranza, E. L. (1990). Attitudes toward Chicanos by students in Mexican American Studies classes: A research note. *Hispanic Journal of Behavioral Sciences, 12,* 397–407.

Luzzo, D. A. (1992). Ethnic group and social class differences in college students' career development. *The Career Development Quarterly, 41,* 161–173.

Marcia, J. E. (1966). Development and validation of ego identity status. *Journal of Personality and Social Psychology, 3,* 551–558.

Marcia, J. E. (1980). Identity in adolescence. In J. Adelson (Ed.), *Handbook of adolescent psychology* (pp. 159–187). New York: Wiley.

Marin, G., & Marin, V. M. (1991). *Research with Hispanic populations.* Newbury Park, CA: Sage.

Matute-Bianchi, M. E. (1986). Ethnic identities and patterns of school failure among Mexican descent and Japanese American students in a California high school: An ethnographic analysis. *American Journal of Education, 95,* 233–255.

Mena, F. J., Padilla, A. M., & Maldonado, M. (1987). Acculturative stress and specific coping strategies among immigrant and later generation college students. *Hispanic Journal of Behavioral Sciences, 2,* 207–225.

Montalvo, F. F. (1991). Phenotyping, acculturation, and biracial assimilation of Mexican Americans. In M. Sotomayor (Ed.), *Empowering Hispanic families: A critical issue for the 90's* (pp. 97–120). Milwaukee: Family Service of America.

Multon, K. D., Brown, S. D., & Lent, R. W. (1991). Relation of self-efficacy beliefs to academic outcomes: A meta-analytic investigation. *Journal of Counseling Psychology, 38,* 30–38.

National Commission for Employment Policy. (1982). *Hispanics and jobs: Barriers to progress* (NCEP Report No. 14). Washington, DC: National Commission for Employment Policy.

Neggy, C., & Woods, D. J. (1992). A note on the relationship between acculturation and socioeconomic status. *Hispanic Journal of Behavioral Sciences, 14,* 248–251.

Ogbu, J. U. (1992). Understanding cultural diversity and learning. *Educational Researcher, 21,* 5–14.

Olivas, M. A. (1986). *Latino college students.* New York: Teachers College Press.

Olmedo, E. L. (1979). Acculturation: A psychometric perspective. *American Psychologist, 34,* 1061–1070.

Osipow, S. H. (1975). The relevance of theories of career development to special groups: Problems, needed data, and implications. In J. S. Picou & R. E. Campbell (Eds.), *Career behavior of special groups: Theory, research, and practice* (pp 9–22). Columbus, OH: Charles E. Merrill.

Osipow, S. H. (1983). *Theories of career development.* Englewood Cliffs, NJ: Prentice-Hall.

Penley, L. E., Gould, S., De la Vina, L., & Murphy, K. (1989). An early career focused study of Hispanic college graduates in business. *Hispanic Journal of Behavioral Sciences, 11,* 366–380.

Phinney, J. S. (1989). Stages of ethnic identity development in minority group adolescents. *Journal of early Adolescence, 9,* 34–49.

Phinney, J. S. (1990). Ethnic identity in adolescents and adults: Review of research. *Psychological Bulletin, 108,* 499–514.

Phinney, J. S. (1991). *The multigroup ethnic identity measure: A new scale for use with adolescents and adults from diverse groups.* Manuscript submitted for publication.

Phinney, J. S., & Alipuria, L. L. (1990). Ethnic identity in college students from four ethnic groups. *Journal of Adolescence, 13,* 171–183.

Phinney, J. S., & Tarver, S. (1989). Ethnic identity search and commitment in Black and White eighth graders. *Journal of Early Adolescence, 3,* 265–277.

Ponterotto, J. G., & Casas, M. J. (1991). *Handbook of racial/ethnic minority counseling research.* Springfield, IL: Thomas.

Raines, R. T. (1988). The Mexican American women and work: Intergenerational perspective of comparative ethnic groups. In M. B. Melville (Ed.), *Mexicanas at work in the United States* (Mexican American Studies Monograph No. 5, pp. 33–46). Houston, TX: University Of Houston, Mexican American Studies Program.

Ramirez, A. (1988). Racism toward Hispanics: A culturally monolithic society. In P. Katz & D. Taylor (Eds.), *Towards the elimination of racism: Profiles in controversy* (pp. 137–157). New York: Plenum.

Ramirez, M. III (1984). Assessing and understanding biculturalism–multiculturalism in Mexican-American adults. In J. L. Martinez & R. H. Mendoza (Eds.), *Chicano psychology* (pp. 77–94). Orlando: Academic Press.

Relethford, J. H., Stern, M. P., Gaskill, S. P., & Hazuda, H. P. (1983). Social class, admixture, and skin color variations among Mexican Americans and Anglo Americans living in San Antonio, Texas. *American Journal of Physical Anthropology, 62,* 97–102.

Savickas, M. L. (1985). Identity in vocational development. *Journal of Vocational Behavior, 27,* 329–337.

Schulenberg, J. E., Vondracek, F. W., & Crouter, A. C. (1984). The influence of the family on career development. *Journal of Marriage and the Family, 46,* 129–143.

Smith, E. J. (1991). Ethnic identity development: Toward the development of a theory within the context of majority/minority status. *Journal of Counseling and Development, 70,* 181–188.

Solberg, V. S., O'Brien, K., Villareal, P., Kennel, R., & Davis, B. (1993). Self-efficacy and Hispanic college students: Validation of the College Self-Efficacy Instrument. *Hispanic Journal of Behavioral Sciences, 15,* 80–97.

Steinberg, L., Dornbusch, S. M., & Brown, B. B. (1992). Ethnic differences in adolescent achievement; An ecological perspective. *American Psychologist, 47,* 723–729.

Super, D. E. (1957). *The psychology of careers: An introduction to vocational development.* New York: Harper & Row.

Super, D. E. (1990). A life-span, life-space approach to career development. In D. Brown & L. Brooks (Eds.), *Career choice and development* (pp. 197–261). San Francisco: Jossey-Bass.

Super, D. E., & Neville, D. D. (1986). *The Salience Inventory.* Palo Alto, CA: Consulting Psychologist Press.

Super, D. E., Thompson, A. S., & Lindeman, R. H. (1988). *The Adult Career Concerns Inventory.* Palo Alto, CA: Consulting Psychologist Press.

Super, D. E., Thompson, A. S., Lindeman, R. H., Jordaan, J. P., & Myers, R. A. (1981). *Career Development Inventory.* Palo Alto, CA: Consulting Psychologist Press.

Thomas, D. A., & Alderfer, C. P. (1989). The influence of race on career dynamics: Theory and research on minority career experiences. In M. B. Arthur, D. T. Hall, & B. S. Lawrence (Eds.), *Handbook of career theory* (pp. 133–158). Canada: Cambridge University Press.

Tienda, M., & Ortiz, V. (1986). "Hispanicity" and the 1980 census. *Social Sciences Quarterly, 67,* 3–20.

U.S. Bureau of the Census. (1988). *The Hispanic population in the United States: March 1988* (Current Population Report, Series P-20, No 431). Washington, DC: U.S. Government Printing Office.

U.S. Bureau of the Census. (1991). *The Hispanic population in the United States: March 1991* (Current Population Report, Series P-20, No. 455). Washington, DC: U.S. Government Printing Office.

Valdivieso, R., & Davis, C. (1988). *U.S. Hispanics: Challenging issues for the 90's* (Population trends and public policy, No. 17). Washington, DC: Population Reference Bureau. (ERIC Document Reproduction Services No. ED 305 213)

Velez, W. (1989). High school attrition among Hispanic and non-Hispanic White youths. *Sociology of Education, 62,* 119–133.

Vondracek, F. W. (1990). A developmental-contextual approach to career development research. In R. A. Young & W. A. Borgen (Eds.), *Methodological approaches to the study of career* (pp. 25–37). New York: Praeger.

Vondracek, F. W. (1992). The construct of identity and its use in career theory and research. *The Career Development Quarterly, 41,* 130–144.

Vondracek, F. W., Lerner, R. M., & Schulenberg, J. E. (1986). *Career development: A life-span developmental approach.* Hillsdale, NJ: Lawrence Erlbaum Associates.

Wall, J. A., Power, T. G., & Arbona, C. (1993). Susceptibility to antisocial peer pressure in Mexican-American adolescents and its relation to acculturation. *Journal of Adolescent Research, 8,* 403–418.

Weinrach, S. G., & Srebalus, D. J. (1990). Holland's theory of careers. In D. Brown & L. Brooks (Eds.), *Career choice and development* (pp. 37–67). San Francisco: Jossey-Bass.

Young, R. A., & Borgen, W. A. (1990). *Methodological approaches to the study of career.* New York: Praeger.

Young, R. A., & Friesen, J. D. (1990). Parental influences on career development: A research perspective. In R. A. Young & W. A. Borgen (Eds.), *Methodological approaches to the study of career* (pp. 147–162). New York: Praeger.

Young, R. A., & Friesen, J. D. (1992). The intentions of parent in influencing the career development of their children. *The Career Development Quarterly, 40,* 198–208.

Young, R. A., Friesen, J. D., & Pearson, H. M. (1988). Activities and interpersonal relationships as dimensions of behavior in the career development of children. *Youth and Society, 20,* 29–45.

Career Development of Asian Americans: A Research Area in Need of a Good Theory

Frederick T. L. Leong
Felicisima C. Serafica
The Ohio State University

> *At fifteen he was country clerk,*
> *At twenty, provincial court councilor,*
> *At thirty, palace attendant,*
> *At forty, lord governor.*
> —Liu & Lo (1975)

In this anonymous Chinese poem, assumed to have been written between the 3rd century B.C. and the 6th century A.D., a woman describes the progress of her husband's career as a steady rise through the ranks of the governing hierarchy. The poem suggests that even in ancient China the concept of career development was present. However, the smooth career path depicted in this poem was probably limited to a narrow segment of the population. For many, a career in government or in any other field was not a viable option. Even Lao-tzu's teaching (Mitchell, 1988), "In work, do what you enjoy" (p. 8), was probably not feasible for many individuals because choices were limited by one's station in life and other factors. At most, one could hope for an occupation that would provide a livelihood. For numerous individuals, however, even this modest aspiration was not attainable and continued to be so over the centuries.

It was the need to find work that initially brought the Chinese to the United States. The other Asians who came after them—Japanese, Filipinos, Koreans, and Asian Indians—had similar motivations. They came because laborers were needed to work on the plantations and railroads, in mines, factories, and canneries, and on the farms of an expanding nation (Takaki, 1989). Since then, many others have followed; some came by design, responding to new demands for an increased workforce in areas such as health care, whereas others arrived as war refugees. Even now, immigrants continue to arrive from Asia.

Have the descendants of these early immigrants been able to develop the careers that eluded their forefathers? What career choices have they made? What factors influenced these choices? What factors facilitated or impeded attainment of their career goals? As for the immigrants who arrived more recently, how have their careers fared in the transition to a new setting? Are these careers characterized by continuity or discontinuity? Some Asians originally came as students and became immigrants only as they were about to begin their professional careers. Are their career paths different from those of other immigrants? And what about the career development of these recent immigrants' offspring? In this chapter we explore whether the answers to these and other questions can be found in available studies of Asian-American career development.

Asian Americans constitute the fastest growing ethnic minority group in the United States (Kitano & Daniels, 1988); yet, as Leong (1985; Leong & Hayes, 1990) repeatedly observed, very little research has been done on career choice and development in this population. This deficit exists in spite of the high need for career-counseling services expressed by Asian Americans. For example, 34% of Asian-American students taking the Scholastic Aptitude Test (SAT) in 1980 expressed an intention to seek vocational-career counseling when enrolled in college compared to 27% of Whites, 24% of African Americans, and 34% of Mexican Americans (College Entrance Examination Board, 1980). A recent national survey (Brown, Minor, & Jepsen, 1991) found that large percentages of Asian-Pacific Islanders (71%) and Hispanics (75%) reported being interested in getting more information about careers if they could start over. The Brown et al. (1991) study also showed that Asian Americans are acting upon their expressed intentions and interests; they are significantly more likely to report using college career information centers than Euro (21%), African (19%), or Hispanic Americans (15%). However, the information they find may not be as useful to them as it is for their Euro-American peers. Brown et al. (1991) reported that Asian-Pacific Islanders (61%) are significantly less likely than Euro Americans (71%) to report that the information they need was available. When they did come across career information, 83% of Asian Americans thought it was useful, as did 83% of the Hispanics, 88% of African Americans, and 77% of Euro Americans.

To meet the Asian Americans' expressed needs for career counseling, career counselors need information on how Asian-American clients are different from Euro-American students so that culturally relevant and effective services can be provided. The primary aim in this chapter is to analyze and synthesize the available research on career development of Asian Americans, with a view toward identifying the research questions that have been addressed, the theories that guided the research, the conceptual and methodological issues, and areas where further research is needed. The second aim is to propose the broad outlines of a conceptual framework for future research. Several theories are discussed for their potential usefulness for describing and explaining career development of Asian Americans.

RESEARCH ON CAREER DEVELOPMENT OF ASIAN AMERICANS

This review is divided into several sections. The first section deals with studies that describe and explain Asian Americans' career choices among the various occupational fields. The second presents a description of their work adjustment and the explanations that have been advanced to account for it. The third section discusses three issues that cut across career choice and work adjustment: occupational segregation, occupational stereotyping, and occupational discrimination.

Career Interests and Choices

At first glance, it seems that Asian Americans' career choices would be a direct reflection of their career interests. However, as Leong (1982) has pointed out, due to a host of factors that have not yet been empirically investigated, Asian-American career choices may not be consistently related to their career interests. For example, many Asian-American adolescents may be interested in artistic careers (reflected in measured interests) but may eventually choose a career in medicine or engineering (expressed interest or choice) because of parental guidance or pressure. Indeed, a recent study (Gim, 1992) showed a significant correlation between real and ideal choices for Euro- but not for Asian-American students. The same study reported that Asian-American adolescents assign higher ratings than their Euro-American peers to perceived parental pressure as a significant factor influencing their career choice. Their career interests also may not correlate highly with career choices because of factors that exist in the broader social world outside the family. For these reasons, it is important to examine Asian-American career interests and career choices separately.

Career Interests. An early study (Sue & Kirk, 1972) of Chinese-American first-year college students at the University of California, Berkeley, showed that compared to other freshman males they expressed more interest in the physical sciences, applied technical fields, and business occupations and less interest in social sciences, aesthetic cultural fields, and verbal linguistic vocations. Chinese-American females differed from all other females in the same direction and pattern as did their male counterparts. However, they differed from all other females in the degree of domestic versus career orientation as measured by the women's form of the Strong Vocational Interest Blank (SVIB). Chinese-American females were more oriented toward the domestic occupations (housewife, elementary teacher, office worker, and stenographer/secretary) than females in other groups. It would be interesting to see whether this ethnic difference continues to hold throughout the 1990s. In a subsequent report based on the same data set, Sue and Kirk (1973) indicated that Japanese Americans and Chinese Americans differed from all other first-year students at the University of California in the same direction, but the former consistently occupied an intermediate position between the two other groups in their responses to the SVIB. In addition, Japanese-American females, unlike the Chinese-American females, did not differ significantly from the other groups in the degree of their interest in domestic occupations.

Career Choices. The occupational distribution for Asian Americans in the 1980 census provides some information about their career choices. Hsia (1988) analyzed the data for nine major occupational groupings and found that Asian Americans were more likely than Euro Americans to be in three of them: professional (18% vs. 12.8%), technical (5.5% vs. 3.1%), and service (15.6% vs. 11.6%) occupations. Conversely, there were fewer Asian than Euro Americans in sales (8.4% vs. 10.7%), production/craft (8.4% vs. 13.4%, and operator/laborer (14.2% vs. 17.1%) occupations. Hsia (1988) also provided similar data on specific Asian-American subgroups (Japanese, Chinese, Filipino, Korean, etc.). The greater tendency for Asian Americans to work in the professional and technical occupations and lower tendency to enter sales and laborer occupations are consistent with the pattern of career interests observed earlier by Sue and Kirk (1972, 1973).

The apparent consistency between career interests and career choices among Asian Americans suggests that career decision making should be an easy task for them. However, a different picture emerges from an analysis of archival data on the help-seeking behavior and problem perception of 3,050 Asian-American clients seen at a university student development center in Hawaii (Tracey, Leong, & Glidden,1986). The sample included eight ethnic groups: White, Chinese American, Filipino American, part Hawaiian, Korean American, Japanese American, Asian-American White mix, Asian-American mix.

Tracey et al. (1986) found that problem endorsement rates differed significantly among the groups on each of the eight problem areas. Asian

Americans were more likely to present vocational and career problems to a counselor than personal-emotional problems. Academic/career concerns were overendorsed by all the Asian-American students and underendorsed by the Whites. Those problems reflecting intra- or interpersonal concerns were disproportionately overendorsed by the Whites and fairly uniformly underendorsed by the Asian Americans. The Filipino-American and Asian-American White-mix students' endorsements of intra- or interpersonal concerns fell between those of the White students and the other Asian-American groups.

Whereas Asian-American clients are more likely to endorse academic/vocational concerns as most important, they did so to a lesser degree if they had previous counseling. However, they were less likely than White clients to have had previous counseling. These findings suggest that counseling helps to moderate the academic/vocational concerns of Asian Americans. Because this ethnic group tends to underutilize counseling services, high school and university career counselors may have to be more proactive through programs designed to promote career awareness, facilitate decision making, and encourage use of career guidance services by Asian-American students and parents.

What accounts for the career interests, choices, and vocational problems of Asian Americans? In the next section, influences within the family and in the larger society that contribute to the observed patterns are explored.

Family Influences on Career Development. Asian-American parents are inclined to provide strong parental guidance, particularly in regard to careers. They are aware that discrimination in the world of work is quite common, and that their children would have an easier time if they were in a respected and autonomous profession in which many Asian Americans have already succeeded. Hence, they may be more likely than their Euro-American counterparts to exert direct influence on the career aspirations and choices of their children. Asian-American youth would be more apt than their Euro-American peers to defer to parental guidance given the values placed by Asian cultures on respecting authority and submitting to the wisdom of the elderly.

Social and behavioral scientists (e.g., Sue & Morishima, 1982) have long acknowledged that the family plays a more central role in the lives of Asian Americans than is true for Euro Americans; yet there has been very little research on its influence on the career choices and behaviors of Asian Americans. In one of the few empirical studies, Johnson et al. (1983) studied the roles of family background, cognitive ability, and personality as predictors of educational and occupational attainment in a sample of male and female Americans of European (AEA) and Japanese (AJA) ancestry. The family background indices (years of education of fathers and mothers, paternal occupation) were consistently positively correlated with subjects' educational attainment. The correlations of the family background items with occupational attainment were similar to those found for educational attainment and were consistent across ethnicity, in spite of the AJA parents coming from a lower socioeconomic stratum than the AEA parents. A father's occupational status was found to have an influence on the educational and occupational status of his adult children, although it was not as strong as is usually assumed.

Cognitive variables, particularly verbal ability, and personality variables such as "ego organization" and "intraception," a measure of rebelliousness, were also correlated with attainment in both education and occupation. The authors concluded that family background, cognition, and personality are related to educational attainment, which in turn is the strongest predictor of occupational attainment, over and above the effect of family background and cognitive ability. In many cases, correlations were higher for the AJA group than for the AEA. The finding that educational attainment is the best predictor of occupational attainment validates the emphasis that Asian-American parents place on academic achievement, particularly for youths who cannot expect to become part of a family business and must therefore make their own way in the broader world of work.

Many Asian Americans do enter family businesses. Wong (1985) described a model of the Chinese family firm. Prototypically, the father-entrepreneur is the founder of the business. The entire business rests on the father's shoulders. This centralizes decision making and minimizes delegation of responsibility to subordinates. But there can emerge a tug-of-war between the father-entrepreneur and the sons who will inherit the business someday. The father often does not want to retire for fear of losing face or having the company fail. If fate intervenes by removing him, his children inherit the business.

Once the sons take over, a consensus among them cannot be taken for granted. Because the business is shared equally among the children, power becomes decentralized and weakened. The power of the new chief executive is greatly curtailed. He no longer enjoys his predecessor's flexibility in reinvestment and transferring funds laterally. The results are segmentation, a more outward expansion of the enterprise, and a reduction in the flexibility for reinvestment and risk taking. The relationships among Chinese brothers are brittle but the family bonds become even more fragile among the first cousins if the latter remain in the same jia (or Chinese family). Depending on the relationships among family members, the family business will either remain strong and prosper or be run into the ground. The fate of the Chinese family firm is less certain compared to its Japanese counterpart. Because the Japanese practice the right of primogeniture, only the male heir inherits so it is easier for ownership and management of the family business to remain intact. In either case, not all the children develop careers within the family business. Because of dissatisfaction and perhaps even internal strife in the case of the Chinese or, if they are Japanese, because they are younger sons, they seek other career opportunities.

In choosing a career, Asian-American youth must confront the task of selecting one that is of interest to them and at the same time acceptable to their parents. This is not an easy task, particularly because Asian-American parents who are recent immigrants or refugees may not be aware of the career opportunities available to their children. However, as shown by Evanoski and Tse (1989), a career awareness program for Asian-American parents can remedy this problem. The goals of their career awareness programs for Chinese and Korean-American parents in 1985 to 1986 and 1986 to 1987 were: (a) to establish a linkage whereby role models of similar cultures and backgrounds could use their prestige and knowledge to inform parents of career opportunities for their children, and (b) to explain the concept of the community college and academic and career programs, thus offering a great variety of career choices to newly arrived immigrants and their children.

Combined data from evaluation surveys completed by 550 participants in 1985 and 1986 and 801 in 1986 and 1987 showed that parents learned more about new jobs for themselves and their children (90+%), became better informed about the employment outlook for particular occupations and the anticipated salary schedules (86%), were more knowledgeable about the educational requirements of the occupations discussed (85%), and were more informed about the kinds of financial aid available for college for themselves and for their children (94%). Authors identified several factors critical to the program's success: the concept of a bilingual role model, materials written in the native language of the target group, and linkage with community organizations of the target population. A replication ought to include a pretraining assessment of parents' and children's knowledge and attitudes about occupations, salaries, and college financial aid so that pre- and posttraining comparisons can be made. A follow-up could examine use of knowledge gains.

Work Adjustment and Vocational Problems

Studies on the work adjustment of immigrants from the Pacific and Asia are reviewed in this section. For a review of the work adjustment problems of Southeast-Asian immigrants and refugees, see Leong's (in press) chapter in the *Handbook of Asian American Psychology*.

Job-Related Stress. There is some evidence that Asian Americans do perceive themselves to be underemployed at work. Brown et al. (1991) found that Asian-Pacific Islanders (47%) were less likely than Euro Americans (54%), African Americans (60%), or Hispanics (63%) to report that their skills were being used very well. More Asian-Pacific Islanders also reported experiencing stress on the job than members of other minority groups. African Americans (59%) and Hispanics (61%) were significantly more likely than Euro Americans (46%) and Asian-Pacific Islanders (48%) to report little or no job stress.

The sources of stress on the job for Asian Americans have yet to be identified. One possible source is cultural conflict. For example, cultural differences regarding the importance of face may induce stress in Chinese Americans. Redding and Ng (1982) contended that "face" is particularly salient for the Chinese and is a key to explaining much of their behavior. "Face" operates in the Chinese business context and is a powerful mediating force in social interaction, in business transactions, or in social situations inside formal organizations. The Chinese concept of face is the individual's assessment of how others close to him see him. It has two dimensions: *lien*, which refers to good moral character, is more ascribed than achieved; whereas *mien-tzu*, which refers to reputation based on one's own efforts, is more achieved than ascribed. The great importance of trust in Chinese business relationships and the resulting informality as to contracts and agreements rest on the common adoption of lien as a moral foundation.

The salience of face was demonstrated by Redding and Ng (1982) in a study of Chinese middle-level executives in Hong Kong. The reported reactions to losing face were shame (100% of respondents), worry (99%), feelings of uneasiness, anxiety, and tension (98%), difficulty in concentrating on work (72%), and symptoms such as blushing (64%). The main effect is short term. Long-term effects, such as loss of appetite or sleep, were reported as probable by only 33% and 21% of the respondents, respectively.

When asked if having face influenced success in daily business transactions and negotiations, the response was 100% strongly positive. Equally strongly negative (97%) was not having face. The process of being given face during a transaction was also seen as highly favorable (96%). To have one's face challenged or deliberately destroyed was seen as highly unfavorable (100%). If one is being given face, one gives it back in return (100%). If one's face is being challenged or attacked, one retaliates by destroying the other's face in return (80%) or by simply not giving face (20%).

Content analysis of the incidents investigated themes. These were classifiable into two groups: *how* and *why* face operates, and *where* and *when* it operates. The results suggest that, although there is some advantage in using face in business transactions, more commonly there is a fundamental clash between the behaviors needed when taking face into account and those needed to meet the rational needs of the organization. To paraphrase Redding and Ng (1982), the entry of Asian Americans into the Western bureaucratic form of organization brings Oriental values of a different and not so simple classifiable nature into a clash with two Western values, rationality and individualism. On these grounds, until the Asian American adapts to the Western managerial system, this clash of values may induce stress.

Stress among Asian Americans may be induced not only by the nature of the job, but also by whether a job enables a worker to meet obligations to the extended family, a culturally valued responsibility. Yu and Wu (1985) examined the relationship between unemployment, marital status, and discomfort experienced by Chinese-American adults when providing support to their parents and parents-in-law in a sample of American-born (24%) and naturalized Chinese Americans (76%) who were either married or single, employed or unemployed.

For the entire sample, regardless of the country of birth, Yu and Wu (1985) explored the effects of gender and employment status on the discomfort level related to meeting the financial needs of parents. Employment status had a significant effect, with the unemployed experiencing more discomfort. Because a higher percentage of employed, compared to unemployed, respondents actually gave financial support and helped to meet the housing needs of their parents, they reported lower levels of discomfort.

When financial and housing assistance for in-laws was examined in the subgroup of married individuals, only employment was significantly associated with discomfort level about providing financial aid to in-laws. Employed respondents had lower levels of discomfort than the unemployed. Gender was associated with providing financial support to in-laws, more females (94%) than males (86%) doing so. The discriminating factor in meeting aged relatives' needs was providing financial aid to parents-in-law; respondents who did not give support to their parents-in-law reported higher levels of discomfort than those who did, regardless of whether they gave support to or lived with their own parents. Among the 72 married couples, husband's and wife's discomfort levels were highly correlated, .61 for financial aid and .52 for in-laws living with the couple. Finally, one spouse's discomfort in meeting such needs affected the discomfort level of the other spouse.

Occupational Prestige-Related Problems. Kincaid and Yum (1987) examined some of the socioeconomic consequences of migration to Hawaii for first-generation immigrants from Samoa, Korea, and the Philippines in contrast to resident Japanese and White-Americans who were born in Hawaii or migrated there from Japan or the U.S. mainland. Males and females were equally represented in each ethnic group except for the Filipino sample that was only 36% male. Native language speakers from the same ethnic group interviewed subjects individually at home. Filipinos had the lowest average level of education—8 years compared to 11 for Samoans, 12 for Koreans, 13 for Japanese, and 15 years for Whites. This order of educational experience corresponds exactly to the order of the average occupational status of these ethnic groups.

Kincaid and Yum (1987) identified several main consequences of migration. First, there was intensification of the differences in occupational prestige between the Whites and Japanese on the one hand, and the three immigrant groups on the other. The mean occupational prestige of all three immigrant groups and the Whites drops substantially with the first job in Hawaii compared to the last job held before migration. The drop is most severe for Koreans and least severe for Filipinos. From the first job to the job they held at the time of the study, there were some gains in occupational prestige but not to the premigration level. Whites regained the most, 5.3 points of the 5.8 points lost in their first postmigration job. Second, there was a striking decrease in occupational status of Korean men relative to Whites from the U.S. mainland, and the decrease in the mean occupational prestige of Samoan men relative to Filipino men. The third most important consequence is the overall difference in occupational mobility across the four immigrant groups after they arrive in Hawaii. Whites reported the highest incidence of outstanding personal achievement, 13% compared to 3% for Japanese, 2% for Koreans, 1% for Filipinos, and no occurrence at all for Samoans.

With the lowest percentage of both spouses working and the highest percentage of both spouses not working, Samoans had an annual family income extremely low compared to other ethnic groups, with 76% earning less than $10,000 a year. They make greater use of the Social Security Administration (29%) than the Filipinos (25%) and Koreans (3%).

Not surprisingly, the Samoans as a group experienced greater amounts of stress than any of the other groups, as measured by the proportion of occurrence of stressful life events. Second were the Koreans, then the Whites, then the Japanese, followed by the Filipinos. As a group, Samoans experienced a degree of stress that was almost three times as great as that of Filipinos, and over twice that of the Japanese. Despite this degree of stress, only 5% expressed any dissatisfaction; 43% of the Samoans said that they were "very much satisfied" with their life in Hawaii, quite comparable to the percentages for Filipinos and Whites. The highest percentage of dissatisfaction (21%) and lowest percentage of satisfaction (7%) was found among the Koreans, the group that had the second highest stress score and the greatest degree of incongruity in occupational prestige of jobs held before and after migration.

Gender-Related Issues. Fujii, Fukushima, and Change (1989) gave a 90-minute semistructured interview to 10 Asian-American female psychiatrists ranging in age from 26 to 44, with a mean age of 35. Included in the sample were 2 Chinese, 2 Filipino, 4 Japanese, 1 Vietnamese, and 1 Korean. As a general rule, families of the women had disapproved of their career choice. There is not as much respect for psychiatrists in the United States and Asia as there is for surgeons. In both geographical settings, psychiatry is not considered a "typical" choice for Asians. At work, racism and stereotyping (positive and negative) by residence faculty, colleagues, and patients appeared to be present, albeit sometimes subtly. Some of the women felt "pushed" into minority issues or felt pressure to behave in a certain way. Nonetheless, all the women reported satisfaction with their professional lives and were deeply committed to their profession. Foreign medical school graduates (FMGs) relied on family and religion to help them through difficult times, whereas non-FMGs coped in ways more similar to those of their mainstream colleagues.

Occupational Segregation, Stereotyping, and Discrimination

Occupational Segregation. Several investigators demonstrated that Asian Americans are overrepresented in some occupations while being underrepresented in others (Chun, 1980; Hsia, 1988; Sue & Kirk, 1972, 1973). Such a skewed distribution of any group in the occupational structure indicates occupational segregation that could be the result of differential, including restricted, access to various occupations. Hsia (1988) provided a good illustration of the overall pattern of occupational segregation among Asian Americans by presenting a table of the representation index (RI) for Asian Americans in various occupations. For Asian Americans, the RI, a single numerical representation of the degree of segregation, is derived by dividing the percentage of Asian Americans in a particular occupation by the percentage of Asian Americans in the total civilian labor force, then multiplying the result by 100. For example, an RI of 100 for Asian Americans in a particular occupation means that they are represented according to their proportion in the general population, whereas an RI of 200 means that twice the number of Asian Americans relative to their proportion in the population are in that particular occupation.

Asian Americans in the occupational group, physicians, have the highest RI (537). Representation of Asian Americans in the physician group is five times more than expected given their representation in the general U.S. population. The other occupations in which Asians are highly segregated into include medical scientist (RI = 372), physicist and astronomer (RI = 357), biological and life scientist (RI = 316), engineers (RI = 293), architects (RI = 251), accountants and auditors (RI = 202). The occupational categories in which Asian Americans are underrepresented or segregated out of include lawyers (RI = 41), judges (RI = 35), chief executive officers and general administrators (RI = 60).

More recent data from the National Science Foundation (1990) provided further evidence of occupational segregation for Asian Americans. In 1988, Asian Americans, who comprise about 2% of the overall U.S. population, accounted for 5% of the total scientists and engineers in the United States. In the same year, the index of dissimilarity between Asian and Euro Americans was 16, that is, 16% of Asian Americans would have to change fields to produce a distribution similar to that for Euro Americans. Compared to Euro Americans, Asian Americans are more likely to be engineers than scientists and, among scientists, to be computer specialists rather than environmental specialists. Among Asian Americans who hold the PhD, more than three fifths are either life or physical scientists.

Chun (1980) attributed occupational segregation to societal and cultural barriers to Asian Americans' occupational aspirations. A national survey (U.S. Commission on Civil Rights, 1978) revealed that among all ethnic minorities the Chinese, Filipino, and Japanese Americans exhibited the highest levels of occupational segregation. We propose that occupational segregation may also reflect U.S. immigration policy formulated in response to labor needs in this country. Rather than reflecting the career choices of a random sample of Asian Americans, occupational segregation may be more indicative of the choices made by policymakers about who among the Asians would be given preference in immigrating to the United States after World War II. A comparison of occupational distributions for Asian Americans prior to and after World War II, particularly after passage of the 1965 Immigration Act, might help to shed light on this issue. So would a study comparing the career choices and occupations of Asian Americans who have been in the United States for one versus three or more generations.

The observed pattern of occupational segregation is consistent with Asian Americans' ethnic and cultural background that emphasizes reserve and formality in interpersonal relations, inhibition of strong feelings, restraint, and obedience to authority. Together, social anxiety and occupational segregation have important consequences for early career development. First, Asian Americans lack access to certain professionals (e.g., lawyers, psychologists, social workers, etc.) from their own culture who, besides providing more culturally congruent services, could serve as occupational role models. Second, internal and external occupational stereotypes may develop and result in additional occupational barriers.

Occupational Stereotyping. It has been suggested that Asian-American overrepresentation in certain fields and underrepresentation in others may result from occupational stereotyping. However, almost no empirical study of this phenomenon had been undertaken until Leong and Hayes (1990) investigated it in a sample of White male (46%) and female (54%) college students. Presented a profile of a high school senior, described as either male or female and White or Asian, subjects rated on a scale of 1 to 7 (a) how well qualified the student was to seek *training* in certain occupations, (b) the probability of *success* in 16 different occupations, and (c) how likely this individual was to be *accepted* by his or her co-workers in those occupations.

Race had a significant main effect of race only on "probability of success." Asian, compared to Euro Americans, were seen as being less likely to succeed in insurance sales, but more likely to be successful as engineers, computer scientists, and mathematicians. Race did not interact significantly with gender, which had significant main effects on both "qualified to seek training" and "probability of success." For the dimension of "likely to be accepted," neither the main effects nor the interaction were significant. The lack of significant race by gender interactions suggests that gender stereotyping by occupations may operate for both population groups.

Further research is needed to determine how widespread these occupational stereotypes are before accepting the generalizability of the current findings. It would be important, for example, to determine whether stereotypes regarding the probability of Asian-American success in certain occupations are held also by teachers, guidance counselors, career education specialists, and other individuals in the school system who are responsible for providing career guidance, and even by Asian Americans themselves. If occupational stereotyping is confirmed in subsequent studies, its determinants and the process whereby it is formed will have to be investigated. The modification of occupational stereotypes needs to be explored in carefully designed intervention studies. The psychological impact of these occupational stereotypes on Asian Americans, including their career choices, has to be assessed.

Occupational stereotypes suggest that the occupations held by Asian Americans may not reflect their actual career interests. Because of occupational stereotypes held by others (e.g., guidance counselors) or by themselves, some or even many Asian Americans may choose careers not on the basis of their interests and abilities but because they have been given the impression that their ethnic membership is closely related to success or failure in an occupation. This impression, in turn, could lead to occupational segregation.

The pattern of occupational stereotyping (i.e., the perception of Asian Americans as being more qualified to enter and likely to succeed in the physical, biological, and medical sciences and less qualified to enter or be successful in the verbal, persuasive, social careers such as a lawyer, judge, or teacher) parallels the pattern of occupational segregation. On one hand, this parallelism suggests a numerical basis for occupational stereotyping of Asian Americans; on the other hand, it could mean that occupational segregation occurs because of occupational stereotyping. Still another possibility is that the relationship between occupational stereotyping and occupational segregation might be a reciprocal one. More empirical studies of the relationship are needed. Most likely, occupational stereotyping is only one of several factors contributing to occupational segregation.

Occupational Discrimination. Based on the occupational distributions for Asian Americans presented previously, one can see why the concept of "model minority" (Petersen, 1966) has been applied to this population. The myth that Asian Americans are a successful minority has been well documented and discussed within the social science literature (Kim, 1973; Leong, 1985; Owan, 1975). Many have questioned the myth, arguing that the stereotypes do not generalize to all Asian Americans and pointing out that labelling Asian Americans as a successful or model minority has resulted in their being neglected in research or intervention programs (Chun, 1980; Hsia, 1980; Kim, 1973; Leong, 1985; Minatoya & Sedlacek, 1981; Owan, 1975; Sue & Kitano, 1973; Sue, Sue, & Sue, 1975; Sue & Wagner, 1973).

Using the criterion of occupational attainment alone, Asian Americans as a group appear to have fared quite well relative to other minority groups. However, such an observation overlooks important intragroup differences. For example, whereas Asian Americans as a group constitute 18.3% of all individuals in professional occupations relative to 12.3% for Euro Americans, only 8.8% of Vietnamese Americans are in professional occupations. Furthermore, 29.3% of Vietnamese and 20.5% of Korean Americans are in operator/laborer occupations compared to 17.1% for White Americans and 14.2% for Asian Americans overall. The model minority concept also ignores the problem of discrimination against Asian Americans. Being successful is no guarantee against prejudice and discrimination.

Leong and Raote (1992) used some national data sets to challenge both the successful minority myth and the economic uniformity myth regarding Chinese Americans. The successful minority myth maintains that Asian Americans have been able to utilize their own resources to achieve high levels of educational and occupational attainment relative to other minority groups. The economic uniformity myth consists of Asian Americans' assumption that economic returns from investment in education is uniformly consistent across all groups within the United States. Put differently, it is the assumption that there is a positive correlation between education and income, and that the degree of this correlation is equal between different racial/ethnic groups. As Siegel (1965) pointed out, this assumption did not apply to African Americans back in the early 1960s. Everything else being equal, African Americans pay a price for being African American. More specifically, Siegel (1965) found that it cost African Americans approximately $1,000 for being African American. A 1970 update of the Siegel (1965) study found that African Americans still paid a price for being African American, and the cost had even increased from $1,000 in 1965 or $1,380 in 1969 dollars to $1,647 in 1970, an increase of $267 (Johnson & Sell, 1976).

When viewed in isolation, data on both educational attainment and occupational status present a rather positive picture of the Chinese American, and one can readily understand how they can be viewed as a successful minority (Leong & Raote, 1992). However, a close examination of data reveals that this is not really true. To investigate occupational discrimination against Chinese Americans, Leong and Raote (1992) calculated the cost of being a Chinese American as well as that of being African American using data from two reports: the Survey of Income and Education (SIE) collected in 1976 (U.S. Commission on Civil Rights, 1978), and a report based on the SIE data set written by Hirschman and Wong (1981), who examined the socioeconomic achievements of foreign-born Asian Americans. Leong and Raote (1992) examined the adjusted mean earnings of the Chinese, African, and Euro Americans with the level of education, occupation prestige, and number of hours/days worked, statistically controlled for with multiple regressions. These analyses essentially revealed what each group made while working in the United States if everything else was held constant. Everything else being equal, Euro-American males made $11,427, African-American males made $9,741, and Chinese-American males made $8,817. In other words, it cost Chinese-American males $2,610 for being Chinese. For African Americans, the cost was $1,686.

These figures provide an index of racial income inequity and also challenge the economic uniformity assumption concerning the education–income correlation. More specifically, it reveals that Chinese-American men are not all that successful. In fact, with the same level of education, age, occupational prestige, and amount of time worked, Chinese-American men lose much more than African Americans. This surprisingly high level of inequity for Chinese-American men warrants not only a reversal of the successful minority myth for this particular Asian group, but also Chinese Americans' reevaluation of their underlying assumption of an automatic relationship between levels of educational attainment and economic success in the United States.

Many Asian-American families have used education as a primary route to upward mobility within American society. Although these families and their children, through their conscientiousness and persistence, have achieved a considerable amount of "success" in educational and occupational attainment, they have been unknowingly discriminated against by the U.S. economic and occupational systems for a long time. The concept that Asian Americans are a successful or model minority has often covered up the occupational constraints and inequities experienced by this ethnic group (Chun, 1980). A recognition and redress of this "hidden cost" for being Chinese Americans is long overdue. However, Asian Americans first need to be educated about the disparity within the economic system and be informed that the "educational route" by itself is insufficient, and that a parallel "political route" is also necessary if they are to attain success within American society.

Evidence that Asian Americans may have comparable or even higher academic competencies and yet be paid less than Euro Americans comes from another national data set. The National Science Foundation (1990) reported that Asian-American psychologists only make 66% of Euro-American psychologists' salary even though the entry level for both groups is the doctorate. Other findings suggest occupational discrimination against Asian-American scientists and engineers within our universities. Among doctoral scientists and engineers in 4-year colleges and universities in 1987, Asian compared to Euro Americans were less likely to hold tenure (43% vs. 57%) and hold the rank of full (36% vs. 42%) or associate (22% vs. 24%) professors. A higher proportion of Asian Americans are in nontenure track positions (12% vs. 9%). The disparities exist despite the fact that Asian Americans enter colleges and universities with much higher academic credentials (course grades and SAT/GRE scores) than Euro Americans.

Investigations into the factors behind the apparent discrepancies in salary, tenure, and promotion of Asian Americans whose credentials are comparable to those of Euro Americans are needed. Of particular importance also would be the levels within an occupation where discrimination begins to occur. In a laboratory simulation study, Carroll, Feren, and Olian (1987) found no evidence of prejudice against Asian Americans as managers in a sample of 267 individuals who were about to enter organizations in junior capacities. In this sample, personal liking and acceptance of an Asian manager as a work colleague, boss, and mentor were primarily related to the manager's interpersonal competence. Also, women preferred non-Anglo-Saxon (Asian or Hispanic) managers as mentors perhaps because, as suggested by another finding from this study, they are more sensitive than men in their reactions to the manager's interpersonal competence. Women typically responded more extremely to manifestations of managers' high and low interpersonal competence.

The Carroll, Feren, and Olian (1987) study raises additional research questions. Are these findings from a laboratory simulation replicable in actual work situations? If replicated, are the favorable perceptions of Asian Americans held by junior-level personnel shared by senior-level personnel, particularly managers or administrators who make decisions regarding assignments, promotions, and salary increases?

Conceptual and Methodological Issues

In general, research on career development of Asian Americans may be characterized as sparse and fragmented. It lacks coherence because there is no critical mass of studies focusing on a particular topic, and, furthermore, there has been no programmatic research. To date, description rather than explanation appears to have been the aim in this research.

A serious conceptual limitation in current research on Asian-American career development is the lack of a theoretical framework. A possible reason for this atheoretical state of the field is that most of the studies have not really been conducted by behavioral scientists whose primary research interest is career development. The researchers represent different disciplines and, within a discipline (e.g., psychology), various specialities. What they have in common is an interest in the adaptation of Asian Americans. It is not surprising, therefore, that their research questions and hypotheses have not been derived from contemporary theories of career development, formulated mainly by psychologists. In addition, these theories or models were proposed to describe and explain career development in Euro Americans, so their validity for Asian Americans remains questionable. However, if a theory has never been tested in a particular population, its questionable validity ought to lead to a test of its potential usefulness rather than outright rejection. Studies can be designed to test the cultural validity of a theory for Asian-American subgroups and, if it is not, to determine what modifications are needed to make it more culturally relevant as well as culturally appropriate for career interventions. Research on Asian-American career development has to progress from a sole focus on information gathering to theory building. Given the availability of career development theories, a deductive as opposed to an inductive approach might be a more efficient way to develop a theory of Asian-American career development.

Another conceptual issue is a tendency on the part of many investigators to equate ethnicity with culture. Ethnic group differences are interpreted as being indicative of cultural differences. Investigators rarely assess the cultural variables that are assumed to underlie ethnic group differences.

The review of research also revealed several methodological issues that have to be addressed in order to improve our scientific database on the career behavior of Asian Americans. Most of the available studies used a heterogeneous sample of Asian Americans or Asian Americans/Pacific Islanders. Potential differences between Asians and Pacific Islanders and between subgroups within each of these larger populations were ignored. The results of future research would be more meaningful if the samples are more homogeneous (e.g., Chinese Americans or Native Hawaiians). Census data collected since 1980 lend themselves to this more refined level of analysis; there are separate categories for Asians and Pacific Islanders, and for subgroups within each of these two larger population groupings.

Another methodological issue is that previous studies often failed to give adequate attention to moderating variables. Foremost among these is the research participant's American generational status that is particularly important in the study of career development because the occupational levels of different migration waves varied. With some exceptions, immigrants from Asia prior to World War II were less educated than those who came after. Furthermore, regardless of educational level, they encountered more occupational barriers and discrimination than later immigrants. It is possible that their career paths and those of their descendants might differ from those of immigrants who arrived after World War II, particularly after 1965.

Within the same generational status, acculturation is a potential moderating variable. The extent to which an individual has become knowledgeable about and incorporates the culture of the dominant ethnic group in American society is bound to influence his or her occupational interests, aspirations, choices, and behavior. Hence, research on career development of Asian Americans must consider the potential moderating effect of acculturation upon a career variable.

Ethnic identity is yet another potential moderating variable in the career development of individuals with the same generational status. It refers to one's sense of belonging as part of an ethnic group and includes those aspects of the self such as beliefs, perspectives, attitudes, feelings, and behaviors that are derived from ethnic group membership. Ethnic identity is related to but not identical with acculturation. Although high acculturation may co-occur with low ethnic identity, it is still possible for someone who is highly acculturated to retain a strong sense of identification with his or her ethnic group. Ethnic identity influences various career variables in different degrees. Its influence is most often seen in career choices. For example, a reason commonly given by ethnic minority high school graduates who choose careers in human services is that they wish, eventually, "to help my people."

Socioeconomic status (SES) is still another potential moderator of career behavior. It is particularly important that research on Asian Americans and other ethnic minority groups separate the effects of ethnicity and

SES. In previous research, effects of these two variables are often highly confounded. Thus, we still do not know to what extent the career patterns observed in Asian Americans are due to the fact of their being from the lower working classes or to their being from a distinct cultural group.

Perceived minority status is also a potential moderating variable in career development. It refers to an individual's perception that his or her ethnic group, in addition to being numerically in the minority compared to one or more groups, is also discriminated against and even oppressed. Because it embodies the notion that ability, hard work, and perseverance are not enough to bring about career success, perceived minority status can have a particularly damaging psychological effect on an individual's career self-efficacy and, consequently, on development. At the very least, it dampens career aspirations, exploration, and planning for legitimate occupations; at the worst, it redirects the individual toward antisocial career paths. The effects of perceived minority status are often confounded with those of ethnic minority membership and SES. It is important to separate it out because ethnic minority members, even those from a low socioeconomic status, may not perceive themselves as objects of discrimination and oppression. Some Asian Americans claim that they have not experienced any discrimination.

A final methodological issue that has to be solved in future research on Asian-American career development is instrumentation. First, there is the problem of evaluating the validity for Asian Americans of various career assessment instruments. For example, very few validity studies have been done to determine if Holland's classification system as represented in the Vocational Preference Inventory (VPI), Self-Directed Search (SDS), or the Strong Interest Inventory (SII) is appropriate for Asian Americans as a group. It is critical to establish the appropriateness for Asian Americans of existing career assessment instruments. If these are not and they cannot be modified to become more appropriate, then new instruments will have to be constructed. Second, there is the task of developing accurate and reliable measures of moderating variables such as acculturation, ethnic identity, social class, and minority status. For example, there is a need for a short, reliable, practical social class measure. Such a measure can be used across various studies and across various groups to provide comparable data on the effects of this very important moderating variable. Although there have been several attempts to develop measures of acculturation and ethnic identity (Phinney, 1992; Suinn, Ricard-Figueroa, Lew, & Vigil, 1987), there is still room for improvement. Definitional problems and failure to fully take into account the development progression of the variables being measured are among the shortcomings of existing measures.

FUTURE RESEARCH ON ASIAN-AMERICAN
CAREER DEVELOPMENT

Directions

Two related but separate programs of research are indicated by the preceding review of research. Primarily, there is a need for theory-based, programmatic research aimed at description and explanation of career development among Asian Americans. A parallel need is for a systematic program of instrument development directed toward constructing reliable and culturally valid measures with appropriate age and gender norms that can be used with Asian Americans. Issues related to instrument development have been discussed previously so this section focuses on research questions.

Research on Asian Americans to date lacks a developmental perspective. The precursors of career development as seen in children's emerging interests and the evolution of career maturity in adolescence have been neglected. Similarly, the work adjustment, career changes, and career advancement of adult immigrants to the U.S. mainland has received very little consideration. There is a need for studies that examine career development at different phases of the life span, particularly studies that employ cross-sectional and longitudinal designs. As proposed by Vondracek, Lerner, and Schulenberg (1986), the initial development of a vocational role and the progression of a career or vocation over time can be conceptualized as one strand in a person's development and examined in the same manner as other strands (e.g., cognitive development). Career development has bidirectional links to other strands and to a changing social context that is permeated in varying degrees by one or more cultures. A full understanding of career development among Asian Americans requires a life-span developmental-contextual framework.

Thus far, researchers have failed also to address to address the differential issues associated with American generational status. Some career issues are common to all generations. Regardless of the country of birth and rearing, childhood is the period for emergence of the precursors of career development: competencies (e.g., knowledge, abilities, skills, talents), personality (e.g., traits, interests, values), self-concept (e.g. self-description, self-esteem, self-efficacy), and task orientation (e.g., study skills, work habits, and attitudes). Adolescence brings with it a heightened awareness that one is expected to make a vocational choice. This adds impetus to the development of career maturity (i.e., the competence to meet the socially prescribed developmental task, which, at adolescence, is the crystallization of a vocational preference). Certain competencies, personality characteristics, self-attributes, work habits, and attitudes that have developed relatively independent of one another now converge in a focus on the task of choosing a vocation or career. In late adolescence and early adulthood, the tentative career choice is implemented by the individual's undertaking the necessary career preparation and, upon its completion, finding a job, adjusting to work, and learning what is required to advance and succeed.

Adulthood, for the American-born and/or -reared Asian Americans, may be a period characterized by a continuous process of establishing oneself and advancing within an occupation. However, it may involve a series of short-term temporary positions for Asian Americans who become immigrants only after completing their graduate or professional training. Many spend years in a series of postdoctoral fellowships, research associateships, or postresidency medical fellowships while they search for permanent positions. When they do find a permanent position, work adjustment, consolidation, and advancement may be a slower and more difficult process for them due to a variety of reasons. For Asian Americans who immigrated to the United States after having settled in a job within a chosen field and embarked on consolidation or advancement, certain career issues such as finding a job in the chosen occupation, meeting certification or licensing requirements, retraining if barriers to career continuity cannot be overcome, and work adjustment assume great importance. In sum, career tasks assume varying degrees of salience for Asian Americans as a function of the life stage when they enter the American labor force.

The role of various explanatory factors may differ also among generations. For example, the family's influence on career choice and the career decision-making process may wane in succeeding generations of Asian Americans. Greater attention to generational differences in career issues will provide more meaningful information about career development in this population. It will increase our understanding of the similarities and differences between Asian Americans and other ethnic groups with respect to career development. It may even identify the particular generation when the career pathways of Asian Americans converge with those of Euro- and other American ethnic groups.

Theoretical Perspectives

Research on Asian-American career development is best approached from an interdisciplinary framework, particularly one that combines psychological, sociological, and economic theories. The immigration of Asian Americans to the United States has been and continues to be linked to this nation's labor needs. Furthermore, subtle racial discrimination and occupational stereotyping may present barriers to their entry and advancement in certain occupational fields. Thus, no explanation of their career development would be complete unless it took into account the influence of occupational structures, social organizations, and public policies. For purely pragmatic reasons, however, our presentation is limited to psychological theories. It is difficult enough to attempt an integration of several theories within a discipline, let alone to take on theories from another discipline. What is being proposed here is the nucleus of a conceptual framework that eventually might integrate theories from other disciplines.

Several major psychological theories have guided research on career development in the United States, particularly among Euro Americans. These theories have been categorized by Osipow (1990) as (a) developmental, (b) trait-oriented, (c) reinforcement-based, and (d) personality focused. Osipow (1990) also noted that, although each of the major perspectives initially had a particular emphasis, subsequent reformulations based on research have enhanced their similarities. Important differences remain, however, and we are inclined to agree with Holland (1992) that theoretical convergence would not be a productive strategy at the present time. Thus, instead of aiming for a tightly knit integration of these theories into a conceptual framework, our more modest goal is to discuss how certain theories representing the developmental, trait-oriented, and reinforcement-based perspectives can be used together to initiate a program of research on career development of Asian Americans. Several reviews (e.g., Brown & Brooks, 1990; Osipow, 1983) have assessed the extent to which these theories (a) meet the formal criteria of a good theory, (b) are supported by research evidence, and (c) deal with contextual issues such as gender, class, minority status, race, ethnicity, and culture. Hence, our presentation highlights only those aspects of these theories that hold promise for the study of career issues that are central to Asian Americans. Specifically, they were chosen for what they might be able to contribute to a description of the career development sequence, career choice and decision making, and work adjustment. One or more of these issues is highly salient for at least one of the three identified categories of Asian Americans: the American-born and/or -reared, the postgraduate or postprofessional training immigrant, and the "mid-career" immigrant. Although the applicability of these theories to Asian Americans and other ethnic minority groups has been criticized (Fitzgerald & Betz, 1992; Smith, 1983), they can serve as starting points for investigating universals in career development. Research on career development of Asian Americans asks the following questions: In what ways is the career development of Asian Americans similar to that of all other ethnic groups? In what ways is it similar only to that of some ethnic groups or some members of an ethnic group? In what ways is it unique?

Describing Career Development Sequences. Ideally, a career can be envisioned as an individual's life work, embarked upon during one's youth and sustained with notable advances until late in life or even till death. As noted earlier, this concept of a career as life's work was held by the ancient Chinese and, very likely, by Asians in other countries, too. For many Asian Americans, a life-span career remains a meaningful concept. Among contemporary theorists, only Super (1957, 1980) has proposed a detailed description of the career development sequence across the life span. In his most recent formulation of the theory, Super (1990, 1992) described the career development process as a series of life stages or a maxicycle involving a sequence of growth, exploration, establishment, maintenance, and decline. As depicted in the Life Career Rainbow (see Fig. 3.1), the stages coincide with an individual's position in the life space, the temporal context, and the social roles he or she plays, the social context (Super, 1980).

Across the life span, both the individual and the environment change in a reciprocal fashion. As the individual's developmental status changes, so do the expectations that the environment or society have of him or her. In regard to career development, these expectations are translated into developmental tasks, unique to each stage, that confront the individual. Initially, five tasks were proposed: crystallization of a vocational preference (approximately 14 to 18 years), specification of a career choice and undertaking career preparation or training (18 to 21 years), implementation of a career choice by completing training and starting relevant employment (21 to 25 years), stabilization through settling down within a field of work (25 to 35 years), and consolidation of status and advancement (30 to 40 years). In a subsequent reformulation of the theory, Super (1990) identified developmental tasks in middle (45 to 65 years) and late (over 65 years) adulthood. The interaction between individual and developmental task has specific outcomes (e.g., a career choice, work satisfaction, etc.).

Successful accomplishment of a developmental task depends on the individual's career maturity, a multidimensional construct representing one's readiness to cope with the task. More specifically, career maturity represents a constellation of career-related physical, psychological, social, and behavioral characteristics; psychologically, it has both cognitive and affective aspects. Variations in rate and degree of success in coping with developmental tasks arise from individual differences in career maturity. Super (1990) emphasized that career maturity does not increase monotonically. Implicit in his theorizing, however, is the notion of hierarchically ordered levels of career maturity; characteristics related to success in coping with the demands of earlier stages and substages, especially the most recent one, are integrated into the next level (Super, 1990).

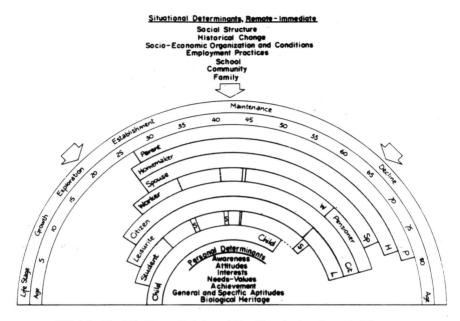

FIG. 3.1. The Life-Career Rainbow: Nine life roles in schematic life space. From "A Life-Span, Life-Space Approach to Career Development," by D. E. Super, 1980, *Vocational Behavior*, 16, p. 285. Copyright 1980. Reprinted by permission.

The maxicycle described by Super (1980) may be applicable to the career development of American-born or foreign-born but American-reared Asian Americans whose careers may be characterized by the continuity implicit in the maxicycle. Japanese Americans, the group with the least influx of new immigrants since 1924 and perhaps the most acculturated among the various Asian-American groups (Daniels, 1988), may come closest to achieving this type of developmental sequence. Still, the rate at which Japanese and other Asian Americans progress through the sequence might differ from that of Euro Americans at a certain stage or consistently throughout the life span. Reports of a "glass ceiling" for Asian Americans (Miller, 1992; Sue, Zane, & Sue, 1985) suggest that the rate and level of advancement for this population might differ from that of Euro Americans. More specifically, even Asian Americans whose families have been in the United States for generations may move through the Establishment stage and advance to the Maintenance stage at a slower pace than their Euro-American peers.

The theory also provides a means of characterizing the career developmental sequence of Asian Americans within a stage. Because each stage is further subdivided into substages or phases, within-stage development can be studied in terms of progress through the different substages (e.g., through the fantasy, tentative, and realistic phases of the exploratory stage). Development within a stage may also be studied as to whether the process conforms to Super's (1990) hypothesized minicycle, that is, each stage has its own cycle of growth, exploration, establishment, maintenance, and decline, followed by a transition to the next stage. The minicycle concept may be applied to all Asian Americans to describe the developmental process at any major career stage, to assess its rate, or to determine the influential factors. It may be particularly useful in studying the career transitions that occur as a result of migration. Regardless of whether career continuity (same occupation or occupational field) or discontinuity is the consequence of migration for adults, their progress through a new job in the host country will probably entail a process of growth, exploration, establishment, maintenance, and decline, although what is involved at each phase has yet to be operationalized.

Asian-American societies, just like American society, also specify developmental tasks that must be accomplished at different periods of the life span. However, we do not know whether the career developmental tasks for a particular period are the same or different for Euro Americans and a specific Asian-American group. Although it may be said with a fair degree of certainty that the crystallization of a vocational preference is perceived in both cultures to be the central task of adolescence, it is more difficult to speculate about the similarity in developmental tasks for other periods. According to Super (1980), developmental tasks are defined in relation to social roles. With increasing age, the number of roles increase and these various roles interact in different ways. Depending on the individual's position in the life space and other factors, the different roles assume varying degrees of salience that have implications for career development. At a particular stage, the central developmental tasks might be different for Euro Americans and an Asian-American group because of different cultural values attached to social roles. Super's (1990) specification of the developmental tasks at each stage offers a starting point for investigating the similarities and differences.

The concept of career maturity also holds some promise for the study of Asian Americans. The anxiety that Asian-American college students show over vocational career concerns (Tracey et al., 1986) suggests that many feel unprepared to cope with the central career developmental tasks facing them, possibly because they must face tasks imposed by the larger society dominated by Euro Americans. For Asian Americans, Super's (1990, 1992) theorizing offers a potentially useful framework for conceptualizing the developmental sequence of career maturity and its relationship to successful attainment of career developmental tasks throughout the life span.

The life-span, life-space approach to career development offers a useful framework for describing sequential patterns but it may be less powerful in explaining and predicting certain career variables such as career choice, career decision making, and work adjustment. Like other career development theorists, Super (1990) accounts for the career pattern (i.e., the occupational level attained and the sequence, frequency, and duration of trial and stable jobs) of the individual's parental SES, intellectual ability, education, skills, personality characteristics, and career opportunities. It is the self-concept, however, that is the central explanatory construct in his theory.

In the initial application of self-concept to career development, it was conceptualized solely as self-description (Super, Starishevsky, Matlin, & Jordaan, 1963), operationalized as dimensions or attributes. The concept has been broadened to include metadimensions such as self-esteem (Super, 1990) and career self-efficacy (Super, personal communication, April 23, 1992). It is now so broad that Super (1990) thought self-concept theory might be more appropriately called personal construct theory. Within the theory, self-concept accounts for career preferences and the eventual specific career choice. It also serves as the explanatory construct for work satisfaction that is hypothesized to depend on the extent to which a work setting or an occupation permit implementation and further development of the self-concept. Additionally, it is employed as a motivational construct for career development across the life span. According to Super (1957), a career can be portrayed as the life course of a person encountering a series of developmental tasks and coping with them in such a way as to become the kind of person he or she wants to be. Career development over the life span is essentially a sequential process of developing and implementing a series of occupational self-concepts (Super et al., 1963).

It is questionable whether the self-concept as an explanatory construct holds the same power for Asian as for Euro Americans. The theory's proposition that implementation of the self-concept, operationalized as one's attributes or combinations of attributes, is the motivating force behind career development may be less applicable to Asian Americans reared in a culture that emphasizes a collective rather than the individualistic orientation favored in Euro-American culture. The Asian emphasis on modesty and self-effacement might moderate the individualistic tendency to engage in self-expression even in American-born and/or American-reared Asian Americans. Perhaps, with increasing acculturation and assimilation, career development may also become primarily a vehicle for an implementation of Asian Americans' self-concept. This, however, remains to be empirically verified.

Social role, a concept also incorporated into the theory, might hold more promise as an explanatory construct. For Asian Americans reared in the traditional manner, career development may be more closely linked to the fulfillment of social roles and the observance of such values as filial piety and reciprocal obligations within the family. In other words, self as dutiful son, nurturing father, and proud clan member may be what is being implemented. Career choice and career advancement may be seen more as means of providing for one's own family, helping one's siblings, and fulfilling one's responsibility to care for parents in their old age than as ways of implementing self-attributes such as gregariousness. Asian Americans may be more inclined to consider the continuity of family tradition (e.g., a family of physicians) when making a career choice. They may value career success and advancement more for the honor bestowed on the family than as expressions of their individuality. The importance of social roles and family expectations as determinants of career development among Asian Americans warrants further investigation.

For Asian Americans and all other groups, the potential usefulness of the self-concept as an explanatory construct for career choice is also limited by how it has been operationalized within the theory. The emphasis on dimensions or even metadimensions, both of which tend to be numerous, makes relating the self-concept to the content of a specific career choice a more complicated task. Furthermore, although Super (1990) indicated that the theory is less concerned with matching than with sequential changes in the self-concept as related to changes in career situations, operationalizing these sequential changes in self-dimensions in a manner that can be easily related to changes in career situations remains a formidable task. Fortunately, career development theory now embraces occupational matching theory (Super, 1990), so Holland's (1973, 1985) typology, a more efficient yet theoretically meaningful approach, can now be used for the study of career choice among Asian Americans within the broader life-span framework.

Career Choice. The primary goals of the theory of vocational choice and behavior (Holland, 1973, 1985; Weinrach & Srebalus, 1990) are to describe and explain career choice, and to predict career achievement, satisfaction, stability, and change. All these are central issues for Asian Americans. Holland (1985) contended that career choice is not a random event, although chance plays a role. Personality is a major determinant of career choice, the latter being an expression of personality. This relationship between personality traits and career choice is mediated by vocational interests. Thus, an individual's vocational interests can be used to make inferences about his or her personality. Holland (1985) assumed that in American society, most persons can be categorized as having one of six personality types: realistic, investigative, artistic, social, enterprising, or conventional. Usually, a person's personality pattern would reveal that one of the six types predominates but might also show subtypes. A complete profile would include characteristics of all six types, but a subtype emerges from the three most prevalent types found in an individual.

Before Holland's (1985) theory can be applied to Asian Americans, it must be empirically demonstrated that his typology holds true for representative samples drawn from a particular subgroup of Asian Americans and from this population as a whole.

According to Holland (1985), each of the personality types relates to the environment in a particular way. Because similarities attract, a particular environment comes to be populated by individuals of a corresponding type, thereby creating an environment in which individuals with a particular personality type dominate. This, in turn, attracts more individuals of that type because people search for environments that will enable them to exercise their skills and abilities, express their attitudes and values, and take on problems and roles to their liking, a phenomenon called "niche-picking" (Scarr & Macartney, 1983). Environments, therefore, can be classified also in a manner similar to that of personalities. There are six kinds of environments: realistic, investigative, artistic, social, enterprising, or conventional. The latest description of personality and environment types may be found in Holland (1985).

The relationships among personalities or environments are depicted in a hexagon. Holland (1985) posited that the relationships within and between types or environments can be ordered according to a hexagonal model in which the distances between the types or environments are inversely proportional to the theoretical relationships between them (p. 5). The degree of similarity (as indexed by correlations) among personality or environment types can be inferred from the distance between them on the hexagon. The degree of personality consistency is indicated by how close the types that figure in an individual's personality appear on the hexagon. The closer they are to one another, the higher the degree of consistency in the individual's personality. Personality types or environments vary in degree of differentiation. An individual or environment in which all types are equally represented is relatively undifferentiated, whereas one in which one or more types dominate would be more differentiated. Personality types or environments can be characterized also in terms of their respective identities. An individual's identity is indicated by possession of a clear and stable picture of one's goals, interests, and talents. An environment's identity is denoted by the clarity, stability, and integration of its goals, tasks, and rewards.

As stated earlier, different personality types require different environments. Hence, the concept of congruence is important in career choice. Congruence is indicated by the degree of similarity between an individual's personality and the environment in which he or she works. Optimal congruence or a perfect fit is present when personality and environment types are identical, as when a realistic personality works in a realistic environment. The next-highest congruence or next-best-fit is found when, as depicted in the hexagon, the individual's personality type is adjacent to an environment type. The least degree of congruence occurs when personality and environment types are at opposite points on the hexagon. The congruence between an individual's personality and job environment can predict occupational achievement, stability, and satisfaction. Syntheses of research evidence (Holland, 1985; Osipow, 1983; Weinrach & Srebalus, 1990) reveal that, indeed, congruence is related to vocational maturity and predicts career achievement, stability, satisfaction, and adjustment. Studies of congruence might clarify whether occupational segregation reflects choice on the part of Asian Americans or is the result of other factors such as parental pressure, occupational stereotyping, or discrimination. With ability, training, and experience held constant, an examination of the role of congruence relative to structural variables in predicting career achievement might increase our understanding of "the glass ceiling" that Asian Americans purportedly encounter (Miller, 1992). The construct of congruence might also be used to investigate the relative contributions of personality and family influences on career choice.

In Holland's view, career development is influenced by intelligence, gender, social class, and organizational structures. He sees culture influencing career development through its influence on personality development. Furthermore, he views culture's influence on personality development as being mediated by gender. He has not addressed the role of culture in creating environments, perhaps because he sees environments as the result of personality types getting together and, therefore, the effect of culture is mediated by personality types. However, a work environment evolves into a whole that is more than just the sum of the resident personality types. It has its own values and practices that may be influenced more by one culture than another. As suggested by the study of Chinese managers described earlier (Redding & Ng, 1982), enterprising Chinese immigrants working in an enterprising environment might still behave differently from their Euro-American counterparts, because of different culturally determined ideas about the business–customer relationship. Furthermore, a work environment may be altered as more members of a different culture, albeit representing the same personality type, begin to reach a critical mass in that setting. Last, a work environment may be deliberately changed through the introduction of concepts and practices from another culture, to attain an organizational goal such as increased productivity. Both personality and work environment interact in a cultural context that affects their congruence and, ultimately, the worker's career satisfaction, achievement, and stability.

Career Decision Making. In addition to providing a useful means of assessing person–environment match in vocational choice, vocational choice theory has some propositions about the conditions under which decisions about career choices are made. It is postulated that the degree of differentiation and the hierarchy established among types in the individual's personality influence the decision-making process. The greater the degree of differentiation in the individual and the clearer what the dominant type is, the easier it is to make a choice. Less differentiation is associated with more vacillation on the part of the individual making the choice. Differentiation and hierarchy are also related to what the individual will do if there are environmental barriers (e.g., occupational opportunity structures) to implementation of the dominant personality type. If there is a clear-cut hierarchy, the individual will choose the second type, but if there is not, then vacillation will also ensue.

A career decision is a at least a two-step process. The first step is establishing the personality–environment match. The second step involves making a decision about the entry level. Holland proposed that for each environment type, there is a hierarchy of occupational levels. Intelligence and self-evaluations are the bases for a decision about level. However, this decision is also likely to be influenced by socioeconomic factors and opportunity structure, particularly among ethnic minority groups. The duration and cost of career preparation, as well as occupational barriers against entry or advancement of a particular group, might influence someone to enter a lower level occupation as opposed to a higher one more suitable on the bases of intelligence and personality.

The theory does not delineate the specific mechanisms underlying career choice and transitions in career development. This lack also characterizes the life-span, life-space approach. Super (1990) acknowledged that developmental theory has tended to neglect the processes whereby career mini- and maxidecisions are made. Because occupational-matching theory, grounded as it is in differential psychology, has shown a similar neglect, propositions from social learning theory and other theories that describe and explain decision-making processes would have to be incorporated into any evolving theory of career development among Asian Americans. Such an addition would not raise any internal contradictions, as career development theory has also embraced decision-making theory (Super, 1990).

The social learning theory of decision making (Krumboltz, 1979; Krumboltz, Mitchell, & Jones, 1976; Mitchell & Krumboltz, 1990) is an attempt to apply social learning theory to career decision making. It is hypothesized that the development of career preferences and skills and the selection of a particular career are influenced by learning experiences. Empirical demonstration of this hypothesis, however, is difficult if not impossible because, as Mitchell and Krumboltz (1990) themselves acknowledged, the possibilities for the nature and scheduling of the patterns of stimuli and reinforcement are nearly infinite in variety, particularly in the naturalistic setting. The acquisition of career preferences, skills, career choice, and decision-making skills may be more complex than can be explained by learning principles alone.

However, the theory does specify the task approach skills relative to career decision making (Krumboltz & Baker, 1973). These include recognizing an important decision situation, defining the decision or task manageably and realistically, examining and accurately assessing self-observations and world-view generalizations, generating a wide variety of alternatives, gathering needed information about the alternatives, determing which information sources are most reliable, accurate, and relevant, and planning and carrying out this six-sequence of decision-making behaviors. Research is needed as to whether Asian Americans who possess these skills to a greater degree than their peers arrive at a career choice more readily and with a higher degree of career certainty. These skills may be particularly important for Asian Americans when someone with a clear-cut personality type has to choose the entry level within the matching environment type, a poorly differentiated personality vacillates about choices, and there are environmental barriers (e.g., occupational opportunity structures) to implementation of the dominant personality type. For Asian Americans, the social learning theory of decision making might be most useful in intervention research aimed at facilitating career decision making, enhancing career certainty or decidedness, and maintaining career choices.

Work Adjustment. After a career choice is made, the requisite training is completed, and a job is found comes the crucial question: Can the individual find happiness or satisfaction? Super's (1990) propositions regarding work satisfaction seem too general as a source of specific hypotheses that can be easily tested. Work satisfaction is hypothesized to depend upon the extent to which the individual finds adequate outlets for abilities, needs, values, interests, personality traits, and self-concepts. Furthermore, work satisfaction (and adjustment, by implication) is seen mainly from the worker's viewpoint.

For Asian Americans who attach great importance to the employer–employee relationship, the employer's approval or satisfaction with employee is equally important. Moreover, because job tenure may be more precious to the immigrant than self-concept implementation, the extent to which his or her work satisfies the employer is critical. Many immigrants have been known to work under arduous conditions that diminish rather than enhance their self-esteem. Because they are determined to survive and support their families in this new country, it is critical that they satisfy the employer to retain their jobs. To them, employer approval and job tenure mean work adjustment and, in turn, adaptation to the host country. The study of Asian-American career development, particularly among adult immigrants, must incorporate concepts and propositions dealing with satisfaction of both the worker and the employer. The theory of work adjustment (TWA) provides a potentially useful framework.

A basic assumption of the TWA (Dawis, 1984; Lofquist & Dawis, 1969) is that each individual is motivated to achieve and maintain correspondence with his or her environment. Implied herein is the importance of a harmonious relationship between individual and environment, a notion that is consistent with Confucian and other Asian philosophies (Cleary, 1992). In work, correspondence is a matter of the individual fulfilling the requirements of the work environment, and the work environment fulfilling the requirements of the individual. Work adjustment denotes the individual's attempts to achieve and maintain a correspondence with the work environment. The individual is operationalized as a work personality, representing work-relevant abilities, needs, and personality styles. The work environment represents occupational ability requirements and occupational reinforcement patterns. Environments also vary in style.

Four style variables moderate the person's interaction with the environment: celerity, or the speed of initiating interaction with the environment; pace, or the intensity (energy level) of the interaction; rhythm, or the pattern of pace in the interaction (whether steady, cyclical, or erratic); and endurance, or the sustaining of the interaction. Thus, persons with the same abilities and values (i.e., personality structure) can have different personality styles such that they differ in their behavior, and therefore in their behavioral outcomes. Different environments, too, have different styles.

According to the theory, an individual's work adjustment at any point in time is indicated by his or her concurrent levels of satisfactoriness and satisfaction. Satisfactoriness is defined in terms of the correspondence between an individual's abilities and the ability requirements of the work environment, provided that the individual's needs correspond with the reinforcer system of the work environment. Satisfaction is determined by the correspondence between the reinforcer system of the work environment and the individual's needs, provided that the individual's abilities correspond with the ability requirements of the work environment. The correspondence between work personality and work environment predicts satisfactoriness and satisfaction. Similarly, correspondence also predicts job tenure, which is a joint function of satisfactoriness and satisfaction.

The work adjustment process is conceptualized within a systems model in which the driving force is achieving and maintaining correspondence, and the parameter value on which the system converges is satisfaction. TWA predicts four targets of change for adjustment behavior: response requirements, response capability, reinforcer requirements, and reinforcer capability, which yield two modes of adjustment: the active mode when the change is effected in the environment, and the reactive mode when the change is effected in the person. If locus of change is crossed with locus of *initiative* for change, there are four modes of adjustment. When dissatisfaction is experienced by the person or the environment, adjustment behavior is activated. Depending on adjustment style, it may be flexibility, an initial tolerance for dissatisfaction or perseverance, a continuing tolerance for dissatisfaction past the flexibility threshold. Adjustment behavior can be directed toward changing the person, a reactive mode, or changing the environment, an active mode. If directed toward the person, the targets of change are response requirements and response capability; if directed toward the environment, the targets are reinforcer requirements and reinforcer capability. Crossing locus of change with person or environment as locus of initiative for change yields four modes of adjustment.

On the question of the theory's applicability to Asian Americans, Dawis (1992) claimed that TWA stands by its individual differences tradition; persons are viewed as individuals, not as members of groups. Despite evidence that Asian Americans may differ from members of other ethnic groups in their occupational values (Gim, 1992; Leong & Tata, 1990), ethnicity—as well as gender, national origin, religion, age, sexual preference, and disability status—is considered irrelevant because it is an inaccurate and unreliable estimator of skills, abilities, needs, values, personality style, and adjustment style. The individual's present status, the result of response and reinforcement history, is what counts.

Concluding Statement

A review of relevant research suggests it is high time that theoretically based programmatic research on career development of Asian Americans is initiated. Studies can test competing theories to assess their usefulness for describing and explaining an aspect of Asian-American career development (e.g., career choice). If no particular theory can fully account for a certain aspect of career development, then studies could explore which theories can be used together to provide a more complete explanation. The modifications needed to make a theory more culturally relevant could also be tested. It is hoped that, eventually, the findings can be integrated into a comprehensive yet coherent and heuristic theory about career development and vocational behavior in this population.

REFERENCES

Brown, D., & Brooks, L. (Eds.). (1990). *Career choice and development.* San Francisco: Jossey-Bass.

Brown, D., Minor, C. W., & Jepsen, D. A. (1991). The opinions of minorities preparing for work: Report of the second NCDA National Survey. *Career Development Quarterly, 40,* 5–19.

Carroll, S. J., Feren, D. B., & Olian, J. D. (1987). Reactions to the new minorities by employees of the future: An experimental study. *Psychological Reports, 60,* 911–920.

Chun, K. T. (1980, Winter–Spring) The myth of Asian American success and its educational ramifications. *IRCD Bulletin,* pp. 2–13.

Cleary, T. (1992). *The essential Confucius.* San Francisco: Harper.

College Entrance Examination Board. (1980). *National college-bound seniors, 1980.* Princeton, NJ: Author.

Daniels, R. (1988). *Asian America: Chinese and Japanese in the United States since 1850.* Seattle: University of Washington Press.

Dawis, R. B. (1984). *A psychological theory of work adjustment.* Minneapolis: University of Minnesota Press.

Dawis, R. B. (1992, April). *Career choice and development theory and the theory of work adjustment.* Paper presented at the Conference on Convergence in Theories of Career Choice and Development, Michigan State University, East Lansing, MI.

Evanoski, P. O., & Tse, F. W. (1989). Career awareness program for Chinese and Korean American parents. *Journal of Counseling and Development, 67,* 472–474.

Fitzgerald, L. F., & Betz, N. E. (1992, April). *Career development in cultural context: The role of gender, race, class and sexual orientation.* Paper presented at the Conference on Convergence in Theories of Career Choice and Development, Michigan State University, East Lansing, MI.

Fujii, J. S., Fukushima, S. N., & Chang, C. Y. (1989). Asian women psychiatrists. *Psychiatric Annals, 19,* 633–638.

Gim, R. H. C. (1992, May). *Cross-cultural comparison of factors that influence career choice.* Paper presented at the Association for Asian American Studies Conference, San Jose, CA.

Hirschman, C., & Wong, M. G. (1981) Trends in socioeconomic achievement among immigrants and native born Asian Americans 1960–1976. *Sociological Quarterly, 22,* 495–514.

Holland, J. L. (1973). *Making vocational choices.* Englewood Cliffs, NJ: Prentice-Hall.

Holland, J. L. (1985). *Making vocational choices: A theory of vocational personalities and work environments* (2nd ed.). Englewood Cliffs, NJ: Prentice-Hall.

Holland, J. L. (1992, April). *Separate but unequal is better.* Paper presented at the Conference on Convergence in Theories of Career Choice and Development, Michigan State University, East Lansing, MI.

Hsia, J. (1980). *Cognitive assessment of Asian Americans.* Paper presented at the National Institute of Education, National Center for Bilingual Research Symposium on Bilingual Research, Los Alamitos, CA.

Hsia, J. (1988). *Asian Americans in higher education and at work.* Hillsdale, NJ: Lawrence Erlbaum Associates.

Johnson, M. P., & Sell, R. P. (1976). The cost of being Black: A 1970 update. *American Journal of Sociology, 82,* 183–90.

Johnson, R. C., Nagoshi, C. T., Ahern, F. M., Wilson, J. R., DeFries, J. C., McClearn, G. E., & Vanderberg, S. G. (1983). Family background, cognitive ability, and personality as predictors of educational and occupational attainment. *Social Biology, 30,* 86–100.

Kim, L. C. (1973). Asian Americans: No model minority. *Social Work, 18,* 44–53.

Kincaid, D. L., & Yum, J. O. (1987). A comparative study of Korean, Filipino, and Samoan immigrants to Hawaii: Socioeconomic consequences. *Human Organization, 46,* 70–77.

Kitano, H. H., & Daniels, R. (1988). *Asian Americans: Emerging minorities.* Englewood Cliffs, NJ: Prentice-Hall.

Krumboltz, J. D. (1976). A social learning theory of career decision making. In A. M. Mitchell, G. B. Jones, & J. D. Krumboltz (Eds.), *Social learning theory and career decision making* (pp. 19–49). Cranston, RI: Carroll Press.

Krumboltz, J. D., & Baker, R. D. (1973). Behavioral counseling for vocational decision. In H. Borow (Ed.), *Career guidance for a new age* (pp. 235–283). Boston: Houghton Mifflin.

Krumboltz, J. D., Mitchell, A. M., & Jones, G. B. (1976). A social learning theory of career selection. *Counseling Psychologist, 6,* 71–81.

Leong, F. T. L. (1982). *Differential career development attributes of Asian American and White college students.* Unpublished master's thesis, University of Maryland, College Park.

Leong, F. T. L. (1985). Career development of Asian Americans. *Journal of College Student Personnel, 26,* 539–546.

Leong, F. T. L. (in press). Career development of Asian Americans. In L. C. Lee & N. W. S. Zane (Eds.), *Handbook of Asian American psychology.* Hillsdale, NJ: Lawrence Erlbaum Associates.

Leong, F. T. L., & Hayes, T. J. (1990). Occupational stereotyping of Asian Americans. *Career Development Quarterly, 39,* 143–154.

Leong, F. T. L., & Raote, R. (1992). *On the hidden cost of being a Chinese American.* Unpublished manuscript, The Ohio State University, Department of Psychology, Columbus.

Leong, F. T. L., & Tata, S. P. (1990). Sex and acculturation differences in occupational values among Chinese American children. *Journal of Counseling Psychology, 37,* 208–212.

Liu, W., & Lo, I. Y. (Eds.). (1975). *Sunflower splendor.* New York: Anchor Press/Doubleday.

Lofquist, L. H., & Dawis, R. V. (1969). *Adjustment to work.* New York: Appleton-Century-Crofts.

Miller, S. K. (1992). Asian-Americans bump against glass ceilings. *Science, 258,* 1224–1228.

Minatoya, L. Y., & Sedlacek, W. E. (1981). Another look at the melting pot: Perceptions of Asian American undergraduates. *Journal of College Student Personnel, 22,* 328–336.

Mitchell, L. K., & Krumboltz, J. D. (1990). Social learning approach to career decision making: Krumboltz's theory. In D. Brown & L. Brooks (Eds.), *Career choice and development* (pp. 145–196). San Francisco: Jossey-Bass.

Mitchell, S. (1988). *Tao te ching.* New York: Harper & Row.

National Science Foundation. (1990). *Women and minorities in science and engineering.* Washington, DC: Author.

Osipow, S. H. (1983). *Theories of career development* (3rd ed.). Englewood Cliffs, NJ: Prentice-Hall.

Osipow, S. H. (1990). Convergence in theories of career choice and development. *Journal of Vocational Behavior, 36,* 122–131.

Owan, T. (1975). *Asian Americans: A case study of benign neglect* (Occasional Paper No. 1). Chicago: Pacific/Asian American Mental Health Research Center.

Petersen, W. (1966, January 6). Success story, Japanese American style. *New York Times Magazine.*

Phinney, J. S. (1992). The multigroup ethnic identity measure: A new scale for use with diverse groups. *Journal of Adolescent Research, 71,* 156–176.

Redding, S. G., & Ng, M. (1982). The role of "face" in the organizational perceptions of Chinese managers. *Organization Studies, 3,* 201–219.

Scarr, S., & Macartney, K. (1983). How people make their own environments: A theory of genotype → environment effects. *Child Development, 54,* 424–435.

Siegel, P. N. (1965). On the cost of being a Negro. *Sociological Inquiry, 35,* 41–57.

Smith, E. J. (1983). Issues in racial minorities' career behavior. In W. B. Walsh & S. H. Osipow (Eds.), *Handbook of vocational psychology* (Vol. 1, pp. 161–221). Hillsdale, NJ: Lawrence Erlbaum Associates.

Sue, D. W., & Kirk, B. A. (1972). Psychological characteristics of Chinese-American students. *Journal of Counseling Psychology, 19,* 471–478.

Sue, D. W., & Kirk, B. A. (1973). Differential characteristics of Japanese-American and Chinese-American college students. *Journal of Counseling Psychology, 20,* 142–148.

Sue, S., & Kitano, H. H. (1973). Stereotypes as a measure of success. *Journal of Social Issues, 29*, 83–98.

Sue, S., & Morishima, J. K. (1982). *The mental health of Asian Americans*. San Francisco: Jossey-Bass.

Sue, S., Sue, D. W., & Sue, D. (1975). Asians as a minority group. *American Psychologist, 30*, 906–910.

Sue, S., & Wagner, N. (Eds.). (1973). *Asian Americans: Psychological perspectives*. Palo Alto, CA: Science & Behavioral Books.

Sue, S., Zane, N. W. S., & Sue, D. (1985). Where are the Asian American leaders and top executives? *P/AAMHRC Research Review, 4*, 13–15.

Suinn, R. M., Ricard-Figueroa, K., Lew, S., & Vigil, P. (1987). Suinn-Lew Asian Self Identity Acculturation Scale: An initial report. *Educational and Psychological Measurement, 7*, 401–407.

Super, D. E. (1957). *The psychology of careers*. New York: Harper & Row.

Super, D. E. (1980). A life-span, life-space approach to career development. *Journal of Vocational Behavior, 16*, 282–298.

Super, D. E. (1990). A life-span, life-space approach to career development. In D. Brown & L. Brooks (Eds.), *Career choice and development* (2nd ed., pp. 197–261). San Francisco: Jossey-Bass.

Super, D. E. (1992, April). *Developmental theory*. Paper presented at the Conference on Convergence of Theories on Career Choice and Development, Michigan State University, East Lansing, MI.

Super, D. E., Starishevsky, R., Matlin, N., & Jordaan, J. P. (1963). *Career development: Self-concept theory* (CEEB Research Monograph No. 4). New York: College Entrance Examination Board (CEEB).

Takaki, R. (1989). *Strangers from a different shore*. Boston: Little, Brown.

Tracey, T. J., Leong, F. T. L., & Glidden, C. (1986). Help seeking and problem perception among Asian Americans. *Journal of Counseling Psychology, 59*, 49–58.

U.S. Commission on Civil Rights. (1978). *Social indicators of equality for minorities and women*. Washington, DC: Author.

Vonracek, F. W., Lerner, R. M., & Schulenberg, J. E. (1986). *Career development: A life-span developmental approach*. Hillsdale, NJ: Lawrence Erlbaum Associates.

Weinrach, S. G., & Srebalus, D. J. (1990). Holland's theory of careers. In D. Brown & L. Brooks (Eds.), *Career choice and development* (pp. 37–67). San Francisco: Jossey-Bass.

Wong, S. (1985). The Chinese family firm: A model. *British Journal of Sociology, 36*, 58–72.

Yu, L. C., & Wu, S. (1985). Unemployment and family dynamics in meeting the needs of Chinese elderly in the United States. *Gerontologist, 25*, 472–476.

Applications of Psychological Theories for Career Development With Native Americans

Marilyn J. Johnson
Pueblo of Acoma, NM

Jody L. Swartz
William E. Martin, Jr.
Northern Arizona University

This chapter includes a brief description of Native Americans in relation to several socioeconomic indices. Aspects of education and early work experience additionally are presented in view of their impact on career development followed by a description of an acculturation continuum. Then, three psychological theories (person–environment theory, social learning theory, and ecological psychology theory) are described. Finally, the three theories are discussed as they apply to the career development of Native Americans.

NATIVE AMERICANS

The American Indian and Alaska Native population of the United States is 1.9 million (U.S. Bureau of the Census, 1990a). This represents a 38% increase of self-identified American Indians from the 1980 U.S. Census as compared with an overall increase of 9.8% in the U.S. general population. The population of Native Americans and Alaska Natives occurs through self-identification in the U.S. Census, where individuals identify themselves as members of a specific tribe. This tribal identification has legitimized the tribal distinctions.

Terms used to describe the Native population of the United States include *American Indians* and *Native Americans*, both of which are used in this chapter. Although these terms describe collectively the Native population, it is not a homogeneous group. There are 318 federally recognized tribes such as Apache, Hopi, Navajo, Sioux, Blackfeet, Acoma, and Choctaw and 200 Alaska Native entities (Bureau of Indian Affairs, 1993). Each tribe possesses social and religious characteristics differentiating them from one another. Finally, the degree to which they maintain their native languages and customs affects the economic conditions of each tribe.

Therefore, it is essential to recognize the distinct cultures and languages of the tribes. Cultural heritage is the composite of one's values, beliefs, morale, art, and cultural habits of a people. Tribes are further defined by family systems and social organization, health and medicine, and religion. In particular, the extended family system is operative for most tribes (Pedigo, 1983). There are nearly 200 languages within the American Indian populations; however, the number of fluent and proficient speakers is diminishing. As the languages fade, the survival of cultures are jeopardized because languages are the basis for knowledge and practice of traditions, customs, religion, and other aspects of culture leading to the term *endangered cultures* (Hodgkinson, 1990).

Based on the 1990 U.S. Census, nearly two thirds (62.3%) of Native Americans live in urban areas, whereas the remainder live on reservations or other similar areas. The 10 states with the highest population of Native Americans are Oklahoma, California, Arizona, New Mexico, Alaska, Washington, North Carolina, Texas, New York, and Michigan. The 10 reservations with the highest populations are: Navajo (Arizona, New Mexico, Utah), Pine Ridge (South Dakota), Fort Apache (Arizona), Gila River (Arizona), Papago (Arizona), Rosebud (South Dakota), San Carlos (Arizona), Hopi (Arizona), Blackfeet (Montana), and Zuni (New Mexico).

Nearly two thirds of the Native-American population live in urban areas for various reasons. Many move to urban areas for training, college, and employment to enable support of their families. Although the urban areas are the employment sites, many return home on weekends or holidays to maintain family and cultural ties. Still, there are others who have assimilated to the extent that they know little of their culture, nor perhaps care to claim their Native-American heritage (Ambler, 1990).

Native Americans who live on reservations consider the tribal community as a social and economic base. When one says, "I'm going home," it is typically in reference to their home reservation. Unlike many non-Indian families, home depends on the present locale of the family, which will likely be different than one's birthplace. Reservation communities are also the center of cultural activities, not merely a land base.

SOCIOECONOMIC CONDITIONS

American Indians are further characterized by factors of health, income, education, and family systems. As a population, the median age of Native Americans is 7 years younger (23.5 years) than the national average (30.5

years). More specific examples of the median age of Native Americans by state are South Dakota, 18.6 years; Arizona, 19.9 years; and New Mexico, 20.3 years (U.S. Bureau of the Census, 1990b).

Of Native families, an average of 23% are headed by single women, although it may range as high as 31% (New York) and 38% (South Dakota). High fertility rates are often a tandem circumstance. The poverty rate of American Indian families is twice the rate (23.7%) of the general population (10.3%) (U.S. Bureau of the Census, 1990b). Native Americans in South Dakota experience a rate of poverty at 47.5%, whereas the rate in Arizona was 44%, and 40.2% in New Mexico. These factors are often associated with a lower level of socioeconomic conditions and is of particular concern because it tends to limit educational and employment opportunities.

Health

The birth rate is significantly higher among American Indians. For every birth in the United States, two were born to Alaska Natives. The birth rates for Alaska Natives was 36.5 per 1,000 population, 27.5 for American Indians, and 15.6 for the U.S. population. The infant mortality rate of American Indian children (9.8 per 1,000 live births) is below the national average (10.4 per 1,000 live births); however, the death rate for American Indian adults (571.7 per 100,000) is higher than the general population (535.5 per 100,000) (Indian Health Service, 1990). The life expectancy of Native Americans is 10 years less than the national average. The high death rates for adults especially over the age of 45 years is attributed, in part, to alcohol-related deaths such as accidents, cirrhosis, or other trauma. In addition, there is a high rate of suicide among youth (Hodgkinson, 1990).

Education

Although the number of Native Americans receiving bachelor- and graduate-level degrees is increasing (Carter & Wilson, 1992), the U.S. Census (1980) indicated that only 56% of American Indians and Alaska Natives over the age of 25 years had completed 4 or more years of high school. This compares with 66.5% for the general U.S. population. Although there are regional and tribal differences, of the 10 largest reservations, less than half had earned a high school diploma (Carter & Wilson, 1992). The dropout rate for Native Americans is 35.5% compared with the U.S. rate of 28.8% (National Center for Education Statistics, 1988). One notable observation was that Native-American high school sophomores were less likely to complete high school than students of other races. For example, 67% of the 1980 Native-American high school sophomores graduated in 1982, compared to 86% for Whites, 78% for African Americans, 72% for Hispanics, and 93% for Asians (Johnson, Joe, Locust, Miller, & Frank,

1987). The percentage of high school graduates vary by state. In the state of California 65.5% of Native Americans over the age of 25 years were high school graduates, whereas 38.5% of Indians in North Carolina had achieved this milestone (White, 1990).

The educational level of Native Americans is a gatekeeper. For those who graduate from high school, the door cracks open to some opportunities. For Indian students who can show evidence of a degree, the door opens to a broader range of social and economic options. In communities where few jobs exist, individuals who have dropped out of high school prior to graduation must accept the lowest paying jobs or those of a temporary nature.

Employment Issues

The choice of residence, urban or reservation community, appears to significantly impact socioeconomic conditions. Specifically, the unemployment rate for American Indians living on a reservation is higher than for those living in urban areas. The unemployment rate for Indians living on reservations is 45%, which is 37% greater than the average unemployment rate in the United States. Likewise, the income level for urban workers is higher than for reservation-based workers. Fourteen percent of those who stay on the reservation have incomes of less than $2,500 per year compared with 5% of the U.S. general population. The high rate of poverty is a reflection of the high unemployment rates.

Economic Issues

There is a high level of variation in tribes' responses to the economic development for their people. The variation in economic development stems, in part, from politically influenced decisions on business such as tribal business priorities for provision of jobs and sharing of benefits rather than on profits. Additionally, obstacles such as weak or limited managerial skills, stability of leadership, and an unskilled or unreliable labor force significantly impair tribal business development.

Business development on reservations is typically limited or lacking. Based on a study by the Council of Energy Resource Tribes (1983), the lack of businesses on reservations posed two particular problems. Money that flows into the reservation, regardless of its source (i.e., government, mining activities, welfare, etc.), finds its way to off-reservation pockets such as banks, or grocery, clothing, and liquor stores. A second problem is the underdeveloped state of businesses on reservations, which limits the possibility of support of tribal programs through taxation. Thus, federal funds must be used for basic services, rather than for economic development.

Several tribes have energy resources consisting mostly of oil and gas. Uranium and coal have been mined on a few reservations; diminished demand and falling prices for uranium have resulted in most of the closures. Logging activities or mining occurs on a limited number of reservations. Tribes that cannot rely on the yield of mineral, timber, or other resources rely on federal funds or other sources.

Subsequently, tribal businesses have a greater likelihood of success when they were administered by the tribes. Specifically, tribal businesses were more likely to achieve (a) transfer of skills and information to the tribe, (b) transfer control to the tribe, (c) enhancement of local and tribal employment, and (d) reduction of tribal financial leakages. Further, tribal businesses were successful when economic, social, and cultural factors received parallel consideration; absence of such consideration resulted in failure (Ruffing, 1979). Example of a failed initiative through the Economic Development Administration is federally financed tourism facilities that lacked adequate planning and design (Checchi & Company, 1977). In addition, tribal administration had limited knowledge and experience in the operation of a business, and in some instances the projects proceeded in the absence of feasibility studies or in spite of weak reports.

Business Development Today

Several tribes have defied obstacles and developed business enterprises that have been profitable and have provided an employment base for their tribal members. These tribal business enterprises have survived through persistence, leveraging of capital to establish the businesses, and partnerships with those who have expertise. Examples of such businesses are Passamaquoddies of Maine, Mississippi Band of Choctaws, Ak-Chin in Arizona, and Confederated Tribes of the Warm Springs Reservation in Oregon (White, 1990).

Acculturation Continuum

Career development in Native Americans is affected by the range of socioeconomic, education, and health variables previously discussed. Another aspect that influences vocational choice and career development is the degree to which one adheres to the traditions and custom's of one's culture and language. The degree to which one maintains or adheres to cultural heritage is difficult to define by tribe, in view of the number of Native-American tribes and Alaska-Native entities, or even from an individual perspective. Likewise, the perception of strong adherence to culture

culture in one tribe may be viewed as a characteristic of acculturation in another tribe.

The degree of adherence to cultural heritage or perhaps the degree of Indianness can best be described as being on a continuum. Ryan and Ryan (cited in LaFromboise, Trimble, & Mohatt, 1990) modified an earlier scheme developed by Spindler and Spindler (cited in LaFromboise et al., 1990) that offers a perspective of Indianness based on acculturation.

1. Traditional—These individuals generally speak in their Native language and know little English. They observe "old time" traditions and values.

2. Transitional—These individuals generally speak both English and their Native language in the home. They question basic traditionalism and religion, yet cannot fully accept dominant culture and values.

3. Marginal—These people may be defensively Indian, but are unable to either live the cultural heritage of their tribal group or to identify with the dominant society. This group tends to have the most difficulty coping with social problems due to their ethnicity.

4. Assimilated—Within this group are the people who, for the most part, have been accepted by the dominant. They generally have embraced the dominant culture and values.

5. Bicultural—Within this group are those individuals who are, for the most part, accepted by dominant society. Yet, they also know and accept their tribal traditions and culture. They can thus move in either direction, from traditional society to dominant society with ease. (pp. 6–7)

THE PATH TO CAREER DEVELOPMENT

Native Americans of high school age are faced with decisions about post-high school options and career choice. These decisions are premised on one's knowledge about the world of work and awareness of occupations. Native-American students, however, make these decisions with limited information or lack of it. In view of the high dropout rates among Indian students and high unemployment rates, the number of working models may be limited, resulting in restricted knowledge about the world of work (Martin, 1991). The knowledge or experience of occupational options may be limited to those that one recognizes in his or her own community (i.e., teacher, social worker, nurse), or those in which Native Americans are working. Martin identified factors that affect career development among Native Americans living on reservations. The factors were discussed according to the areas of world of work knowledge, external pressures, and assessment.

The findings of several studies have shown that Native Americans living on reservations often have limited exposure to a wide range of occupations in the world of work that can lead to less than optimal *work knowledge* that negatively affects vocational decision making (Epperson & Hammond, 1981; Gade, Fuqua & Hurlburt, 1984; McDiarmid & Kleinfeld, 1986). Narrow information about occupational possibilities may result in job choices that do not adequately reflect an individual's capabilities or potentials, which subsequently lowers self-image and promotes a lack of vocational confidence (Krebs, Hurlburt, & Schwartz, 1988).

Limited world of work knowledge among Native Americans living on reservations is largely due to *external pressures* such as environmental constraints that include high unemployment rates and limited job opportunities. A source of strength for coping with these external pressures is found in traditional beliefs and practices associated with family, tribal activities, religious beliefs, and the land itself. These traditional beliefs and practices, however, may take precedence over an individual's career development. Morgan, Guy, Lee, and Cellini (1986) concluded that many Indian people view family, home, and community as the center of their existence rather than a job or a career.

Another complication in the process of assisting Native Americans who live on reservations toward optimal career development relates to culture fair *assessment* issues. Studies have shown limitations related to assessment practices in the areas of language (Nye, 1988; Tanner & Martin, 1986), general ability (McShane, 1980; Sidles, MacAvoy, Bertson, & Kuhn, 1987), vocational interest (Epperson & Hammond, 1981; Gade et al., 1984), and personality (Hoffman, Dana, & Bolton, 1985; Pollack, & Shore, 1980). The common limitations to assessment identified in these studies relate to interference from cultural and language differences.

To summarize, Native Americans live within complex social networks that often involve learning traditions and customs through modeling and experientially based learning. Whereas Native Americans share many common group characteristics, they also reflect diverse cultural and linguistic characteristics.

Three psychological theories are discussed next that provide a foundation for understanding the career development needs of Native Americans. Current approaches to career development are firmly rooted in trait–factor theory that emphasizes a person–environment matching process. A more complete understanding of this person–environment matching process for traditional Native Americans takes shape when considering their unique learning experiences and ecological contexts. Social learning and ecological psychology theories are also described to account for unique contextual dimensions of Native Americans who embrace traditional beliefs and practices at varying degrees.

PERSON–ENVIRONMENT THEORY

Career theories that focus on the person–environment relationship have their roots in the trait–factor approach to vocational guidance. Frank Parsons, the originator of the trait–factor approach to career counseling, is credited with pioneering the vocational guidance movement in America (Brown, 1990; Williamson, 1965). Indeed, Parsons's approach is credited with integrating the concept of individual differences with the concept of job analysis to produce a true reasoning model of occupational exploration. Specifically, trait–factor theory is based on the premise that individuals, when given the opportunity to possess accurate information about themselves and various occupations, can make rational vocational decisions (Brown, 1990).

In addition, it is posited that there are four basic assumptions underlying trait–factor theory (Klein & Weiner, 1977): (a) Individuals possess measurable traits; (b) occupations require individuals to have specific traits; (c) each individual can match their traits to a specific job; and (d) individuals who closely match their unique characteristics to a corresponding occupational field are more apt to derive greater success and satisfaction from their work.

With growing interest in differential psychology and the study of individual differences, the work of Paterson and Williamson added to Parsons' conception of the vocational guidance process. Specifically, Paterson and his associates at the University of Minnesota provided trait–factor theory with a psychometric basis for measuring an individual's unique constellation of traits (Dawis, 1992). As a result, vocational counselors were provided with a comprehensive classification system for occupations (i.e., Dictionary of Occupational Titles) and a variety of measurements designed to aid in the guidance process (e.g., instruments designed to assess personality structure, interests, and special aptitudes). Equally important were Williamson's contributions as spokesman for trait–factor theory (Brown, 1990). Williamson is credited for expanding trait–factor theory into a more comprehensive counseling process.

HOLLAND'S THEORY OF CAREER DEVELOPMENT AND CHOICE

Evolving out of Parsons's trait–factor theory is Holland's (1973, 1985) theory of vocational personalities and work environments. Specifically, Holland's theory emphasized the importance of person–environment fit in career choice and development. Indeed, Holland proposed that individuals with certain definable characteristics are attracted to and best suited for jobs with similar traits (Yost & Corbishley, 1987).

Implicit in Holland's theory is the concept of structural-interaction that is characterized, according to Weinrach and Srebalus (1990), as "an explicit link among various personality characteristics and corresponding job titles and . . . organization of a massive number of data about people and occupations" (p. 40). Accordingly, four basic assumptions underlie the structure of Holland's (1973) theory: (a) the manner in which individuals interact with their environment can be characterized as a type; (b) work environments can be characterized in a similar manner; (c) people search for environments that will enable them to express their personality style; and (d) with knowledge of the individual's personality type and the characteristics of the work environment, outcomes such as vocational choice, success, job change, personal competence, and other types of personal behavior can be predicted.

Holland (Holland & Gottfredson, 1981) proposed that an individual's personality, in part, results from interactions with his or her environment. Specifically, individuals are reinforced by parents, teachers, peers, and community members for performing certain behaviors more than others. Likewise, modeling of certain behaviors, by influential individuals, impacts an individual's preference for performing that behavior. Subsequently, the individual's incorporation of the behaviors into his or her repertoire leads to the development of a typological cluster of personality traits.

Personality Types

Based on the first and second underlying assumptions, Holland proposed that both individuals and work environments have specific, measurable characteristics. Accordingly, Holland identified six personality types and work environment types (i.e., realistic, investigative, artistic, social , enterprising, and conventional).

According to Holland (Yost & Corbishley, 1987), although individuals have one dominant personality type, it is rare for a person to be adequately categorized by this one type alone. Therefore, Holland proposed that individuals have one predominant type and one or two less dominant types. Based on an individual's three highest scores, a three-letter summary code is derived.

Holland's Hexagon

In addition to the categorization of personality types, Holland proposed that the types can be conceived of as forming a hexagonal shape. According to Prediger, Swaney, and Mau (1993), Holland's hexagon is a two-dimensional structure (orientation toward data/information and toward things/people) that reflects the relationships among the six types. The following four concepts are used in the interpretation of an individual's personality type:

1. According to Holland (Herr & Cramer, 1992), *consistency* is regarded as the similarity between the individual's codes on the hexagon. Specifically, the closer together an individual's codes are, the more consistent they are perceived to be.

2. Holland's concept of *differentiation* can be operationally defined as the difference between the individual's highest and lowest summary code. According to Holland (1985), varying degrees of vocational differentiation lead to different outcomes. As such, individuals with high differentiation are said to evidence a clear picture of their vocational interests, abilities, and goals and are more likely to attain educational and vocational success. Conversely, individuals with low differentiation are perceived as poorly defined and possibly lacking in vocational identity (Holland, 1985).

3. Holland (1973) posited that "different types require different environments" (p. 5). As such, *congruence* is conceptualized as the similarity between the individual's personality type and that of their work environment. Specifically, individuals of a specific personality type working in a similar environment are said to have high congruence (e.g., a social type in a social environment).

4. Holland (1985) suggested that individuals with a clear picture of their vocational interests, abilities, and goals are said to have a vocational *identity*. According to Weinrach and Srebalus (1990), identity relates to commitment, level of career decision, and life satisfaction. Conversely, lack of an identity indicates role confusion, lack of confidence, and impaired decision-making ability.

Process

Holland's theory proposed that individuals will tend to look for environments where they can express their particular personality style (Herr & Cramer, 1992). Specifically, the focus in counseling is on ascertaining the individual's personality type and providing the individual with information about environments that are conducive to success for that type. As such, Holland's (1973) theory emphasized the provision of vocational assistance via (a) clear and usable organization of occupational information, (b) explanation of and interpretation of data gained from assessments, and (c) facilitation of vocational development through individualized assistance for individuals who are experiencing difficulties.

Therefore, individuals, who have a clear conception of their personality style and have knowledge regarding appropriate work environments, are likely to make an accurate occupational choice without extensive guidance from a counselor. However, individuals without full recognition of their personality style are more apt to make either inappropriate occupational decisions or lack the requisite ability to make any decision (Herr & Cramer, 1992). As such, the role of the counselor is to aid individuals in determining their personality type through interest inventories that utilize the Holland typology (e.g., self-directed search [SDS], strong interest inventory [SII], Campbell skill and interest survey [CSIS]), interpret the information, and utilize the information to guide individuals in finding occupations that will allow them to express their style.

Theory of Work Adjustment

Drawing on the traditional trait–factor emphasis on differential psychology and individual differences, Dawis and Lofquist (1984; Lofquist & Dawis, 1969) developed a comprehensive theory of work adjustment that adds learning and personality to the conception of the person–environment approach. Indeed, according to Lofquist and Dawis (1972), the premise on which the theory of work adjustment (TWA) was developed is that "each individual seeks to achieve correspondence with their environment" (p. 5). As such, TWA strives to examine the relationship between the adjustment of the individual's dynamic personality and that of the work environment (Tinsley, 1993). Accordingly, TWA can be described in terms of its central constructs: work personality, reinforcement, correspondence, and satisfaction/satisfactoriness.

1. Work Personality. Central to TWA is the concept of *work personality*. According to Lawson (1993), work personality can be defined as abilities and skills an individual brings to a job and the needs and values that must be met by the work environment. The work personality can best be understood in terms of two concepts: structure and style. According to Lofquist and Dawis (1969), the individual's personality structure is comprised of unique abilities, needs, and the interaction between his or her abilities and needs. However, the concept of personality structure simply characterizes the individual's specific traits. Subsequently, the concept of personality style is utilized to describe both the individual's style of responding and style of reacting to stimulus conditions (Lofquist & Dawis, 1969).

2. Reinforcement. According to Dawis, Dohm, and Jackson (1993), *reinforcement* is the primary basis for work behavior. Specifically, an individual's work performance and subsequent job satisfaction are impacted by three aspects of reinforcement: reinforcement requirements, reinforcer class, and reinforcement patterns. Reinforcement requirements are those needs and values that the individuals hope to have met through their work environment. Reinforcer class refers to specific conditions in the work environment (e.g., job security, working conditions, and compensation) that can be used to predict job satisfaction. Finally, reinforcement patterns delimit the rate at which an individual's reinforcement requirements are achieved.

3. Correspondence. *Correspondence* occurs when an individual fulfills the demands of the work environment and the work environment meets the needs of the individual. Indeed, correspondence is a dynamic process of corresponsiveness characterized by a reciprocal relationship where the individual and the work environment change to meet each other's needs.

4. Satisfaction and Satisfactoriness. *Satisfaction* and *satisfactoriness* relate to the evaluation of the extent to which the individual and the work environment meet each other's needs (Bizot & Goldman, 1993). Specifically, satisfaction is an individual's internal evaluation regarding the extent to which a work environment provides his or her requisite reinforcement. Correspondingly, satisfactoriness is the external evaluation of the individual's ability to satisfy the requirements of the work environment.

Process

According to Osipow (1990), Lofquist and Dawis's TWA is most appropriate for the mature worker. However, Lofquist and Dawis (1969) delineated a process that enables individuals to predict their success in a given work environment. In addition, they note that there are six basic procedures related to the vocational counseling process: (a) assessment of the individual's personality in terms of structure an style; (b) examination of both the client's vocational and personal problems, goals, and his or her capacity for successful remediation of problems and attainment of goals; (c) obtain a personal history of the client, including reinforcement patterns, educational, social, and work history; (d) acquisition of information on the client's current abilities and needs; (e) generation of a variety of appropriate occupational alternatives; and (f) assist the client in exploration of occupational alternatives that are most likely to lead to correspondence, adjustment, and satisfaction within the work environment.

SOCIAL LEARNING THEORY

Social learning theory (SLT), in the broadest sense, is concerned with how social values and roles are acquired by the individual (Levine & Sandeen, 1985). It posits that individual's personalities are shaped by their unique learning experiences. Specifically, an individual's personality develops from interactions with the environment, Yost and Corbishley (1987) said: "People learn by both responding to and acting on their environment."

SLT, which is most commonly associated with the work of Bandura (1977), is rooted in reinforcement theory and traditional behavior theory. According to Bandura (1985), "humans come with few inborn patterns . . . people must develop their basic capabilities over an extended period, and they must continue to master new competencies to fulfill changing demands throughout their life-span" (p. 88). Specifically, Bandura (1985) proposed that individual behavior results from a reciprocal determinism; individuals encounter experiences from which they incorporate behaviors, based on reinforcement contingencies, into their unique repertoire of behavioral responses that then serve to create a new environment that provides the individual with new learning experiences.

Regardless of the specific learning experience involved, there are central processes that act to either increase or inhibit the likelihood that an individual will perform a behavior. Specifically, perpetuation or extinction of the behavior depends on how the action was reinforced. Behavior that receives positive reinforcement is likely to be repeated. By repeating the behavior, the individual's performance of the behavior becomes more adept and the behavior itself becomes intrinsically interesting so that the individual no longer needs external reinforcement to perform the behavior (Mitchell & Krumboltz, 1990).

It is from an individual's observations and interactions with other people that he or she derives cognitive processes (beliefs, values, and expectancies) that determine how an environmental event is perceived and subsequently serve as guides for future action (Bandura, 1985). According to Bandura (1985), an individual has the ability to symbolically test hypotheses that enables them to determine possible outcomes while avoiding the actual performance of the behavior. However, judgments based on learning experiences are not always rational and well reasoned. Indeed, as individuals have the capacity to filter experiences and infer causation based on their cognitive schema, they too have the ability to utilize faulty logic and inadequate information in their assessment of a particular event or personal behavior. Additionally, individuals often misperceive events that then produce erroneous beliefs about themselves and the world around them (Bandura, 1985).

Integral to Bandura's SLT is the concept of triadic reciprocality or reciprocal determinism; the belief that behavior, cognitions and environment interact to produce a subsequent behavior. Indeed, Bandura (1985) posited that none of the three can be adequately understood in isolation; rather they all work together to determine and explain human behavior (Hergenhan, 1982).

SLT of behavior (Bandura, 1977), as interpreted and applied by Krumboltz, Mitchell, and Jones (1976), has been found to be effectively utilized in promoting career decision making. Krumboltz's SLT of career decision making (CDM) is primarily concerned with why people enter into certain educational and occupational fields and why they may alter their educational and occupational paths at certain points in their lives (Krumboltz, 1981).

Key Concepts

According to Krumboltz et al. (1976), the individual's unique career decision-making processes are influenced by the interaction between both individual and environmental factors: genetic endowment and special abilities, environmental events, learning events, and task approach skills. Based on the interaction between these factors, the individual derives generalizations, both of self and the world, that then reciprocally influence the individual's approach to new learning experiences and ultimately affects one's aspirations, actions, and future career path (Krumboltz, 1981).

Genetic Endowment and Special Abilities

Genetic endowment and special abilities are inherited qualities that may serve to limit or enhance an individual's interest in and ability to perform certain occupational or educational tasks. Genetic endowment encompasses those characteristics of an individual that are generally unchangeable (e.g., gender, ethnicity, physical disabilities) or that a person can choose to develop (e.g., special talents and skills). An individual's interests and skills may develop as a result of being afforded the opportunity to profit from certain environmental events based on his or her inherited predispositions. Similarly, certain individuals are born with greater or lesser ability to profit from environmental learning experiences (Mitchell & Krumboltz, 1990). Consequently, individuals with special abilities (e.g., intelligence, muscular coordination, musical ability) may have derived these abilities from an interaction between inherited predispositions and certain environmental events.

Environmental Conditions and Events

The career decision-making path of an individual may be impacted by social, cultural, political, economic, and natural forces (Krumboltz, 1981). Specifically, environmental conditions and events refers to specific situational variables that are out of an individual's control (e.g., number and nature of job opportunities; training opportunities, cultural values; changes in social organizations; family training experiences and resources; educational system; and neighborhood and community influences; Krumboltz, Mitchell, & Gelatt, 1975).

Learning Experiences

According to Krumboltz et al. (1976), individual learning is comprised of a unique repertoire of responses that individuals have compiled throughout their lifetime. Derived from traditional learning theory, Krumboltz identified two types of past learning experiences that impact an individual's unique path in career decision making: instrumental and associative.

1. *Instrumental learning* is characterized by individuals' acting on their environment, which in turn produces certain consequences that may either positively or negatively reinforce the action. Specifically, individuals are more likely to develop preferences for behaviors that are positively reinforced and will tend to avoid those for which they were either punished or received no reward (Krumboltz & Nichols, 1990).

2. *Associative learning* occurs when an individual attributes a positive or negative meaning to a previously neutral stimulus. According to Mitchell and Krumboltz (1990), the individual associates some previously affectively neutral event or stimulus with an emotionally laden event or stimulus. Whether an event or stimulus is associated with a positive or negative outcome affects how an individual views that event; events that are positively reinforced will tend to elicit positive responses from the individual.

Task Approach Skills (TAS)

Interactions between genetic and environmental factors produce skills that an individual brings to each new task or problem (e.g., work habits, performance standards and values, perceptual and cognitive processes, and emotional responses; Krumboltz et al., 1976). TASs, which affect each activity in which the individual engages, are modified based on the differential outcome of the particular task (Krumboltz et al., 1976). Indeed, Krumboltz et al. (1976) noted that "TASs are both factors which influence outcomes and outcomes in themselves" (p. 73).

TASs are learned cognitive and emotional responses that are utilized by individuals to make judgments about their past behaviors and to formulate predictions of future events. Krumboltz et al. (1976) noted that the nature of any task approach skill is the result of a myriad of sequential learning experiences to which an individual has been exposed. According to Krumboltz (1981), individuals can choose to acquire and utilize certain TASs that will aid them in performing behaviors that affect the career path they choose to follow. Specifically, these skills both build on the competencies currently in individuals' repertoire and enable them to complete the necessary tasks related to future career decision making.

According to Krumboltz and Baker (1973), several TASs are important in the career decision-making process: value clarifying, goal setting, alternative generating, estimating, predicting future events, reinterpreting of past events, choosing from alternatives, information seeking, planning, and generalizing.

Self-Observation Generalization

Self-observation generalizations (SOGs) are generalizations made by individuals about the nature of their attitudes and the extent of their skills. In addition, SOGs serve to influence the outcome of new learning experiences and cognitive processes that result from prior learning experiences:

1. SOGs about *task-efficacy* are individuals' appraisal of whether they possess the skills necessary to perform a task. Accordingly, individuals compare their performance with some observable standard of performance and formulate conclusions about themselves and their competence based on this appraisal.

2. SOGs about *interests* are a result of learning experiences that impact whether or not individuals will perform certain activities. These are seen as the intermediate step between prior learning experiences and future learning experiences individuals undertake due to their interests. Specifically, an individual who perceives, through actions or observations, an event being positively reinforced will be more apt to show interest in performing the actions associated with that event.

3. SOGs about *personal values* are characterized by individuals' assessment about or their attitudes toward the merit of certain behaviors, events, or outcomes (Mitchell & Krumboltz, 1990). Personal values are the result of both instrumental and associative learning experiences that serve to reinforce the positive value of certain tasks and skills.

According to Krumboltz et al. (1975), individuals often do not remember the actual performance of the behavior, but rather they remember and generalize the feedback they received regarding their performance. Individuals may experience a discordance when they compare themselves with standards that may be inappropriate, inaccurate, or unrealistic for their personal situation. Similarly, people experience conflict when they accept others' possibly biased or inaccurate evaluations of their performance (these may be either positive or negative judgments of the individual's abilities and aptitudes).

World View Generalizations

Similar in nature to SOGs are world view generalizations (WVG). Based on past learning experiences, individuals make observations about the world in which they live. According to Krumboltz (Mitchell & Krumboltz, 1990), individuals utilize these observations to generalize and predict what may occur in the future and in other environments. WVGs include, but are not limited to, generalizations regarding the worth and characteristics about occupations, work environments, and educational fields. Similar to SOGs, WVGs can be both accurate appraisals and misperceptions of the environment. In addition, the accuracy of WVGs depends on the type and number of learning experiences to which individuals have been exposed and on which they subsequently base their observations.

Action

Krumboltz (1981) noted that CDM is primarily interested in entry behaviors. Entry behaviors are those behaviors that serve to initiate career-relevant actions and are often the consequences of TASs and SOGs. As a result of learning experiences, preferences for a particular occupation will be developed and will be evidenced by the individual's overt behaviors. Specifically, action is characterized by the individual's application of overt behaviors, which build on one another, in their progression toward attainment of a career goal.

Process

According to Krumboltz (1979),

> The general picture of career development presented here is that of an individual inheriting a given structure, being placed in an environment which provides a variety of events and conditions that facilitate or limit activities, and being exposed to a set of learning experiences, some provided by culture and some self-initiated. These learning experiences generate self-observation generalizations and task approach skills which lead to specific career related actions. (p. 39)

Adding to his conception of the career development process, Krumboltz (1994) noted that the goal of career counseling is "to facilitate learning of skills, interests, beliefs, work habits, and personal qualities that will enable clients to create a satisfying life within an ever changing work environment."

According to CDM theory, career development is characterized as a life-span process that takes into consideration the continuous reciprocal nature of the four key concepts and outcomes of an individual's learning experiences. Individuals who seek guidance in the career decision-making process may be experiencing difficulties in one or more of the four outcome areas: SOGs, WVGs, TASs, and actions that impede their ability to progress through the CDM process.

Several approaches have been utilized to evaluate the validity of an individual's generalizations. Assessment via psychometric instruments (Mitchell & Krumboltz, 1990) and established therapeutic approaches (Keller, Biggs, & Gysbers, 1982) have proven to be successful modes of intervention. Additionally, Krumboltz (1994) has suggested several cognitive intervention methods that may provide both insight and understanding into the client's generalizations: goal clarification, cognitive restructuring, disputing, and narrative analysis.

In addition to problems generated from faulty cognitive processes, individuals may possess inadequate TASs. Specifically, individuals may have difficulty delineating their interests, may be unaware of or be incapable of acquiring available resources, or they may simply lack knowledge about what skills are necessary for CDM. Accordingly, it is important for the counselor to get a clear appraisal of the client's TASs. In addition to psychometric measures, Krumboltz (1994) has indicated that assessment and development of TASs can be obtained through role playing, desensitization, paradoxical intention, and assumption testing.

ECOLOGICAL PSYCHOLOGY THEORY

The conception that individuals' developmental process is influenced by their interaction with their environment has long been accepted by behavioral researchers. As such, there is an abundance of theoretical applications and research supporting this concept. However, the predominant focus of traditional research and theories has been on the properties of the person. Indeed, Bronfenbrenner (1979) asserted that "there has been a hypertrophy of research focusing on the properties of the person and only the most rudimentary conception and characterization of the environment in which the person is found" (p. 16).

Ecological Approaches

Collectively, ecological psychology theories endeavor to compensate for the paucity of research on the characteristics and impact of the environment. Specifically, ecological theories, in the broadest sense, strive to explain the natural patterns of stimuli, both social and physical, that exist in the individual's immediate environment and subsequently impact the individual's behavior and experience (LeCompte, 1972). As such, ecological approaches can be said to examine both the match or mismatch between an individual and the reciprocal nature of the person–environment association (Fine, 1985).

Lewin's field theory (1951) is conceived of as the earliest theoretical approach that falls under the auspices of ecological psychology. Specifically, Lewin's approach emphasizes the role of the individual's phenomenological environmental situation in gaining a better understanding of the individual. Similarly, Barker's (1968) theoretical approach, which focuses on delineating the characteristics and laws of the environment, underscores the necessity of understanding the environment to discern the individual's pattern of behavior. Additionally, the systems ecological perspectives (SEP), although recognizing both the internal and external forces that impact an individual's behavior, emphasizes the importance of acknowledging the reciprocal relationship between the individual and the various systems in which they function to ascertain both the direct and indirect factors that impact the individual's functioning.

Key Concepts

The ecological approaches share several key characteristics: Individuals do not exist or act in isolation; rather, they function within an interrelated system of relationships; individual behavior is impacted by both internal (psychological) and external (environmental) forces; and individuals' behavior is a result of attempts to maintain homeostasis in their environment (Wicker, 1979).

Lewin's Field Theory

Lewin emphasized the individual's life space in his or her conceptualization of the field or environment. According to Lewin (1951), an individual's life space consists of the individual and his or her subjective psychological environment, such that the individual's life space can be adequately examined in terms of three qualities: existence, interdependence, and contemporaneity. Specifically, Lewin utilized the concept of existence to refer to both direct processes (e.g., needs, goals, cognitive structure) and indirect processes (e.g., social, economic, physical events) that affect the individual. According to Lewin, the parts of individuals' life space are to some degree interdependent; that is, the way individuals respond to events is based, to some extent, on their perception of their environment. Such that individuals belonging to a social or cultural group will view their behavior in terms of their perception of expected group norms and will modify their behavior or respond to their environment accordingly. Additionally, based on the concept of contemporanaiety, behavior can be explained only by the properties of the environment that are determined to be present at the same time as the behavior. As such, an individual's actions can be explained by the singular and/or synergistic effects of cultural and social forces that are occurring in their environment at any given time.

Barker's Ecological Theory

Although Barker (1968) concurred with Lewin's assertion that a person's momentary behavior is determined by his or her life space, he further stated that "if we wish to understand more than the immediate . . . behavior, . . . knowledge of the ecological environment is essential. . . . Development is not a momentary phenomenon, and the course of the life-space can only be known within the ecological environment in which it is embedded" (p. 9). Accordingly, Barker's ecological approach emphasized the importance of understanding the ecological environment. Specifically, Barker posited that the environment is comprised of several behavior settings or small ecosystems that call forth particular behavior. According to Barker (1968), it is neither possible nor inherently advantageous for researchers to adequately analyze naturally occurring individual behavior variation and patterns by neglecting the impact of the functioning environment.

Indeed, Barker noted that how physical or social characteristics of a setting determine the individual's behavior is evidenced by the individual's adaptation or adjustment to his or her environment (Wandersman, Murday, & Wadsworth, 1979). Specifically, when individuals either adapt (individual modifies their behavior to fit the environment) or adjust (individual manipulates the environment based on their needs) their behaviors, they are striving to retain synomorphy (or fit) with their environment. In this manner, individuals' synomorphic relationship with their environment draws on both of Lewin's (1951) concepts of interdependence and contemporaneity; that is, individuals are affected by their prior knowledge of and current changes in their environment, and, conversely, the environment is impacted by changes in the individual (Barker, 1968). Consequently, this interplay between individuals and their environments is a continuous process whereby individuals seek to maintain homeostasis within their system and subsystems.

Systems Ecological Perspective

A logical outgrowth of Lewin's (1951) and Barker's (1968) work in ecological psychology is the SEP. Conceptually similar to their foundational theories, SEPs perceive behavior to be determined by both internal and external characteristics of the interaction between the individual and the environment. In addition, SEPs add to the traditional ecological psychology theories that focus on environments the emphasis of studying the total of interacting systems in which the individual functions. Specifically, Bronfenbrenner's theory of human ecology (1979, 1980), Attneave's ecological network theory (ENT; Attneave, 1990; Attneave & Speck, 1974), Henggeler's (1989, 1993) multisystemic theory, and Rappaport's (1987) theory of empowerment can all be characterized as SEPs.

Bronfenbrenner's Theory of Social Ecology

Bronfenbrenner's (1979, 1980) theory of human ecology seeks to explain how the larger context in which individuals function impacts the reciprocal relationship of the individuals and the dynamic properties of the immediate settings in which they live (Bronfenbrenner, 1979).

Ecological Structures

Similar to Lewin's concept of existence (1951) and based on Barker's (1968) ecological environment, Bronfenbrenner posited that the individual's environment can be divided into four embedded environmental structures that act reciprocally to influence the individual: Microsystem, comprised of the more intimate aspects of the individual's development in the family and workplace, which includes goals-directed behavior, interpersonal relationships, and system-defined roles and experience; Mesosystem, consisting of the link between the individual's multiple microsystems; Exosystem, comprised of events that do not directly affect or are not directly affected by the individual; Macrosystem, consisting of the cultural and societal belief systems and underlying ideologies that may be present at the other levels but that inherently influence individuals' functioning within their microsystem (Herr & Cramer, 1992).

Adding to Bronfenbrenner's conception of the nested nature of the ecological environment, Attneave's ecological network therapy (ENT; Attneave, 1990; Attneave & Speck, 1974) recognizes the importance of assessing the impact of various roles and consequences within a system and endeavors to delineate the roles in which each individual member functions. Attneave (1990) devised a family network map that depicts the individual's core network in terms of embedded levels or rings: The innermost ring is comprised of members of the household; the second level consists of significant people with whom the individual has frequent contact; the third level is comprised of people with whom the individual has a casual relationship but are seen fairly often; and the outermost ring consists of those people with whom the individual has distant relationships and are seen only on special occasions. Individuals are classified according to their relationship to the individual and are identified according to their family roles and relationships to the nuclear family (e.g., "his girlfriend," "Uncle's neighbor"; Attneave, 1990). In addition to the nested arrangement of the core network, Attneave (1990) further organized the individuals into three categories: On the left side of the structure are family and kin; on the right side of the structure are other individuals; and at the bottom of the structure is an area where the individual can place people they either do not like or with whom they are uncomfortable.

Other systemic approaches related to Family Network Maps are genograms and ecomaps. A genogram is a three-generational graphic representation of a client's family of origin. Okiishi (1987) demonstrated the use of a genogram as a tool in career counseling. She used a three-step career-counseling process with the genogram that involved (a) construction of the genogram, (b) identification of occupations, and (c) exploration with the client. Another technique is the ecomap, which is a visual drawing of all external resources utilized by an individual. Goodluck (1991) conducted a study with vocational rehabilitation counselors to determine the effectiveness of both genograms and ecomaps to assess American Indian families who have a member with a disability. The researcher (Goodluck, 1991) reported some resistance in using the tools: "This change of working from the individual perspective to multi-family units requires an ideological shift from a medical individual focused model to a system focused empowerment based model" (p. 63).

Behavior

According to Bronfenbrenner (1979), as individuals move through their ecological space, they are both a product of and a producer of change. Indeed, Bronfenbrenner characterizes the process of mutual accommodation as replete with ecological transitions. Specifically, an ecological transition occurs whenever there is a change in individuals' position (i.e., roles, setting, or both) within their ecological environment. As such, individuals' transition from one role or setting to another can be characterized as individuals attempt to both accommodate or adjust to their changing environmental situation and thus can be further conceived of as individuals attempt to maintain homeostasis within their environment.

According to Bronfenbrenner (1979), the human behavior of interest to ecological psychologists is the individual's molar activities or ongoing behavior that possesses both momentum and a perception of meaning for individuals in the microsystem. Molar activities can impact the individual's relations, (i.e., interpersonal structures such as dyads where two or more individuals work together in a shared activity). According to

Bronfenbrenner (1979), an individual's participation first in observational dyads, where the individual both observes the activity of another person and is acknowledged as doing so; then in joint dyads, where the individual participates in the activity with the other person; and, subsequently, in primary dyads, in which a mutual strong bond is developed and which is present outside the work setting, impacts his or her development.

Rappaport's (1987) theory of empowerment adds to Bronfenbrenner's conception of molar activities the phenomena of empowerment. According to Rappaport, empowerment is conceived of as a multilevel construct that is concerned with the relationships within and between the various levels of systemic influences (e.g., individuals, communities, social policies) and is viewed as the goal of any interaction (i.e., outcome of dyad). Accordingly, Rappaport (1987) posited that individuals and communities that work together in common processes (e.g., work community) are more likely to develop a sense of empowerment. Rappaport (1987) also emphasized the intrinsic value of an individual's participation in the process; individuals derive more meaning from activities in which they play an important role (e.g., participation in a joint or primary dyad) and subsequently are more likely to be empowered.

Similarly, Henggeler's multisystemic model builds on Bronfenbrenner's assessment of the systemic nature of the environment, incorporates Attneave's conception of the embedded nature of individuals within the person's various systems, and is both parallel to and expands upon Rappaport's premise of empowerment (Henggeler, Melton, & Smith, 1992). Specifically, Henggeler (1993) asserted that the individual and other significant people are more likely to be empowered when they are engaged in the change process. As such, intervention with an individual is conceived of as a process of recognizing both individual and systemic strengths that can be utilized to remedy difficulties within the individual's systems.

Process

Based on an ecological perspective of intervention, vocational guidance can be conducted according to an adaptation of Ryan's (1974) six functions of a systematic approach:

1. Establish a conceptual framework—examine the individuals value and belief structure and identify systems and roles.
2. Possessing information—obtain information related to aspects of the community, social structures, and organizations.
3. Assess needs—compare the ideal situation with knowledge of what is currently occurring, ascertain discrepancies, obtain input from significant others.

4. Formulate plan—specify appropriate goals, objectives, and method of implementation.

5. Implement plan—may include such activities as educational or technical training, and job preparation activities (e.g., resume writing, role playing of interview situation).

6. Evaluate plan—evaluate plan according to goals and objectives, revise if necessary.

APPLICATION OF PSYCHOLOGICAL THEORIES TO THE CAREER DEVELOPMENT OF NATIVE AMERICANS

Person–Environment

Theories that fall under the auspices of person–environment emphasize the need to consider an individual's inherent differences in the career development process. Maintaining this perspective is particularly important when working with Native Americans because of the variability in their cultural background. The behavioral repertoire and resulting vocational personality typology cluster is quite different for a person growing up in a rural reservation community who practices traditional tribal customs compared to an individual who grew up in a large city and has had no teaching about tribal beliefs and practices. Thus, it is especially important for Native Americans who are in the process of career decision making to integrate their unique personal, environmental, and cultural characteristics into the process.

Specifically, Holland and Gottfredson (1981) asserted that ethnic identity contributes to the individual's development of a personality type in the same manner that environment and learning influence development. When working with Native Americans, two components of the vocational guidance process are important: assessment of their current status, that is, full exploration of the effects of their history and socialization process; and formulation of an instrumental career development plan that will enable the individual to conceive of possible areas of vocational development (Holland & Gottfredson, 1981). Accurately linking an individual's characteristics to corresponding job titles (structural interaction) is especially important where job opportunities are limited as is the case in many reservation communities. An accurate person–job match will result in individual satisfaction and work environment satisfactoriness.

Integral to the person–environment approach is the assessment of the individual's knowledge of the world of work. As such, Native Americans can be at a disadvantage in career development due to their limited level of knowledge about vocations and careers. These individuals often have underdeveloped vocational identities resulting in inaccurate vocational self-estimates concerning vocational skills and interests as well as unclear career goals. Therefore, a considerable amount of attention in the vocational guidance process with Native Americans should focus first on ascertaining the individual's breadth of knowledge regarding occupations and subsequently providing experiences that may include, but are not limited to, tryout experiences, career exploration seminars, career information interviews, exposure to career information (e.g., occupational information publications and computerized career guidance systems), and job shadowing (Martin, 1991). Indeed, the absence of occupational knowledge or experience may inhibit or skew the individual's vocational decision making. Additionally, Martin maintained that more extensive knowledge about their vocational options is likely to enhance the individual's ability to make enduring career choices.

In addition, Native Americans' choices of vocations will likely be impacted by family or social factors. High unemployment in reservation communities will make relocation to urban areas a viable option. However, this must also be weighed against the cultural and family support base that may hold particular significance and importance for many Native Americans. Some individuals attempt to resolve these concerns by working in urban areas and commuting 60 or 70 miles to work each day.

The person–environment approaches emphasize the use of psychometric instruments to assess various aspects of the individual's career development process. As such, it is important to note that research regarding the appropriateness of using norm-referenced tests with Native Americans has been mixed (Gade, Fuqua, & Hurlbert, 1984; Hurlbert, Schulz, & Eide, 1985). Specifically, cultural influences and effects of socialization processes may be reflected in the individual's test profile (Anastasi, 1988; Gade et al., 1984). However, Martin (1991) and Gade et al. (1984) suggested techniques that may compensate for possible cultural and language biases. Specifically, Martin (1991) suggests utilizing item analysis following test administration; this allows the counselor to ascertain any discrepancies between the individual's understanding of the items and his or her responses. Additionally, Gade et al. (1984) asserted that employment of local norms may facilitate short-term generation of career alternatives and long-term decrease in occupational stereotypes.

Social Learning Theory

Social learning theory is premised on the concepts that although an individual has a complement of genetically determined characteristics and abilities, it is the individual who will "respond(ing) to and act(ing) on their environment" (Yost & Corbishley, 1987). Modeling of behavior- and experiential-based learning was the primary avenue through which many Native people have learned their traditions and customs (LaFromboise et al., 1990). One learns through experience that in a given circumstance, there is an appropriate response or action.

As Native-American youths exposure to a variety of occupations is restricted (Martin, 1991), there is a scarcity of learning experiences related to nontraditional occupations. As such, Herring (1990) suggested the utilization of Native-American occupational role models from nontraditional occupations. Through modeling, an individual is exposed to multiple vicarious learning experiences that may benefit his or her career decision-making process.

Through CDM, an individual draws on one's own repertoire of experiences rather than trying to fit into a predefined set of circumstances. In view of the recognition of one's experiences, interventions based on this theory would be less culturally biased (LaFromboise et al., 1990). Family and community input could also facilitate the behaviors or responses that would be most appropriate in reaction to the environment.

Social learning theory provides a template upon which some career outcomes can be described. For example, a Native American may experience and observe the limited frequency in which Indian people make career decisions in the technical or scientific fields (i.e., medicine, biomedical engineering, psychologist). Instead, one sees Native Americans as teachers, teacher aides, janitors, bus drivers, and so forth; therefore these are career options available or accessible to Native Americans. The notion of being a physician may seem an inaccessible career option if one has not seen Native Americans in such career roles.

Relative to career decisions, the social learning theory has broader application. Given the narrower range of Native Americans in varied occupations, students have limited sources from whom they can obtain information about essential educational preparation, degree requirements, and the type of work and responsibilities associated with such a career choice. Students might instead draw on sources of information that may be inadequate, skewed, or incorrect.

Ecological Psychology Theory

The network approach that provides therapy or counseling with a therapist serving as facilitator and the social network of family, extended family, or friends works to address the crisis. The individual's needs are addressed, not in isolation, but within the context of his or her social network—family or community (LaFromboise et al., 1990).

This approach has particular relevance and/or compatibility to Native Americans who generally view themselves as a member if some social system—family, tribe, or community. It is not unusual to be identified as a member of an extended family, or as a member of a clan, or tribe. Simon Ortiz, Acoma poet, used the term *Howbah Indians* (approximate translation is all of us Indians) in one of his poems suggesting that Indian people are connected or related in some way.

The ecological network therapy has additional appeal because of the prescribed dynamics for arriving at solutions. Individuals receiving therapy with their families are involved in the process to resolve issues and to implement strategies to remedy or modify problem situations. Past patterns of interaction between Native Americans and non-Native people minimize the opportunities for joint efforts at problem solving and for implementation.

CONCLUSION

The three theories described in this chapter have varied appeal and application to Native Americans for facilitating vocational choices and promoting career development. Given the number of tribes, cultures, languages, and individual differences, it is difficult to prescribe one best method. Rather, the psychologist should make efforts to identify the extent to which a Native person has significant ties to family, community, or tribe and the importance of each to the individual. The social, economic, and cultural base of support may have heightened importance for those who have particular roles or responsibilities within their families or tribes. Others, however, may function independent of family or other cultural influences. This may reflect an individual preference or it may suggest limited ties with their tribe or cultural group.

The skilled psychologist will seek to connect, listen, and communicate effectively with the client. The psychologist must exhibit respect and concern for the client. The applications to Native Americans as described in this chapter provide options for responses that are premised on theories of broad-based use. It is intended that this chapter will serve as a template for further discussion.

REFERENCES

Ambler, M. (1990). *Breaking the bonds: Indian control of energy development.* Lawrence: University Press of Kansas.
Anastasi, A. (1988). *Psychological testing.* New York: Macmillan.
Attneave, C. L. (1990). Core network intervention: An emerging paradigm. *Journal of Strategic and Systemic Therapies, 9*(1), 3–10.
Attneave, C. L., & Speck, R. V. (1974). Social network intervention in time and space. In A. Jacobs (Ed.), *Groups as agents of change.* New York: Behavioral Publications.
Bandura, A. (1977). *Social learning theory.* Englewood Cliffs, NJ: Prentice-Hall.

Bandura, A. (1985). Model causality in social learning theory. In M. J. Mahoney & A. Freeman (Eds.), *Cognition and psychotherapy* (pp. 81–99). New York: Plenum.

Barker, R. (1968). *Ecological psychology*. Palo Alto, CA: Stanford University Press.

Bizot, E. B., & Goldman, S. H. (1993). Prediction of satisfaction: An 8-year follow up. *Journal of Vocational Behavior, 43,* 19–29.

Bronfenbrenner, U. (1979). *The ecology of human development*. Cambridge, MA: Harvard University Press.

Bronfenbrenner, U. (1980). Ecology of childhood. *School Psychology Review, 9*(4), 294–297.

Brown, D. (1990). Trait–factor theory. In D. Brown & L. Brooks (Eds.), *Career choice and development* (2nd ed., pp. 13–36). San Francisco: Jossey-Bass.

Bureau of Indian Affairs. (1993). *Federally recognized tribes.* Washington, DC: U.S. Department of Interior, Bureau of Indian Affairs.

Carter, D. J., & Wilson, R. (1992). *Minorities in higher education. 1991 tenth annual status report.* Washington, DC: American Council on Education.

Checchi and Company. (1977). *The gift that hurt the Indians: A report about federally financed tourism on Indian reservations.* Washington, DC: The Ford Foundation and Bureau of Indian Affairs.

Council of Energy Resource Tribes. (1983, October). *Tribal self-government: A self-sufficiency analysis* (by Ahmed Kooros & Anne C. Seip). Denver, CO: DOI Task Force.

Dawis, R. V. (1992). The individual differences tradition in counseling psychology. *Journal of Counseling Psychology, 39*(1), 7–19.

Dawis, R. V., Dohm, T. E., & Jackson, C. R. (1993). Describing work environments as reinforcer systems: Reinforcement schedules versus reinforcement classes. *Journal of Vocational Behavior, 43,* 5–18.

Dawis, R. V., & Lofquist, L. H. (1984). *A psychological theory of work adjustment.* Minneapolis: University of Minnesota Press.

Epperson, D. L., & Hammond, D. C. (1981). Use of interest inventories with Native Americans: A case for local norms. *Journal of Counseling Psychology, 28*(3), 213–220.

Fine, M. J. (1985). Intervention form an ecological perspective. *Professional Psychology: Research and Practice, 16*(2), 262–270.

Gade, E. M., Fuqua, D., & Hurlburt, G. (1984). Use of the Self-Directed Search with Native American high school students. *Journal of Counseling Psychology, 31*(4), 584–587.

Goodluck, C. T. (1991). *Utilization of genograms and eco-maps to assess American Indian families who have a member with a disability: Making visible the invisible.* Flagstaff: Northern Arizona University, Institute for Human Development, American Indian Rehabilitation Research and Training Center. (Available from the American Indian Rehabilitation Research and Training Center, Institute for Human Development, Northern Arizona University, P.O. Box 5630, Flagstaff, AZ 86011).

Henggeler, S. W. (1989). *Delinquency in adolescence*. Beverly Hills, CA: Sage.

Henggeler, S. W. (1993). An ecological approach to treatment. *The Scientist Practitioner, 3*(1), 10–17.

Henggeler, S. W., Melton, G. B., & Smith, L. A. (1992). Family preservation using multisystemic therapy: An effective alternative to incarcerating juvenile offenders. *Journal of Consulting and Clinical Psychology, 60*(6), 953–961.

Hergenhan, B. R. (1982). *An introduction to theories of learning* (2nd ed.). Englewood Cliffs, NJ: Prentice-Hall.

Herr, E. L., & Cramer, S. H. (1992). *Career guidance and counseling through the life-span: Systematic approaches* (4th ed.). New York: Harper Collins.

Herring, R. D. (1990). Attacking career myths among Native Americans: Implications for counseling. *The School Counselor, 38,* 13–18.

Hodgkinson, H. L. (1990). *The demographics of American Indians: One percent of the people; fifty percent of the diversity.* Washington, DC: Institute for Educational Leadership.

Hoffman, T., Dana, R. H., & Bolton, B. (1985). Measured acculturation and MMPI-168 performance of Native American adults. *Journal of Cross-Culture Psychology, 16*(2), 243–256.

Holland, J. L. (1973). *Making vocational choices: A theory of careers.* Englewood Cliffs, NJ: Prentice-Hall.

Holland, J. L. (1985). *Making vocational choices: A theory of vocational personalities and work environments* (2nd ed.). Englewood Cliffs, NJ: Prentice-Hall.

Holland, J. L., & Gottfredson, G. D. (1981). Using a typology of persons and environments to explain careers: Some extensions and clarifications. In D. H. Montross & C. J. Shinkman (Eds.), *Career development in the 1980's: Theory and practice.* Springfield, IL: Thomas.

Hurlbert, G., Schulz, W., & Eide, L. (1985). Using the Self-Directed Search with American Indian high school students. *Journal of American Indian Education, 35*(1), 34–41.

Indian Health Service. (1990). *Trends in Indian health.* Rockville, MD: U.S. Department of Health and Human Services.

Johnson, M. J., Joe, J., Locust, C., Miller, D., & Frank, L. (1987). Overview of the American Indian population and the influence of culture on individuals with disabilities. In J. C. O'Connell (Ed.), *A study of the special problems and needs of American Indians with handicaps both on and off the reservation* (Vol. II, pp. 1–13). Flagstaff: Northern Arizona University, Native American Research and Training Center; Tucson: University of Arizona Native American Research and Training Center.

Keller, K. E., Biggs, D. A., & Gysbers, N. C. (1982). Career Counseling from a cognitive perspective. *The Personnel and Guidance Journal, 60,* 367–370.

Klein, K. L., & Weiner, Y. (1977). Interest congruency as a moderator of the relationship between job tenure and job satisfaction and mental health. *Journal of Vocational Behavior, 10,* 91–98.

Krebs, E., Hurlburt, G., & Schwartz, C. (1988). Vocational self-estimates and perceived competencies of Native high school students: Implications for vocational guidance counseling. *Canadian Journal of Counseling, 22*(4), 212–225.

Krumboltz, J. D. (1979). A social learning theory of career decision making. In A. M. Mitchell, G. B. Jones, & J. D. Krumboltz (Eds.), *Social learning theory and career decision making.* Cranston, RI: Carroll Press.

Krumboltz, J. D. (1981). A social learning theory of career selection. In D. H. Montross & C. J. Shinkman (Eds.), *Career development in the 1980's: Theory and practice* (pp. 43–66). Springfield, IL: Thomas.

Krumboltz, J. D. (1994, January). *How to explain what career counselors do.* Symposium conducted at the meeting of the National Career Development Association, Albuquerque, NM.

Krumboltz, J. D., & Baker, R. D. (1973). Behavioral counseling for vocational decisions. In H. Borow (Ed.), *Career guidance for a new age* (pp. xx–xx). Boston: Houghton Mifflin.

Krumboltz, J. D., Mitchell, A. M., & Gelatt, H. B. (1975). Applications of social learning theory of career selection. *Focus on Guidance, 8*(3), 1–16.

Krumboltz, J. D., Mitchell, A. M., & Jones, G. B. (1976). A social learning theory of career selection. *The Counseling Psychologist, 6*(1), 71–80.

Krumboltz, J. D., & Nichols, C. W. (1990). Integrating the social learning theory of career decision making. In S. H. Osipow & W. B. Walsh (Eds.), *Career counseling: Contemporary topics in vocational psychology.* Hillsdale, NJ: Lawrence Erlbaum Associates.

LaFromboise, T. D., Trimble, J. E., & Mohatt, G. V. (1990). Counseling intervention and American Indian tradition: An integrative approach. *The Counseling Psychologist, 18*(4), 628–654.

Lawson, L. (1993). Theory of work adjustment personality constructs. *Journal of Vocational Behavior, 43,* 46–57.

LeCompte, W. A. (1972). When the donkey speaks: The perspective of ecological psychology. *Hacettepe Bulletin of Social Science and Humanities, 4*(2), 153–161.

Levine, F. M., & Sandeen, E. (1985). *Conceptualization in psychotherapy*. Hillsdale, NJ: Lawrence Erlbaum Associates.

Lewin, K. (1951). *Field theory in social science*. New York: Harper & Row.

Loftquist, L. H., & Dawis, R. V. (1969). *Adjustment to work: A psychological view of man's problems in a work-oriented society*. New York: Appleton-Century-Crofts.

Loftquist, L. H., & Dawis, R. V. (1972). Application of the theory of work adjustment to rehabilitation counseling. *Minnesota Studies in Vocational Rehabilitation Bulletin, 58*.

Martin, W. E., Jr. (1991). Career development and American Indians living on reservations: Cross-cultural factors to consider. *The Career Development Quarterly, 39*, 273–283.

McDiarmid, G. W., & Kleinfeld, J. S. (1986, May). Occupational values of rural Eskimo. *Journal of American Indian Education*, pp. 23–29.

McShane, D. (1980). A review of scores of American Indian children on the Wechsler Intelligence Scales. *White Cloud Journal, 1*(4), 3–10.

Mitchell, L. K., & Krumboltz, J. D. (1990). Social learning approach to career decision making: Krumboltz's theory. In D. Brown & L. Brooks (Eds.), *Career choice and development* (2nd ed., pp. 143–196). San Francisco: Jossey-Bass.

Morgan, C. O., Guy, E., Lee, B., & Cellini, H. R. (1986). Rehabilitation services for American Indians: The Navajo experience. *Journal of Rehabilitation, 52*(2), 25–31.

National Center for Education Statistics. (1988). *Dropout rates in the US, 1988*. Washington, DC: U.S. Department of Education.

Nye, W. C. (1988). The development of a test of language assessment for Navajo children. In M. J. Johnson & W. E. Martin, Jr. (Eds.), *Final report for September 1983–December 1988* (pp. 59–61). Flagstaff: Northern Arizona University, Institute for Human Development, Native American Research and Training Center. (Available from the American Indian Rehabilitation Research and Training Center, Institute for Human Development, Northern Arizona University, P.O. Box 5630, Flagstaff, AZ 86011)

Okiishi, R. W. (1987). The genogram as a tool in career counseling. *Journal of Counseling and Development, 66*(3), 139–143.

Osipow, S. H. (1990). Convergence in theories of career choice and development: Review and prospect. *Journal of Vocational Behavior, 36*, 122–131.

Pedigo, J. (1983). Finding the meaning of Native American substance abuse: Implications for prevention. *Personnel and Guidance Journal, 61*, 273–276.

Pollack, D., & Shore, J. H. (1980). Validity of the MMPI with Native Americans. *American Journal of Psychiatry, 137*(8), 946–950.

Prediger, D., Swaney, K., & Mau, W. (1993). Extending Holland's hexagon: Procedures, counseling applications, and research. *Journal of Counseling and Development, 71*(4), 422–428.

Rappaport, J. (1987). Terms of empowerment/exemplars of prevention: Toward a theory for community psychology. *American Journal of Community Psychology, 15*(2), 121–148.

Ruffing, L. T. (1979). Dependence and underdevelopment. In R. D. Ortiz (Ed.), *Economic development in American Indian reservations*. Albuquerque: University of New Mexico Native American Studies Development Series.

Ryan, T. A. (1974). A systems approach to career education. *Vocational Guidance Quarterly, 22*(3), 172–179.

Sidles, C., MacAvoy, J., Bertson, M., & Kuhn, A. (1987). Analysis of Navajo adolescents performance on the Raven Progressive Matrices. *Journal of American Indian Education, 27*, 1–8.

Tanner, D. C., & Martin, W. E., Jr. (1986). Services and training needs in communicative problems and disorders for rehabilitation professionals serving Native Americans. *The Journal of Rehabilitation Administration, 10*(4), 117–123.

Tinsley, H. E. (1993). Editorial: Special issue on the theory of work adjustment. *Journal of Vocational Behavior, 43,* 1–4.

U.S. Bureau of the Census. (1990a). Statistical Abstract of the United States, 1990. Washington, DC: U.S. Government Printing Office.

U.S. Bureau of the Census. (1990b). Characteristics of American Indians by tribe and selected areas. Washington, DC: U.S. Government Printing Office.

Wandersman, A., Murday, D., & Wadsworth, J. C. (1979). The environment–behavior–person relationship: Implications for research. *Environmental Design Research Association, 10,* 162–174.

Weinrach, S. G., & Srebalus, D. J. (1990). Holland's theory of careers. In D. Brown & L. Brooks (Eds.), *Career choice and development* (2nd ed., pp. 37–67). San Francisco: Jossey-Bass.

White, R. H. (1990). *Tribal assets: The rebirth of native America.* New York: Holt.

Wicker, A. W. (1979). Undermanning theory and research: Implications for the study of psychological and behavioral effects of excess human populations. *Representative Research in Social Psychology, 4,* 185–206.

Williamson, E. G. (1965). Vocational counseling: Trait–factor theory. In B. Stefflre (Ed.), *Theories of counseling* (pp. 193–213). New York: McGraw-Hill.

Yost, E. B., & Corbishley, M. A. (1987). *Career counseling.* San Francisco: Jossey-Bass.

II

ASSESSMENT AND INTERVENTION

5

Career Intervention Strategies and Assessment Issues for African Americans

Sharon L. Bowman
Ball State University

Many of us absorbed a certain message about work when we were growing up: Go to school, get a good education, find a good job, and you will be satisfied for life. This message, the cornerstone of the Protestant work ethic, teaches us that work should be the main focus, if not the defining point, of our lives. That message also presumes that everyone has equal opportunity to earn the education necessary to enter the desired career. What that work ethic message ignores, however, is a second message that African Americans and members of other ethnic minority groups also hear on a daily basis. They are often told, subtly or overtly, that there are only certain careers open to them because of their ethnicity. This message becomes painfully clear when African Americans seek same-race role models in various careers, often resulting in few or no available resources. This message is evident when African Americans receive negative feedback about careers that their peers, or their elders, do not perceive as possible for members of their group. It is evident when entering a career in which there are few ethnic minorities, and receiving the message that one's hiring occurred only because of race, as though the new employee had no "real" qualifications. Finally, this message is evident when some African Americans find themselves in a position that forces them to interact in a system that is alien, and possibly hostile, to achieve status. Is it any wonder, then, that many African Americans select occupations to which they have already been exposed by other members of their community, occupations that, in general, are of a working-class or service-based level?

Vondracek and Schulenberg (1992) reported that "career intervention efforts have been criticized as being focused too narrowly" (p. 292). They suggested that interventions have failed to consider the broader human developmental framework when seeking to effect positive changes. Interventions already take into account age-graded influences that may covary with chronological age (as most career development theories do), but should also include history-graded influences that covary with biocultural change (e.g., the Persian Gulf War, the recession, or the L.A. riots, which may have unique effects on career development), and nonnormative influences that do not occur in any particular pattern (i.e., any random events that may have an effect, such as the early loss of a parent). Counselors should take into consideration the "normal" events that differ in prevalence for various ethnic groups. For example, national unemployment rates fluctuate over time, but the levels of unemployment for African-American and Hispanic teenagers, especially males, are consistently high. Counselors must incorporate these realities into their design of career interventions.

Brown, Minor, and Jepsen (1991) summarized the results of the National Career Development Association's national survey. Among the 1,350 adults surveyed, members of ethnic groups were more likely to say they needed help in finding out information about jobs than were Whites (44% of African Americans, 36% of Asian Americans, 35% of Hispanic Americans, 25% of Whites). Although all ethnic groups agreed on the need for increased attention to career development in the schools, a higher proportion of African Americans endorsed this statement than other groups. This attention includes assistance in choosing a career, developing non-college-bound students' job skills, placement for graduates and dropouts, use of occupational information, developing interviewing skills, and preparation for college. The need for more, and more effective, interventions as a means of exposure to new ideas is evident.

Fretz (1981) defined a *career intervention* as "any activity or program intended to facilitate career development; interventions may be as brief as administering and presenting results of an interest inventory or as extensive as a full year's curriculum in career development" (p. 78). Spokane (1991) concurred, noting that career interventions may include anything from training about effective decision making to focused intensive counseling to resolve career difficulties and may include techniques (applying career intervention principles such as inventories), strategies (plans of action intended to change the individual, group, or organization's vocational behavior), or programs (a compilation of techniques used to alter the behavior of group in a specific setting over a period of time). The goal of career interventions, regardless of the counselor's theoretical background, is to help the client(s) identify the career that is the best fit, leading to beneficial career outcomes (Spokane, 1991). Using these definitions and goals as the foundation for this review, the remainder of this chapter addresses factors to consider when counseling African Americans, issues in career assessment, and types of career interventions that may be more effective with an African-American clientele.

FACTORS INVOLVED IN COUNSELING AFRICAN AMERICANS

Presently, the largest ethnic minority in the United States, the African-American population, is also the most researched ethnic minority group. Vontress (1979, cited in Zunker, 1990) suggested that African Americans may feel like outsiders in the public school system and are treated differently than Whites. This group receives inferior educational opportunities as compared to Whites, which in turn affects their occupational opportunities. Stereotypes about the types of jobs that African Americans traditionally hold, coupled with the lack of visible role models in nontraditional fields, add to the perception of a limited opportunity structure.

African Americans, as a group, tend to be more group centered, sensitive to interpersonal matters, and to value cooperation (Sue & Sue, 1990), in contrast to White values of individuality, uniqueness, and competition. As members of a group that has suffered racist behavior from Whites, they tend to be more wary of White interactions, and African American–White interactions may be more formal than in-group interactions (depending on the racial identity level of the participants).

Racial Identity Development

An area that is rarely included in the career intervention literature is racial identity development, which has consequences for counseling and for career choice. Several models of racial identity development exist, including that of Atkinson, Morten, and Sue (1989), which identifies five stages of racial identity development. In the interest of brevity, the stages are only briefly described here; the reader is directed to Atkinson et al. (1989) for further information. The first stage is conformity, in which the African-American person accepts the dominant (White) culture's value system and its perception of ethnic minorities. The second stage, dissonance, occurs as the individual learns that the messages gleaned from the dominant society about African Americans are not necessarily accurate or complete, resulting in an examination of one's belief system.

In resistance and immersion, the individual focuses on dispelling the previously accepted "myths" from the dominant system and learning more about African-American heritage. During introspection, the individual again questions "blind" acceptance of a particular cultural system without examining its merits on a personal basis, leading to a reexamination of beliefs. In the final stage, synergistic articulation and awareness, the individual's values are truly a result of personal examination instead of blind acceptance of any cultural group's beliefs, resulting in a positive identification with African Americans and comfort with values of other cultural groups.

How does the client's racial identity level affect career interventions? The racial identity literature indicates that stage of racial identity is related to preference for a counselor of a particular ethnicity (cf. Helms, 1986, 1991; Pomales, Claiborn, & LaFramboise, 1986). This preference should be considered when operationalizing career strategies; for some clients information will be more salient when presented by another African American. This is especially true for clients in the resistance and immersion stage, who may not trust presenters or counselors of any racial group except their own.

The racial identity levels of counselors may also have an effect on career intervention strategies. African-American counselors do not hold a monopoly on racial sensitivity simply because they are members of a minority group. They, too, may be in any of the aforementioned stages, and their level of development may, in turn, influence their interactions with their African-American clients. For example, African-American career counselors in the conformity stage may not perceive certain occupations to be open to, or appropriate for, African Americans, so they may subtly dissuade clients from certain career paths. Clients in racial identity stages that are incongruent with the career counselor's stage, as noted earlier, may be less likely to pay heed to the counselor's suggestions or directions.

Racial identity issues also arise for White counselors that may, in turn, affect career interventions with African-American clients. Helms (1991) provided a five-stage model of White racial identity, and details how Caucasian counselors may respond to African-American clients (see Helms for further information on these stages). In contact, Whites have a naive understanding of the implications of their interactions with African Americans; "they" are different, and there is a curiosity about what makes "them" different. Career counselors in this stage may downplay the importance of race in this stage, and may not recognize their own biases. In disintegration, Whites focus, for the first time, on the meaning of whiteness in the United States, resulting in negative feelings about their race. Whites may overidentify with African Americans, treat them in a paternalistic manner, or retreat from them altogether. As career counselors, overidentifying or being paternalistic to clients can be a quick way to discredit oneself, and to lose the client's respect. Such treatment is still stereotypic and does not recognize the client's individuality.

In Stage 3, reintegration, a White person will act in a pro-White, anti-African-American manner. He or she will be overtly or covertly biased against and fearful of African Americans and may avoid them as much as possible. As career counselors, such biases may affect the types of choices promoted to African-American clients, or the quality of the inter-action. In the pseudo-independent stage, Whites begin to accept racial differences, at least on an intellectual level. They are again curious about African Americans, but at a deeper level than that of the contact stage; they will prefer to associate with African Americans who are "like" them in some way. As career counselors, this intellectual understanding will probably lead to an increased awareness of racial issues in career devel-opment and choice, but no emotional connection. Finally, in autonomy, Whites resonate to racial issues on both an intellectual and emotional level. There is a genuine acceptance, both of one's own whiteness and of others as African Americans. A person in this stage seeks diversity and understands that norms differ across cultures. A career counselor in this stage of racial identity development should be the most comfortable in discussing racial factors with African-American clients.

Obviously, there are a finite number of combinations of career coun-selor and client racial identity dyads. Some of these combinations will be complimentary, and few problems will result from these interactions. Other combinations, however, will be antagonistic, and the result may be a prematurely terminated relationship, or, at worst, a client who has been misguided into an unsatisfactory career. The type of intervention used may mediate this process. In one-on-one counseling situations, con-flicts among racial identity levels may be more pronounced, whereas racial identity levels of career client and career counselor may be an indirect issue in group or workshop situations. Career counselors should become aware of the idea of racial identity and its possible effects on the success of career interventions.

Role Models

The counseling literature is filled with studies demonstrating the impor-tance of family members (cf. Anderson, 1980; Smith, 1980) and other models (Hawks & Muha, 1991) to our career choices. These people influ-ence our decisions, in both a positive and a negative manner, as we struggle to chart our personal career path. Career theorists stress the importance of modeling to career development; yet there is little effort in practice to provide role models for ethnic minority clients, at least as reported in the voluminous career literature. Given the low number of ethnic minority men and women in many professional fields, not to mention in graduate school, ethnic minority models of both sexes should be included in career interventions. Dunn and Veltman (1989) noted that members of ethnic minority groups (with the exception of Asian Americans) are more likely to enter culturally traditional areas like business, social work, humanities, and teaching (i.e., social, conventional, and enterprising Holland work environments) where role models already exist. The U.S. society is increasingly geared toward technological careers, however, an area that presently provides very few role models for ethnic minorities. Increasing the prominence of the existing African-American models in technological areas is one way to encourage more African Americans to consider these fields as possible careers.

D'Andrea and Daniels (1992), among others, noted the importance of providing models of the same ethnicity as the clients, and Betz and Fitzgerald (1987) stressed the importance of providing models of the same gender. McDaniels and Gysbers (1992), in addition, stressed the need to provide race- and gender-appropriate models when working with ethnic minority females to increase awareness of career choices. Authors such as Griffith (1980), Yang (1991), and Herring (1990) stated that counselors must consider the level of acculturation, or identification with and acceptance of the dominant cultural system, for clients as a part of any career intervention.

The preference for counselors of a particular ethnicity may be similar to a preference for same-ethnicity role models in occupations; depending on racial identity stage, some clients may seek same-ethnicity role models, whereas others may have no preference or may shun same-ethnicity role models. Career counselors, to be most effective, should help African-American clients identify the role models, both positive and negative, who are salient to their work choices, and to examine the effects those models have had on their decision-making process. Clients with limited or foreshortened horizons (Gottfredson, 1981) should be directed toward African-American models (and gender-appropriate models, if possible) in a variety of areas, to open new areas for discussion and to develop contacts for future plans.

As Thomas and Alderfer (1989) reported, career counselors should also discuss the importance of mentors in the workforce. In many careers, having a mentor is extremely vital to success and advancement in the field, and to successfully negotiate the potential difficulties in one's career path. African Americans, however, with the low number of available role models in many areas, may perceive themselves as having few choices for mentors or may not understand the importance of having a mentor. This is especially true if they have difficulty trusting White co-workers and superiors as mentors. In fact, Thomas (1986; cited in Thomas & Alderfer, 1989) reported that African Americans tended to have same-race mentors outside their department, possibly meeting a psychosocial need for developmental relationships, whereas having Caucasian sponsors or mentors within the department, which may be an organizational necessity. Career counselors working with African Americans about to enter or already in the workforce must remember that the mentoring process does not cease upon graduation, and that clients may not understand the advantages and disadvantages of developing connections to a variety of people.

African-American Women

Career interventions developed for women tend not to discuss ethnic minority issues, nor do ethnic minority career interventions tend to examine gender issues. In response, Gainor and Forrest (1991) described a model to explain African-American women's self-concept as a combination of multiple self-referents (Brown-Collins & Sussewell, 1986, cited in Gainor & Forrest, 1991). These referents would include the psychophysiological referent, or one's knowledge of oneself as a woman; the African-American referent, or one's knowledge of oneself as African American (both in comparison to other African Americans and to Whites); and the myself referent, or one's knowledge of oneself as an unique being. Gainor and Forrest (1991) stated that career counselors should identify the various referents that form an African-American woman's self-concept and career choice when designing career interventions and should allow women the opportunity to discuss the implications of each of the referents on their career options.

Jordan (1991) discussed some of the issues faced by African-American women. The initial focus of the women's movement was for rights that African-American women did not consider relevant. For example, one of the movement's early goals was achieving the right to work, which was something many African-American women of all socioeconomic status (SES) levels had done all their lives. Jordan also noted that counseling theories, both career and personal, assert the need to establish trust as a precursor to the actual work of counseling. Yet, many African Americans have a "healthy paranoia" when dealing with Whites, and do not develop trust easily. Work with an African-American woman may move at a slower pace, especially if the career counselor is White, until trust is developed. The counselor should address the issues about both race and gender in the world of work.

Women may bring a number of issues to counseling. First, it has been reported that women tend to have lower career aspirations than men (Kerr, 1983), and that there are gender-typed differences between African-American men's and women's choices, even if both select prestigious career areas (Grevious, 1985). Women also tend to see family as more important than career issues (Coombs, 1979; DiBenedetto & Tittle, 1990). The latter can be even more of an issue when dual career families are discussed; issues are raised when trying to balance two careers and a family (Herr & Cramer, 1988), and/or when child care is a primary directive (Zunker, 1990). Women may also carry some stereotypes about women's choices that may effectively lower their self-esteem and keep them from seriously considering careers for which they may be suited (Eccles, 1987; Isaacson & Brown, 1993). According to Gottfredson (1981), women develop a personal understanding of what women can do and what men can do at a very early age. Career counselors working with African-American female clients should include these issues when discussing career and life roles, and be prepared to challenge stereotypical statements that may be prematurely restricting career options.

Finally, when examining women's issues, career counselors must also be aware of the federal discrimination laws that protect women in the workplace (Zunker, 1990). Women who are new entrants into the world of work, displaced homemakers, or women attempting to change jobs after holding one position for a long period of time, may have no understanding of what behaviors or questions are considered discriminatory. Career counselors are responsible for addressing this topic, both on the basis of gender and on the basis of race.

ISSUES IN CAREER ASSESSMENT

With the existence of two high-quality vocational journals (*Journal of Vocational Behavior* and *Career Development Quarterly*), and the recent introduction of the *Journal of Career Assessment*, one would expect to find a high number of articles focused on the assessment of ethnic minority career development. Indeed, one does find a high number of "assessment" articles, a broad definition including everything from career maturity to decision-making styles to vocational instruments. What is missing from many of those articles, however, is a focus on ethnic minority development. Phillips, Strohmer, Berthaume, and O'Leary (1983) commented on the relative lack of research in this area, noting a need for the literature to keep pace with a developing interest in vocational behavior for ethnic minorities.

Hoyt (1989) concurred with Phillips et al.'s (1983) perceptions. He recalled a commitment made by the National Vocational Guidance Association (now the National Career Development Association) to strive to eradicate sexism and racism and scrutinized all issues of the Association's journal, *Career Development Quarterly* (previously *Vocational Guidance*

Quarterly), for evidence of this commitment. The percentage of articles related to African Americans was three times higher in Volumes 17 to 35 (up to September 1987) than it was in Volumes 1 to 16 (2.6% and 0.8%, respectively); the percentage of articles on other ethnic minority groups remained almost immeasurable across the years (Volumes 1–16, 0.5%; Volumes 17–35, 0.6%). The percentage of articles on gender stereotyping more than doubled between Volumes 1 to 16 and 17 to 35 (4.5% and 10.6%, respectively). Given the rise of women in the workforce, and the predictions about the growth of the ethnic minority population in the near future (Hoyt, 1989), these percentages do not seem nearly large enough. Hoyt, Subich (1989), and Lee (1989) all agreed that the failure of the vocational literature to acknowledge the vocational barriers faced by women and ethnic minorities does a disservice to both groups. They challenged the career development profession to turn their attentions to these issues. The following sections examine some of what is known about assessment with African Americans.

Career and Educational Aspirations

For many adults, career and educational aspirations helped shape their vocational existence today, according to most of the popular vocational theories. When it comes to African Americans' aspirations and expectations, however, relatively little is known. Payton (1985) commented that African-American women did not aspire to traditionally female occupations, such as nursing, teaching, and social work, as much as their predecessors did; instead they showed interest in business and engineering careers. African-American women's educational aspirations were on par with the aspirations of African-American men; many expected to earn graduate- or professional-level degrees.

Unlike Payton (1985), Grevious (1985) expected the occupational aspirations of African-American men to be higher than those of African-American women. She found that both groups aspired to prestigious occupations; men's aspirations, however, were even higher than women's aspirations. Gender differences existed in the respondents' preferences for gender-typed occupations and in the selection of neutral specialties. For example, women aspired to public school teaching, especially in elementary schools, whereas men aspired to college teaching. Aspiring female medical students tended to choose pediatrics and psychiatry as specialties, which are less respected areas in the medical profession; men chose those same areas and also more respected specialties such as general surgery, neurosurgery, and internal medicine.

Bronzaft (1991) questioned African-American, White, and Hispanic female college students between the ages of 17 and 25 about their attitudes toward marriage, family, and career aspirations. She found that the majority of these young women intended to go on to graduate school. The majority of the African-American women aspired to academic (26%), business (30%), or professional (doctor, lawyer, dentist, etc.; 24%) careers, percentages similar to those of Hispanic and White women; 13% were planning nursing careers (a percentage equaling that of Hispanic and White female aspirants combined). Most of the sample expected to combine marriage and family with work; none indicated that they intended to limit themselves to home and family obligations. Ethnic minority women expected less help with household responsibilities from their husbands than did White women, and African-American women expected the least amount of child-care help from their extended families. The latter finding was surprising, given the importance of extended family connections to African Americans; Bronzaft (1991) suggested that her respondents may not be cognizant of the importance of child-care assistance in the lives of working women, because they are still in school.

Another, older study of aspirations, expectations, and attainment was conducted by Cosby, Thomas, and Falk (1976). They surveyed lower SES African-American and White college-age respondents (4 years post-high school) to determine how their present aspirations differed from those expressed in high school. The percentage of African-American respondents who had aspired to (65%), expected (37%), and attained college degrees were lower than the equivalent percentages for White respondents (70%, 50%, and 14%, respectively). The percentage of African-American respondents who had aspired to (34%), expected to (24%), and actually attained (2.6%) professional or technical occupations were also lower than the equivalent percentage for White respondents (48%, 30%, and 10%, respectively). The authors also found that 84% of African-American and 80% of White respondents still aspired to higher status occupations than those presently held; 65% of the total sample expected to exchange occupations for one with higher status.

Jacobs, Karen, and McClelland (1991) analyzed data from the National Longitudinal Study of Young Men, which began in 1966 and continues to survey the original cohort on an annual or biannual basis. Jacobs et al. (1991) expected to find race and class differences in vocational aspiration levels. They reported moderate differences by race for most of the occupational categories utilized. White males were consistently more likely to aspire to professional and managerial occupations, whereas African-American males were more likely to aspire to other white-collar occupations, craft, and other blue-collar occupations. Over the years, White males tended to hold to higher status occupational aspirations, whereas African-American males tended to hold to lower status occupational aspirations. Results for both groups were moderated by SES. It also appeared that African-American respondents with high levels of education were at least as likely as Whites to hold professional aspirations, regardless of socioeconomic background. In other words, from a sociological perspective, helping students achieve a higher education seems to be one of the best ways to ensure that they will have high level professional aspirations.

Although it certainly appears that African Americans have high career and educational aspirations, there are clearly some gender differences in their level and direction. It should also be stressed that socioeconomic status is a moderator of aspirations and expectations and in the future should be examined in conjunction with race and ethnicity in the career literature.

Vocational Interests

The study of interests may well encompass more of the vocational literature than any other topic. A recent book on the practice of career assessment (Lowman, 1991) provides practitioners with an assessment model and up-to-date literature supporting his tenets. A search of the table of contents, index, and the chapters and examples provided, however, yielded no mention of ethnic or racial issues in assessment. Given that many questions can be raised about test bias, linguistic differences, and functional and conceptual equivalence across vocational instruments (Fouad, 1993), this omission has serious consequences. Many practitioners turn to career inventories as a quick way to assess respondents' interests, or to predict future success and satisfaction (Spokane, 1991). A lack of awareness on the counselor's part of the potential biases evident in the inventories used may result in the dissemination of misleading information to ethnic minority career clients at best, or potentially damaging information at worst.

Any attempt to describe the literature on all career inventories in popular usage and relevance for African Americans would be beyond the scope of this chapter. Instead, a brief discussion of one of the more popular instruments, the Strong Interest Inventory (Hansen & Campbell, 1985), is provided here as an example of the present state of the literature. The reader is encouraged to examine the test manual of the vocational instrument in which he or she is interested to begin the search for evidence of that instrument's cultural validity and relevance.

Strong Interest Inventory (SII).   The SII is the direct descendant of the Strong Vocational Interest Blank (SVIB), which has been in existence for men and women since the 1930s. It is probably the most widely used interest inventory in college counseling centers (Zytowski & Warman, 1982) and has generated an impressive amount of validity data. Unfortunately, when Carter and Swanson (1990) set out to review the validity articles on the SII and its predecessors that focused on African-American samples, they were only able to locate only eight such studies. They also noted that the most recent manual for the SII (Hansen & Campbell, 1985) does not report racial or ethnic characteristics for the general reference or occupational criterion norm groups. The manual does indicate that the SII has been used successfully in other countries, and that translated versions do exist. There is no simple way, however, to determine how comparable the norm group is to a sample of U.S. ethnic minority respondents.

Carter and Swanson (1990) first reported on five studies on the psychometric properties of the SVIB. Although these studies concluded that the SVIB had predictive validity, the authors identified sampling problems with the studies that called such conclusions into question. The validity studies tended to use small samples of African Americans, typically males; these samples were usually compared to larger White samples. Such samples may not provide an adequate picture of African Americans' interest patterns, especially for females.

Carter and Swanson (1990) located three studies utilizing the SII. In one, Hines (1983; cited in Carter & Swanson, 1990) reported moderate predictive validity with African-American male and female college students. In addition, he reported gender differences in his sample (although his sample was overwhelmingly female), and significant differences between his sample and the women- and men-in general samples on the Basic Interest scales. Carter and Swanson (1990) noted that Hines' study suggests the need for an African-American reference group on the SII.

Howard (1981; cited in Carter & Swanson, 1990) reported that gender was a more important predictor of measured interests than race for college students; however, African-American females did demonstrate a discrepancy between their measured and expressed interests. Their measured interests were more similar to those of White females, whereas their expressed interests were more similar to those of White males, a discrepancy that warrants further study. Finally, Yura (1985; cited in Carter & Swanson, 1990) reported no racial differences on the Academic Comfort and Introversion–Extroversion scales, but did find differences on three of the six general Occupational Theme scales and 11 of 23 Basic Interest scales. Carter and Swanson (1990) summarized their review by noting that the consistent difference in interest patterns among Whites and African Americans may reflect within-group cultural characteristics for African Americans, their understanding of the occupational opportunity structure, or, as with White males and females, differences in socialization experiences. In any case, they concluded that the SII has demonstrated little psychometric validity for its use with African Americans to date.

Kapes and Mastie (1988) warned that one should not confuse popularity of a vocational instrument with effectiveness.

Tomlinson and Evans-Hughes (1991), noting the scarcity of multicultural literature on the validity of the SII, focused specifically on the Academic Comfort and Introversion–Extroversion scale scores of first-year African-American, White, and Hispanic college students enrolled in a summer orientation program. Their results suggested that ethnicity and gender do influence career interest and choice. Past research on the Academic Comfort scale indicated that women have higher scores (show more comfort) than men. In this study, White and Hispanic women tended to score higher than White and Hispanic men. For African-American men and women, however, the opposite was true. Tomlinson and Evans-Hughes (1991) suggested that this might be the result of social desirability, or that African-American males were more comfortable in the academic setting than were other groups of males. The authors caution that these scores were hard to interpret, however, because the Academic Comfort scores for the sample as a whole were low.

Tomlinson and Evans-Hughes (1991) also reported that African-American women had higher scores on the Introversion–Extroversion scales than did African-American men. This indicated that the women were more introverted and "were more likely to prefer working with a combination of interests involving people, ideas, and things, whereas African-American men were more likely to prefer working with others or in people-oriented occupations" (p. 154). White and Hispanic women tended to score toward the extroverted direction, whereas their male counterparts tended toward a more introverted direction; this is the pattern reported in past research. The authors commented that, whereas their sample was predominantly African American, limiting some of the statistical power of the analyses, ethnic and gender differences do appear to exist for the SII. Again, there is a suggestion that African-American women have patterns more similar to those of White men than to other groups. This suggestion deserves further exploration. It is also time to explore whether the interest patterns adhered to in vocational theories and research are indeed valid representations of African-American career development and choice.

Career Maturity

Career maturity has been defined as the accomplishment of developmental tasks, and the behavior manifested in coping with the tasks of a given life stage (Naidoo, 1993). It has been assessed by a number of authors, across a wide variety of populations within and outside the United States. In searching through the literature, however, few references to the career maturity of African Americans could be located. Many of these studies used African-American participants as a comparison group for Whites, fostering an expectation that one group would be "more" mature than the other group. This approach does not take into consideration the validity of the measures used, or within-group differences in socialization that may affect how career maturity is manifested.

Westbrook, Sanford, Merwin, Fleenor, and Gilleland (1988) investigated whether the ability to make appropriate career choices for others and the ability to make appropriate choices for oneself were related for African-American and White ninth-grade students. The assumption was that the ability to make choices for others, as measured by the Goal Selection subtest of the Career Maturity Inventory (CMI; Crites, 1978), is a valid measure of one's own career maturity. Westbrook et al. (1988) found that there is no relationship between the ability to make appropriate choices for others and to make them for oneself (as measured by determining the appropriateness of one's aspirations based on one's abilities and expressed interests) for African-American students; there was a small but significant relationship for White students. In fact, the two measures of career maturity used in this study did not correlate with each other, an indication that they measure different constructs. A replication of this work by Westbrook, Sanford, and Donnelly (1990) found no correlations between the two measures of career maturity for ninth graders, regardless of ethnicity or gender. These studies are a strong reminder to select a career maturity instrument that accurately measures the construct for the population with which it is to be used.

Dillard (1976a, 1976b) and Lawrence and Brown (1976) reported that SES status was correlated with career maturity for urban and suburban African-American students. Dillard and Perrin (1980) found that the career maturity scores of White high school students were higher than those of African-American high school students; however, the mean vocational aspiration levels for White males were lower than those of African-American and Hispanic males. No such differences were reported for females. McNair and Brown (1983) also found that White high school students scored higher on career maturity measures than African-American students; females scored higher than males. Overall, the career maturity literature to date indicates that race or ethnicity, gender, and SES are factors in predicting career maturity levels, and should be taken into account in future studies in this area.

Conclusions

This brief examination of the career assessment literature was certainly not meant to cover all aspects of assessment. There are several other areas that deserve mention, including (but not limited to) the role of education in assessment, the salience of "work" in African Americans' lives as compared to other roles that may carry more weight, and a more lengthy examination of the state of assessment instruments as they relate to African Americans. What this section has provided, however, is some idea of how far the literature has to go in its awareness of ethnic/racial issues. The literature abounds with studies that have examined only White samples, or did not report the race of the sample (leading to an assumption that the group was White). Very few studies were reported that included African Americans, either as a comparison group or to examine within-group differences. Such differences do exist (e.g., suburbia provides a very different experience than the inner city, regardless of race); those differences must be identified before between-group comparisons can rightfully be made. Such an approach may lead to the development of African-American career theories (Griffith, 1980), or at minimum, different norm groups for African Americans.

TYPES OF CAREER INTERVENTIONS

Having now identified several factors relevant to African-American career development, how does this population fare in the career intervention literature? Most career theories suggest similar practical implications for counselors (Yost & Corbishley, 1987). First, career decisions are based on a lifetime of experiences, not a single isolated moment, so counselors should explore significant elements in the client's past as clues to future decisions. Second, work can either enrich or impoverish people's lives, leading counselors to explore the client's expectations for inter- and intrapersonal satisfactions. Third, counselors need information on assessing career-appropriate skills and on locating up-to-date information about careers. Finally, counselors recognize that, even if the "career of best fit" is identified, clients are not always in a position to enter that career immediately (or possibly, ever), because of immaturity, environmental constraints, or personality flaws. Most theories suggest that these vocational barriers be removed or circumvented. Career counselors translate these implications into specific interventions to aid the client's development.

The majority of interventions fall into one of three categories: individual, self-directed CDM, and group interventions. These approaches may parallel the process of psychotherapy, but differ in that more structure is required of the career counselor. Spokane (1991) noted: "the focus is clearer, the client's goal is always implicit (even when unstated), and the available technology results in less available interventions than in psychotherapy" (p. 29). This structure can make the career counselor's job easier, because there is less variability to contend with, but can also cause complacency and lull the career counselor into believing that a pat or uniform approach will work with all clients, regardless of race, gender, age, and so on.

Individual Interventions

In many cases, counseling, be it for personal or career concerns, is provided on a one-on-one basis. Peterson, Sampson, and Reardon (1991) listed the characteristics of individual career counseling. This approach can adapt to a variety of vocational identity, career maturity, and career decisiveness issues. Its content can adapt to a greater diversity of individual needs. Scheduling is easier and faster than with group approaches, and there is less competition for external information resources. Individual career counseling is also easily adaptable to multidisciplinary service approaches (including career counselors, family therapists, psychologists, physical and occupational therapists, social workers, rehabilitation counselors, and educators). An individual career counselor must have an extensive knowledge of mental health issues, because career counseling is sometimes used as a steppingstone to a discussion of non-career-related personal issues. Finally, individual career counseling is more expensive, because of the lower cost–benefit ratio, than group interventions.

Individual career counseling generally has distinct phases or stages. Spokane (1991) described a three-stage (or phase) model: beginning, activation, and completion. The beginning phase contains three subphases: opening (establishing the basis of counseling), aspiring (exploring career aspirations), and loosening (exploring conflicts raised by the aspirations). The activation phase defines the "work" of counseling, as the client examines incongruencies between interest, abilities, values, and personality and specific job requirements. This stage requires a strong level of support and encouragement, as the client's anxiety is increased at this point. This phase has three subphases: assessment (use of inventories to set a cognitive structure), inquiry (formation and testing of hypotheses), and commitment (making compromises to reach a preliminary commitment). The third phase, completion, is reached when the client's attitudes, emotions, and behaviors are consistently geared toward a satisfactory career choice. The subphases here include execution (performance of behaviors leading to career choice) and follow-through (continued compliance after counseling termination). Other models follow this general idea but include additional stages (cf. Peterson et al., 1991; Yost & Corbishley, 1987).

No models of individual career counseling were identified that directly address ethnic/cultural issues. Yost and Corbishley (1987), however, noted that members of ethnic minority groups may face internal and external constraints on their career choices. Past experience (direct or vicarious) with discrimination may result in anxiety about one's options and lowered self-esteem. As Gottfredson (1981) noted, the result may be foreclosed horizons, or a tendency to set one's sights lower than necessary. It is also possible that ethnic minority clients will encounter discrimination from employers in the form of increased negative responses, unreasonably low salaries, or work below one's ability levels.

Individual career counseling may benefit African-American clients in several ways. It is most useful for African-American clients who are less career mature, indecisive, or have a less-than-adequate vocational identity. African-American clients who are uncomfortable with the idea of "counseling" may prefer to meet with someone one-on-one to discuss career issues (on the other hand, many clients may feel more comfortable in a group situation, where they meet peers who are experiencing similar levels of career confusion). African-American clients' individual needs and concerns can be addressed more easily in individual sessions. In group situations, it may be next to impossible to address all the issues that a particular client may have; some issues may be too personal to discuss, or not relevant to the rest of the group members.

Issues regarding perceptions of certain occupations as "open" or "closed" to African Americans, the lack of available African-American role models, and messages regarding work that the client may hold or may perceive society as holding about African-American employees are all possible topics of discussion. The client may also raise issues about family dynamics; for example, a potential career path may conflict with the family's values or physically take the client away from the family unit. For many African Americans, connections to extended family are most salient, and, whereas the family may encourage education, they may not encourage moving far away from the family. The career counselor may need to help an African-American client gather information about the world of work, especially if the client's background is such that she or he was not exposed to a wide variety of career models. The client may also need to work on vocational and overall self-concept and learn how one's self-concept affects perceptions of work roles.

Yost and Corbishley (1987) stated that career counselors must address such issues in a realistic manner. Not every African-American person will experience difficulty or discrimination in his or her career goals because of race, so the counselor should not make a blind assumption that such difficulties have occurred or will occur. The career counselor should, however, assess the potential for such difficulties with the client by examining both the messages that the client is telling her- or himself, and the messages that the employers may be sending. Counselors working with African-American clients, therefore, must expand their knowledge base to have some awareness of these difficulties, and some awareness of community resources to use when their personal knowledge base falls short.

In addition, career counselors must be aware of and sensitive to the impact of ethnic differences and similarities between themselves and their clients. Communication and understanding can be hampered or enhanced by differences in life experiences, values, goals, or attitudes toward work. For example, an African-American career counselor from a middle SES background will probably have had different life experiences and been exposed to different work attitudes than an African-American client from a lower SES background.

Self-Directed Career Decision Making

For individual clients who have an adequate level of career maturity, are not indecisive, and are developing a vocational identity, self-directed CDM could be helpful. Some clients have the requisite skills to make an appropriate vocational decision, but need to spend time seeking the information necessary to make an informed decision. Self-directed clients require very little of a counselor's time, in contrast to other career clients, needing nothing more than brief guidance on where to locate resources. Such a client will be at a higher level of readiness than clients involved with other types of interventions. This approach has some of the advantages of individual career counseling (e.g., adaptability to diverse needs, no scheduling problems) and is more cost effective (Peterson et al., 1991).

At issue, however, is the helpfulness of self-directed CDM to African-American clients. As reported earlier (Brown et al., 1991), African-American adults do not believe they have access to enough career information to make a valid decision. Clients who have not been exposed to a variety of career options and role models throughout their lives may not have the requisite background to make good career decisions. In addition, if they have questions regarding the racial "climate" in a particular occupation, or they hold discouraging messages about the acceptability of African Americans in a particular position, or if they have prematurely foreclosed their options and are seeking careers below their potential, self-directed approaches will not meet their needs. Career counselors will need to make themselves available to deal with such issues. They may, in fact, want to ascertain whether their African-American clients are truly ready for self-assessment approaches, or if more exploration is needed first.

Group Approaches to Career Counseling

Holland, Magoon, and Spokane (1981) noted that group treatments are becoming more popular with practitioners. This category of interventions includes courses, seminars, workshops, job finding and interviewing training, values clarification groups, and special courses for designated groups such as women, ethnic minorities, and retirees. The authors (Holland et al., 1981) reported that the beneficial effects of any intervention strategies include "exposure to occupational information; cognitive rehearsal of vocational aspirations; acquisition of some cognitive structure for organizing information about self, occupations, and their relations; [and] social support or reinforcement from counselors or workshop members" (p. 285). When attempting to affect the vocational behavior of ethnic minorities, counselors should additionally focus on the client's identification as a member of a particular racial and gender group, and the meaning that identification has for the client.

Peterson et al. (1991) stated that career counseling with homogeneous groups allows for peer feedback and observational learning while demonstrating that career problems are common. There are some prepackaged career programs designed for group use (cf. Azrin & Besalel, 1980; Daane, 1972). Group career counseling is a more cost effective approach because information is quickly disseminated to groups instead of individuals; however, the ability to meet individual needs decreases as the group grows and as the degree of structure increases. The potential for delay in providing services, as individuals wait for a group to form, is another drawback.

African Americans, as noted earlier in this chapter, tend to be more group oriented. As such, many African-American clients may find group career interventions more comfortable, taking the focus away from them as individuals and fostering a sharing of the work and the process among the group. African Americans, when in more racially homogeneous groups, also tend to be more open to discussion. They may share information and feel more comfortable discussing topics raised by the group facilitator or career counselor in a group format. African Americans, in general, will prefer a more interactive process instead of a didactic, lecturing style and will seem to learn more from the former. African Americans also prefer a more directive style, in general, than do Whites, so group approaches can be an ideal learning experience.

The career intervention literature has several avenues that remain unexplored for ethnic minorities. One difficulty is that authors often neglect to report the race of participants; in some cases they do not even collect such information. Readers cannot assume that the results of such studies are relevant to groups other than the White middle-class population. This is of particular concern when trying to locate published interventions, successful and unsuccessful, that have been utilized with an African-American population. The interventions that follow were among the few located in which the participants' race was reported. Only one of the interventions utilized a multicultural approach to career counseling; it is encouraging to note such initiative in the literature.

Group Interventions

Dunn and Veltman (1989) stated that restrictive choice patterns may be caused by a lack of academic preparation, underdeveloped interests, career-planning knowledge, or perceptions of opportunity, all areas that are positively affected by career interventions. To counteract the latter two obstacles, the authors developed a career intervention program facilitated by representatives from university faculty and counselors, local industry, city government, public service organizations, and area high schools. Twenty African-American and two Asian-American low-income high school juniors participated in a 2-week workshop focusing on science, math, and engineering, including academic tutorials on note-taking, calculator use, and computer use and programming. The students also participated in three 2-hour career exploration groups. The final part of the program was a paid internship, spent shadowing engineers in research development activities. The students were pre- and posttested on the CMI, and their scores rose significantly over time on the decisiveness, involvement, and orientations scales. There was a slight increase in competence scores, and a slight, nonsignificant decline in independence scores. The latter score may stem from a newfound recognition that career decisions do not have to be made alone, and that others can assist in the decision-making process. The students indicated that they had made some career-related decisions and perceived themselves as having more control of their decisions; they also demonstrated a more positive interest in work. Dunn and Veltman (1989) did not report a cultural component in their program, nor did they report a follow-up of their students; the latter is a particular drawback to demonstrating the program's long-term effectiveness.

Rea-Poteat and Martin (1991) developed a 2-week summer program, "Taking Your Place: Exploring Technology and Tomorrow," to encourage 7th- through 10th-grade girls to explore technological occupations. The program included "80 hours of activities such as business and industry visitations, technical and tradeshop 'hands-on' activities at a local community college, as well as self-concept building exercises" (p. 183). They stated that career interventions for females should include both self-concept-building exercises and career-building activities.

Every female applicant was admitted to Rea-Poteat and Martin's (1991) program, which had been offered at least once per summer since 1986. Each session included approximately 25 to 30 girls of all SES levels. They were typically 14 or 15 years old; 57% were White, and the other 43% were members of other ethnic groups. This program consisted of a "demonstration" component, including fieldtrips to work sites; an "instruction" component, including classroom learning and hands-on applications (computer usage, radio assembly); and a "counseling activities" component, including group exercises, individual counseling, and lectures and discussions about women's involvement in nontraditional occupations. The girls reported overwhelmingly positive perceptions of the program, professing greater confidence in making choices and in potentially selecting nontraditional occupations. As with Dunn and Veltman (1989), the authors did not follow up on their participants' subsequent career-related behaviors, nor did they describe any area of the program that related specifically to potential issues for the ethnic minority participants.

D'Andrea and Daniels (1992) described inner-city youth as an "endangered species" and asserted that creative career development programs should be designed to reach them. Their program, entitled "I Have a Future Program," was based at Meharry Medical College in Nashville. Their primary goals were to increase availability of direct vocational development services to the inner-city community, to incorporate community counseling services, and to infuse multiculturalism into the program design. The 8-week course (twice per week, 2 hours per session) for 40 teens, 14 to 17 years old, was designed to promote career awareness, teach pre-employment skills, increase personal discipline, and cultivate problem-solving skills. This was a cooperative project with community residents and church leaders (role models with significant influence in the African-American community), public housing and elected officials, human service professionals, and private industry.

This program combined traditional counseling strategies with a cooperative group approach that D'Andrea and Daniels (1992) believed might be more conducive to African-American youths' learning styles. This included group exercises, role playing, African-American guest speakers, and skills training (assertiveness and communication). In addition, D'Andrea and Daniels included a multicultural component in their program by incorporating Atkinson et al.'s (1989) stages of identity development into their planning, acknowledging that students in different stages of development will have different needs. They tried, therefore, to focus on identity development and to help facilitate students' movement through the various stages. They also utilized the seven principles of life, based on the work of Kunjufu (1986), throughout discussions; these principles reflect a community-centered viewpoint that is representative of an Africentric world view. This program reported successful changes in students' perceptions of work and of their place as African Americans in the work world. Again, no follow-up was provided.

One program that did complete a follow-up is the Pre-College Program by Kammer, Fouad, and Williams (1988), designed to promote "successful completion of high school and eventual graduation from college of students from disadvantaged backgrounds who show academic potential in

mathematics and natural sciences" (p. 41). This summer program emphasized upgrading skills and provided tutorial support, career awareness
seminars, advising, and career counseling for participants. The authors
surveyed 157 former participants in the program, of whom 50% ($n = 80$)
were African American, 31% ($n = 50$) were White, 5% ($n = 8$) were Hispanic, 5% ($n = 8$) were Asian, 3% ($n = 4$) were Native American, and 6%
($n = 9$) were "other." None of the students had dropped out of high
school; 117 had graduated, and the remainder were still in high school.
In contrast, the average high school dropout rate in the students' school
system is 12%.

Of the high school graduates, 73% ($n = 85$) had attended a postsecondary school; several had graduated from vocational schools or from 4-year
colleges. For the total sample, 86% expressed career choices that require
postsecondary training or were presently undecided about career choice
but intended to attend a postsecondary school. Kammer et al. (1988) also
asked these former participants to indicate whether they were satisfied
with the Pre-College Program on a scale from 1 to 5, with 5 indicating
the most satisfaction; the average rating was 4.3. The former participants
also indicated that the program had been very helpful with their entry
into college (average rating of 4). Although race was not directly examined
in this study, most of the students were ethnic minority group members.
The high levels of graduation, postsecondary school attendance, and satisfaction with the program cannot be ignored in this context.

Final Counseling Considerations

From a sociological perspective, Hotchkiss and Borow (1990) noted that
career counselors should be involved in the following tasks. First, they
must inform ethnic minority clients about potential barriers to career
attainment and help them develop strategies to circumvent them. Second,
career counselors must provide direct advocacy for clients who are having
difficulty negotiating the system. Third, they should work to reduce racial
and ethnic barriers to success whenever possible (e.g., by assisting in
school-to-work transitions). Finally, they should help raise clients' educational aspirations as a way of expanding vocational opportunities.

Hawks and Muha (1991) added that counselors should emphasize stu-
dent-generated versus counselor-generated knowledge in their career interventions. Students can be encouraged to independently generate information about their interest areas, and to locate ethnic minority role
models in those areas. Clients have more of an investment in the process
if they are learning how to do it for themselves instead of relying on
spoon-fed information. Hawks and Muha (1991) further stated that career
counselors should incorporate the student's language style and culture

into programs. This may be very difficult for many career counselors, because it requires an increased awareness of their own cultural differences and accompanying biases. This includes paying attention to such things as some African Americans' preference for interactive, structured group approaches, and for social occupations. Sometimes this preference for social occupations, however, is based on perceived opportunity, not interest, so career counselors must explore such issues with their clients to determine whether they stem from foreshortened horizons (Gottfredson, 1981) or actual interest. Career counselors must also be aware of racial identity stages and their implications on career choice and development and be prepared to work with the client's level of development.

Hawks and Muha (1991) also stated that the minority community, especially parents, should be included in career programs. Employers and other workers can serve as excellent role models for students and can be utilized in the planning stages of designing a career program. African-American parents tend to have aspirations for their children as high as those of White parents, although they cannot always present a similar variety of role models. African-American children also tend to look to their parents and extended family for career advice, so involving the parents in career programs helps them serve as informed resources and decision makers.

Finally, Hawks and Muha (1991) proposed that counselors view problems as external or systemic problems instead of flaws within the student, then use that viewpoint to challenge students to overcome those problems. If racism or other institutional factors are deemed insurmountable by both the client and the career counselor, or if the career counselor subtly or overtly denies that racism exists in the workforce, it is unlikely that the client will develop strategies to compensate and overcome these barriers. Career counselors may sometimes lower their expectations for African-American clients or neglect to provide critical feedback as a way of protecting the client. These behaviors are as discriminatory as denial or blaming the client for the problem. Career counselors must take care to be aware of these behaviors and attitudes and actively work to avoid them in their counseling work.

Griggs and Dunn (1989) reported that, in general, African-American middle and high school students tend to process and retain information better when it is presented in an auditory manner and has a verbal conceptual orientation. African-American students also tend to prefer "hands-on learning activities, report persistence in learning or a willingness to sustain studying beyond the required time or until task completion, and prefer formal study arrangements" (p. 152). The authors noted that, whereas these are generalities, career counselors would benefit from taking these points into consideration when designing interventions.

Zunker (1990) listed five developmental strategies that career counselors could attend to in their work. The first strategy is the development of a vocational self-concept, or paying attention to feelings of personal inadequacies that may affect their perceptions of current and future work roles. Second, help clients become more internally directed or take control of their career direction instead of continuing less productive life patterns. Third, aid clients in learning about job opportunities, including learning about and utilizing job search plans to gather information about trends in the labor force. Fourth, focus on clarifying motivational aspirations, including an examination of low expectations and fear of failure and how to resolve them. Fifth, help clients learn to interact in a Caucasian society, including developing and maintaining one's identity while developing relationships in the work environment. Zunker (1990) described these as module topics for use in group counseling interventions, but they are equally applicable strategies for individual interventions.

CONCLUSIONS

Information pertaining directly to African-American career interventions and assessment is sparse. It appears, from the literature, that either very few career counselors and researchers are working in this area, or very little of their work is being published. For example, the vocational literature has scarcely addressed racial identity and its potential effects on career counseling, development, and decision making. This topic seems to be a valid one for further research.

Similarly, we have little follow-up information on the group career interventions that are described in the literature. Fretz (1981) and Spokane (1991), among others, emphasized that intervention programs should be evaluated for their short- and long-term effectiveness. Several of the programs described in this chapter did not include formal evaluations or did not follow up with their participants to gauge long-term effects. In addition, some programs did not focus on race as a variable, even when a large proportion of their participants were ethnic minorities. There is no way, as yet, to gauge whether culturally relevant programs are more effective than generic programs for African Americans. It is suggested that this issue be examined in future studies.

Finally, as a practice implication, career counselors are liable to see an amazing array of clients (based on race, age, gender, or sexual orientation). It is the counselors' responsibility to understand that their clients, coming from different cultures, have different needs, expectations, and biases toward work. They may also have different learning styles. As Yost and Corbishley (1987) noted, it is impossible for a career counselor to know everything about every culture. It is, however, permissible to admit, to oneself and to the client, that the counselor is not all knowledgeable. When working with African-American clients, counselors who can acknowledge their own biases and attempt to form a collaborative relationship with the client and her or his community, as opposed to utilizing a limited, one-size-fits-all strategy, will be more likely to perceive their clients as individuals with a particular cultural background (instead of representatives of all African Americans).

In addition, practitioners must develop a working knowledge of the assessment literature on African Americans, especially as it relates to the specific assessment instruments used in their work setting. If norms are not available, it is the practitioners' ethical responsibility to aid in the development of such norms. Many of the questions raised in this chapter can be resolved through a collaborative effort between practitioners, who have the data, and researchers, who may have more time to put it to use.

REFERENCES

Anderson, K. L. (1980). Educational goals of male and female adolescents: The effects of parental characteristics and attitudes. *Youth and Society, 12*, 173–188.

Atkinson, D. R., Morten, G., & Sue, D. W. (1989). A minority identity development model. In D. R. Atkinson, G. Morten, & D. W. Sue (Eds.), *Counseling American minorities* (pp. 35–52). Dubuque, IA: Brown.

Azrin, N. H., & Besalel, V. A. (1980). *Job Club counselor's manual: A behavioral approach to vocational counseling.* Baltimore: University Park Press.

Betz, N. E., & Fitzgerald, L. F. (1987). *The career psychology of women.* San Diego: Academic Press.

Bronzaft, A. L. (1991). Career, marriage, and family aspirations of young Black college women. *Journal of Negro Education, 60*(1), 110–118.

Brown, D., Minor, C. W., & Jepsen, D. A. (1991). The opinions of minorities about preparing for work: Report on the second NCDA national survey. *Career Development Quarterly, 40*(1), 5–19.

Carter, R. T., & Swanson, J. L. (1990). The validity of the Strong Interest Inventory with Black Americans: A review of the literature. *Journal of Vocational Behavior, 36*, 195–209.

Coombs, L. C. (1979). The measurement of commitment to work. *Journal of Population, 2.*

Cosby, A. G., Thomas, J. K., & Falk, W. W. (1976). Patterns of early adult status attainment and attitudes in the nonmetropolitan South. *Sociology of Work and Occupations, 3*, 411–428.

Crites, J. O. (1978). *Administration and use manual* (2nd ed.). Monterey, CA: CTB/McGraw-Hill.

Daane, C. J. (1972). *Vocational Exploration Group.* Tempe, AZ: Studies for Urban Man.

D'Andrea, M., & Daniels, J. (1992). A career development program for inner-city youth. *Career Development Quarterly, 40*(3), 272–280.

DiBenedetto, B., & Tittle, C. K. (1990). Gender and adult roles: Role commitment of women and men in a job family trade-off context. *Journal of Counseling Psychology, 37*, 41–48.

Dillard, J. M. (1976a). Relationship between career maturity and self-concepts of suburban and urban middle- and urban lower-class preadolescent Black males. *Journal of Vocational Behavior, 9*, 311–320.

Dillard, J. M. (1976b). Socioeconomic background and the career maturity of Black youths. *Vocational Guidance Quarterly, 25*, 65–70.

Dillard, J. M., & Perrin, D. W. (1980). Puerto Rican, Black, and Anglo adolescents' career aspirations, expectations, and maturity. *Vocational Guidance Quarterly, 28*, 313–321.

Dunn, C. W., & Veltman, G. C. (1989). Addressing the restrictive career maturity patterns of minority youth: A program evaluation. *Journal of Multicultural Counseling and Development, 17*, 156–164.

Eccles, J. S. (1987). Gender roles and women's achievement-related decisions. *Psychology of Women Quarterly, 11*, 135–172.

Fouad, N. A. (1993). Cross-cultural vocational assessment. *Career Development Quarterly, 42*, 4–13.

Fretz, B. R. (1981). Evaluating the effectiveness of career interventions. *Journal of Counseling Psychology, 28*(1), 77–90.

Gainor, K. A., & Forrest, L. (1991). African American women's self-concept: Implications for career decisions and career counseling. *Career Development Quarterly, 39*(3), 261–272.

Gottfredson, L. S. (1981). Circumscription and compromise: A developmental theory of occupational aspirations. *Journal of Counseling Psychology, 28*(6), 545–549.

Grevious, C. (1985). A comparison of occupational aspirations of urban Black college students. *Journal of Negro Education, 54*, 35–42.

Griffith, A. (1980). Justification for a Black career development. *Counselor Education and Supervision, 19*(4), 301–310.

Griggs, S. A., & Dunn, R. (1989). The learning styles of multicultural groups and counseling implications. *Journal of Multicultural Counseling and Development, 17*, 146–155.

Hansen, J. C., & Campbell, D. P. (1985). *Manual for the SVIB–SCII* (4th ed.). Palo Alto, CA: Consulting Psychologists Press.

Hawks, B. K., & Muha, D. (1991). Facilitating the career development of minorities: Doing it differently this time. *Career Development Quarterly, 39*(3), 251–260.

Helms, J. E. (1986). Expanding racial identity theory to cover counseling process. *Journal of Counseling Psychology, 33*, 62–64.

Helms, J. E. (1991). *Black and White racial identity: Theory, research, and practice.* Westport, CT: Greenwood.

Herr, E. L., & Cramer, S. H. (1988). *Career guidance and counseling through the life span: Systematic approaches.* Glenview, IL: Scott, Foresman.

Herring, R. D. (1990). Attacking career myths among Native Americans: Implications for counseling. *The School Counselor, 38*, 13–17.

Holland, J. L., Magoon, T. M., & Spokane, A. R. (1981). Counseling psychology: Career interventions, research, and theory. *Annual Review of Psychology, 32*, 279–305.

Hotchkiss, L., & Borow, H. (1990). Sociological perspectives on work and career development. In D. Brown & L. Brooks (Eds.), *Career choice and development* (pp. 262–307). San Francisco: Jossey-Bass.

Hoyt, K. B. (1989). The career status of women and minority persons: A 20-year retrospective. *Career Development Quarterly, 37*, 202–212.

Isaacson, L. E., & Brown, D. (1993). *Career information, career counseling, and career development.* Needham Heights, MA: Allyn & Bacon.

Jacobs, J. A., Karen, D., & McClelland, K. (1991). The dynamics of young men's career aspirations. *Sociological Forum, 6*(4), 609–639.

Jordan, J. (1991). Counseling African American women: "Sister-Friends." In C. C. Lee & B. L. Richardson (Eds.), *Multicultural issues in counseling: New approaches to diversity* (pp. 51–63). Alexandria, VA: American Association for Counseling and Development.

Kammer, P. P., Fouad, N., & Williams, R. (1988). Follow-up of a pre-college program for minority and disadvantaged students. *Career Development Quarterly, 37*, 40–45.

Kapes, J. T., & Mastie, M. M. (Eds.). (1988). *A counselor's guide to career assessment instruments* (2nd ed.). Alexandria, VA: The National Career Development Association.

Kerr, B. A. (1983). Raising the career aspirations of gifted girls. *Vocational Guidance Quarterly, 32,* 37–43.

Kunjufu, J. (1986). *Motivating and preparing Black youth to work.* Chicago: African American Images.

Lawrence, W., & Brown, D. (1976). An investigation of intelligence, self-concept, socioeconomic status, race, and sex as predictors of career maturity. *Journal of Vocational Behavior, 9,* 43–51.

Lee, C. C. (1989). Needed: A career development advocate. *Career Development Quarterly, 37,* 218–220.

Lowman, R. L. (1991). *The clinical practice of career assessment: Interest, abilities, and personality.* Washington, DC: American Psychological Association.

McDaniels, C., & Gysbers, N. C. (1992). *Counseling for career development: Theories, resources, and practice.* San Francisco: Jossey-Bass.

McNair, D., & Brown, D. (1983). Predicting the occupational aspirations, occupational expectations, and career maturity of Black and White male and female tenth graders. *Vocational Guidance Quarterly, 32*(1), 29–36.

Naidoo, A. V. (1993). *Factors affecting the career maturity of African American university students: A causal model.* Unpublished doctoral dissertation, Ball State University, Muncie, IN.

Payton, C. R. (1985). Addressing the special needs of minority women. *New Directions for Student Services, 29,* 75–90.

Peterson, G. W., Sampson, J. P., & Reardon, R. C. (1991). *Career development and services: A cognitive approach.* Belmont, CA: Wadsworth.

Phillips, S. D., Strohmer, C., Berthaume, B. L. J., & O'Leary, J. C. (1983). Career development of special populations: A framework for research. *Journal of Vocational Behavior, 22,* 12–29.

Pomales, J., Claiborn, C. D., & LaFramboise, T. D. (1986). Effects of Black students' racial identity on perceptions of White counselors varying in cultural sensitivity. *Journal of Counseling Psychology, 34,* 123–131.

Rea-Poteat, M. B., & Martin, P. F. (1991). Taking your place: A summer program to encourage nontraditional career choices for adolescent girls. *Career Development Quarterly, 40*(2), 182–188.

Smith, E. R. (1980). Desiring and expecting to work among high school girls: Some determinants and consequences. *Journal of Vocational Behavior, 17*(2), 218–230.

Spokane, A. R. (1991). *Career intervention.* Englewood Cliffs, NJ: Prentice-Hall.

Subich, L. M. (1989). A challenge to grow: Reaction to Hoyt's article. *Career Development Quarterly, 37,* 213–217.

Sue, D. W., & Sue, D. (1990). *Counseling the culturally different: Theory and practice.* New York: Wiley.

Thomas, D. A., & Alderfer, C. P. (1989). The influence of race on career dynamics: Theory and research on minority career experiences. In M. B. Arthur, D. T. Hall, & B. S. Lawrence (Eds.), *Handbook of career theory* (pp. 133–158). New York: Cambridge University Press.

Tomlinson, S. M., & Evans-Hughes, G. (1991). Gender, ethnicity, and college students' responses to the Strong–Campbell Interest Inventory. *Journal of Counseling and Development, 70,* 151–155.

Vondracek, F. W., & Schulenberg, J. (1992). Counseling for normative and nonnormative influences on career development. *Career Development Quarterly, 40*(4), 291–301.

Westbrook, B. W., Sanford, E. E., & Donnelly, M. H. (1990). The relationship between career maturity test scores and appropriateness of career choices: A replication. *Journal of Vocational Behavior, 36,* 20–32.

Westbrook, B. W., Sanford, E. E., Merwin, G., Fleenor, J., & Gilleland, K. (1988). Career maturity in grade 9: Can students who make appropriate career choices for others also make appropriate career choices for themselves? *Measurement and Evaluation in Counseling and Development, 21,* 64–71.

Yang, J. (1991). Career counseling of Chinese American women: Are they in limbo? *Career Development Quarterly, 39*(4), 350–359.

Yost, E. B., & Corbishley, M. A. (1987). *Career counseling: A psychological approach.* San Francisco: Jossey-Bass.

Zunker, V. G. (1990). *Career counseling: Applied concepts of life planning.* Pacific Grove, CA: Brooks/Cole.

Zytowski, D. G., & Warman, R. E. (1982). The changing use of tests in counseling. *Measurement and Evaluation in Guidance, 15,* 147–152.

6

Career Behavior of Hispanics: Assessment and Career Intervention

Nadya A. Fouad
University of Wisconsin-Milwaukee

Hispanics in the United States are a very diverse group of people who are descendants of individuals from Central or South America. They tend to share a common language (Spanish) and religion (Roman Catholic), although Brazilians speak Portuguese and some Hispanics practice other religions. According to Marin and Marin (1991), Hispanics share cultural values that "remain strong and personally significant across generations" (p. 2). Marin and Marin also noted that the label *Hispanic* is one that is not universally adopted by those to whom it applies, and that the term connotes an *ethnic group* rather than a *racial group*. This latter point is of importance because Hispanics actually comprise many racial groups, particularly White, African American, and indigenous Native American, and the use of the term *Hispanic* in research studies or census/demographic data is sometimes confused with that of a racial group rather than an ethnic group. This needs to be considered when working with Hispanic Americans as well as when interpreting conclusions based on data collected on them.

Arbona (this volume) thoroughly described the history of diverse groups of individuals who are considered Hispanic and presented compelling statistics that impact on the career development of Hispanic Americans. As a group, Hispanics are a very diverse group with respect to socioeconomic status (SES) and education, although 26% live below the poverty level and have lower levels of educational attainment than non-Hispanics. Hispanics tend to be concentrated in service, unskilled, and skilled occupations, rather than in managerial, technical, or professional areas, and Arbona (this volume) concluded that Hispanics have lower occupational and professional attainment than non-Hispanics even though they have similar rates of participation in the labor force. Whereas these statistics describe a group that has significant problems, they do not adequately capture the complex interplay of individual and institutional reasons for the problems.

Research on the career assessment of Hispanics has described their lower educational and occupational attainment, and delineated possible causes of these problems, as well as described differences across ethnic groups on career-related variables (e.g., vocational interests). The few career interventions have implemented programs to counteract possible causes for those problems (e.g., increasing math and science achievement and career awareness). Most of the research on Hispanics has focused on the individual, although some authors (e.g., Casas & Ponterotto, 1984; Ochoa, 1985) have identified institutional problems and barriers. It is beyond the scope of this chapter to thoroughly describe the structural barriers to change that exist for Hispanics (i.e., discrimination, prejudice, inferior education policies and practices), but the reader is encouraged to keep those in mind when considering assessment and intervention for Hispanic/Latino clients.

The chapter is organized into four major sections. The first focuses on group differences in the assessment of career-related variables. Investigation primarily has focused on vocational interests, but there is some research on vocational aspirations and the educational experiences of Hispanics, as well as on gender differences between Hispanic men and women.

A second section reviews the scant literature available on career interventions with Hispanics. Much of the discussion centers on increasing math and science career awareness and achievement to counteract the underrepresentation of Hispanics in these career areas.

The third section discusses career counseling with Hispanics. An overview of cultural values is given, and a discussion of issues for counselors of Hispanics focuses on the implications of cultural values, at the same time acknowledging the large amount of variability within the Hispanic population.

In the final section, I draw conclusions about the research and make specific recommendations for counselors and researchers in working with and studying Hispanics.

GROUP DIFFERENCES IN CAREER-RELATED VARIABLES

Ten years ago, Phillips, Strohmer, Berthaume, and O'Leary (1983) wrote about the state of affairs in the career development of special populations. They lamented the lack of research in this area, although they noted a growing interest in cross-cultural vocational behavior and expressed concern that research designs be thoughtful and considered. They recommended that research seek both to describe career behavior and then to explain the behavior. The past decade has indeed seen a moderate growth in research of the career behavior of racial/ethnic groups, although much of the research is rather narrowly focused on the differences among minority groups on a particular variable. Little work has focused specifically on Hispanics, and an initial perusal of the literature results in an impression of a scattershot approach to answer the question, "Does Hispanic vocational behavior fit the models we have?" However, in the absence of a strong knowledge of Hispanic career behavior, initial research must be exploratory, and although the research reviewed in this chapter has not followed the excellent framework laid out by Phillips et al. (1983), it has not been totally atheoretical. Most of the studies on interests, for example, have focused on Holland's (1985) theory of vocational types. In addition to the assessment of interests, some researchers have investigated vocational aspirations, and others have examined the educational experiences of Hispanics in an attempt to explain the differences in educational attainment among minority group members.

Interests

Researchers investigating the applicability of interest assessment across cultures have used two methods. One has been to explore the similarity of interest patterns across cultures, usually comparing profiles or scale scores in two or more ethnic groups (e.g., Harrington & O'Shea, 1980). Others have studied the structure of interests across groups to determine the validity of the theoretical structure in various subgroups (e.g., Fouad, Cudeck, & Hansen, 1984).

Harrington and O'Shea (1980) presented intercorrelations among Career Decision-Making System (CDM; Harrington & O'Shea, 1976) subscales for four subgroups of Hispanics: Puerto Ricans, South Americans, Cubans, and Chicanos. Harrington and O'Shea used a validated Spanish translation of the CDM (which measures Holland's types) and found that the combined group correlations were very similar to intercorrelations measured by the Vocational Preference Inventory (VPI; Holland, 1965) for Whites. Intercorrelation matrices were not presented for the South American or Cuban samples (both samples were less than 30), but were presented for the Mexican American and Puerto Rican combined gender samples with similar results. Harrington and O'Shea were exemplary in their detailed presentation of the translation procedure for the CDM and in their delineation of the subgroups within the Hispanic population. They concluded that their data support the construct validity of the instrument with Spanish-speaking clients.

Turner and Horn (1975) investigated correlations between Guilford–Zimmerman Temperament Survey (Guilford & Zimmerman, 1949) and the Kuder Occupational Interest Survey-DD (KOIS; Kuder, 1968), which also explored gender differences. They assigned subjects to a Holland type and, using discriminant analysis, they differentiated among the six types on the basis of the Guilford–Zimmerman Temperament Survey. They used six types for men and three types for women. Fewer types were used for women because of small sample sizes within the codes of Realistic, Investigative, and Artistic. They were unable to differentiate the Conventional group for males from the other groups, but were able to do so for the other five types, finding personality types uniquely characterizing each group. Female types were not significantly discriminated, leading Turner and Horn to question the generalizability of Holland's types to Mexican-American women. Two general concerns with this research raise questions about any conclusions about women in the study, however. The first is the inadequate explanation of the assignment of Holland codes to occupations listed on the KOIS. How occupations are assigned to a Holland code will clearly affect the discrimination among types for women. The second and related concern is the restricted range of occupations for women in the study.

Montoya and DeBlassie (1985) compared Strong–Campbell Interest Inventory (SCII; Hansen & Campbell, 1985) General Occupational Theme and Introversion–Extroversion (I–E) scale scores between White and Hispanic college students. The authors found no differences between ethnic groups on any of the scales measured, but one gender difference: males scored higher on the Realistic theme, corroborating previous findings of gender differences in this theme (Hansen & Campbell, 1985). Although the authors' explanation of this difference as "due to the nature of the types of occupations listed under this theme, which call for a person to be rugged and physically strong in addition to working outdoors and typically with large machinery" (p. 287) is technically accurate, the impression left is gender stereotypic. The authors concluded that their results indicate that "Hispanics are becoming bicultural and combining their values with the values of the mainstream cultures" (p. 288). This is an extraordinary statement that goes beyond their data, because they did not report measuring acculturation or values.

Tomlinson and Evans-Hughes (1991) also found a gender difference on the Realistic theme in a study of group differences among Hispanics, African Americans, and Whites attending a summer orientation program. Hispanics were predominantly Puerto Rican and were the smallest group ($N = 14$) of the 77 subjects in the study. No differences were found across ethnic groups in a 2×3 ANOVA on General Occupational Theme scores, IE scores or on Academic Comfort (AC) scores. An interaction effect was found between gender and ethnicity for all these scales, such that African-American males scored higher on AC, more extroverted on the IE scale, and lower on the Artistic theme. Thus, the authors replicated the previously mentioned findings of similarity of scale scores between Hispanic and White groups.

Similarity of scale scores also has been investigated across national borders, specifically in Mexico. The findings of Fouad, Hansen, and Arias-Galicia (1986, 1989) may have some application to the Hispanic populations in the United States (Fouad & Hansen, 1987). Testing the hypothesis that vocational interests are more similar across cultures in areas based on natural, universal laws (e.g., math and science) than those interests based on human laws (e.g., teaching, management), they found that engineers were indeed more similar than lawyers across cultures (Mexico and the United States), and that similarity was greater within the occupational group than within the cultural group (Fouad, Hansen, & Arias-Galicia, 1986). Fouad and Hansen (1987), however, found that predictive validity was still quite high for both groups, concluding that the SCII may be transferred into Mexico for both occupations of Law and Engineering. Following up with an investigation of professional engineers, Fouad et al. (1989) found that engineers in Mexico and the United States were very similar on all scales related to the profession of Engineering, such as Realistic and Investigative General Occupational Themes, and the Mechanical Activities Basic Interest Scale. The groups differed, however, in their avocational interests, with Mexican engineers having much broader avocational interests. These findings support the similarity of Hispanic populations and Whites on various scales of the Strong Interest Inventory (SII).

A different approach to similarity of vocational interests has been taken by several investigators to determine the similarity in the structure of interests across ethnic groups. Specifically, these studies have examined the validity of Holland's (1985) theory, which has postulated a structure underlying interests. In this structure, six personality types are ordered around a hexagonal shape, with the assumption that adjacent types are more similar and types opposite each other on the hexagon are least similar.

Lamb (1976) found no differences across ethnic groups (Hispanic, African-American, and Asian college students were compared to Whites) in the structure of interests. Fouad et al. (1984) used confirmatory factor analysis in an investigation of the structural analysis of the English and Spanish forms of the SCII correlated .79 and concluded that the data fit Holland's (1985) model.

Fouad and Dancer (1992a), examining the structure of interests of the U.S. and Mexican professional engineers used in Fouad et al.'s study, found that the structure of interests is very similar across the two cultures.

Preliminary results of the investigation of interest patterns and the structure of interests for Hispanics and Whites indicate little differences in interests across these two ethnic groups. More study is necessary, however, to determine whether similarity is modified by SES, geographic region, acculturation of Hispanic individuals, or number of generations in the United States, among other variables. As Fouad and Dancer (1992a) noted, the continued use of interest inventories across cultures both within and outside the United States depends on the validity of the assumption that individuals across cultures view occupations and interests in the same way, as well as on the belief that the structure of interests is the same across cultures. They expanded on this issue in a response to a series of reactions to their 1992(a) paper (Fouad & Dancer, 1992b). In their response, they questioned whether Holland's theory is universal, or whether it "ethnocentrically define[s] the structure of interests by a White standard against which all deviations are abnormal" (p. 224).

Vocational Aspirations

A number of studies have investigated the vocational aspirations of His-panics. Arbona (1990) thoroughly reviewed the literature in this area, and I do not replicate her review of the early research on occupational aspi-rations, except to note that many early studies concluded that poor edu-cational and occupational achievement for Hispanics were related to their cultural values and fatalism, which has been refuted in later studies and does not adequately account for the impact of environmental barriers.

Arbona (1990) concluded her review of the aspiration literature for Hispanics by noting that their aspirations are high, but that there are mediating factors in their expectations of attaining their goals. Thus, help-ing children to aspire to a variety of occupational goals is not enough to influence their entry into those areas, because something occurs to keep them from expecting to reach their goals.

Two recent studies indicate that one of those factors may be self-efficacy. Lauver and Jones (1991) supported this in an investigation of perceived career options and self-efficacy in rural Native-American, White, and Hispanic 9th- and 11th-grade boys and girls. The authors found differences across ethnic groups in range of perceived career options and demon-strated that strength of self-efficacy and gender were significant predictors of range of perceived career options for Hispanic males and females.

In a well-designed study, Church, Teresa, Rosebrook, and Szendre (1992) also investigated the relationship between self-efficacy and occu-pational consideration in a study of minority high school equivalency students. They found a strong relationship among these variables, but found no differences due to ethnicity. They also found that interests, self-efficacy, and perceived incentives satisfaction predicted the range of occupations a student was willing to consider.

Although some have investigated self-efficacy in relation to occupational consideration and aspiration, Arbona (1989) investigated the reality of the labor market for Hispanics, demonstrating differences in level and type of work (coded by Holland type) across ethnic and gender groups. She found that Hispanics are overrepresented in low-level Realistic jobs and underrepresented in all other levels and types of work.

Arbona and Novy (1991) followed this up to examine the relationship between aspirations, expectations, and the reality of the labor market for Mexican-American, White, and African-American college students. Arbona and Novy found no ethnic or gender differences in type of careers to which students aspired, and only slight differences in career expectations. They did find a traditionally stereotypic trend for Mexican-American men and women, in that men aspired to and expected to work in primarily Realistic occupations more than did Mexican-American women, and the women aspired to and expected to work in Social and Conventional occupations more than Mexican-American men. An additional finding was that there was a stronger association between gender and expectations than there is between gender and aspirations, and that this association is higher for Mexican Americans than it is for Whites. Comparing the expectations of students in the study to the distribution of jobs in the labor market, Arbona and Novy found a close approximation. Thus, students may moderate their vocational aspirations with information about the labor market, particularly with the lack of available Hispanic role models in a variety of occupational areas.

Similar to Arbona and Novy's (1991) finding, gender differences in the stereotypic direction were also found for Hispanic girls and women by Frost and Diamond (1979), indicating that Hispanic girls may aspire to a restricted range of occupations. Frost and Diamond's findings for Hispanic girls were somewhat contradictory, in that Hispanic girls chose stereotypical female occupations (e.g., nurse, teacher) more than neutral or stereotypical male occupations (e.g., police officer), but they also found that Hispanic girls who stereotyped male children's jobs (e.g., mowing the lawn) were less likely to stereotype female adult jobs.

Dillard and his colleagues (Dillard & Campbell, 1981, 1982; Dillard & Perrin, 1980) investigated aspirations of Puerto Rican adolescents and adults, examining the influence of the parents on children, and examining the relationship between aspirations and values. Dillard and Perrin (1980) found no ethnic differences for females on career aspirations, but found that White boys had lower career aspirations than African-American or Puerto Rican boys. Dillard and Perrin also examined the contribution of SES to career aspirations, career expectations, and career maturity and found that it contributed 3.3%, 3.2%, and 5% of the variance to each of these variables, respectively, with higher SES related to higher levels on each variable.

Dillard and Campbell (1982) turned their attention to the career aspirations and values of Puerto Rican, White, and African-American adults. These participants were adult family members of Dillard and Perrin's study. No differences were found in career aspirations among women of different ethnic groups, but a statistically significant difference was found for men: African-American men had a higher level of career aspiration than White men. Puerto-Rican and African-American men and women had higher levels of career values than White men and women.

Fields (1981), Soto (1988), and Dillard and Campbell (1981) investigated the impact of parents' behavior on children's vocational aspirations. Dillard and Campbell (1981) put parental and children's data together to investigate the impact of parents' career behavior on their children's aspirations, and found a relationship between their mothers' aspirations and adolescents' aspirations. Thus, Dillard and Campbell's hypothesis that children expect to enter areas that their parents aspire for them may be true for these Puerto-Rican children.

Fields (1981), however, argued that much of the variance in the occupational aspirations of white-collar African-American and Mexican-American children will be explained by their parents' perceptions of opportunities. He found that ethnicity was related to mothers' perceptions and values, but not related to mothers' aspirations for children. He also found that occupational aspirations of children appear to be influenced by maternal aspirations and values differentially. Fields explained these findings in terms of acculturation, concluding that Mexican-American mothers do not pass their perceptions of limitations and frustrations to their children, rather fostering their children's belief in individual success and achievement. It should be noted that these are 1966 data in urban California. It is conceivable that a more current replication of this study may find different results.

Soto (1988) examined differences in home environment for higher and lower achieving Puerto-Rican children, focusing on parent's aspirations for themselves and for their children. Parental influence was clearly a factor in achievement for these children.

The literature reviewed previously indicates that Hispanic children often have higher aspirations than they do expectations of achieving those goals, but some research indicates that aspirations themselves may decline as individuals interact with environmental and institutional barriers. Holsinger and Chapman (1984) supported these findings in a longitudinal study on Mexican-American and White college students' occupational aspiration, finding a differential decline in aspiration, with more decline for Mexican Americans, and more decline for females than males. Hispanic students in the study experienced more educational barriers (e.g., nonacademic tracking) than did the Whites, and had lower achievement scores. The study did not control for SES, which may have confounded the results.

Portes, McLeod, and Parker (1978) investigated Hispanic male immigrant aspirations upon arrival to the United States and compared aspiration to occupational attainment for Hispanics of the same subgroup who were already U.S. residents. They found that Cuban and Mexican aspirations were similar to the distribution of employment of U.S. residents who were Cuban and Mexican American. Income aspirations were much higher than actual income attained by the U.S. residents. Education, English proficiency, and previous occupational attainment were predictors of aspirations. The authors (Portes et al., 1978) concluded that their findings contradict the popular notion that immigrants come to the United States with unrealistic expectations of "streets paved with gold," but rather the results support the "fundamental rationality with which aspirations for life in a new country are formulated" (p. 257). They also indicated that aspirations decline as individuals come face to face with the reality of life as an Hispanic immigrant.

The literature on the vocational aspirations of Hispanics indicates that aspirations of Hispanic adolescents and adults are as high, if not higher, than White or African-American adolescents and adults. There is a moderator variable, however, between career aspiration and career expectation in that Hispanic career expectations tend to be lower than aspirations. The moderator variable may perhaps be related to career self-efficacy, which in turn may be predicted to be related to parental aspirations and expectations, particularly maternal aspirations and occupational perceptions. The moderator variable could also be accurate perceptions of environmental and institutional barriers.

Educational Experiences

The past decade has seen a growth in the concern voiced about educational barriers for Hispanics (e.g., Olivas, 1986; Orum, 1986; Weyr, 1988). Documentation of the educational attainment—or lack thereof—of Hispanics has been thorough, and much literature has focused on possible or probable causes of the problems. Thomas and Gordon (1983) found that the link between educational attainment and occupational attainment is mediated by educational expectations and gender for Hispanics, and that this is true for Hispanics more than for African Americans and Whites. Nonetheless, the link between educational and occupational attainment is strong enough that the educational experiences of Hispanics are clearly relevant to their career development.

The most recent data from the 1990 census indicate some gains for Hispanics in educational attainment (U.S. Bureau of Census, 1991). The educational gains that Hispanics have accomplished are tempered, however, by comparison to non-Hispanic populations. Examination of more detailed educational data indicate that Hispanic children are more likely to be delayed a grade level or more than Whites (Orum, 1986), with 25% two or more years below grade level (Vincent & Orum, 1984). Forty-nine percent of Hispanics do not complete high school, and Orum (1986) indicated that many of those who drop out do so before 10th grade. Dropout rates vary widely by state and local conditions, but in some inner-city areas dropout rates are as high as 80% (Dryfoos, 1990).

Dryfoos cogently described the antecedents and consequences of dropping out of high school. Short-term consequences of leaving school include unemployment, low wages, depression, alienation, and delinquency. Long-term consequences include no entrance to the work force, low earnings, poor health, welfare dependency, marital instability, and later regrets and emotional cost.

The literature on vocational aspirations indicate that Hispanic children and their parents have high hopes for their futures, which is contraindicated for some by dropping out of high school. Whereas early studies blamed parental practices or cultural values (e.g., Evans & Anderson, 1973), more recent studies show that both individual and institutional factors interact to affect students leaving high schools before completion. Ortiz (1986) reported the High School and Beyond study as identifying personal factors affecting dropping out, such as high absenteeism, poor academic performance, pregnancy, suspensions, low parental involvement, or low self-esteem. Ochoa (1985) documented the multitude of environmental and institutional factors that contribute to noncompletion of high school, including "tracking," or the disproportionate placement of Hispanic students in low-ability groups or vocational programs, highly segregated schools, poor student–teacher interaction and low teacher expectations, poor perceptions by teachers of non-English speakers, and poor or no counselor interactions.

Consequences of dropping out of high school limit the choices of Hispanic students. Noncompletion obviously affects college entrance, but also limits entrance to the military, which has been an alternate avenue for White and African-American dropouts (Santos, 1986).

Hispanic students who do attend college are more likely to attend 2-year community colleges than 4-year institutions (Hickey & Solis, 1990; Santos, 1986). Hickey and Solis (1990) discussed a report commissioned by the Carnegie Foundation that examined the factors related to college selection, which included parental influence, proximity to family, economic situation of family, and financial aid. Ortiz (1986) indicated that although some students who enroll in 2-year institutions transfer to 4-year universities, Hispanic students are less likely to transfer than other students and are less likely to complete college than White students. Ortiz identified the lack of financial aid as one of the barriers to success in postsecondary education for Hispanics, as well as high school preparation and admissions testing.

The preceding factors related to overall educational attainment for Hispanic groups also applies to participation performance in math and science education, and the subsequent entry into math and science careers. Rendon (1985) described student- and institution-related factors in Mexican-American participation and achievement in math and science. The former category includes socioeconomic status, academic deficiencies, and student attitudes towards math and science. Hispanic groups tend to be less well prepared academically and, as discussed earlier, more likely to be "tracked" into a noncollege preparatory program. This is of particular concern in math and science areas, where some researchers have found that Hispanic students stop taking math and science courses in junior high (Valverde, 1984). In addition to factors for low rates of academic participation already discussed, Valverde also identified the problems of teaching math in a language in which the student is not familiar, using culturally inappropriate curricular material and instructional methods, poor teaching quality, and teaching to the same cognitive styles as sources of underachievement for Hispanics in math and science.

Some researchers have investigated noncurricular variables affecting math and science participation. Valverde (1984) identified lack of role models and mentors and poor counseling as possible reasons for underrepresentation of Hispanics in math and science areas, as well as discrimination and poor career information. Others have investigated science attitudes. Walker and Rakow (1985) investigated Hispanic youth's attitudes toward science, using data from the National Assessment of Educational Progress with a small sample of 9-year-olds, and larger groups of 13- and 17-year-olds over 5 years (1976–1981). They compared Hispanic (primarily Mexican-American) boys and girls to African-American and White youth, asking students their attitudes toward science classes, science teachers, science as a career, and the overall value of science. Hispanic women had the least favorable attitudes toward science in ages 9 and 13, with their unfavorable attitude continuing at age 17. Hispanic males and females remained relatively stable in their attitudes toward science classes, with males slightly higher than the national average, and females lower. Their attitudes toward science teachers increased between ages 13 and 17, with Hispanic females starting with the least favorable rating of all groups (54% favorable) and ending at age 17 close to the national average at 66%. It is not clear whether there is a selection of only those students who are currently in science classes, which would tend to distort the final results because Hispanic students in general take fewer science classes as they move through school. Interestingly, Hispanic females tended to feel more positively toward science careers from ages 13 to 17, whereas males felt less favorable. This trend for a gender difference across time was true for all ethnic groups.

Mestre and Royer (1992) took an interesting approach to the problem of underrepresentation of Hispanics in math and science. They reviewed studies that address the problem and concluded that language proficiency mediates complex cognitive tasks. This was corroborated by studies in which Hispanic students were more likely to exhibit linguistic errors than White students. They discussed the Science Verification Technique to measure reading and listening comprehension.

Math and science achievement may also be affected by factors that have been found to positively affect overall Hispanic educational achievement. These include cultural integration (Buriel, 1984; Chavez & Roney, 1990), higher SES (Nielson, 1986), and parental support, especially maternal support and involvement (Gandara, 1982). To gain more information on the attributes and concerns of minority students who have succeeded in high school, Kerr, Colangelo, Maxey, and Christensen (1992) examined the characteristics of academically gifted minority students. They analyzed the data from the top 5% of students who had taken the American College Testing (ACT) program college entrance assessment who were minority group members. They identified nearly 800,000 students, 2.5% (19,717) of whom identified themselves as Mexican American, and 1.1% of whom identified themselves as Puerto Rican/Hispanic (8,622). Kerr et al. (1992) noted the relationship between SES and education in the underrepresentation of Hispanic and African-American groups among the top 5% of ACT scorers. They found no significant differences due to ethnicity in choice of college major, although they expressed concern at the lack of interest in education as a major. Investigating the need for services expressed by students, they found that Hispanic and Mexican-American students were more interested in financial aid and employment, as well as in independent study and honors programs than majority students.

Review of the literature on educational experiences of Hispanics indicates that educators and policymakers need to review current practices to retain more Hispanic students in school and to more effectively promote their achievement. Ochoa (1985) recommended examining those policies that promote English monolingualism, that perpetuate views of cultural differences as deficits, and that support the suggestion that dominant values are superior to others. Rather, he recommended multilingual systems, cultural pluralism, all children having equal access to resources, and the use of testing to identify strengths rather than weaknesses. He also supported recognition of different learning styles, holding the staff accountable for grade-level proficiency for all students, and the incorporation of community and parent involvement into the curriculum and programs.

Gender Differences

Issues for Hispanic women have received an increasing amount of attention in the past decade. Casas and Ponterotto (1984) and Chacon, Cohen, and Strover (1986) pointed out that Chicanas are severely underrepresented in institutions of higher education and are at the lowest levels of occupational attainment and poverty. Casas and Ponterotto (1984) undertook an investigation to determine a profile of the "typical" Chicana attending college. They found she was in her mid- to late 20s, coming from a family of six, and she was not the oldest child. She was not married and was living with her family. She received "Bs" in high school and was maintaining that average in college. She identified her high school preparation as inadequate. She expressed concerns about financial resources. Casas and Ponterotto made the following recommendations to promote Chicana entry to and retention in college: financial aid, vigorous recruitment, supportive reentry programs, advising, support services specific for Chicanas, and task forces to change representation on campuses.

Chacon et al. (1986) conducted an in-depth study of the variables that affect Chicana progress in higher education. They found a major predictor of program progress (which they linked to eventual persistence in higher education) was amount of domestic labor that was differential by gender: Chicana women worked an average of twice as much in domestic activities as did men in the same marital category (single, married, married with children). Women who spent more hours in domestic activities were less likely to progress academically. They also found gender differences in parental support. Although the majority of students of both sexes reported support from both mothers and fathers, women reported more discouragement. Women also reported more stress than men due to financial concerns and feeling academically unprepared, supporting the concerns noted by Casas and Ponterotto (1984).

Vasquez (1982) also identified role conflict, financial aid, and admissions criteria as barriers to education for Mexican-American women. She recommended a variety of ways to facilitate greater retention in higher education, including role models, encouragement from parents, teachers, and counselors, and help in dealing with discrimination and isolation.

CAREER INTERVENTIONS

Career interventions are programs designed to increase specific career-related outcomes. Interventions may range from training in career decision making and problem solving, counseling, group test interpretation, or a variety of other strategies or techniques (Spokane, 1991). Outcomes may include increasing achievement in one or more curricular areas (e.g., math or science), changing attitudes toward work and schooling, increasing occupational knowledge and awareness, or helping students acquire specific skills such as job interviewing or resume writing.

Unfortunately, very few career interventions have focused specifically on Hispanic groups. Bowman (1993), in a review of career interventions with all racial/ethnic minorities, found fewer than 10 career interventions that used ethnic minority participants, and only one that focused specifically on Hispanics. Evans and Burck's (1992) finding that career education interventions have a positive effect on academic achievement is an indication of the potential impact of career interventions for Hispanics.

Rodriquez and Blocher (1988) investigated two interventions to increase the career maturity of Puerto Rican women. The control group was a regular college orientation program with no emphasis on career planning. Outcome measures were career maturity measured by the Career Development Inventory (CDI; Super, Thompson, Lindeman, Jordaan, & Myers, 1981) and locus of control measured by the Personal Orientation Inventory (Shostrum, 1974). They found that both interventions increased career maturity and produced a significant change to a more internal locus of control. They did not find differences between treatment groups, even though the Adkins program was specifically designed for a disadvantaged population. Fitzgerald and Rounds (1989) in their review of vocational literature for 1988 noted that, although Rodriquez and Blocher found no differences between treatment groups, the data did not indicate an increase in student career decision-making knowledge or skills.

Other career interventions have focused specifically on addressing the underrepresentation of Hispanics (and other minority populations) in math and science careers. Lockheed, Thorpe, Brooks-Gunn, Casserly, and McAloon (1985) reviewed programs designed to address gender and ethnic differences in math and science achievement for students in Grades 4 to 8. They concluded that little empirical work has focused on determinants of differences in math and science participation, and that much of the intervention work has emphasized nonintervenable factors rather than intervenable or policy-oriented factors. Their study expressed concern about the large number of studies that did not hold constant those variables known to be correlated with gender or ethnicity, such as the age difference between girls and boys in the same grade, and causal attribution of differences to factors uncorrelated with achievement. They found that the following factors positively affected math and science performance: enrollment in relevant classes, using the language with which students are comfortable, extracurricular experiences with math, technology, and science, hands-on activities, peer learning, and helping students to develop positive expectations.

One program has focused on developing career awareness and fostering self-efficacy in high school choice. Fouad (in press) designed an intervention (called *career linking*) to promote the math and science career awareness of a culturally diverse group of inner-city middle school students (24% were Mexican American). The intervention combined printed career information, speakers and role models, field trips, and curricular integration of career awareness. The program was found to increase student knowledge of careers, and students implemented that knowledge in choice of high school congruent with interests. Students performed better in math and science courses than a control group, but not enough to counteract an overall downward trend in grades from the beginning to the end of the year. Following up the students 2 years later, Fouad found that they had chosen different and more difficult math courses than the control group as sophomores in high school. This program did not involve extracurricular activities, nor did it incorporate enough adaptation of students' culture into the curriculum. Additional improvements would have been in promoting more parent involvement, and employing a control group in measuring the attitudinal variables.

A perusal of the literature indicates few additional descriptions of programs designed to promote math and science achievement and career awareness for Hispanic subgroups, and those few do not present outcome data on their programs. Undoubtedly, funded programs report outcome measures to funding agencies, but it is difficult to evaluate the overall programs without any quantitative measures on achievement, career maturity, knowledge acquisition, or skill development. Rendon (1985) described several intervention programs without referring to specific outcome data, although she recommended evaluating each program on a variety of dimensions. She identified key elements of successful models to promote math and science, and, although it is not specified how she determined a program was successful, it may be useful to briefly delineate those elements. She emphasized that a program should be central to the mission of the school, and that all faculty should be integrally involved in the program. She identified the most successful programs as those linking a school with a university, particularly in promoting precollege activities for students. The most successful programs appear to be those that work with younger children, particularly middle and elementary school-age youth, and those programs appear to target those students that are in the above-average-ability groups. Rendon cogently pointed out the need for programs to work with middle- and below-average-ability groups as well. Successful models incorporate Mexican-American history and experience into math and science curriculum, include hands-on activities, and have a literacy, communication, and computer-skills component. The student support component includes parental involvement, creates networks and peer tutoring, personalized counseling, role models, and includes remedial and enrichment opportunities.

Clearly, there is a strong need for increased career interventions with Hispanics. We must know if the process of career counseling that we have established with clients from the majority culture is appropriate with Hispanic clients. We need to know if we can effectively intervene institutionally to promote educational and occupational attainment.

CAREER COUNSELING WITH HISPANICS

The literature reviewed in the previous sections indicates that career counseling with Hispanics is neither guided by empirical evidence of strategies and techniques that have proven effective, nor by knowledge of how assessment tools work across cultures. Rather, career counselors working with Hispanics must have some knowledge of cultural values of Hispanics, and a sensitivity to the very large within-group variability on all dimensions. This section briefly discusses cultural values, assessment with Hispanic clients, and general concerns for career counselors.

A brief case study may help to illustrate some of the issues in working with a Hispanic client. Juana is a 15-year-old Mexican American, oldest daughter of six children. Her father is a sheet metal worker, and her mother died in escaping from Mexico. She is currently living with her father and stepmother, her siblings, and two half-siblings. She is struggling with what to do after high school. Her grades are excellent, although she is frequently absent from school when needed to babysit. She is expected to go home after school each day to care for the children, and her family has no expectations for her to go to any postsecondary schooling. She, however, would like to continue her education, if not at a university, at a vocational-technical school. She is not sure what she would like to do for a living, but has a sense that "there is more." She has a boyfriend, Mario (age 21), who wants to get married, but she feels she is too young.

Career counseling with Juana started with a discussion of how she felt about even asking the question "What should I be when I grow up?" She felt guilty for considering anything other than "ama de casa" (housewife). If she married Mario, she would be fulfilling her family's expectations, and Mario was making a good living as a mechanic so they could continue to help her family. But still, she felt she needed to do something else and finally decided she could continue with career counseling because maybe she could also work to help the family with money. Assessment results indicated she had high abilities in math, science, and perceptual abilities, with interests in the Realistic, Investigative, and Conventional themes. She agreed to explore occupations in nontraditional areas such as engineering and electronics technician, as well as in the traditional areas of secretary.

She returned to her counselor excited about engineering and electronics technician. This posed a real problem for her, though, because she was scared that she would not receive any support from her family or Mario, and she decided that she would not continue her schooling without their support.

Cultural Values

This case study brings out several cultural variables, many that may be related to Juana's Hispanic cultural values. Carter (1991) reviewed the literature on cultural values and concluded that there are, indeed, differences among cultures in value orientations, but that those differences between groups mask large within-group variation. Factors that may affect values within a group include demographic variables (such as age, SES, generational status, and/or education) and psychological variables (such as racial/ethnic identity). Nonetheless, awareness and knowledge of differences in cultural values will help counselors work with Hispanic clients.

Carter (1991) reviewed studies based on Kluckhohn and Strodtbeck's (1961) model of value orientations, in which they proposed that cultures differ on five dimensions: view of human nature (as evil, good, or mixed), relationship with nature (subjugation to nature, mastery over nature, or harmony with nature), time sense (present, future, past), activity (being, being-in-becoming, or doing), and social relations (lineal, collateral, individualism). Klukhohn and Strodtbeck (1961) and Szapocznik, Scopetta, Arannadle, and Kurtines (1978) found that the White middle-class U.S. culture is characterized by a mixed view of human nature, belief in mastery over nature, future time orientation, emphasis on doing, and emphasis on the individual. Investigators of the Hispanic culture have found that it differs from the U.S. mainstream culture on every dimension (Kluckhohn & Strodtbeck, 1961; Papajohn & Spiegel, 1975; Szapocznik et al., 1978). Papajohn and Spiegel found that Puerto Ricans believe that human nature is evil, which is not necessarily generalizable to all other Hispanic cultures, because the other two studies did not investigate that dimension. All three studies found that Hispanics believe that humans must live in harmony with nature, that one must live in the present rather than have a future orientation, that there is an emphasis on being rather than on doing, and that in social relations an individual's goals are subordinate to the group goals (collateral).

Marin and Marin's (1991) term for the collateral value is *allocentrism*. The impact of this value in career counseling may be a decreased emphasis on individual decision making. This was seen in Juana's case with the influence her family and Mario had on her decision. Career counselors who work with traditionally Hispanic clients may need to approach decision making from the perspective of a larger group, finding out the opinions of parents, family members, and so on. Not all Hispanic clients will approach decision making in this way, and some may be very interested in making individual career decisions that go against the group norm or expectation. However, even those clients who have chosen to adopt an approach to career decision making more similar to the dominant culture may face a clash in cultural values, and a sensitive counselor may help them resolve those conflicts.

Related to allocentrism is *familismo* or individuals' strong affiliation with their nuclear and extended families (Marin & Marin, 1991). This involves obligations to provide material and emotional support to the family. It also is typical that the first avenue for help (financial or emotional) is the family. Implications for the career counselor, again, may include the importance of familial perceptions on career choice. Career counselors also may find Hispanic clients placing more weight on familial issues than White clients in the final career-related decision, such as proximity to family or ability to support family members in choice of job. Juana, for example, considered the impact of her possible financial help for her family as an acceptable reason to pursue her options.

Also related to familismo and allocentrism is *simpatia* or the need to make relationships pleasant and smooth, and the need for social affiliations. Counselors will note a tendency for socially desirable responses, in an interview as well as on assessment instruments given (Marin & Marin, 1991). Clients may be uncomfortable with direct interpersonal confrontations and may avoid conflicts rather than address them. Juana was less likely to confront and contradict her family about her desires to continue her education. Rather, she clearly stated she would continue only if she had their support.

Respeto (respect) refers to the cultural value placed on appropriate deference paid to an individual's gender, generation, and role within the family network (Comas-Diaz, 1992; Sue & Sue, 1990). This may also refer to the hierarchical nature of relationships within the traditional Hispanic family. Traditionally, men, the elderly, and parents are given more authority. Children are "seen and not heard" and are typically not given a voice in decisions. This hierarchy is violated when children are asked to translate for parents because then children are given control of the information flow. Typically, counselors are granted respect and are seen as authority figures. Juana viewed her father, her future husband, and her counselor as sources of authority and was quite uncomfortable with the notion that she could make a decision by herself.

Gender roles were briefly discussed earlier in its impact on educational attainment for Hispanic women. One of the most often stereotyped views of the Hispanic culture is that of *machismo*, and the two standards of behavior held for men and women. *Machismo* is the term used to connote maleness, sexuality, and men as providers for their family (Comas-Diaz, 1992; Marin & Marin, 1991; Sue & Sue, 1990). The standard of behavior for men is one of considerable freedom, whereas women traditionally are expected to be submissive, passive, and dependent. However, these roles are changing, particularly with interaction with the mainstream White culture (Comas-Diaz, 1992). Counselors must be careful not to assume that clients will adopt a traditional view of gender roles. On the other hand, for those clients who do hold traditional gender-role ideologies, counselors must be careful that they not impose their own views of egalitarian relationships on their clients. Whether or not clients wish to change their gender roles are their own decision, and not their counselor's. As is the case when working with girls and women, though, counselors should work to increase an Hispanic female's awareness of her options, ensuring that she has information about nontraditional occupations as well. Counselors thus will give a client more knowledge on which she may make an informed choice. Counselors may also be called upon to help her sort out the consequences of her decision. Knowledge of some of the cultural values discussed here may help a counselor's awareness of some of those consequences. Juana's career counselor worked to encourage her to learn more about the nontraditional areas of engineering and electronics technician, but did not dissuade her from learning more about more traditional areas of clerical work.

In all the aforementioned cultural values, the adoption of the values for the client may depend in part on his or her level of acculturation. Acculturation is the process of becoming changed as a result of being in a new culture and may be viewed as the extent to which an individual changes: language use, cognitive style, personality, identity, attitudes, and stress (Marin & Marin, 1991). Acculturation has been shown to affect a wide variety of variables and will clearly affect the impact of traditionally Hispanic cultural values on an individual's behavior. It is extremely important that counselors incorporate acculturation as a variable in their work with Hispanic clients, and that they approach each individual without preconceived stereotypic notions.

Assessment

Assessment plays a large role in career counseling (Brown & Brooks, 1991). Career counselors may use assessment to help a client identify occupational interests, differentiate between vocational and avocational pursuits, explode occupational options under consideration, identify irrational beliefs, determine skills and abilities, clarify values, or determine interpersonal perceptions. Fouad (1993) delineated several issues of concern in using assessment across cultures. She discussed the impact of cultural variables on the assessment process, adopting Walsh and Betz's (1990) broad model of assessment: problem clarification, information gathering, understanding the problem, and coping with the problem. She also pointed out areas for counselors to consider in adopting an instrument for use with a population other than the population on which it was normed (e.g., using a standardized vocational interest inventory with a minority group member).

Specifically in using assessment tools with Hispanic clients, career counselors must evaluate the client's proficiency with English and determine whether a Spanish version of an instrument may be more appropriate. Spanish translations have been validated for the SII (Hansen & Fouad, 1984) and the CDM (Harrington & O'Shea, 1980), and other instruments may also report Spanish translations. Counselors must consult the manual of instruments they are adopting to determine if a translation exists, and, if so, how it was validated (Fouad, 1993). They must also consider test-taking response sets (Prince, Uemura, Chao, & Gonzales, 1991) which Marin and Marin (1991) indicated for Hispanics may be biased by social desirability. Counselors must determine if there are appropriate norms for use with Hispanic clients, or if they must use White norms. Prince et al. (1991) raised an interesting point in the need to determine the reference group of the client, asking the client to whom they should be compared: White or Hispanic. In other words, will the client be interested in knowing the answer to, Am I different from Hispanics (and which subgroup)? or Am I different from Whites? It is important to have studies of predictive validity to help answer both questions.

The role of assessment in counseling with Hispanic clients may be different than with White clients. Traditional Hispanic clients will not be amenable to a "three interviews and a cloud of dust" career-counseling process (opinions vary whether anyone is amenable to this approach). Rather, counselors must take care to explain the purpose of the instrument, and how it may be used to help clients explore various options. It is important that career counselors ask the client to whom, if anyone, he or she typically turns for help in making decisions, and what factors must be considered in making this decision. Clearly, in Juana's case, the assessment tools helped to point to some particular occupational areas, but career counseling also included helping Juana to work through her conflicts about her desires versus her family's expectations for her.

Juana's family did not encourage her to continue her education. Rather, they felt that it was important that she stay home to take care of her siblings until she got married. They did not encourage her to finish high school, but did not actively dissuade her either. Her boyfriend was encouraging her to finish high school, but not to go into "men's" work. Juana came back to her career counselor with great concerns about how to resolve this conflict between what she thought might be best for her future, and what she was being told at home and by Mario. Eventually, Juana and her career counselor worked together to help her sort out that she did want to continue her education after high school, and that she did want to go into an engineering program. Juana also worked with her career counselor and teachers at school to help convince her family that this decision would help her family in the long term, and that she would continue to live at home and maintain her responsibilities toward her siblings. She was granted a scholarship, is now in her junior year in electrical engineering at a large urban university, and has maintained a B grade-point average as of this writing. She continues to report, however, difficulty in juggling her responsibilities at home (babysitting and financial support) with her work at school. She has not continued her relationship with Mario because he did not like her decision, and she complains that she is somewhat lonely.

CONCLUSIONS AND RECOMMENDATIONS

The overwhelming conclusion that may be drawn from the literature reviewed on vocational interests, vocational aspirations, and educational achievement is that we do not know enough to make substantive statements about the career behavior of Hispanics. We do not know whether extant career theories fit for Hispanic groups and subgroups, we do not know whether a wide range of the instruments used in career counseling have the same meaning and interpretation for Hispanics, and we do not know if our assumptions about the relationships among various factors related to career decision making are appropriate for this population.

We may, however, draw a limited set of conclusions from the research conducted on the career behavior of Hispanics. Preliminary studies indicate that vocational interest inventories appear to be appropriately transferred from White population to the Hispanic population. Comparison of scale scores and intercorrelations among scales across cultures indicates similarity of scores across cultures. Also, structural analyses indicate that the underlying structure of interests is quite similar across White and Hispanic cultures.

Hispanic children have high vocational aspirations that are somehow moderated by self-efficacy, or realistic perceptions of opportunities, or by a discriminatory educational or occupational environment. The group's lack of high educational achievement is of great concern, particularly in the areas of math and science achievement. Concomitantly, the occupational achievement of Hispanics is disproportionately in unskilled and semiskilled Realistic areas for males and in Conventional areas for women. Unfortunately, the scant literature on career interventions give us little guidance in concrete remedies for these problems.

The literature points to some areas for recommended change. These are presented with an urgent plea that researchers turn their attention to assessing these recommendations:

1. Career counseling must take place within a cultural context. Counselors must become comfortable and knowledgable about their *own* values and ethnicity before competently working with clients of other cultures (Sue, Arrendondo, & McDavis, 1992). Clients bring their ethnic identity as well as their individual identities into counseling, and both must become a part of the counseling process. Hispanic clients will bring their cultural values to counseling with them. These values may be of the traditional Hispanic culture, but also may not be traditional. Counselors must be knowledgable enough and sensitive enough to incorporate individual values and cultural values without stereotyping the client. Leong (1993) called this "creative uncertainty," the need to be creative as we approach career counseling without certainty about the client's background and values. Thus, we have an uncertainty that is guided by our own knowledge and the client's willingness to tell us about the role culture plays for him or her.

2. The career counseling process must be flexible enough to incorporate familial and group-related variables, rather than a sole focus on individual factors in decision making.

3. Assessment tools must be evaluated for appropriateness in use across Hispanic cultures. Previous research may point to similarity in interests across cultures, but more research is needed to determine the limitations that may be due to acculturation, language proficiency, SES, geographic location, or generational status. Research also is needed on instruments assessing vocational maturity, work values, or personality variables.

4. More research is needed to determine effective career interventions. Underlying this is the need for knowledge about various contributing factors to educational and occupational attainment and choice. Do the same factors contribute to career choice for Hispanics? If the same factors contribute to career choice, do they contribute the same weight (e.g., do Hispanics place the same weight on values as Whites?)? Until we know what factors operate in career choice, we cannot design effective career interventions.

5. Immediate intervention is needed, however, to retain Hispanic students in school and to promote their selection of math and science courses.

This is particularly true of math courses that serve as *gatekeepers*: courses that are prerequisites for many technical school and university majors. Curricula that incorporate culturally appropriate strategies and techniques and hands-on activities that also infuse career awareness are strongly recommended. Also recommended are the creation of cohorts and fostering of cooperative learning that support Hispanic cultural values. Strong student support and parental involvement are strongly encouraged.

6. The preliminary literature on the relationship of self-efficacy to career choice indicates the need to help students' self-efficacy. Can we design effective interventions to increase self-efficacy?

7. Preliminary studies indicate that Hispanic students receive inadequate career counseling in high schools and colleges (Callejas, 1985; McKenna & Ortiz, 1988). Much more effort is needed to provide more culturally sensitive career counseling at all levels of education. This includes classroom guidance activities, individual counseling, and group counseling with a focus on career awareness, career exploration, and helping students develop culturally appropriate career decision-making skills. The latter will incorporate personal relationships and familial influences on current decision-making models. Career counselors may need to be multilingual to effectively deliver their services, and they may need to design new delivery methods (Prince et al., 1991). Research should also focus on the role that counselors play in "tracking" Hispanic students into noncollege preparatory classes, especially in math and science.

8. Counselors need to help Hispanics, particularly Hispanic females, explore a wide variety of careers and make particular efforts to increase their awareness of nontraditional careers.

These recommendations are not exhaustive, nor are they in any order of priority. The most critical conclusion is that we must examine the career behavior of Hispanics much more carefully. We cannot assume that career-counseling strategies and techniques developed for use with middle-class Whites will be effective with all populations. It is important, though, that as we research and study Hispanic career behavior we keep Phillips et al.'s (1983) recommendations in mind. We must first describe Hispanics' career behavior, then develop models to explain their career choices, which may then be tested empirically and refined.

Clearly, our agenda for the next decade is to demonstrate how models of career development, choice, and adjustment incorporate variables of culture, race, and ethnicity. Unless we begin to do this in a substantive way, our models will explain the career behavior of increasingly fewer members of the U.S. population.

REFERENCES

Arbona, C. (1989). Hispanic employment and the Holland typology of work. *The Career Development Quarterly, 37*, 257–268.

Arbona, C. (1990). Career counseling research and Hispanics: A review of the literature. *The Counseling Psychologist, 18*, 300–323.

Arbona, C., & Novy, D. M. (1991). Career aspirations and expectations of Black, Mexican American, and White students. *The Career Development Quarterly, 39*, 231–239.

Bowman, S. L. (1993). Career intervention strategies for ethnic minorities. *The Career Development Quarterly, 42*, 14–25.

Brown, D., & Brooks, L. (1991) *Career counseling techniques.* Boston: Allyn & Bacon.

Buriel, R. (1984). Integration with tradtional Mexican-American culture and sociocultural adjustment. In J. E. Martinez (Ed.), *Chicano psychology* (2nd ed., pp. 95–129). San Diego: Academic Press.

Callejas, J. J. (1985). *The career guidance and counseling of in-school Hispanics: Some practical theoretical considerations.* Paper presented at the annual conference of the American Vocational Association, Atlanta, GA.

Carter, R. T. (1991). Cultural values: A review of empirical research and implications for counseling. *Journal of Counseling and Development, 70*, 164–173.

Casas, J. M., & Ponterotto, J. G. (1984). Profiling an invisible minority in higher education: The Chicana. *The Personnel and Guidance Journal, 63*, 349–353.

Chacon, M. A., Cohen, E. G., & Strover, S. (1986). Chicanas and Chicanos: Barriers to progress in higher education. In M. A. Olivas (Ed.), *Latino college student* (pp. 296–324) New York,: Teachers College.

Chavez, J. M., & Roney, C. E. (1990). Psychocultural factors affecting the mental health status of Mexican American adolescents, In A. R. Stiffman & L. E. Davis (Eds.), *Ethnic issues in adolescent mental health* (pp. 73–91). Newberry Park, CA: Sage.

Church, A. T., Teresa, J. S., Rosebrook, R., & Szendre, D. (1992). Self-efficacy for careers and occupational consideration in minority high school equivalency students. *Journal of Counseling Psychology, 39*, 498–508.

Comas-Diaz, L. (1992). Counseling Hispanics. In. D. R. Atkinson, G. Morten, & D. W. Sue (Eds.), *Counseling American minorities: A cross-cultural perspective* (4th ed., pp. 245–264). Dubuque, IA: Brown.

Dillard, J. M., & Campbell, N. J. (1981). Influences of Puerto Rican, Black, and Anglo parents' career behavior on their adolescent children's career development. *The Vocational Guidance Quarterly, 29*, 139–148.

Dillard, J. M., & Campbell, N. J. (1982). Career values and aspirations of adult female and Male Puerto Ricans, Blacks, and Anglos. *Journal of Employment Counseling, 19*, 163–170.

Dillard, J. M., & Perrin, D. W. (1980). Puerto Rican, Black, and Anglo adolescents' career aspirations, expectations, and maturity. *The Vocational Guidance Quarterly, 28*, 313–321.

Dryfoos, J. G. (1990). *Adolescents at risk: Prevalence and prevention.* New York: Oxford University Press.

Evans, F. B., & Anderson, J. G. (1973). The psychocultural originals of achievement and achievement motivation: The Mexican-American family. *Sociology of Education, 46*, 396–416.

Evans, J. H., Jr., & Burck, H. D. (1992). The effects of career education interventions on academic achievement: A meta-analysis. *Journal of Counseling and Development, 71*, 63–68.

Fields, A. B. (1981). Some influences upon the occupational aspirations of three white-collar ethnic groups. *Adolescence, 16*, 663–684.

Fitzgerald, L. F., & Rounds, J. B. (1989). Vocational behavior, 1988: A critical analysis. *Journal of Vocational Behavior, 35*, 105–163.

Fouad, N. A. (1993) Cross-cultural vocational assessment. *Career Development Quarterly, 42.*

Fouad, N. A. (in press). Career linking: An intervention to promote math/science career awareness. *Journal of Counseling & Development.*

Fouad, N. A., Cudeck, R. A., & Hansen, J. C. (1984). Convergent validity of the Spanish and English forms of the Strong–Campbell Interest Inventory for bilingual Hispanic high school students. *Journal of Counseling Psychology, 31,* 339–348.

Fouad, N. A., & Dancer, S. L. (1992a). Cross-cultural structure of interests: Mexico and the United States. *Journal of Vocational Behavior, 40,* 129–143.

Fouad, N. A., & Dancer, S. L. (1992b). Rejoinder: Comments on the universality of Holland's theory. *Journal of Vocational Behavior, 40,* 220–228.

Fouad, N. A., & Hansen, J. C. (1987). Cross-cultural predictive accuracy of the Strong–Campbell Interest Inventory. *Measurement and Evaluation in Guidance, 20,* 3–10.

Fouad, N. A., Hansen, J. C., & Arias-Galicia, F. (1986). Multiple discriminant analysis of cross-cultural similarity of vocational interests of lawyers and engineers. *Journal of Vocational Behavior, 28,* 85–96.

Fouad, N. A., Hansen, J. C., & Arias-Galicia, F. (1989). Cross-cultural similarity of vocational interests of professional engineers. *Journal of Vocational Behavior, 34,* 88–99.

Frost, F., & Diamond, E. E. (1979). Ethnic and sex differences in occupational stereotyping by elementary school children. *Journal of Vocational Behavior, 15,* 43–54.

Gandara, P. (1982). Passing through the eye of the needle: High-achieving Chicanas. *Hispanic Journal of Behavioral Sciences, 4,* 167–179.

Guilford, J. P., & Zimmerman, W. S. (1949). *The Guilford–Zimmerman Temperament Survey: Manual of instruction and intepretation.* Beverly Hills, CA: Sheridan Supply.

Hansen, J. C., & Campbell, D. P. (1985). *Manual for the SVIV–SCII* (4th ed.). Stanford, CA: Stanford University Press.

Hansen, J. C., & Fouad, N. A. (1984). Translation and validation of the Spanish form of the Strong–Campbell Interest Inventory. *Measurement and Evaluation in Counseling and Development, 16,* 192–197.

Harrington, T. F., & O'Shea, A. J. (1976). *Manual for the Harrington/O'Shea System for career decision-making.* Moravia, NY: Chronicle Guidance.

Harrington, T. F., & O'Shea, A. J. (1980). Applicability of the Holland (1973) model of vocational development with Spanish-speaking clients. *Journal of Counseling Psychology, 27,* 246–251.

Hickey, C. A., & Solis, D., (1990). *The recruitment and retention of minority trainees in university affiliated programs—Hispanics* (M. L. Kuehn, Ed.). Madison: University of Wisconsin-Milwaukee.

Holland, J. L. (1965). *Manual for the Vocational Preference Inventory.* Palo Alto, CA: Consulting Psychologists Press.

Holland, J. L. (1985). *Making vocational choices: A theory of vocational personalities and work environments* (2nd ed.). Englewood Cliffs, NJ: Prentice-Hall.

Holsinger, D. B., & Chapman, D. (1984). Students' aspirations and choice of college type. *College Student Journal, 18,* 87–93.

Kerr, B., Colangelo, N., Maxey, J., & Christensen, P. (1992). Characteristics of academically talented minority students. *Journal of Counseling & Development, 70,* 606–609.

Kluckhohn, F. R., & Strodtbeck, F. L. (1961). *Variations in value orientations.* Evanston, IL: Roe Paterson.

Kuder, G. F. (1968). *Occupational Interest Survey: General manual.* Chicago: Science Research Associates.

Lamb, R. R. (1976). *Validity of the American College Testing Inventory for minority group members* (American College Testing Res. Rep. 72). Iowa City, IA: American College Testing Program.

Lauver, P. J., & Jones, R. M. (1991). Factors associated with perceived career options in American Indian, White, and Hispanic rural high school students. *Journal of Counseling Psychology, 38,* 159–166.

Leong, F. T. L. (1993). The career counseling process with racial/ethnic minorities: The case of Asian Americans. *Career Development Quarterly, 42,* 26–40.

Lockheed, M. E., Thorpe, M., Brooks-Gunn, J., Casserly, P., & McAloon, A. (1985). *Understanding sex/ethnic related differences in Mathematics, Science and Computer Science for students in grades four to eight.* Princeton, NJ: Educational Testing Service.

Marin, G., & Marin, B. V. (1991). Research with Hispanic populations. *Applied Social Research Methods Series* (Vol. 23). Newbury Park, CA: Sage.

McKenna, T., & Ortiz, F. I. (Eds.). (1988). *The broken web: The educational experiences of Hispanic American women.* Encino, CA: Floricanto Press.

Mestre, J. P., & Royer, J. M. (1992). Cultural and linguistic influences on Latino testing. In G. D. Keller, J. R. Deneen, & R. J. Magallan (Eds.), *Assessment and access: Hispanics in higher education.* New York: State University of New York.

Montoya, H., & DeBlassie, R. R. (1985). Strong–Campbell Interest Inventory comparisons between Hispanic and Anglo college students: A research note. *Hispanic Journal of Behavioral Science, 3,* 285–289.

Nielsen, F. (1986). Hispanics in high school and beyond. In M. A. Olivas (Ed.), *Latino college students* (pp. 71–103). New York: Teachers College Press.

Ochoa, A. (1985). Problems of access to higher education for students of non-White ethnic backgrounds. *Excellence Through Equity, 2,* 20–25.

Olivas, M. A. (1986). *Latino college students.* New York: Teachers College Press.

Orum, L. S. (1986). *The education of Hispanics: Status and implications.* Washington, DC: National Council of La Raza.

Ortiz, V. (1986). Generational status, family background, and educational attainment among Hispanic youth and non-Hispanic White youth. In M. A. Olivas (Ed.), *Latino college students* (pp. 29–46). New York: Teachers College Press.

Papajohn, J. C., & Spiegel, J. P. (1975). *Transactions in families.* San Fransisco: Jossey-Bass.

Phillips, S. D., Strohmer, C., Berthaume, B. L. J., & O'Leary, J. C. (1983) Career development of special populations: A framework for research. *Journal of Vocational Behavior, 22,* 12–29.

Portes, A., McLeod, S. A., Jr., & Parker, R. N. (1978). Immigrant aspirations. *Sociology of Education, 51,* 241–260.

Prince, J. P., Uemura, A. K., Chao, G. S., & Gonzales, G. M. (1991). Using career interest inventories with multicultural clients. *Career Planning and Adult Development Journal, 7,* 45–50.

Rendon, L. I. (1985). *Preparing Mexican Americans for mathematics—and science-based fields: A guide for developing school and college intervention models.* Las Cruces: New Mexico State University Press.

Rodriguez, M., & Blocher, D. (1988). A comparison of two approaches to enhancing career maturity in Puerto Rican College women. *Journal of Counseling Psychology, 35,* 275–280.

Santos, R. (1986) Hispanic high school graduates: Making choices. In M. A. Olivas (Ed.), *Latino college students* (pp. 104–130). New York: Teachers College Press.

Shostrum, E. L. (1974). *Personal Orientation Inventory.* San Diego: Educational and Industrial Testing Service.

Soto, L. D. (1988). The home environment of higher and lower achieving Puerto Rican children. *Hispanic Journal of Behavioral Sciences, 20,* 161–167.

Spokane, A. R. (1991). *Career intervention.* Englewood Cliffs, NJ: Prentice-Hall.

Sue, D. W., Arrendondo, P., & McDavis, R. J. (1992). Multicultural counseling competencies and standards: A call to the profession. *Journal of Multicultural Counseling and Development, 70,* 477–486.

Sue, D. W., & Sue, D. (1990). *Counseling the culturally different: Theory and practice* (2nd ed.). New York: Wiley.

Super, D. W., Thompson, A. S., Lindeman, R. H., Jordaan, J. P., & Myers, R. A. (1981). *Career Development Inventory*. Palo Alto, CA: Consulting Psychologists Press.

Szapocznik, J., Scopetta, M. A., Arannadle, M. A., & Kurtines, W. (1978). Cuban value structure: Treatment implications. *Journal of Consulting and Clinical Psychology, 46,* 961–970.

Thomas, G. E., & Gordon, S. A. (1983). Evaluating the payoffs of college investments for Black, White, and Hispanic students (Rep. No. 344). Baltimore: Johns Hopkins University, Center for Social Organization of Schools.

Tomlinson, S. M., & Evans-Hughes, G. (1991). Gender, ethnicity, and college students' responses to the Strong–Campbell Interest Inventory. *Journal of Counseling & Development, 70,* 151–155.

Turner, R. G., & Horn, J. M. (1975). Personality correlates of Holland's occupational types: A cross cultural study. *Journal of Vocational Behavior, 6,* 379–389.

U.S. Bureau of Census. (1991). *The Hispanic population in the United States*. Washington, DC: U.S. Government Printing Office.

Valverde, L. A. (1984). Underachievement and underrepresentation of Hispanics in mathematics and mathematics-related careers. *Journal for Research in Mathematics Education, 15,* 123–133.

Vasquez, M. J. T. (1982). Confronting barriers to the participation of Mexican-American women in higher education. *Hispanic Journal of Behavioral Sciences, 4,* 147–165.

Vincent, A., & Orum, L. S. (1984). *Selected statistics on the education of Hispanics* (Hispanic Statistic Services Report No. 6). Washington, DC: National Council of La Raza.

Walker, C. L., & Rakow, S. J. (1985). The status of Hispanic American students in science: Attitudes. *Hispanic Journal of Behavioral Sciences, 7,* 225–245.

Walsh, W. B., & Betz, N. E. (1990). *Tests and assessment* (2nd ed.). Englewood Cliffs, NJ: Prentice-Hall.

Weyr, T. (1988). *Hispanic USA: Breaking the melting pot*. New York: Harper & Row.

Career Assessment and Intervention With Asian Americans

Frederick T. L. Leong
The Ohio State University

Ruth H. Gim-Chung
Pomona College

In providing information about career assessment and intervention with Asian Americans, this chapter is divided into two sections. The first section is concerned with career assessment with Asian-American clients. Existing research on career assessment with Asian Americans is reviewed, and the problems and general guidelines for conducting career assessment with Asian Americans is presented. The second section discusses the process and outcome issues involved in providing career interventions for Asian Americans.

CAREER ASSESSMENT

Career assessment as a prelude to intervention has typically focused on several related dimensions such as career development, career interests, values, needs, and personality. This section of the chapter discusses the issues and problems in the assessment of those five dimensions as they pertain to Asian Americans.

Assessment of Career Maturity

Research on career choice and development has been dominated by three major theoretical perspectives: (a) the person–environment interaction model as exemplified by Holland's model, (b) the developmental approaches as exemplified by Super's theory, and (c) social learning approaches as delineated by Krumboltz and Mitchell (see Brown & Brooks, 1990). Within the developmental perspective, the level and correlates of career maturity has been the most researched construct. Crites (1978) defined career maturity as having definite career choices, making consistent choices over time, and making choices that are realistic.

In a study examining the differential career development attributes of Asian-American and European-American college students, Leong (1991) used the Crites's (1973) career maturity inventory (CMI): attitude scale; Harren's (1978) assessment of career decision-making (CDM) style subscale; and Holland, Daiger, and Power's (1980) my vocational situation (MVS) on a sample of 83 European-Americans (46% male and 54% female) and 63 Asian-Americans (38% male and 62% female) college students. The Asian Americans were primarily of Chinese and Korean descent. The Asian Americans exhibited higher levels of dependent decision-making styles than European Americans. Asian Americans also scored lower on career maturity. There were no significant cultural differences for vocational identity. Asian-American college students, when compared to their Euro-American peers, do show some significant differences on career development attributes and occupational values. These differences could be due to the Asian-American culture placing a greater emphasis on a collectivistic orientation in decision making and could possibly be influenced by the acculturation process.

Although Holland's theory focused primarily on career choice and not career development, he also developed with colleagues a measure of vocational identity that is a construct similar to Super's concept of career maturity. Holland et al. (1980) defined vocational identity as an awareness of and the ability to specify one's own interests, personality characteristics, strengths, and goals as they relate to career choices. Fretz and Leong (1982) have found that the CMI (attitude subscale) and MVS (which measures Holland's vocational identity levels) are moderately correlated ($r = .43$). In a different college sample, Leong and Morris (1989) found that the CMI and the Vocational Identity scale of the MVS were highly correlated ($r = .69$). No study has yet examined the correlation between these two measures among Asian Americans. Interestingly, whereas Leong (1991) found that Asian Americans were significantly lower than European Americans in career maturity, no significant ethnic differences were found in vocational identity. How two different measures of career development can provide different results for Asian Americans points to the complexity of assessing career development as well as the potential influence of cultural differences in either the measures themselves, the construct, or both.

The major implication of this study for counseling is that Asian Americans do seem to have differential career development attributes when compared to European Americans. Career counselors need to be mindful that Asian Americans may have preferences for different decision-making processes and may on the surface appear less "career mature" than European Americans. However, it should also be recognized that most of the career maturity models and measures have been developed from a Euro-American middle-class value orientation that may not be appropriate for Asian Americans. Future research on the career development attributes of Asian Americans needs to examine this pattern of results and more directly test cultural differences in career decision-making styles and career maturity levels.

Assessment of Career Interests

Since the 1970s, there has been only a handful of studies on career interest patterns of Asians Americans with psychometrically validated instruments. In a review of the literature on the career development of Asian Americans, Leong (1985) was able to identify only three published empirical articles and one dissertation related to the career interest of Asian Americans. In the first study of Chinese Americans at University of California, Berkeley, consisting of the School and College Ability Tests (SCAT), the Strong Vocational Interest Blank (SVIB), and the Omnibus Personality Inventory (OPI), Sue and Kirk (1972) found that Chinese-American males showed more interest in physical sciences, skilled technical trades, and business occupations than all other males. They tended to be less interested in social service and welfare, sales or business contact, and verbal/linguistic occupations. The Chinese-American males' vocational interests appeared more masculine than all other males. Also, Chinese-American males seemed to aspire to a lower level of occupational status and responsibility.

Generally, Chinese-American females were more oriented toward the domestic occupations. Besides this, Chinese American females exhibited more interest in technical-applied fields, biological and physical sciences, business and clerical activities, and less interest in aesthetic/cultural fields, social sciences, and verbal-linguistic vocations. Chinese-American students were less oriented to theoretical, abstract ideas and concepts and tended to evaluate ideas on the basis of their immediate practical application more than did all other students. Chinese-American males did not differ from all other males in interest in scientific activities employing logical, analytical, and critical thinking. Chinese-American females, however, scored much lower on this dimension.

In the second study that focused on both Chinese and Japanese Americans, Sue and Kirk (1973) found a similar pattern of vocational choice between the two groups of Asian-American men. The exception was that the Japanese-American men did not express greater interest than did Euro-American men in physical sciences or lower interest in the social sciences. In addition, Japanese-American women did not express greater interest than did Euro-American women in domestic fields. The authors explained these differences between the Chinese- and Japanese-American participants as differential rates of acculturation and assimilation into American society, with the Japanese Americans having a higher rate of acculturation.

In the third study, using a typological analysis of the same Chinese- and Japanese-American men who participated in the study discussed earlier, Sue and Frank (1973) found that these students clustered into groups with characteristics quite different from those of Whites. They confirmed the findings of the other two studies and concluded that those occupations that require "forceful self-expression, interaction with people, and communication in oral or written form" are the ones that Asian Americans feel most uncomfortable with and are most likely to avoid, given their preferences for "structured, logical, concrete and impersonal" work activities (p. 141).

The results of Sue and Kirk's study regarding the career interest patterns of Asian Americans have yet to be replicated with a larger and more representative sample of Asian Americans. It would also be important to cross-check these patterns with Asian-American samples from other parts of the country because all these previous studies have been limited to California. A replication would also allow us to determine if the interest patterns found by Sue and Kirk in the 1970s have held consistent across the years or if there have been significant shifts over the two decades.

In an unpublished dissertation on career development of Asian Americans, Kwak (1980) also examined the vocational interests of Asian-American youths, using Holland's Self-Directed Search (SDS; 1974). He found that the Asian-American students revealed vocational types predominantly in the investigative (25.8%) and social (25%) categories. In another unpublished study, Leong (1982) used the Vocational Preference Inventory (VPI) to assess interests patterns within Holland's model and found that Asian-American students at the University of Maryland had measured interests patterns that were predominantly in the investigative (30%) and social (21%) areas. These results are consistent with Kwak's (1980) earlier study. More recently, Leung, Ivey, and Suzuki (in press) used an occupations list (155 occupations) that was categorized according to Holland's classification system and found that Asian Americans were more likely than European Americans to have considered Investigative occupations and less likely to have considered Enterprising occupations. No ethnic differences were found for Social occupations.

Interestingly, when Leong (1982) examined the Asian-American students' expressed interests (i.e., what career fields they say they are interested in pursuing) in contrast to the measured interests (what the VPI said they were interested in), a different picture emerged. Over 50% of the Asian-American students reported interest in Investigative careers (versus 30% measured interests) and only 7% expressed interest in Social careers (versus 21% measured interests). This discrepancy between measured and expressed interest among Asian-American students is a significant clinical phenomena worthy of further investigation.

In a technical report by the American College Testing (ACT) service, Lamb (1976) analyzed the structural validity of Holland's model of career interests for the four ethnic minority groups including Asian Americans. He found that the hexagonal structure was consistent across all the minority groups with the exception of the Native-American group. In other words, the internal structure of Holland's model was the same for Asian Americans as for White, African-American, and Hispanic-American high school students. Unfortunately, this study was based on a relatively small sample of Asian Americans ($n = 102$).

Another approach to understanding the career interests of Asian Americans would be to examine the courses they take and the academic majors they choose while in high schools. Data from a recent National Science Foundation (NSF; 1990) report indicated that:

Fully twice the proportion of Asian Americans as European Americans had a calculus course while in high school: 36 percent versus 18 percent. Asian Americans were also more apt to have been in honors math courses.... Whereas almost all students had taken biology, Asian Americans reported taking a chemistry or physics course more often than European Americans. (p. 41)

As for intended undergraduate major, Asian Americans were twice as likely to choose an engineering discipline. Within the sciences, Asian Americans tended more toward biology and computer science than European Americans. Asian Americans' greater interest in scientific majors was also paralleled by a high level of educational aspiration. More than 2 out of every 5 Asian-American freshmen planned their highest degree to be either a doctorate or a medical degree compared to 1 of 5 European Americans (NSF, 1990, p. 43).

According to the NSF (1990) report:

Coincident with their higher degree aspirations, over one-third of Asian American freshmen plan to become either engineers or physicians; this fraction compares to only about a tenth of European Americans. Among other careers, Asian Americans choose elementary or secondary teaching as their probable profession to a much lesser extent than do European Americans: 2 percent versus 9 percent. (p. 43)

Assessment of Occupational Values

On the whole there has also been a lack of empirical studies on the work values of Asian Americans. In an early dissertation, Tou (1974) compared the work value orientations of Chinese-American and Euro-American seventh- and eighth-grade students in Catholic schools and designed a career intervention. Using Super's (1970) work values inventory she found that cultural influences were associated with the Chinese-American students' work value orientations. The intervention involved administering the SDS in an attempt to increase the Chinese Americans' awareness of work value alternatives. A small increase in awareness was produced, but it was not statistically significant.

In a more recent study, Leong and Tata (1990) conducted a study to determine what work values were important to Chinese-American children. The relation between the Chinese-American children's level of acculturation and work values was also examined. Gender differences in work values among Chinese-American fifth and sixth graders were studied as well. In this study, 177 Chinese-American fifth and sixth graders in a Los Angeles inner-city elementary school were given the Ohio work values inventory (OWVI) and the Suinn-Lew Asian self-identity acculturation scale (SL-ASIA). The OWVI yields scores on 11 scales. The two most important values for Chinese-American children were money and task satisfaction. Object orientation and solitude appeared to be of considerably lower importance. Boys valued object orientation, self-realization, and ideas/data more than did girls. Girls valued altruism more than did boys. These sex differences may represent non-culture-specific gender differences in work values. The Chinese-American children were also divided into three groups according to their SL-ASIA scores: the low-acculturation group, the medium-acculturation group, and the high-acculturation group. Significant acculturation differences were found for only self-realization. Highly acculturated Chinese-American children valued self-realization more than low-acculturation Chinese-American children. Self-realization seems to be more a part of the Euro-American than the Chinese-American culture.

Knowledge of this pattern of occupational values among Chinese-American children can serve as advance organizers for counselors who help this group of minority children with their career planning. The challenge lies in broadening the occupational options for Chinese-American children while still respecting their cultural values, which may underlie their occupational values.

In another study that examined both career development variables and occupational values Leong (1991) used Rosenberg's (1957) occupational values scale to compare the work values of 83 European-American (46% male and 54% female) and 63 Asian-American (38% male and 62% female) college students. The results related to the career development variables were discussed previously. In terms of values, following the pattern used by Rosenberg (1957), clusters of occupational values were formed for analyses in the study: the Social cluster, the Extrinsic cluster, the Self-Expression cluster, the Power cluster, and the element of Security. The comparison of the two racial/ethnic groups revealed that Asian Americans showed significant differences in terms of placing greater emphasis on the Extrinsic values than European Americans. Asian Americans also significantly valued more Security than European Americans. Hence, Asian-American college students, when compared to their Euro-American peers, do show some significant differences on occupational values. These differences could be because of the Asian American's culture placing greater emphasis on pragmatism, a collectivistic orientation in decision making, and a mindset influenced by the immigration experience. The major implication of this study for counseling is that Asian Americans do seem to have differential occupational values when compared to European Americans. Career counselors need to find ways of using a sufficiently structured approach that is mindful of the occupational values of Asian Americans. Asian-American clients may not appreciate counselors who directly or indirectly promote the use of a more intrinsic set of work values that guide their career decision making.

In a more recent study, Gim (1992) used Nevill and Super's (1986) Values Scale to compare Asian Americans, African Americans, Chicanos, and European Americans. She found significant ethnic differences in Material and Work environment value scales (from factor analyses), with Asian Americans placing a higher value on Material than European Americans. This finding is consistent with Leong and Hayes's (1990) study using the Rosenberg occupational values scale, although the factor scales are not identical (Material versus Extrinsic Values). Gim (1992) also found that the Work environment was more important for Asian Americans than for European Americans.

Assessment of Personality Variables

In a review of the literature on the career development of Asian Americans, Leong (1985) noted that there were three personality variables that were repeatedly referred to in various studies concerning the vocational behavior of Asian Americans. These three personality variables were locus of control, social anxiety, and intolerance of ambiguity. With regard to locus of control, different studies have pointed out that Asian Americans tend to be less autonomous, more dependent , and more obedient to authority (Meredith, 1966; Sue & Kirk, 1972, 1973) Meredith's study (1966), which used the 16 Personality Factor Questionnaire, found that Japanese-American students were more "submissive, diffident, and regulated by external realities" than Euro-American students.

Relatedly, Sue and Kirk (1972) administered the Omnibus Personality Inventory to 236 Chinese-American students and found that they were significantly more conforming and socially introverted than Euro-American students. They went on to suggest that this high level of conformity may be due to the traditional Chinese cultural values of respect for authority and submergence of individuality. These findings suggest that Asian Americans, or at least Chinese and Japanese Americans, are more externally oriented in terms of how they view issues of control and reinforcement. In fact, Hsieh, Shybut, and Lotsof (1969) had already discovered that Chinese Americans do score higher on Rotter's locus of control scale (i.e., more external) than European Americans. As suggested by Leong (1985), if indeed Asian Americans have an external locus of control, it could certainly affect not only their career decision-making style but also the nature and scope of their career choices.

Social anxiety was the second personality characteristic that Leong (1985) had identified as a converging theme within the literature. Besides clinical impressions that Asian Americans are more emotionally withdrawn, socially isolated, and verbally inhibited (Bourne, 1975; Sue & Sue, 1974), various empirical studies using objective and standardized personality instruments have found that Asian Americans do experience a greater degree of social anxiety. Sue and Sue (1974), in an MMPI comparison of Asian-American and Euro-American students, found that the former exhibit greater social introversion.

In another study using the omnibus personality inventory, Sue and Kirk (1972) found that Chinese-American students were significantly more inhibited, more impersonal in their interpersonal relations, and appeared less socially concerned with other people. In a related study using the same database, Sue and Kirk (1973) found a similar pattern of social introversion and withdrawal among both Chinese- and Japanese-American samples. They concluded that the social discomfort experienced by these Asian-American students may be due to conflict between the informal nature of social relationships within American culture and their own more formal and traditional cultural values.

Leong (1985) also found that Fenz and Arkoff (1962) provided additional confirming data on this social anxiety/discomfort phenomenon among Asian Americans. Administering the Edwards personal preference schedule (EPPS) to their subjects, Fenz and Arkoff (1962) found that both

Chinese and Filipino Americans (and to a lesser extent Japanese Americans) scored higher on the deference and abasement scales than European Americans. The Asian ethnic groups also scored lower on the exhibition and aggression scales. In a later study that also used EPPS with Japanese and European Americans as subjects, Connor (1975) found that the former exhibited greater need for deference, order, and abasement.

Sue (1975), in his chapter in Picou and Campbell's book, *Career Behavior of Special Groups*, already pointed out the relevance of Asian Americans' social anxiety to their career aspirations and plans. Sue (1975) observed that Asian Americans tend to withdraw from social contacts and responsibility. Sue (1975) went on to assert that the tendency of Asian Americans to choose occupations in the physical sciences and technical trades may be due to this social anxiety, discomfort, and inhibition. In any event, Sue noted that Asian Americans are underrepresented in the social sciences and other vocations that require verbal/persuasive skills and high levels of social interaction, such as law and psychology.

Recently, Leung et al. (in press) tested these themes in the personality-career literature identified with a sample of 149 Asian-American college students. By having these students rate a list of occupations according to whether they have ever considered each of them, Leung et al. (in press) found partial support for what they labeled the "personality structure hypothesis." The 155 occupations on the list were categorized according to Holland's classification. They found that Asian Americans were more likely than European Americans to have considered Investigative occupations and less likely to have considered Enterprising occupations. No significant ethnic differences were found for the other Holland types. The authors interpreted the lack of differences in the remaining types, especially in Social-type occupations, as providing only partial support because they were expecting the Asian Americans to be less interested in Social occupations than European Americans. However, this test of the personality structure hypothesis was limited by the fact that Holland's single-code classification system is too broad to capture the potential cultural differences and to test the hypothesis directly. For example, in terms of testing the social anxiety hypothesis among Asian Americans (Leong, 1985), Holland's single-code Social category consists of jobs that involve a great deal of social interaction (e.g., nurse, counselor, social worker) as well as jobs with only moderate amounts of social contact (e.g., cook, dog catcher, and editorial assistant).

Besides the personality dimensions identified by Leong (1985), Hsia (1980) also discussed the role of a field-independent cognitive style among Asian Americans in the occupational segregation and limited occupational mobility among Asian Americans. She noted that given their field-independent orientation, Asian Americans were much more likely to be limited to scientific and technical careers and were not likely to be successful in the people-oriented occupations, such as managerial and administrative positions that require the more field-dependent cognitive style. The relationship between field-dependence–independence and occupational choices has already been examined and the evidence supports Hsia's observation, and her hypothesis is definitely worthy of further exploration with various Asian-American samples. Her observation about cognitive style and career choices also points to the need to examine the role of cognitive styles in the career choices and behaviors of Asian Americans.

Some of the data from personality inventories already provide some support for her and Leong's (1985) hypotheses about personality variables' influence on the career behavior of Asian Americans. For example, the Sue and Frank study (1973), which was done on 69% of entering freshman males at Berkeley in California in the fall of 1966, found that Asian males leaned toward occupations encompassing routine, business-detail activities. They were overrepresented in engineering and underrepresented in the social sciences. Asian-American men tended to score low in autonomy, and they tended to be more conforming, more obedient to authority, and more connected to familial control. They tended to dislike ambiguity. They also experienced strong feelings of isolation, loneliness, and rejection.

Similarly, Sue and Kirk (1972) found that Japanese-American students were less oriented to theoretical, abstract ideas and concepts than Euro-American students. Japanese-American students also tended to dislike ambiguity in favor of structured situations. They were likely to evaluate ideas based on immediate practical applications and were more socially conforming.

In a study examining the influence of the gender-role identity and occupational attainment of Asian-American women's psychological well-being, Chow (1987) tested three hypotheses: (a) both masculine and androgynous Asian-American women would have a higher level of occupational attainment than those with feminine and undifferentiated gender-role identity; (b) androgynous Asian-American women would have a higher level of self-esteem and greater work satisfaction than those with other gender-role identities; and (c) the higher the level of occupational attainment secured by Asian-American women, the higher their level of self-esteem and work satisfaction. A survey of 161 Asian-American women (Chinese, Japanese, Korean, and Filipino) were rated for occupational attainment, work satisfaction, and self-esteem. Most of the subjects were employed full time and information was obtained through the BSRI, the Self-Esteem scale, and interviews. The results of the study supported all three of the hypotheses just stated. Chow also questioned Bem's assertion that androgyny benefits behavioral adaptivity and personal competence because it was masculinity and not androgyny that was linked to the greatest occupational attainment among Asian-American women. However, this study points to androgyny as being a positive and healthy state for women as androgynous Asian-American women scored high in self-esteem. Interestingly, feminine women scored higher in both self-esteem and work satisfaction than masculine women. This is perhaps due to the stronger emphasis of femininity in women that is placed by Asian culture. The results indicate that both masculine and feminine qualities are important for the career development and physiological well-being of Asian-American women. Chow also suggested that enhancing both androgyny and occupational status would improve the self-esteem and work satisfaction of Asian-American women.

Guidelines for Career Assessment with Asian Americans

Based on both the preceding review of empirical studies of career assessment and on clinical experience, the following general guidelines on conducting and using career assessment with Asian Americans are offered. First, given the lack of cultural norms and empirical research demonstrating the cultural validity of career instruments, use of such instruments needs to be undertaken with considerable care and caution. This is particularly important because we know so little about Asian Americans' attitudes toward psychological testing, their familiarity and comfort level with tests, and how they actually approach tests. For example, we do not know if social desirability operates to the same degree and in the same way for Asian Americans as for European Americans.

Second, counselors need to be alert to the multiple sources of bias that may be operating in the assessment process. Given the basic assumptions of psychometrics, it is probable that there are sources of bias within our theories of career choice and development (e.g., the American emphasis on individualism versus the Asian emphasis on collectivism). These biases in turn are operationalized and expressed in our instruments. Lonner and Ibrahim (1989) and Fouad (1993) have already delineated many of the equivalent problems in using instruments with culturally different clients. Biases may also operate in the attitudes and expectations of counselors who are trained in primarily Western models of counseling (e.g., leaving home during the 20s is quite normative in American experience, whereas many Asian cultures encourage extended families living together or living at home until marriage).

There are certain elements in Asian Americans' test-taking attitude that are important to keep in mind. Asian Americans tend to live within authoritarian family and social systems and are therefore less likely to question or challenge the counselor who is viewed as an authority figure.

Therefore a counselor's assignment of a test to an Asian-American client without sufficient explanation may result in premature termination because the client may have been placed in a catch-22 situation. To refuse to take the test would be to challenge the counselor; to take the test may go against the client's fears (e.g., what hidden problems would the test uncover about me), expectations (e.g., I did not really come to take a test but just to find out which is the best medical schools to apply to in New England), or attitudes toward tests (e.g., I do not believe these tests will really help me but I cannot tell that to my counselor); given such a dilemma many Asian-American clients may choose not to return to subsequent sessions. Therefore, the assignment of career tests and the meaning of that assignment need to be carefully explored and executed with Asian-American clients.

Finally, cultural factors are likely to influence the test interpretation and feedback session for Asian Americans. For example, as pointed out by Sue and Morishima (1982) and by Redding and Ng (1982), "maintaining face" and avoiding "loss of face" are very important dimensions of interpersonal relations for Asian Americans. Leong (1993) also pointed out the importance and prevalence of subtle and indirect forms of communication among Asian Americans. Violations of these and similar cultural norms and expectations during the assessment process would prevent the effective use and interpretation of career assessment tools for this minority group. Personality studies of Asian Americans (see Leong, 1985) have indicated that Asian Americans, relative to European Americans, are less tolerant of ambiguity. In general, more structured approaches to test interpretation would be better received by Asian Americans than unstructured exploratory approaches. Many of the issues highlighted by Leong (1993) as it relates to the career counseling process with Asian Americans also applies to career assessment with Asian Americans.

CAREER COUNSELING WITH ASIAN AMERICANS

The degree of applicability of existing theories of career development and counseling to minority populations has been questioned (Fitzgerald & Betz, 1992; Smith, 1983). Whereas the traditional focus that has been on individual factors such as values, attitudes, and abilities is important, a broader set of social, cultural, and historical variables that impinge on career choice and career development process needs to be considered when working with Asian-American and other minority populations. Their bicultural and minority experience, and their historical legacy as a particular racial and ethnic group in the United States are the contextual elements that shape the lives and vocational choices of Asian Americans.

The following discussion focuses on factors affecting career counseling with Asian Americans in light of these broader social, cultural, and historical conditions. First, significant dimensions of diversity within the Asian-American population are discussed followed by culturally related factors that affect career-counseling process and outcome. Finally, specific career intervention strategies in working with Asian Americans are presented.

Diversity Within the Asian-American Population

The term *Asian American* is deceptive in its simplicity in that it belies a sense of homogeneity that in reality does not exist. In various governmental and institutional applications of the term, it includes persons from over half the globe, stretching from the islands of Micronesia to the Middle East. Until recently, even the field of psychology subscribed to the prevailing myth of homogeneity—the stereotypic belief that Asian Americans are all alike. Racial minorities are often perceived as unidimensional beings with race as the only or primary dimension of salience. Other dimensions of diversity such as ethnicity, gender, and class have been largely ignored. These dimensions, as they relate to Asian Americans, are briefly considered.

Ethnicity

To assume that Asians, and consequently Asian Americans, are all alike is as unacceptable a notion as assuming that all Europeans are alike. There needs to be a recognition of the fact that there are distinct ethnic groups within the Asian-American population, each with its own unique history and culture. According to the 1980 census, 53 different national and ethnic origins are included in the term *Asian Pacific Islander*. A closer examination of just one of these groups reveals not only ethnic diversity but also the range of differences within just one subgroup. For example, the Chinese-American community is the most diverse among the Asian-American groups. Although the Chinese were the first to migrate to the United States, they also constitute a significant portion of the most recent immigrants. Thus, this community has the greatest generational and acculturation range of all the Asian-American groups. In addition, Chinese immigrants come from different countries of origin, including Mainland China, Taiwan, Hong Kong, Malaysia, Singapore, and Vietnam. These different nationalities further diversify an already complicated system of dialects, thus making intercommunication within one ethnic group a challenge.

There is evidence of ethnic group differences in areas related to career development. A study by Mizokawa and Ryckman (1990) revealed a complex pattern of differences in causal attributions for academic performance among the major Asian-American ethnic groups. Korean Americans gave the highest effort attribution in doing well in language arts and social sciences, whereas Vietnamese Americans gave the lowest effort attribution. Ethnic group differences can also be observed in educational achievement. Data on percentage of the population with 4 or more years of education after high school in the age group of 25 and older revealed that Asian-Indian males have the highest rate at 68% and Vietnamese-American males the lowest at 18% (Hsia, 1988). A study by Gim, Atkinson, and Whiteley (1990) also revealed ethnic group differences in both type and severity of problems experienced by college students. Southeast Asians indicated both greater number and severity of problems. For Japanese and Chinese Americans, academic/career problems were most salient, whereas for Southeast Asians, Filipinos, and Korean Americans, financial concerns were most salient. However, in attitudes toward seeking psychological services, no ethnic group differences were observed (Atkinson & Gim, 1989). This indicates that, whereas it is important to be cognizant of distinct ethnic groups within the Asian-American population, the conditions under which ethnicity is a significant factor in relation to various aspects of psychological functioning remains unclear.

Level of Acculturation

Although it is important to be aware of distinct ethnic group differences in career counseling, a more important distinction to make is that of acculturation level (Leong, 1985). This is a concept that cuts across ethnic groups. Although generation and acculturation are interrelated in that generational level has been identified as one of the best indicators of acculturation level (Lai & Sodowsky, 1992), acculturation level is a more robust and accurate construct to employ. The lack of conceptual precision in generational level is best evinced by the use of the term *1.5 generation* within the Korean-American community. This term is employed to distinguish between foreign born who came as adults versus those who came at a young age. Although both are technically first generation, there is usually a significant difference between these two groups. Thus, the term *1.5* is an attempt within the community to make a distinction between acculturation levels within a single generation.

Several studies indicate the salience of the acculturative dimensions in various aspects of counseling process and outcome. A series of studies revealed that acculturation level is highly significant in relation to attitudes toward seeking psychological help (Atkinson & Gim, 1989), type and severity of problems experienced, willingness to seek help for those problems (Gim, Atkinson, & Whiteley, 1990), and preferences for help providers (Atkinson, Whiteley, & Gim, 1990). Acculturation level was highly significant in all these studies, whereas ethnicity was significant in only one.

Leong and Tata (1990), in a study that examined occupational values in Chinese-American children, observed that the more acculturated the participants the more they valued self-realization. This finding was interpreted in light of established cultural differences on the dimension of individualism versus collectivism (Hofstede, 1980). Self-realization appears to be more a part of Euro-American than Chinese-American culture. As was indicated previously, individualism is preeminent as a cultural value in mainstream American culture, whereas in Chinese and Chinese-American culture there is a more collectivistic orientation. Thus, individuals from the former culture are more likely to view occupational choice as a personal matter and an opportunity for self-expression and self-actualization, whereas individuals from the latter culture may view the same choice in the context of potential contributions and obligations to the group. Indeed, the notion advanced by Super, Starishevsky, Matlin, and Jordaan (1963), that one's career choice is really an implementation of one's self-concept, may not apply equally to individuals from collectivistic cultures. These persons may have concepts that involve subordinating self-realization needs to group needs.

Conceptualization of Acculturation and Biculturality

To fully understand the implications of acculturation in career counseling, it is necessary to briefly consider how acculturation and biculturality are conceptualized. Keefe and Padilla (1987) provided an overview of the evolution in conceptualization of acculturation and cultural identity. Initial models were unidimensional with two cultures serving as polar opposites. It was based on an assimilationist assumption of rejecting the "old" ethnic culture for the "new" mainstream American culture. This evolved into an awareness that the two cultures are legitimate in their own right and that a person can be somewhere in between the two cultural opposites. However, this model was based on an assumption of mutual exclusivity where the more a person accepted one culture the more he or she rejected the other culture. Furthermore, biculturality was defined as being somewhere in between the two cultures or having a balance of both cultures. In contrast, most recent models are based on an orthogonal approach in which the Asian and mainstream American cultures are placed on independent dimensions; thus, a person can be highly acculturated to both mainstream American and Asian culture instead of having to choose between them. The ideal is to be highly acculturated to both cultures rather than one to the exclusion of the other, or, worse yet, to neither culture.

The level of acculturation of the client and how both the client and counselor conceptualize biculturality will have important implications for career intervention. These implications are discussed later in this chapter.

Gender

Gender differences have received minimal interest in the vocational research literature on Asian Americans. The few studies that have included gender provide interesting data regarding paradoxical roles and expectations for Asian-American women. Dixon, Fukuda, and Ignacio (1972) observed that Asian-American females are more likely to choose academic post-high school destinations than males. Another study by Brandon (1991) revealed that young Asian-American females attain a high level of education more quickly than males, particularly among the immigrant generation. Asian-American women simultaneously hold high educational aspirations and traditional values and gender roles. Furthermore, the parents of these women have the same expectations regarding educational attainment for both males and females.

These studies indicate that traditional values regarding education for women are changing; educational attainment is as important for Asian-American women as it is for Asian-American men. However, it remains to be seen whether the goal and purpose of education for women are the same as for men. In the past, the underlying goal of education and occupational attainment was to be a more marketable and desirable wife. However, there is an increasing emphasis on financial independence and security for women in contemporary Asian-American communities. To quote one student: "My mother wants me to be a doctor so that I can find a good husband, and in case anything happens to him or the marriage I can always take care of myself." This indicates both changes in cultural values regarding the role of women as well as changes in economic times where dual income is deemed a necessity rather than a luxury.

Even as Asian-American women are encouraged to strive for the high-status and high-income careers, they may experience conflicts due to expectations to maintain traditional gender roles as wife and mother. In a dual-career marriage, the woman's career is likely to be secondary to the man's. Trying to accommodate the husband's career and maintain traditional gender roles related to the family may limit career opportunities and affect job satisfaction. These issues are not unique to Asian-American women; however, they may be more severe due to greater polarities in cultural values and expectations. Furthermore, these issues are not as clearly identified nor deemed important, and there are fewer role models who have negotiated the difficulties successfully. Asian-American women must also deal with an array of stereotypes that portray them as exotic, subservient, passive, hardworking, and, most recently, as news broadcasters. Whereas some of these images may seem positive and help them obtain entry-level positions, these very images create and perpetuate the glass ceiling that prevents them from exploring the range of occupations and positions that are available to Euro-American men and, to a lesser degree, Euro-American women.

These gender-related factors are mediated by level of acculturation in that these issues may be more salient for immigrant generation and low-acculturated women than for those who are highly acculturated. The challenge for the counselor is to explore these issues without imposing them on the clients, and to be able to recognize the indicators that point to their significance to the client.

Socioeconomic Status

Whereas gender has received only minimal research interest, socioeconomic status (SES) has received nearly nonexistent attention in the vocational literature on Asian Americans. However, the lack of empirical attention does not minimize its importance. Economic difficulty, particularly among recent immigrants, combined with the traditional Asian value of collectivism and the subordination of individual well-being to that of the group has important implications in terms of vocational behavior of Asian Americans. It is not unusual in Asian cultures for families to sacrifice certain members of the family to provide opportunities for another member for the family as a whole to benefit from the latter's success. Traditionally, opportunities for female children have been limited to provide for the males. Furthermore, the difficulties of economic adjustment often lead these families to discourage the children from pursuing careers that require substantial investment in terms of time and education. In one particular case, a Vietnamese-American student pursued college education over the objections of his parents. They urged him to find employment immediately so that he could help provide the basic necessities for his large family. Thus, although education is highly emphasized in the Asian and Asian-American cultures, this is not a universal phenomenon. Access to education is mediated by immigrant status and class background. Even though education may be valued, some families and individuals may not be able to invest in education nor afford to wait for delayed income.

Middle- and upper-class Asian-American families strongly emphasize education and try to provide complete financial support for their children through college. These parents often make great personal sacrifices in terms of time, resources, and leisure opportunities to make sure their children get a good education. In effect, they are making a total investment in their children. In return, they have high expectations of their children, both in terms of academic performance and vocational aspirations. Many of them, regardless of financial means, do not want their children to work for fear it will detract from their studies. Also, parents may not want their children to have serious romantic relationships for the same reason.

If the family's primary income is from a family-owned business, there may be contrasting expectations for the children to invest substantial time in the family business and do well in school. First-generation parents often do not have the language proficiency to manage the business without their children's help. In some cases parents are entirely dependent on the children not only for the management of the business but, in times of economic difficulty, also for basic labor. These conflicting expectations can place tremendous burden on the children. The second author is familiar with many such cases of Asian-American students who, while taking a demanding load of courses in preparation for careers in the medical sciences, were expected to work after hours and on weekends to upwards of 30 to 35 hours. In one particular case, the student did not even have a car and thus had to arrange transportation between school and the family business, which was about 40 minutes driving distance. Although this kind of dilemma is not limited to a particular class, it is more prevalent in the immigrant population and lower SES levels.

The interaction of class and acculturation level has implications for career development of Asian Americans. Acculturation facilitates interaction with mainstream society that would eventually translate into greater opportunities. Those who speak English fluently and understand and adopt mainstream cultural practices and values will naturally find it easier to pursue employment outside the ethnic community and thus consider a wider range of vocational and employment opportunities. However, those who do not speak English fluently and do not feel comfortable with mainstream cultural values may find it more comfortable to work within the ethnic community. These indirect influences on career choice and career opportunities may hinder or facilitate upward socioeconomic mobility.

Implications of Dimensions of Within-Group Differences

The dimensions of ethnicity, gender, class, and acculturation level have important implications for career counseling. As a point of beginning, counselors need to be aware that the Asian-American population is not homogeneous. The greater the awareness of the diversity that exists within the Asian-American population, the more effective the counselor will be because of her or his ability to identify and understand the complex pattern of career issues that are salient for specific subgroups of Asian

Americans. The acculturative dimension is particularly important because the degree to which culturally based issues in career counseling applies to Asian Americans will depend on acculturation level. Greater caution should be used in applying traditional approaches of career counseling to low-acculturated Asian-American clients than to highly acculturated ones.

Given the lack of research on how these dimensions of within-group diversity translate to specific intervention strategies, the most important factor in the process of providing culturally sensitive career counseling is for the counselor to be educated and aware of culturally based factors that affect career development for Asian Americans. The following discussion highlights some of these factors.

Culturally Based Factors That Affect Career-Counseling Process with Asian Americans

In addition to the dimensions of diversity that exists within the Asian-American population, there are a number of important culturally based factors that affect counseling process and outcome. Before these factors are presented, a brief digression on the nature of cultural contrasts is in order.

Any discussion of cultural differences involve generalizations because comparisons are made at the group level and not at the individual level. Thus, the danger of stereotyping and overgeneralizing is inherent. First of all, just as the statistical mean is a representation of the data as a whole, so are descriptions of cultural traits. Second, just as one would not expect every element of the data set to be identical to the mean, not every member of a culture will fit the normative description. Third, cultural differences should be interpreted as a matter of degree rather than discrete categories; that is, to say that Asian Americans are group oriented does not mean that other groups are not. It means that as a group Asian Americans are more collectivistic in their orientation than other groups. Furthermore, the reader is asked to be mindful of the acculturative dimension and understand that cultural contrasts are more applicable to low-acculturated and immigrant Asian Americans than to highly acculturated and later generations.

A Model for Conceptualizing Process and Outcome in Career Counseling with Asian Americans

In a recent article, Leong (1993) applied Sue's (1977) model of cross-cultural counseling to career counseling with Asian Americans. The two underlying dimensions of this model, process and goals, were combined with an appropriateness–inappropriateness dimension to create a fourfold typology: (a) appropriate goals, appropriate process, (b) inappropriate goals, inappropriate process, (c) appropriate goals, inappropriate process, and (d) inappropriate goals, appropriate process. For the ease of discussion, Leong (1993) labeled the quadrants as (a) "On Target" counselor, (b) "Missed by a Mile" counselor, (c) "Good-hearted Bumbler," and (d) "Barking up the Wrong Tree" (see Fig. 7.1). Which quadrant a counselor falls under depends on awareness of cultural differences in style of communication, values regarding the importance of the family, impact of fluency in language, prejudice, and stereotypes, conceptualization of problems, expectations from counseling, and the importance of counselor credibility. These and other factors are discussed next.

Styles of Communication

Differences in communication style between Asian and mainstream American cultures have been widely discussed. In contrast to the direct style of communication preferred by European Americans, Asian cultures prefer an indirect style of communication (Leong, 1993). This derives from the fundamental basis of Confucian philosophy that is harmony and balance. Assertiveness, expressiveness, directness, and openness and other expressions of individuality are seen as potential disrupters of interpersonal harmony. Also, due to the importance of maintaining face and giving face discussed in the previous chapter, Asians may use subtle cues or metacommunication to convey negative content. This has been found

PROCESS

	Appropriate	Inappropriate
Appropriate	On Target Counselor	Good Hearted Bumbler
Inappropriate	Barking up the Wrong Tree	Miss by a Mile Counselor

GOALS

FIG. 7.1. Interactions between culturally appropriate and culturally inappropriate counseling process and goals.

to be true in the clinical setting where it is difficult to obtain direct and accurate feedback about the therapeutic process from Asian-American clients (Kinzie, Leung, Bui, & Ben, 1988). Rather than confront the counselor directly and cause the counselor to lose face, clients may indicate their dissatisfaction through indirect means, most commonly by being noncompliant or simply dropping out of therapy. In fact, Sue and McKinney (1975) observed a higher drop-out rate among Asian Americans compared to European Americans (52% vs. 30%).

A culturally sensitive counselor should be aware of these differences in communication style and consider their impact in the counseling process. In case of uncertainty about the subtext of a particular statement or action, the safest approach is to clarify the meaning with the client and indicate that the need to clarify is out of a desire to be most helpful to the client. Another approach is to invite the client to educate the counselor as to his or her preferred style of communication. Direct confrontation should be used with caution according to the level of acculturation of the client.

In working with Asian-American clients, counselors should be more conscious of their own nonverbal behavior, both intentional and nonintentional ones, as well as those of the client's. The counselor should also be aware of the potential bias in interpreting nonverbal behavior according to mainstream cultural values. For example, lack of direct eye contact may be an act of deference to someone who is older and respected in traditional Asian cultures, but if mainstream norms are applied, then it can be misinterpreted as indication of discomfort or an attempt to hide something. What is being suggested here is a general increase in awareness of the *potentially* greater role of nonverbal behavior in the counseling relationship and not a hypervigilance and questioning of every move that the client makes.

The Role of the Family

The collective rather than individualistic orientation evident in Asian and Asian-American cultures translates into the family, particularly parents, playing an important role in career development process of Asian Americans. In a comparative study of factors that influence career choice among African Americans, Asian Americans, Chicano/Latinos, and European Americans, Asian Americans were the only group to rank parental pressure as one of the top five most influential factors (Gim, 1992). Because parents see their children as an extension of themselves, and the success of the children a direct reflection on the parents, many traditional Asian-American parents believe that it is their right to direct and influence important decisions of their children such as career and spousal choice. The mainstream American value of individualism and self-determination comes into direct conflict with this traditional value. Asian Americans who are exposed to and internalize the mainstream value often experience conflict with parents who do not abide by this value. It is common to find in an educational environment Asian-American students who experience great distress due to conflict with parents over major and career choice. Some parents bribe and even threaten to disown their children to coerce them to pursue careers that are desired by the parents. Students who experience these kinds of pressures sometimes lie to their parents about how well they are doing in school for fear of reprisal and disappointing them.

In light of the significant role that parents may play in career development of Asian Americans, counselors need to be aware of their own values regarding individualism and autonomy, and the danger of imposing these values on the client. One of the most common culturally insensitive comments made to Asian Americans by well-intended friends and professionals is: "It's your life, do what you want to do, don't let other people rule your life." Such a response would be indicative of a "Missed by a Mile" counselor (Leong, 1993).

However, just because there is a cultural basis for an issue does not automatically make it acceptable. Each culture has both functional and dysfunctional aspects. Even issues that have a healthy cultural basis can be distorted, exaggerated, or go beyond the range of appropriateness within that culture. Whereas the counselor cannot make such a judgment for the client, the counselor can help the client explore this possibility, help him or her to see the consequences of certain kinds of values and behaviors, provide alternative values and behaviors for the client to consider, and, finally, support the client in making the best choice he or she can at that time. Certainly, this is a challenging task, particularly for someone who is not familiar with the culture. Great care and caution should be used in the process because the danger of imposing one's own values and expectations on the client is always lurking. Nonetheless, at times, the role of the counselor requires her or him to invite the client to reevaluate even culturally based behaviors.

Impact of Language, Prejudice, and Stereotypes

In addition to the impact that parents or the family as a whole may have on various aspects of career development of Asian Americans, they are also affected by a broader set of factors. Developing fluency in English is a major challenge for the immigrant population. Lack of confidence in one's ability to express oneself may lead individuals to consider a limited range of vocations. Immigrant parents, based on their own experience of prejudice and discrimination due to the language factor, may encourage their children to pursue careers in science and engineering because of their perception that both the preparation and practice in these careers are less language dependent and thus more "safe" than careers in the Social and Enterprising Holland codes.

Language ability of the client can also be a factor in the counseling process, particularly because more than 50% of the Asian-American population is foreign born (Kitano & Daniels, 1988). Counselors need to be vigilant to resist the natural temptation to patronize someone who is not able to speak fluently, make a more negative assessment of competence and ability based on this one factor, or track them into careers that are deemed to be "safe."

Prejudices experienced by Asian-American clients can have a wide range of effect on career-related issues. One of the reasons for many Asian Americans pursuing high-status and high-income careers is to protect themselves against such experiences. Although these careers do not provide absolute protection, they do offer greater protection than many other vocations. This is a rationale often used by immigrant parents to encourage their children to pursue a career in medicine.

An awareness of one's own prejudices and biases is a requisite characteristic of an ethical counselor. In working with Asian-American clients, one way for prejudices to affect the counseling process is for the counselor to subscribe to stereotypic images of Asian Americans. A common image of Asian Americans is that of the model minority that emphasizes educational attainment, particularly in the math and sciences. The most insidious aspect of stereotypes is that it imposes an external reality on a person; others define who and what a person is by their expectations. Individuals may strive to fulfill these stereotypic expectations or define themselves in opposition to them. In either case, the net effect is the same; they are being shaped by an external force. Many Asian-American students comment on the devastating effect of a comment such as, "You're Asian, you should be doing well in math." Often, the internalized message from such a statement is, "There must be something terribly wrong with me if all Asians are supposed to excel in math but I'm not." Others, in their reaction against the stereotype, are actually proud of the fact that they do not do well in math and even intentionally do poorly in it. Counselors need to examine their own prejudices and stereotypes and make sure that they are not "tracking" Asian Americans into stereotypic areas or imposing their stereotypic images on Asian-American clients.

Conceptualization and Identification of Problems

The underutilization of general psychological counseling and overutilization of academic/career counseling among Asian Americans has been documented (Sue & Kirk, 1975; Sue & Sue, 1974). Stigma associated with having psychological problems, beliefs regarding their origin, and culturally prescribed ways of coping with problems all contribute to this pattern.

People who have psychological problems are stigmatized in Asian-American cultures. This stigma is applied not only to the individual but to the entire family. Because of the collective nature of identity, to admit that one has problems causes not only the individual to lose face but the family as a whole. For example, a person and his or her family could be stigmatized as having "bad blood" if that person were to admit to having psychological problems. This affects the way in which Asian Americans conceptualize and identify problems. Tracey, Leong, and Glidden (1986) conducted a study examining help seeking and problem perception among Asian Americans in Hawaii and observed that with the same symptomology of being lonely, having few friends, and not doing well in school, Euro-American students emphasized their feelings of depression and loneliness as the primary reason for seeking help, whereas Asian-American students emphasized academic-related issues for seeking help. This is consistent with the finding that Asian-American students over-utilized academic and career counseling (Sue & Kirk, 1975; Sue & Sue, 1974). This suggests that because academic/career issues are less stigmatizing, many Asian Americans may use this avenue to reach out for help for deeper psychological issues. Thus, career counselors need to be aware of this possibility and know when to refer to the counseling center or work in conjunction with the counseling center staff. Although it is true that career counseling and other psychological counseling are not necessarily distinct and separate enterprises, career counselors need to be able to identify when the career concern is rooted in a deeper psychological issue that merits in-depth exploration.

Given the stigma associated with psychological problems, career counselors need to be aware that Asian Americans may question and resist exploring deeper psychological issues in the context of career counseling or be alarmed by the counselor's suggestion or referral for additional counseling. If the client is clearly in need of additional counseling but is uncomfortable with the idea, the counselor can normalize the process and explain that it is common for people to struggle with psychological problems, explain the ways in which counseling can be helpful, and assure the client of the laws of confidentiality that govern the therapeutic relationship. In most cases, if the counselor establishes a trusting and caring relationship with the client, communicates genuine concern for the welfare of the client, and describes the potential benefits of counseling, the client will tend to respond favorably.

Expectations from Counseling

A study by Yuen and Tinsley (1981) revealed that Asians, in comparison to European Americans, expect to take a more passive role in the counseling process and expect the counselor to be more directive, nurturing, and authoritative. Low-acculturated Asian Americans may expect advice giving from the counselor and prefer a problem-solving approach. This in turn may stem from what has been observed as lower tolerance for uncertainty and ambiguity among Asian Americans than European Americans (Sue & Morishima, 1982).

Given this, Asian-American students may experience greater distress when they are uncertain about future life plans and career goals and prefer a more structured and directive counseling approach. A study by Atkinson, Maruyama, and Matsui (1978) supports this view. Asian Americans, in comparison to European Americans, preferred a structured, logical, and rational counseling approach over one that is reflective, unstructured, and focused on emotions. Leong (1993) stated: "Yet, given Asian Americans' preference for hierarchical relationships, counselors will often be expected to be experts and authority figures" (p. 37). Furthermore, Leong noted that, not only are Asian Americans verbally less expressive and reticent about admitting problems due to the shame it may cause, they are also reluctant to reveal personal and family problems because they view mental health as a matter of discipline, self-control, will power, and the avoidance of morbid thoughts (Lum, 1982; Sue, Wagner, Ja, Margulis, & Lew, 1976). Given such conceptualizations, counselors' attempts to elicit self-disclosure about clients' personal problems may be viewed as attempts to undermine their mental health. One culture's self-examination and self-understanding is another culture's unhealthy self-focus and unnecessary rumination (Leong, 1993).

Thus, in career counseling with Asian Americans, it is important for the counselor to be aware that their expectations from counseling may differ in the way problems are conceptualized, the solutions for the problems, the goals of therapy, and how the goals are achieved. An exploration of these issues at the beginning of the counseling relationship, leading to an agreement on common goal and method, is essential for a successful outcome.

Credibility of the Counselor

According to Sue and Zane (1987), credibility of the counselor is an important aspect of the counseling process. Because of the Asian value of respect for authority, the counselor as an authority and an expert is accorded a certain degree of credibility from the beginning. However, Sue and Zane indicated the importance of converting this ascribed credibility to earned credibility through the process of gift giving. Using a common Asian tradition of gift giving as a metaphor, counselors can give a symbolic gift to their clients to indicate an ability to be helpful. Gifts can be in the form of normalizing the anxiety that a client may experience because she or he does not have a clear idea of what career to pursue, helping the client understand the various stages of career development, and indicating an awareness of how cultural factors may influence career issues. Lack of attention to these factors may be interpreted by the client as poor fit with the counselor or ineffectiveness of the counselor and the counseling process as a whole.

Addressing Value Conflicts in Counseling

Woven throughout the discussion thus far is the inherent danger of imposing Euro-American values on Asian-American clients. By definition, counseling is a value-laden endeavor in which both the process and the goals reflect the mainstream cultural context. Then, how can counselors address culturally based differences that manifest themselves in the counseling process? One approach is to consider the contextual nature of behavior. The following illustration describes how this approach can be applied to a common vocational issue for Asian Americans.

Asian Americans, like other minority groups, encounter a glass ceiling in the workplace. Whereas the model minority image of being hardworking, dependable, and passive may help in getting entry-level jobs, these very same stereotypes prevent them from advancing to management and executive levels because they are seen as lacking the requisite communication, management, and leadership skills. One possible approach in helping clients cope with this barrier is to help them be more expressive and assertive and behave in ways that are consistent with mainstream cultural definition of leadership ability. However, these characteristics may be counter to traditional Asian values, and, thus, to encourage clients to adopt such behaviors is in essence imposing mainstream cultural values and norms. On the other hand, to ignore this context and support the client in maintaining only traditional Asian behaviors would be, although culturally sensitive, doing the client a disservice. This denies the reality of the American work environment and may result in limited opportunities for the client in the long term.

One way of addressing this dilemma is for the counselor to help the client define the nature of the problem, particularly the culturally based aspect of the issue, identify the options in dealing with the issue, be aware of the consequences of these options, empower the client to make the best choice, and support the client in implementing that choice. If, after such a deliberation process, the client chooses to acquire a style of communication valued by the Euro-American culture, it need not be seen as a rejection of traditional values. Both the client and counselor should be mindful of the fact that such choices are contextual. The orthogonal model of cultural identity and acculturation presented previously can be applied in this situation. Individuals can strive to abide by values and norms of both cultures rather than having to choose one over the other. Although some behaviors may be contradictory, the contexts can determine the adaptiveness and appropriateness of behaviors. These behaviors can be framed as skills. Once the skills are acquired, the client can apply them as needed, when appropriate. In the preceding example, the client can choose to be assertive and use a communication style that is valued by the mainstream culture when in a business context but choose to use a culturally consistent set of behaviors when interacting with older members of the ethnic community. The ideal is for the client to have a wide range of behaviors from which to choose so that she or he has the choice of applying them when appropriate. Emphasis is on the contextual nature of behavior and conceptualizing cultural identity on separate and independent dimensions instead of a single dimension with only one way of addressing the dilemma of value conflict in career counseling.

A final caveat to consider is that, although counselors help clients deal with the realities of the workplace and support decisions made by clients to accommodate the culturally based differences in the work environment, counselors should also strive to be advocates for clients and be agents of social change. Counselors need to be proactive agents of change and facilitate modifications in societal structures and institutions so that it will accommodate the multiple cultural perspectives of our increasingly diverse work force.

The degree to which the counselor is aware of the various cultural factors presented, be able to assess their relevance to individual members of the Asian-American community, and apply that awareness to respond appropriately in the counseling process will determine whether or not the counselor is on-target, barking up the wrong tree, good hearted but bumbling, or missed by a mile. At minimum, an awareness of these cultural factors, having an attitude that indicates a desire to be sensitive to these issues, and communicating this desire to the client are the fundamental components of being an on-target counselor.

Career Intervention Strategies

The final section of this chapter highlights specific issues in culturally sensitive career-counseling strategies. In this context, career counseling is broadly defined and not limited to the traditional one-on-one approach.

Encourage Career Exploration. The unequal distribution of Asian Americans across the vocational spectrum is well established. Asian Americans, particularly early generations, tend to consider a limited range of vocations. One way of addressing this issue is to encourage career exploration and consideration of a wider range of career options than the traditionally emphasized ones in the medical sciences and engineering.

Fukuyama and Cox (1992), in their report of the results of the 1989 National Career Development Association/Gallup Poll survey, revealed that 71% of Asian Americans compared to 63% of European Americans said they would like more information on career options if they could choose their careers over again. Interestingly, the same survey revealed that Asian Americans obtained vocational information through college career centers more than any other group (37% for Asian Americans vs. 21% and less for European Americans and other groups). Despite this, only 61% of Asian Americans indicated that the desired vocational information was available to them when they needed it in contrast to 71% of European Americans who indicated the same. These results indicate that Asian Americans do utilize established avenues of obtaining information on careers, and that those who are already in their vocations would have liked more information when they were choosing a career.

Use Structured, Didactic Approaches. Given the stigma associated with seeking counseling and preference for a structured and didactic approach in counseling, interventions that are contextualized as educational may be preferable. Whether in an individual counseling setting or in a group setting, a structured, didactic format allows the participants to obtain helpful information with minimal risk and threat. A positive initial contact of this nature would facilitate behaviors of greater risk such as seeking individual career counseling.

Other educational approaches include informational brochures. Obviously, the more culture specific and the more tailored the information to Asian Americans, the more effective it will be. A focus group of Asian Americans can be used to identify the particular vocational concerns of the target population and design a brochure using a question and answer format that can then be combined with the subsequent interventions.

Group Interventions. The group interventions that target Asian Americans can be risky unless certain precautions are taken. The precautions should include the previous recommendation of using a structured and didactic approach with minimal expectation of self-disclosure, at least in the initial period. Counselors should be particularly sensitive to issues of stigma and loss of face. To traditional Asian Americans the concept of talking about personal issues with a stranger is difficult enough but to do so with a group of strangers who are peers is even more threatening (Leong, 1992). Confidentiality is also an important issue because the ethnic community tends to be small and tight knit. The fear of rumors and circulation of personal information is real, particularly in light of the devastating effects of loss of face for the individual and the family as well.

For group interventions to work, pregroup screening is essential to select group members who would truly benefit from the group process and to orient them to the group counseling process and ensure their comfort with it. An assessment of the acculturation level of the client would serve as a helpful guide.

Outreach. Due to the stigma associated with seeking help and differences in conceptualization of psychological problems, aggressive outreach to the Asian-American population may be needed. Outreach is particularly important for the immigrant population because they may not be aware of the resources that are available to them, and they may still see themselves as guests of this country and thus not entitled to utilize its services. Furthermore, they may assume that existing services cannot be helpful due to differences in culture. Thus, outreach should include a component that indicates awareness of and sensitivity to cultural issues that are related to career concerns. Indicating the potential helpfulness of career services is critical in addition to educating them to the resources that are available to them. Although an Asian American would be most preferred for the outreach, non-Asian Americans can also be effective. In either case, service providers should develop rapport and trust by frequent contact with the community. This is particularly important if the service provider is not an Asian American.

The key to effective outreach with Asian Americans, whether in the broader community or a campus community, is to utilize existing formal and informal networks. On a college campus Asian-American student clubs and organizations are the most effective means of outreach. For many, particularly those who are less acculturated, their lives revolve around these organizations. In the broader communities, outreach through churches and ethnic language school networks is effective.

When targeting an immigrant population, an ethnic-specific approach to both outreach and intervention is recommended, particularly in regions with a large and diverse Asian-American population. Many do not identify with the broader collective term *Asian American* and prefer an ethnic-specific designation, with the exception of the highly acculturated and politically conscious who have a pan-Asian ethnicity. Where possible, an ethnic-specific approach would increase the perception of relevance and potential helpfulness of the services that are being offered.

Use Parents and Role Models. Given a collective identity with the family and the critical role that parents may play in the career development process, interventions that include parents is desirable, particularly in working with the immigrant population and clients that are young in age. Many Asian-American parents encourage their children to pursue

traditionally valued careers because they lack awareness of various career
options and may operate from inaccurate assumptions about nontraditional careers and subscribe to traditional gender-role stereotypes. They
may also be motivated by a limited set of values that emphasize status
and materialism. Although it is not the role of the counselor to impose
different values, yet, counselors can help parents be aware of other value
dimensions such as personal fulfillment, ability to be creative, and compatibility with interest and ability.

When parents are targeted, ethnic-specific and language-specific interventions would be most desirable because many of them do not feel
comfortable with the English language. However, this represents an ideal
scenario where appropriate personnel and resources are available.

In addition to parents, other role models are known to influence career
development regardless of the ethnic group. In keeping with principles
of social learning theory, the target audience must be able to identify
with the models. The models must also have characteristics that are valued by the target population such as status and income, or any other
desired aspect. Role models in nontraditional fields can facilitate career
exploration by being living examples of people who are successful in
their respective areas. Role models can also serve as a source of information and inspiration.

The empirical literature on specific career intervention strategies for
Asian Americans is severely limited. However, the study by Evanoski
and Tse (1989) merits particular attention because it incorporated many
of the elements discussed previously.

CONCLUSION

Cultural sensitivity in career counseling involves two basic components,
culture-specific knowledge and counselor's attitude. An awareness of the
role of culture in various aspects of psychological function is essential to
be a culturally sensitive counselor. This entails a certain degree of culture-specific knowledge about values, norms, and the experiences of
members of a particular group. For Asian Americans, counselors need to
be aware of the dimensions of diversity within the population such as
ethnicity, gender, class, and acculturation level as well as traditional values regarding collective identity, attitudes toward seeking psychological
help, and style of communication.

In addition to culture-specific knowledge, the attitudes of the counselor
are important to culturally sensitive career counseling. An insensitive
approach insists that the client adapt to fit the mainstream values and

norms, whereas the sensitive approach involves working with the client to explore the full range of options available from both or multiple cultures. The emphasis is on the contextual nature of behavior and the adaptiveness of certain behaviors in certain contexts.

The counselor should not be surprised to find that many Asian-American clients are not aware of and not able to articulate the cultural basis of career issues. It is not unusual for clients, regardless of ethnicity, to be unaware of the values and a priori assumptions that shape their world view. The issues presented in this chapter may apply more or less to a single Asian American depending on her or his level of acculturation (and the usual range of individual differences). Because the greatest contrast from mainstream culture will be observed among recent immigrants, and because acculturation is strongly correlated with generational status and years of residence in the United States, the issues presented in this chapter will be most applicable to them. For fourth- or fifth-generation and highly acculturated Asian Americans, these issues may not apply.

The line between cultural sensitivity and stereotyping is a fine one. The information contained in this chapter should be seen as a general guideline rather than an established rule. Counselors should hold them as tentative hypotheses to be tested and verified with each client.

REFERENCES

Atkinson, D. R., & Gim, R. H. (1989). Asian American cultural identity and attitudes toward mental health services. *Journal of Counseling Psychology, 36*, 209–212.

Atkinson, D. R., Maruyama, M., & Matsui, S. (1978). The effects of counselor race and counseling approach on Asian Americans' perceptions of counselor credibility and utility. *Journal of Counseling Psychology, 25*, 76–83.

Atkinson, D. R., Whiteley, S., & Gim, R. H. (1990). Asian American acculturation and preferences for help providers. *Journal of College Student Development, 31*, 155–161.

Bourne, P. (1975). The Chinese student-acculturation and mental illness. *Psychiatry, 38*, 269–277.

Brandon, P. (1991). Gender differences in young Asian Americans' educational attainments. *Sex Roles, 25*, 45–61.

Brown, D., & Brooks, L. (Eds.). (1990). *Career choice and development*. San Francisco: Jossey-Bass.

Chow, E. N. (1987). The influence of sex-role identity and occupational attainment on the psychological well-being of Asian American women. *Psychology of Women Quarterly, 11*, 69–82.

Connor, J. W. (1975). Value changes in third generation Japanese Americans. *Journal of Personality Assessment, 39*, 597–600.

Crites, J. O. (1973). *Career Maturity Inventory*. Monterey: California Testing Bureau, McGraw-Hill.

Crites, J. O. (1978). *Theory and research handbook for the Career Maturity Inventory*. Monterey: California Testing Bureau, McGraw-Hill.

Dixon, P. W., Fukuda, N. K., & Ignacio, R. (1972). Prediction of post-high school destination choice from curriculum, financial need, and students' rating of parents' wishes for post-high school occupation. *The Journal of Experimental Education, 41*(2), 18–22.

Evanoski, P. O., & Tse, F. W. (1989). Career awareness program for Chinese and Korean American parents. *Journal of Counseling and Development, 67,* 472–474.

Fenz, W. D., & Arkoff, A. (1962). Comparative need patterns of five ancestry groups in Hawaii. *Journal of Social Psychology, 58,* 67–89.

Fitzgerald, L. F., & Betz, N. E. (1992). *Career development in cultural context: The role of gender, race, class and sexual orientation.* Paper presented at the Conference on Convergence in Theories of Career Choice and Development, Michigan State University, East Lansing.

Fouad, N. A. (1993). Cross-cultural vocational assessment. *The Career Development Quarterly, 42,* 4–13.

Fretz, B. R., & Leong, F. T. L. (1982). Career development status as a predictor of career intervention outcome. *Journal of Counseling Psychology, 29,* 388–393.

Fukuyama, M. A., & Cox, C. I. (1992). Asian-Pacific Islander and career development. In D. Brown & C. Minor (Eds.), *Career needs in a diverse workforce: Implications of the NCDA Gallup survey.* Alexandria, VA: National Career Development Association.

Gim, R. H. C. (1992, May). *Cross cultural comparison of factors that influence career choice.* Paper presented at the Association for Asian American Studies Conference, San Jose, CA.

Gim, R. H. C., Atkinson, D. R., & Whiteley, S. (1990). Asian American acculturation, severity of problems, and willingness to see a counselor. *Journal of Counseling Psychology, 37,* 281–285.

Harren, V. A. (1978). *Assessment of career decision-making.* Carbondale: Department of Psychology, Southern Illinois University.

Hofstede, G. (1980). *Culture consequences: International differences in work-related values.* Beverly Hills, CA: Sage.

Holland, J. L. (1974). *Self-directed search.* Palo Alto, CA: Consulting Psychologists Press.

Holland, J. L., Daiger, D. C., & Power, P. G. (1980). *My vocational situation.* Palo Alto, CA: Consulting Psychologists Press.

Hsia, J. (1980, September). *Cognitive assessment of Asian Americans.* Paper presented at the National Institute of Education, National Center for Bilingual Research Symposium on Bilingual Research at Los Alamitos, CA.

Hsia, J. (1988). *Asian Americans in higher education and at work.* Hillsdale, NJ: Lawrence Erlbaum Associates.

Hsieh, T. T. Y., Shybut, J., & Lotsof, E. J. (1969). Internal versus external control and ethnic group membership: A cross-cultural comparison. *Journal of Consulting and Clinical Psychology, 33,* 122–124.

Keefe, S., & Padilla, A. (1987). *Chicano ethnicity.* Albuquerque: University of New Mexico Press.

Kinzie, J. D., Leung, P., Bui, A., & Ben, R. (1988). Group therapy with Southeast Asian refugees. *Community Mental Health Journal, 24,* 157–166.

Kitano, H., & Daniels, R. (1988). *Asian Americans: Emerging minorities.* Englewood Cliffs, NJ: Prentice-Hall.

Kwak, J. C. (1980). Vocational development of Asian American youth (doctoral dissertation, University of Wisconsin). *Dissertation Abstracts International, 41,* 1956–A.

Lai, E. W. M., & Sodowsky, G. R. (1992). *Acculturation: An examination of theory, measurement, and sociocultural, mental health, and counseling variables.* Paper presented at the APA Annual Conference.

Lamb, R. R. (1976). *Validity of the ACT Interest Inventory for minority group members* (ACT Res. Rep. No. 72). Iowa City: American College Testing Program.

Leong, F. T. L. (1982). *Differential career development attributes of Asian American and White college students.* Unpublished master's thesis, University of Maryland, College Park.

Leong, F. T. L. (1985). Career development of Asian Americans. *Journal of College Student Personnel, 26,* 539–546.

Leong, F. T. L. (1991). Career development attributes and occupational values of Asian American and White American college students. *The Career Development Quarterly, 39,* 221–230.

Leong, F. T. L. (1992). Guidelines for minimizing premature termination among Asian American clients in group counseling [Special Issue: Group Counseling with Multicultural Populations]. *Journal for the Specialists in Group Work, 17,* 218–228.

Leong, F. T. L. (1993). The career counseling process with racial-ethnic minorities: The case of Asian Americans. *Career Development Quarterly, 42,* 26–40.

Leong, F. T. L., & Hayes, T. J. (1990). Occupational stereotyping of Asian Americans. *The Career Development Quarterly, 39,* 143–154.

Leong, F. T. L., & Morris, J. (1989). Assessing the construct validity of Holland, Daiger, and Power's measure of vocational identity. *Measurement and Evaluation in Counseling and Development, 22,* 117–125.

Leong, F. T. L., & Tata, S. P. (1990). Sex and acculturation differences in occupational values among Chinese-American children. *Journal of Counseling Psychology, 37,* 208–212.

Leung, S. A., Ivey, D., & Suzuki, L. (in press). Factors affecting the career aspirations of Asian Americans. *Journal of Counseling and Development.*

Lonner, W. J., & Ibrahim, F. A. (1989). Assessment in cross-cultural counseling. In P. B. Pedersen, J. G. Draguns, W. J. Lonner, & J. E. Trimble (Eds.), *Counseling across cultures* (3rd ed., pp. 299–333). Honolulu: University of Hawaii Press.

Lum, R. G. (1982). Mental health attitudes and opinions of Chinese. In E. E. Jones & S. J. Korchin (Eds.), *Minority mental health* (pp. 1–189). New York: Praeger.

Meredith, G. M. (1966). Amae and acculturation among Japanese-American college students in Hawaii. *Journal of Social Psychology, 70,* 171–180.

Mizokawa, D. T., & Ryckman, D. B. (1990). Attributions of academic success and failure: A comparison of six Asian American ethnic groups. *Journal of Cross-Cultural Psychology, 21,* 434–451.

National Science Foundation. (1990). *Women and minorities in science and engineering.* Washington, DC: Author.

Nevill, D. D., & Super, D. E. (1986). *The Values Scale.* Palo Alto, CA: Consulting Psychologists Press.

Redding, S. G., & Ng, M. (1982). The role of "face" in the organizational perceptions of Chinese managers. *Organization-Studies, 3*(3), 201–219.

Rosenberg, M. (1957). *Occupations and values.* Glencoe, IL: Free Press.

Smith, E. J. (1983). Issues in racial minorities' career behavior. In W. B. Wash & S. H. Osipow (Eds.), *Handbook of vocational psychology* (Vol. 1, pp. 161–221). Hillsdale, NJ: Lawrence Erlbaum Associates.

Sue, D. W. (1975). Asian Americans: Social-psychological factors affecting their lifestyles. In J. S. Picou & R. E. Campbell (Eds.), *Career behavior of special groups: Theory, research and practice* (pp. 97–121). Columbus, OH: Merrill.

Sue, D. W. (1977). Barriers to effective cross-cultural counseling. *Journal of Counseling Psychology, 24,* 420–429.

Sue, D. W., & Frank, A. C. (1973). A typological approach to the psychological study of Chinese and Japanese American college males. *Journal of Social Issues, 29,* 129–148.

Sue, D. W., & Kirk, B. A. (1972). Psychological characteristics of Chinese-American students. *Journal of Counseling Psychology, 19,* 471–478.

Sue, D. W., & Kirk, B. A. (1973). Differential characteristics of Japanese-American and Chinese-American college students. *Journal of Counseling Psychology, 20,* 142–148.

Sue, D. W., & Kirk, B. A. (1975). Asian Americans: Use of counseling and psychiatric services on a college campus. *Journal of Counseling Psychology, 22,* 84–86.

Sue, S., & McKinney, H. (1975). Asian-Americans in the community mental health care system. *American Journal of Orthopsychiatry, 45,* 111–118.

Sue, S., & Morishima, J. K. (1982). *The mental health of Asian Americans.* San Francisco: Jossey-Bass.

Sue, S., & Sue, D. W. (1974). MMPI comparisons between Asian American and non-Asian students utilizing a student health psychiatric clinic. *Journal of Counseling Psychology, 21,* 423–427.

Sue, S., Wagner, N., Ja, D., Margulis, C., & Lew, L. (1976). Conceptions of mental illness among Asian and Caucasian American students. *Psychological Reports, 38,* 703–708.

Sue, S., & Zane, N. (1987). The role of culture and cultural techniques in psychotherapy: A critique and reformulation. *American Psychologist, 42,* 37–45.

Super, D. E. (1970). *Work Values Inventory.* Boston: Houghton-Mifflin.

Super, D. E., Starishevsky, R., Matlin, N., Jordaan, J. P. (1963). *Career development: Self-concept theory* (Research Monograph No. 4). New York: College Entrance Examination Board.

Tou, L. A. (1974). A study of work orientations of Chinese American and White American students of the 7th and 8th grades in Catholic elementary schools (doctoral dissertation, Catholic University of America). *Dissertation Abstracts International, 35,* 831.

Tracey, T. J., Leong, F. T. L., & Glidden, C. (1986). Help seeking and problem perception among Asian Americans. *Journal of Counseling Psychology, 59,* 49–58.

Yuen, R. K., & Tinsely, H. A. (1981). International and American students' expectancies about counseling. *Journal of Counseling Psychology, 28,* 66–69.

Career Development Assessment and Intervention Strategies With American Indians

William E. Martin, Jr.
Northern Arizona University

The purpose of this chapter is to provide suggestions to improve assessments and interventions during the career development process with American Indians. Initially, the theories that guide the discussion are presented; they are the individual differences tradition, social learning theory, and an ecological perspective. Then, a model for developing a differential assessment and intervention plan with American Indians is outlined accompanied by a discussion. Finally, an example is presented that illustrates how interventions can be identified in conjuction with assessments using the cultural and contextual guide for planning differential assessment and intervention with American Indians.

GUIDING THEORIES

Reflecting on the future impact of the individual-differences tradition on the future of counseling psychology, Dawis (1992) stated: "In counseling practice, one issue connected with individual differences psychology seems likely to overshadow all other future concerns, and that issue is cultural pluralism (or cultural diversity)" (p. 17). He also suggested that research related to individual differences and cultural diversity has had little impact on counseling psychology.

One reason for the seeming lack of substantive progress in increasing our understanding of cultural influences from an individual differences perspective may be the prevalent focus on describing ethnicity from the larger ethnic or racial group view, for example, "Native Americans have these psychological characteristics, whereas White Americans have these. . . ." Ascribing attributes to many or most while focusing less on intragroup variability necessarily leads research away from differential psychology. Some current research, however, is focusing more on intra-group variability and on understanding intersubgroup differences within a larger ethnic group. Cervantes and Acosta (1992) reflected this focus relative to clinical work and research done with Hispanics by stating: "As we have emphasized, there is no one 'Hispanic' population group but rather a population that varies with respect to language, country of origin, and value systems" (p. 216). Likewise, this new emphasis is illustrated in a recommendation from a conference on ethnic minority health issues at which DeAngelis (1992) stated: "When researching ethnic minority groups, it's wise to account for their within-group diversity as well as their similarities, conference participants agreed. Among Native Americans alone, for instance, there are some 509 official nations, tribes and Alaskan villages, each with its own traditions and sometimes language" (p. 32).

The tradition of individual differences in counseling psychology was significantly influenced by the pioneering work in vocational guidance by Frank Parsons during the early 1900s (Dawis, 1992). Parsons established a trait–factor theory of matching personnel traits to job characteristics. Trait–factor theory has evolved over the decades into a more sophisticated matching process. This evolution is best represented by Holland's (1985) theory of vocational personalities and work environments that is probably the most applied theoretical framework for career decision making. This individual differences tradition is very important in providing career counseling to American Indians. The primary attention given to a client is to integrate individual and cultural uniqueness within the career decision-making and job-matching processes. Martin (1991) underscored the importance of an individual-differences perspective in career counseling with American Indians by stating: "Career counselors cannot approach Indian clients as a homogeneous group but instead must be keenly aware of individual differences while at the same time give consideration to potential cultural influences" (p. 280).

Social learning theory has been effectively applied to promoting career development (Krumboltz, 1976) and may be less culturally biased than other intervention theories (Yost & Corbishley, 1987). Social learning theory emphasizes social skills training that is tailored to individual needs. Learning occurs when people both respond to and act upon the environment. Krumboltz identified four factors from social learning theory that impact career decision making. First, an individual's genetic endowment can enhance or limit career opportunities. Genetic factors can be those unchangeable aspects such as gender, race, and disability, or those that can be altered including unique talents. Second, career decisions are in-fluenced by environmental conditions including family and cultural norms, economic conditions, educational background, and socioeconomic status. The third factor that influences career decision making is individ-ual learning. Learning experiences accumulate resulting in an individual's unque set of interests and perceptions of the world of work. Self-obser-vation generalizations are the fourth factor. As individuals compare their own performance and skills with some standard and draw conclusions about themselves and their confidence, they are making self-observation generalizations.

LaFromboise, Trimble, and Mohatt (1990) pointed out that social learn-ing theory interventions can enable members of American Indian com-munities to identify target behaviors that correspond to community-level problems to be solved. For example, if a rural reservation community has a restricted labor market and limited job opportunities, then oppor-tunities can be developed for occupational role-modeling experiences for persons who are in an exploration phase of career development.

The influence of an environment on career decision making for Native Americans living on reservations was illustrated in the previous example. The environment is one of many systems that make up an individual's ecological network. An ecological perspective involves considering the impact and compounding effects of intrapersonal, interpersonal, physical, institutional, and social systems on behavior. Conoley and Haynes (1992) stated that a disturbance that a person may be experiencing should be viewed as discordance in a system. They defined the discordance as a disparity between an individual's abilities and the demands or expecta-tions of the environment—a failure of match between person and system. A suggestion from the conference on ethnic minority health issues refer-enced earlier (DeAngelis, 1992) emphasized the importance of a systemic orientation. This new theoretical approach does not use culture as the primary focus but instead "looks at the system as the center of the prob-lem, with culture attaching to that in various ways" (p. 33).

LaFomboise et al. (1990) discussed network therapy as a "progressive form of counseling intervention that operates on a model similar to and consistent with the more traditional Indian community-oriented guidance system" (pp. 641–642). This approach reflects an ecological perspective viewing persons within the context of the many systems that affect their lives. Certainly, using an ecological perspective is important when coun-seling with any individual. An ecological perspective is especially helpful when there are differences in cultural, home, and family orientations between a counselor and client.

There are salient themes influencing career decision making that cut across the individual-differences tradition, social learning theory, and an ecological perspective. First, there is a value and accent placed on the uniqueness of individuals. Second, there is an awareness of the multitude of traits, factors, and systems that affect career decision making. Third, consideration is given to the collateral affiliation between the person and environment.

DIFFERENTIAL ASSESSMENT AND INTERVENTION WITH AMERICAN INDIANS

Given that professionals must be keenly aware of the individual differences among Indian people, they equally must be mindful of unique cultural influences on decision making and behavior. Five moderating variables are discussed that are important to consider in developing a differential assessment and intervention plan with American Indians: (a) language usage, (b) cultural orientation, (c) home community, (d) family system, and (e) communication style (see Table 8.1).

Language Usage

The extent to which an Indian person uses his or her native language versus English will affect decisions made in the assessment and intervention process. Sources have estimated that there are 206 (American Indian Policy Review Commission, 1977) to 250 (Chafe, 1974) different languages and language dialects spoken by American Indians. Although American Indians differ considerably in personal usage of their native languages, the use of native languages is widespread. Native language usage is common among children and adults from tribes in the Southwest. For example, among Navajo children in the early and middle 1980s, 50% to 95% of them were reported to be bilingual or had low English proficiency (Warner, 1984). Nye (1986) found bilingual Navajo children to perform better on a Navajo version of the Test of Oral Language Development— Primary than on the standard English version. Sidles and MacAvoy (1986) found that two thirds of a sample of bilingual Navajo seventh- and eighth-grade students preferred using their native language.

During a study of adults living in Pueblos of New Mexico that involved in-person interviews, Martin and O'Connell (1986) found that 34% requested that the interviews be conducted in their native language. The plurality of the sample (45%) said that their native language was spoken most in their communities, and 41% reported that native language was the common usage in their homes. A study of urban American Indians residents also showed that a majority of the sample reported being able to speak their native language fluently (Marshall, Johnson, Martin, Saravanbhavan, & Bradford, 1992). Sioux was the native language spoken

TABLE 8.1
Cultural and Contextual Guide for Planning Differential Assessment
and Intervention With American Indians

Language Usage				
	The person's use of language(s) growing up:			
Bilingual	Proficient Native Language	Proficient English		Not Proficient in Either
	The person's use of language(s) now:			
Bilingual	Proficient Native Language	Proficient English		Not Proficient in Either
Cultural Orientation[a]				
	The person reflects Indian culture in the following way:			
Traditional	Transitional	Marginal	Assimilated	Bicultural
Home Community				
	The person grew up:			
On Reservation	Off-Reservation			Both
	The person currently lives:			
On Reservation	Off-Reservation			Both
	The person is planning to live:			
On Reservation	Off-Reservation			Both
Family System				
	The person lives predominantly within a:			
Nuclear Family				Extended Family
Communication Style[b]				
	The person is responsive to:			
Attending Skills	Influencing Skills			Focusing Skills

[a]The operational definition for cultural orientation was taken from Spindler and Spindler (1958), Ryan and Ryan (1982), and LaFromboise et al. (1990).
[b]The operational definition for communication style was taken from Ivey (1983).

by most (78%) of these individuals. As well as using their native language, 100% of the sample reported being able to speak English fluently, 97% could read English, and 96% could write English.

Martin, Frank, Minkler, and Johnson (1988) surveyed rehabilitation counselors from 25 states where 87% of the total national Indian population reside. The counselors were asked to provide their perceptions of factors important in working with American Indians with disabilities. For the counselors working with clients who live on reservation, 67% agreed or strongly agreed that their clients had adequate English proficiency skills and 80% of counselors working with clients who live off reservation also agreed or strongly agreed in their clients' English skills. When American Indian clients did have English proficiency deficits, 85% of the on-reservation and 88% of the off-reservation counselors reported that it was somewhat or very important to remediate the deficits.

Certainly, being bilingual is often viewed as an asset. However, if an individual speaks more than one language but is not fully proficient in any language, then the individual may have communication limitations that can affect optimal personal career decision making. In addition, the quality of services the individual receives in the process of career development may be affected. For example, Tanner and Martin (1986) found that 56% of rehabilitation professionals working with tribes throughout the nation reported that their efforts toward effective rehabilitation were inhibited when clients had limited English or communication disorders.

Assessment Considerations. An early interest in the evaluation process is to identify the intervening effects of language usage not only on a person's career development but also as it mingles with the assessment and intervention processes:

1. Preliminary contacts should be made with the client, client's family members, and referral source to obtain an informal assessment of the client's level of English usage. It may be warranted to use a native-speaking assistant if it appears that an interpreter might enhance communication during the assessment process. The native-speaking assistant must be knowledgeable of psychological and career development constructs and procedures or valuable information may be lost in the translation process. Cervantes and Acosta (1992) reviewed the shortcomings of employing translators or interpreters in the assessment and treatment process.

2. A thorough developmental history of language usage and current usage should be undertaken by interviewing both the client and family members. Acquired information should include: (a) What was the first language used?; (b) Was another language used with the first language?; (c) Did the first language remain the primary language used during childhood?; (d) At what age and where was English introduced?; (e) What language did the family members use in the home?; and (f) What language does the client use cognitively to process various problem-solving situations related to word meaning, narrative analysis, mathematics, hypothesis testing, personal decision making, social situations, and values exploration and clarification? Because these are commonly used constructs in assessment, obtaining qualitative information from the client can help the professional secure a richer understanding of the quantitative results from appraisal instruments. Certain American Indians may be disadvantaged if they process information in their native languages but are expected to perform effectively using English. Efforts to understand the ways these

individuals control the strategies they use for carrying out tasks (meta-cognition) may provide valuable insight to these individuals in bridging cognitive problem solving from a primary language to a secondary language.

3. The client's level of English usage should be obtained through assessments of word recognition, word meanings, spelling, comprehension, narrative analysis, oral language skills, and receptive language skills. Clearly this information is important to identify the appropriate assessment tools to administer. Also, in most work environments and educational settings, including those in reservation communities, there are requirements of varying degrees of English usage skills. Thus, it is important to have a comprehensive assessment of an individual's maximal English usage skills that will be needed in a work setting or used in the pursuit of additional education.

4. For an individual who has demonstrated limitations in the use of English, a careful matching of the English usage requirements of jobs to a client's capabilities is needed. A thorough job analysis generates information related to the requirements of a particular job including a job description, job functions and task elements, level of education, certifications, specific vocational preparation, reasoning development, mathematical development, language development, aptitudes, temperaments, environmental conditions, and physical demands (Blackwell, Conrad, & Weed, 1992). Less comprehensive but useful are the *Dictionary of Occupational Titles* (U.S. Department of Labor [DOL], 1991), *The Selected Characteristics of Occupations Defined in the Dictionary of Occupational Titles* (DOL, 1981), and *The Complete Guide for Occupational Exploration* (Farr, 1993) that provide general job analysis facts including information about the language demands of given occupations. However, to obtain an optimal match between a person who has limited second-language skills in English and a specific job, it is better to conduct an analysis of the functional English skills needed in a particular working environment. Language usage practices at a Kentucky Fried Chicken Restaurant located in certain reservation communities will be different from a similar establishment located in an urban area.

5. Modifying a recommendation from Cervantes and Acosta (1992), when working with a native language proficient/preferred client, it would be helpful for an English-speaking evaluator to check periodically throughout the assessment to see if the client is fully comprehending during the exchange of information.

6. Conventional career assessment instruments may be quite appropriate for those American Indian clients who have the English usage skills

Cultural Orientation

Many cultural factors may contribute to the cultural orientations of Indian people that act as intervening variables in the career development process. In relation to their experiences working with Navajo people, Morgan, Guy, Lee, and Cellini (1986) stated that:

> Many Indians view career development and the choosing of a job differently than most mainstream vocational counselors. For example, reservation Indians view the home, family, and community as the center of their existence, rather than a job, career, or occupation; the latter view is often common among members of the non-Indian population. (p. 28)

Everett, Proctor, and Cartmell (1983) identified these culture values relevant to psychological service delivery to American Indians that were: (a) family structure, (b) childrearing practices, (c) noninterference, (d) giving, sharing, and cooperating, (e) time, (f) aging, (g) religion, and (h) culture conflict. Regarding culture conflict, Everett et al. (1983) stated: "An awareness of varied styles of acculturation is important to the psychologist who wishes to relate across cultures" (p. 601). LaFromboise et al. (1990) presented a useful model for assessing varied styles of acculturation among American Indians. This model consists of the following five delineations of cultural orientations as described in LaFromboise et al. (1990):

> Traditional—These individuals generally speak and think in their native language and know little English. They observe "old-time" traditionalism and religion, yet cannot fully accept dominant culture and values.
>
> Transitional—These individuals generally speak both English and the Native language in the home. They question basic traditionalism and religion, yet cannot fully accept dominant culture and values.
>
> Marginal—These people may be defensively Indian, but are unable either to live the cultural heritage of their group or to identify with the dominant society. This group tends to have the most difficulty in coping with social problems due to their ethnicity.
>
> Assimilated—Within this group are the people who, for the most part, have been accepted by the dominant society. They generally have embraced dominant culture and values.
>
> Bicultural (referred to in Ryan & Ryan, 1982, as transcendental)—Within this group are those who are, for the most part, accepted by the dominant society. Yet they also know and accept their tribal traditions and culture. They can thus move in either direction, from traditional society to dominant society, with ease. (p. 638)

Assessment Considerations. Having a point of reference for a client's cultural orientation can help both the client and the professional infuse culture values into the process of career development. This point of reference, most importantly, should be understood by the client during the process of career decision making. According to Martin (1991), underlying this cultural infusion process is the "perspective that it is the client's right and responsibility to make career choices, it becomes the responsibility of the counselor to assist the client to explore and clarify the alternative decisions and consequences associated with them" (p. 281).

1. The counselor should learn as much as possible about a client's particular tribal customs before the initial interview. This can be done through obtaining selected readings and talking with cultural informants. If a client lives in a reservation community, it is very useful to visit that homeland to begin understanding how environmental factors may influence the career decision-making process.

2. By using background and interview information, it is useful to develop an initial hypothesis as to the cultural orientation (see Table 8.1) of the person with whom you are working. This hypothesis should be one that is tested throughout the assessment process.

3. Developing a thorough case study with a Native-American client is very important to more fully understand how culture may impact career decision making. Whenever possible, the nuclear and extended family members should be involved to enrich one's understanding of the client's cultural background.

4. During the case study process, cultural orientation information should be obtained in several areas: (a) family structure; (b) client perceptions of acculturation; (c) client's involvement in traditional ceremonies; (d) client's financial role within the family structure; (e) client's short-term and long-term goals related to living in homeland (reservation); and (f) client's work-related values including academic achievement, professional status, income, work independence, job-related and upward mobility.

5. It must be remembered that American Indian clients who practice traditional ways may not view the lack of employment as being independent from their culture, religion, family, tradition, and social network (Morgan et al., 1986). Also, one should use caution when discussing traditional healing and medicine practices with traditional American Indian clients. Frank (1987) advised not to explore the topic in the initial interview, but to establish rapport first and then, if the client initiates the topic, explore the possibilities in more detail.

Home Community

The environmental context has an essential influence on the career development of American Indians especially those persons living on or near reservations. The environments in which people live affect their knowledge about the world of work. Martin (1991) stated:

> An individual's knowledge of the world of work partially depends upon the depth and breadth of past work experiences and the degree of exposure to people working in a wide range of occupations. The environments where people live provide the opportunities to obtain work experience and learn about jobs. Individuals living in an environment with high unemployment and limited job opportunities may have a restricted knowledge of the world of work. (p. 274)

Approximately 40% of American Indians live on or adjacent to Indian reservations (Klein, 1990) that are often very rural and located in remote areas. These communities often have hardships that include unemployment rates 5.47 times higher than that of the total civilian labor force (Martin & Frank, 1987), a 1.5 times higher rate of work disability than for the general population (O'Connell, 1987), and more health-related problems at younger ages than does the general population (Maddux, 1987).

Studies of adolescents living on reservations have shown the impact of rural environments upon occupational values and vocational interests. A comparison of occupational values was made between rural Eskimo adolescents to a sample of urban Alaska White adolescents (McDiarmid & Kleinfeld, 1986). Although the two groups' work values were more similar than different, autonomy, leadership, responsibility, and challenge were reported to be lower for the rural Eskimo students. The researchers asserted that these differences were a function of differing experiences that adolescents of both groups had with various occupations. Fewer Eskimo parents held professional or highly skilled jobs that offered more intrinsic satisfaction from work. The researchers concluded that: "Rural Eskimo students might well seek greater intrinsic satisfaction from work if they were more familiar with occupational areas which offer such rewards" (p. 28).

Epperson and Hammond (1981) studied the efficacy of using the Kuder's General Interest Survey, Form E., with a sample of Zuni ninth-grade males and females. They found substantial differences between the Zuni students' scores and national norms and a high proportion of unacceptable V scores. They recommended that the Zuni students would be best served if their interest scores were interpreted using local as well as national norms. They interpreted these findings to be a reflection of cultural or socialization differences between the two populations. Gade, Fuqua, and Hurlburt (1984) also concluded that long-term cultural and socialization experiences contributed to differences in vocational interests scores between a sample of Swampy Cree and Pequis High School students when compared to national norms using the self-directed search (SDS). They also speculated that the results reflected "the limited range of work models found in the far North reserve" (p. 586).

Approximately, 1,200,000 American Indians (60%) live in cities and suburbs across the nation (Klein, 1990). Two barriers to receiving vocational rehabilitation services by Native Americans living in urban areas were a lack of family and cultural support systems and no identified central agency with whom to communicate (White, 1987). Additional barriers, transportation problems, a lack of affordable housing, a lack of outreach from social service agencies, and advocacy services, were identified by Marshall et al. (1992). Strategies to overcome barriers for Native Americans who have relocated from reservation communities to urban areas for vocational training or job placement were identified by Martin et al. (1988). These strategies include: (a) assist clients to establish cultural support networks, (b) coordinate culturally appropriate services, and (c) network services with state and federal service providers to Indian people.

Assessment Considerations. A principle of social learning theory is that learning occurs when people both respond to and act up the environment. Thus, a history of a client's community living experiences is vital to promoting his or her effective career decision making:

1. A complete history of an American Indian client's community living experiences should be obtained. The locations of the client's various home communities and the amount of time spent on and off reservation should be identified. An analysis of all work experiences and vocational training should be conducted.

2. Descriptions of the occupations and work activities of current and past family members should be acknowledged. The same information about significant others such as friends can be helpful.

3. The use of vocational interest inventories can provide useful information. Conventional vocational assessment techniques are suitable for individuals who have the appropriate level of English skills, who are assimilated or bicultural, and who have spent the majority of their life in an urban community. For persons who have lived on reservation most of their lives, conducting one-to-one or small-group interviews using an interest inventory as the SDS can be effective in assessing their knowledge of the world of work. Likewise, picture interest inventories such as the Wide Range Interest and Opinion Test can be used for persons who may have limited English skills. This procedure not only provides assessment information, but it also expands clients' understanding of job options.

4. It is helpful to identify the career developmental tasks that a client is working on. Super (1990) identified stages by age intervals and developmental tasks as part of a life-span, life-space approach to career development. The age intervals by stages are less useful than the development tasks associated with stages. For example, a client appears to be in an *exploration stage* of development (ages 15–24) that includes developmental tasks of crystallizing, specifying, and implementing a vocational preference. It is clear from the case study, however, that he or she has not successfully completed developmental tasks of the *growth stage* (birth to 14), which includes incorporating work as a part of ego ideal and acquiring basic habits of industry. Despite the client's age, then, interventions should focus on completing developmental tasks in the growth stage.

5. It is important to identify where the client wants and plans to live while developing a career. For example, the importance of a social network and traditional value system that are realized in a reservation homeland may be more important to an individual than having a good-paying, high-status job in a city without support networks. The counselor must help the client make the best life choice, not just the best job choice. When a client makes a decision to live on a reservation that has limited job opportunities, then creative job development and traditional work become salient activities for career placement. The counselor must be knowledgeable of the reservation labor market.

Family System

The family structures of American Indians will vary along a continuum from nuclear systems to intricate networks of extended family members. Pedigo (1983) identified the extended family system as the normative base for American Indian society. The extended family system may consist of three or more closely related family units where the family members are considered relatives with the same influence on an individual's life as parents, brothers, and sisters if there is a clan system (Frank, 1987). There may be protocols within individual families for dealing with important issues or problems and seeking help from outside the family (Everett et al., 1983). When a traditional extended-family network exists, individual decision making may be less important than group decision making because the decisions impact the family system, not just an individual. For example, there may be pressure on an individual who has left his or her reservation home for vocational training or a job. If the individual does not return home for important community and family events, family members may perceive this behavior as being disrespectful or reflecting acculturation. On the other hand, if the individual does return home continually for community and family events, teachers or employers may view the individual's behavior as irresponsible. Individuals are likely to be more successful in career decision making if values associated with family, tribal traditions, homeland, and community living are fully explored. This will help the individuals have a more complete view of the consequences associated with their vocational decisions.

Assessment Considerations. Information about the family system is obtained during the assessment of language usage, cultural orientation, and home community as outlined earlier. Trust toward a counselor by members of a client's extended family may be as vital to successful career development as trust from the client:

1. It is important to determine how major decisions are made within a family system and identify who are the primary decision makers. Decisions made by an individual with a counselor may be quickly overruled when introduced to family members. The counselor must be sensitive to how a client's decisions may affect the health and even survival of a family system. For example, if a family depends on a member's income and that individual relocates to another community to acquire vocational training, the family may be endangered by the loss of that individual's income.

2. Besides the financial role made by the client, other family roles and responsibilities need to be assessed. These include caregiving responsibilities to elders and children, leadership roles in family decision making, religious and ceremonial responsibilities, and home maintenance activities.

3. It is useful to find out what family members' expectations are for a client's future career pursuits. Identify the family traditions related to employment and careers and how they may affect career planning.

4. It is very important to determine how family members can provide support to the client in career planning, vocational training, job seeking, job placement, and job retention.

Communication Style

Any time there are differences between clients and professional helpers related to language, culture, environment, or lifestyle, there is an increased possibility for misunderstanding during the communication process. Ivey (1983) pointed out that peoples of differing cultural backgrounds will have differing patterns of communication and differing expectations of the counseling process. In his work with Navajos, Lowrey (1983) found cross-cultural counseling to be beset with poor communication, value differences, conflicting goals, stereotyping, and frequent failures. Martin et al. (1988) found that counseling and interviewing skills were the second most important training need expressed by counselors working with American Indians living on reservations. Even for counselors working with American Indians living off reservations, these skills were ranked third most important.

A microskills approach for intentional interviewing and counseling (Ivey, 1983) provides a useful framework for assessing and adjusting to the unique communication styles of individuals. Ivey (1983) stated that: "Microskills are communication skill units of the interview that will help you develop a more intentional and rounded ability to interact with a client" (p. 4). Microskills can be observed and measured as both a client and a counselor exhibit them during communication. The objective, skill-oriented makeup of this approach is well suited for cross-cultural communication.

Skills such as attending and influencing are used to some extent by persons from all cultures so they can be vehicles to bridge communication across cultural barriers. This approach has built-in safeguards against insensitivity. For example, a technique called client observation skills is used to note gradual or sudden changes in a client's development level that signals the need to shift to another communication style using differing microskills.

There are three major groupings of microskills: attending skills, influencing skills, and focusing skills. The goal of attending skills is simply to listen accurately to the other person from his or her frame of reference. Fundamental to attending skills are attending behaviors that include eye contact, verbal tracking, body language, and vocal qualities. Other attending skills are client observation skills, open and closed questions, encouragers, paraphrasing, summarization, reflection of feeling, and reflection of meaning.

Focusing is a counseling skill that helps a client to develop an awareness of the many factors relating to a problem and to organize thinking. There are six focusing directions that a counselor can take: the client, the main theme or problem, others, mutual issues or group, the counseling relationship, counselor, and the cultural/environmental context.

Influencing skills are advanced counseling skills that attempt to influence a client directly. Ivey (1983) identified eight influencing skills: directives, logical consequences, self-disclosure, feedback, interpretation, influencing summary, information/advice, instruction/opinion/suggestion, and confrontation.

Assessment Considerations. Ivey's model of microskills provides a culture-fair means to functionally assess and modify the communication process to enhance understanding among persons, including those from differing cultural orientations.

1. In keeping with previous recommendations, spending time in interviewing Native American clients and their family members is time well spent to establish rapport, trust, and obtain valuable information. Horan and Cady (1990) stressed the importance of maximizing informal interactions with American Indian clients during the psychological evaluation process. In their experiences with traditional, primarily Navajo, clients they stated: "Many Indian clients respond well to humor during the course of testing. Frequent breaks, a cup of coffee, a chance to swap jokes or small talk in a different setting (e.g., a coffee room) also help to break down anxiety, guardedness, and a perception by the client that the examiner is in an adversarial role" (p. 7).

2. The client's and family members' responsiveness to attending, influencing, and focusing skills should be assessed during formal and informal interviewing. According to Ivey (1983), client observation skills enable the counselor to "note and understand the client and how he or she thinks and behaves in relation to other people and situations" (p. 58). The counselor assesses the client's nonverbal and verbal behavior in response to the counselor's prompts. Also, the counselor identifies any discrepancies in client messages. This process is designed to help the counselor select useful interviewing skills and counseling interventions to facilitate client growth and development.

INTERVENTION EXAMPLE

An example is presented next that illustrates how interventions can be identified in conjunction with assessments using the cultural and contextual guide for planning differential assessment and intervention with American Indians (refer to Table 8.2).

Background and Assessment Information

A 27-year-old, single, American Indian male has been referred for career development counseling. The client is currently living and working within an off-reservation community that is 25 miles from his reservation home. He is employed as a service technician at an automobile service and repair shop and making minimum wage. He wants to move back to the reservation and seek a career in teaching and coaching. Table 8.2 reflects a differential assessment of hypothesized cultural and contextual factors influencing the career development process.

Language Usage. The client grew up in a home where both his Native language and English were spoken. Currently, he speaks his Native language only when he goes home or when tribal members visit him. The

TABLE 8.2
Cultural and Contextual Guide for Planning Differential Assessment
and Intervention With Native Americans

Language Usage			
	The person's use of language(s) growing up:		
Bilingual	Proficient Native Language	Proficient English	Not Proficient in Either
	The person's use of language(s) now:		
Bilingual	Proficient Native Language	Proficient English	Not Proficient in Either

Cultural Orientation[a]				
The person reflects Indian culture in the following way:				
Traditional	Transitional	Marginal	Assimilated	Bicultural

Home Community		
The person grew up:		
On Reservation	Off-Reservation	Both
The person currently lives:		
On Reservation	Off-Reservation	Both
The person is planning to live:		
On Reservation	Off-Reservation	Both

Family System	
The person lives predominantly within a:	
Nuclear Family	Extended Family

Communication Style[b]		
The person is responsive to:		
Attending Skills	Influencing Skills	Focusing Skills

[a]The operational definition for cultural orientation was taken from Spindler and Spindler (1958), Ryan and Ryan (1982), and LaFromboise et al. (1990).
[b]The operational definition for communication style was taken from Ivey (1983).

client completed primary and secondary education using English exclusively at the BIA school on his reservation. His academic potential was average and he excelled in competitive athletics. He typically scored in the lower quartile (national norms) and low average (local school norms) on the national achievement tests that were administered yearly.

His overall English usage skills were tested to be around the fifth-grade level with lowest skills measured in spelling, oral language, and writing skills. There are no identified problems in communicating effectively within his current living and working environments.

Cultural Orientation. Members of the immediate family system practiced both Christian and traditional religious practices while the client was growing up and he continues to do so. The grandparents spent time each week teaching the grandchildren Native language and traditional ways. His family spent the vast majority of time living on the reservation. They would go off reservation primarily for business transactions, to obtain goods and services, and to participate in recreational activities. He currently participates in eight traditional ceremonies each year.

Home Community. The client grew up within a rural reservation community in the western United States with a population of approximately 2,000 residents. The primary employers for reservation residents are the tribal government, BIA, the Forest Service, the tribal community college, and small farmers. The towns surrounding the reservation community are rural with populations of 15,000 or less. The economies of these towns are primarily based in agriculture, forestry, tourism, and transportation. The client currently lives in one of the surrounding rural communities with a population of 8,000. The closest urban community (80,000) is 150 miles from the reservation community. An analysis of the labor market on the reservation established that the tribe is building a new K–8 school to replace the BIA school. The tribal council wants the school to be staffed primarily by tribal members who can carry out the bilingual, multicultural programs that will be implemented.

The client expressed a strong interest in teaching in the new school. The results of a conventional vocational interest inventory using an interview format showed a low, flat profile of interests related to Holland's typology of personalities and work environments. It was clear during the testing that the client had limited knowledge about a wide range of jobs and specific activities and competencies associated with many jobs.

Family System. He was raised with his parents, one grandmother, one aunt, two sisters, and one brother living in the home. Additionally, two grandparents and two uncles with families lived nearby and were a daily part of the family system. His father worked for many years as the custodian at the BIA school. The client's work experience growing up was occasionally assisting his father at the school, cutting and selling wood by the cord, and doing ranch chores.

The client seeks advice and approval from family members, especially his mother, on all major decisions. A significant portion of his salary is contributed to his family through his mother. The client goes to his family's home most weekends. On several occasions during each month, family members stay at his apartment when they go to town.

Communication Style. The client was responsive to some aspects of attending, influencing, and focusing skills (as indicated by the underlines used in Table 8.2). He was responsive to the counselor's typically ex-

pressed attending skills using eye contact, body language, and vocal quality during several one-to-one interviews. With verbal tracking, he shifted
topics abruptly and continually during interactions. He also was not open
to reflection of feeling.

The client was able to focus on the main theme for counseling most
of the time and was able to focus on others and mutual issues between
the counselor and client. He was less able to discuss personal strengths
and weaknesses. The skill that was important for further development
was focusing on cultural/environmental/contextual issues.

He seemed the most amenable to the influencing skills of directives,
information giving, advice, and providing him with a brief summary of
what the counselor said or thought during the interview. The least effective influencing skills were self-disclosure, feedback, and interpretation.
The influencing skill that was lacking but needed to be more fully developed was logical consequences.

Initial Interventions

The following interventions provide examples for incorporating cultural
and contextual variables into the process of establishing a sound career
development plan. Once the career development plan is established, the
counselor needs to provide close monitoring and coordinate support systems to assist the client to implement career development.

1. Before meeting with the client, the counselor needs to obtain information about the client's tribe and reservation community. The counselor
should obtain written accounts, talk with tribal members, and visit the
reservation community. Information obtained should include tribal history, customs, and traditional family structures. Also, information about
economic, labor market, educational, and social systems should be obtained.

2. Initially, the client and counselor need to enhance communication
using logical consequences skills and cultural/environmental/contextual
focusing. The skill of logical consequences encourages the client and counselor to analyze the positive and negative outcomes of decisions. Cul-
tural/environmental/contextual focusing helps direct client conversational
flow. It enables a broadening of perspectives for both the counselor and
the client to understand a presenting problem. The ways in which cultural,
environmental, and contextual factors will influence the client's decision
making are multiple and intricate. Full use of this focusing skill results
in increased cognitive complexity and understanding of difficult decisions.

3. Clearly extended families will be active in the client's decision making and will be affected by his decisions. After rapport and productive communication has been established with the client, the client's mother and father should be talked with to obtain input into decision making for their son. They can also provide information about the client's roles and responsibilities to the extended family system. It will be vitally important to gain their general support and identify specific ways that they will commit to the career development process.

4. The client should enroll in an English class at the tribal community college following an evaluation from the college to identify which class would be the best placement. He would benefit from improving his English usage skills, especially in the areas of oral expression and writing. Increased English skills would enhance vocational upward mobility and would be necessary for success in obtaining postsecondary education.

5. The client needs to expand his global knowledge of the world of work to see more fully the career options available to him. He is in the career life stage of exploration (Super, 1990) and needs to accomplish more fully the crystallizing, specifying, and implementing of a vocational preference. The establishment of a structured reading-discussion method should be implemented using sources of occupational information such as the *Dictionary of Occupational Titles*, the *Occupational Outlook Handbook*, *The Complete Guide to Occupational Exploration*, and occupational videotapes. A group guidance approach would be an effective modality to use. The client should be scheduled to conduct career exploration interviews with individuals performing jobs of interest to the client. These interviews should be scheduled with employees in urban, rural, and reservation communities.

6. The client needs to obtain a focused knowledge of his expressed career interest of teaching. He might interview and job shadow a teacher in the BIA school. He needs to obtain information about the teacher aid certificate training at the tribal community college and teacher preparation requirements at the state teachers' college.

7. If teaching remains a viable vocational preference, the client would benefit from an on-the-job training (OJT) experience working with a teacher. This could be independent from or in concert with the teacher aid certificate training program at the tribal community college. This OJT would provide an opportunity for situationally assessing the multiple interests and skills associated with teaching, including the demands for English usage skills.

8. If teaching at the tribal school remains feasible, the client should enroll in a Native language class at the community college so that he will

be prepared to assist in the implementation of the bilingual, multicultural programs.

CONCLUSION

Culture evolves. Any attempt at capturing what the culture is for a given group of people is imperiled by the inevitable condition of change. Culture is evidenced in differential ways by similar people. Environmental factors and specific characteristics of individuals interplay with culture to create persons who are unique. Psychologists and counselors must understand the culture, environmental factors, and individual characteristics of American Indian clients with whom they work. More importantly, these professionals must help their Native American clients to integrate this information in the process of making optimal career choices and being at ease with the associated consequences.

REFERENCES

American Indian Policy Review Commission. (1977). *Final report* (Vosl. 1 and 2). Washington, DC: U.S. Government Printing Office.

Blackwell, T. L., Conrad, A. D., & Weed, R. O. (1992). *Job analysis and the ADA: A step by step guide.* Athens, GA: Elliott & Fitzpatrick.

Cervantes, R. C., & Acosta, F. X. (1992). Psychological testing for Hispanic Americans. *Applied and Preventive Psychology, 1,* 209–219.

Chafe, W. L. (1974). About language: A richness of words, a Babel of tongues. In J. B. Billard (Ed.), *The world of the American Indian* (pp. 150–155). Washington, DC: National Geographic Society.

Conoley, J. C., & Haynes, G. (1992). An ecological approach to intervention. In C. D'Amato & B. Rothlisberg (Eds.), *Psychological perspectives on intervention: A case study approach to prescriptions for change* (pp. 177–189). New York: Longman.

Dawis, R. V. (1992). The individual differences tradition in counseling psychology. *Journal of Counseling Psychology, 39,* 7–19.

DeAngelis, T. (1992, November). Division 38 conference explores ethnic-minority health issues. *APA Monitor,* pp. 32–33.

Epperson, D. L., & Hammond, D. C. (1981). Use of interest inventories with Native Americans: A case for local norms. *Journal of Counseling Psychology, 28,* 213–220.

Everett, F., Proctor, N., & Cartmell, B. (1983). Providing psychological services to American Indian children and families. *Professional Psychology: Research and Practice, 14*(5), 588–603.

Farr, J .M. (Ed.). (1993). *The complete guide for occupational exploration.* Indianapolis: JIST Works.

Frank, L. W. (1987, Fall). Cultural factors that can affect rehabilitation of American Indians. *UTS'ITISHTAAN'I* (p. 4). Flagstaff: Northern Arizona University, Native American Research and Training Center. (Available from the American Indian Rehabilitation Research and Training Center, P.O. Box 5630, Flagstaff, AZ 86011.)

Gade, E. M., Fuqua, D., Hurlburt, G. (1984). Use of the Self-Directed Search with Native American high school students. *Journal of Counseling Psychology, 31,* 584–587.

Holland, J. L. (1985). *Making vocational choices: A theory of vocational personalities and work environments.* Englewood Cliffs, NJ: Prentice-Hall.

Horan, K., & Cady, D. C. (1990). The psychological evaluation of American Indians. *Arizona Counseling Journal, 15,* 6–12.

Ivey, A. (1983). *Intentional interviewing and counseling.* Monterey, CA: Brooks/Cole.

Klein, B. T. (1990). *Reference encyclopedia of the American Indian* (5th ed.). West Nyack, NY: Todd.

Krumboltz, J. D. (1976). A social learning theory of career selection. *The Counseling Psychologist, 6,* 71–81.

LaFromboise, T. D., Trimble, J. E., & Mohatt, G. V. (1990). Counseling intervention and American Indian tradition: An integrative approach. *The Counseling Psychologist, 18,* 628–654.

Lowrey, L. (1983). Bridging a culture in counseling. *Journal of Applied Rehabilitation Counseling, 14,* 69–73.

Maddux, C. (1987). Analysis of the prevalence of disability among American Indians: School-based data. In J. C. O'Connell (Ed.), *A study of the special problems and needs of American Indians with handicaps both on and off the reservation* (Vol. 2, pp. 98–144). Flagstaff: Northern Arizona University, Native American Research and Training Center, and Tucson: University of Arizona, Native American Research and Training Center. (Available from the American Indian Rehabilitation Research and Training Center, P.O. Box 5630, Flagstaff, AZ 86011.)

Marshall, C. A., Johnson, M. J., Martin, W. E., Jr., Saravanabhavan, R. C., & Bradford, B. (1992). The rehabilitation needs of American Indians with disabilities in an urban setting. *Journal of Rehabilitation, 58,* 13–21.

Martin, W. E., Jr. (1991). Career development and American Indians living on reservations: Cross-cultural factors to consider. *The Career Development Quarterly, 39,* 273–283.

Martin, W. E., Jr., & Frank, L. W. (1987). An analysis of the labor market participation of American Indians with implications for rehabilitation. In J. C. O'Connell (Ed.), *A study of the special problems and needs of American Indians with handicaps both on and off the reservation* (Vol. II, pp. 98–144). Flagstaff: Northern Arizona University, Institute for Human Development, Native American Research and Training Center. (Available from the American Indian Rehabilitation Research and Training Center, Institute for Human Development, Northern Arizona University, P.O. Box 5630, Flagstaff, AZ 86011.)

Martin, W. E., Jr., Frank, L. W., Minkler, S., & Johnson, M. J. (1988). A survey of vocational rehabilitation counselors who work with American Indians. *Journal of Applied Rehabilitation Counseling, 19,* 29–34.

Martin, W. E., Jr., & O'Connell, J. C. (1986). *Pueblo Indian vocational rehabilitation services study.* Flagstaff: Northern Arizona University, Institute for Human Development, Native American Research and Training Center. (Available from the American Indian Rehabilitation Research and Training Center, Institute for Human Development, Northern Arizona University, P.O. Box 5630, Flagstaff, AZ 86011.)

McDiarmid, G. W., & Kleinfeld, J. S. (1986). Occupational values of rural Eskimos. *Journal of American Indian Education, 24,* 23–29.

Morgan, C. O., Guy, E., Lee, B., & Cellini, H. R. (1986). Rehabilitation services for American Indians: The Navajo experience. *Journal of Rehabilitation, 52,* 25–31.

Nye, C. (1986). *Standardization of the TOLD-P for five to eight year old bilingual Navajo children.* Flagstaff: Native American Research and Training Center, Northern Arizona University. (Available from the American Indian Rehabilitation Research and Training Center, Institute for Human Development, Northern Arizona University, P.O. Box 5630, Flagstaff, AZ 86011.)

O'Connell, J. C. (Ed.). (1987). *A study of the special problems and needs of American Indians with handicaps both on and off the reservation* (Vol. II). Flagstaff: Northern Arizona University,

Native American Research and Training Center, and Tucson: University of Arizona, Native American Research and Training Center. (Available from the American Indian Rehabilitation Research and Training Center, P.O. Box Flagstaff, AZ 86011.)

Pedigo, J. (1983). Finding the "meaning" of Native American substance abuse: Implications for prevention. *The Personnel and Guidance Journal, 61,* 273–276.

Ryan, L., & Ryan, R. (1982). *Mental health and the urban Indian.* Unpublished manuscript.

Sidles, C., & MacAvoy, J. (1986). *Navajo adolescents' scores on a primary language questionnaire, the Raven Standard Progressive Matrices (RSPM) and the Comprehensive Test of Basic Skills (CTBS): A correlational study.* Flagstaff: Northern Arizona University, Native American Research and Training Center, and Tucson: University of Arizona, Native American Research and Training Center. (Available from the American Indian Rehabilitation Research and Training Center, P.O. Box 5630, Flagstaff, AZ 86011.)

Spindler, L., & Spindler, G. (1958). Male and female adaptations in culture change. *American Anthropologist, 60,* 217–233.

Super, D. E. (1990). A life-span, life-space approach to career development. In D. Brown & L. Brooks (Eds.), *Career choice and development* (2nd ed.). San Francisco: Jossey-Bass.

Tanner, D. C., & Martin, W. E., Jr. (1986). Services and training needs in communicative disorders for rehabilitation professionals serving Native Americans. *The Journal of Rehabilitation Administration, 10,* 117–123.

U.S. Department of Labor. (1981). *Selected characteristics of occupations defined in the Dictionary of Occupational Titles.* Washington, DC: U.S. Government Printing Office.

U.S. Department of Labor. (1991). *Dictionary of Occupational Titles.* Washington, DC: U.S. Government Printing Office.

Warner, C. (1984). Bilingual instruction and special English training. *Annual Report of the Arizona Department of Education.* Phoenix: Arizona Department of Education.

White, A. (1987). The nature and extent of cooperative efforts by state vocational rehabilitation programs for Indian people who are disabled. In J. C. O'Connell (Ed.), *A study of the special problems and needs of American Indians with handicaps both on and off the reservation* (Vol. II, pp. 145–178). Flagstaff: Northern Arizona University, Native American Research and Training Center, and Tucson: University of Arizona, Native American Research and Training Center. (Available from the American Indian Rehabilitation Research and Training Center, Box 5630, Flagstaff, AZ 86011.)

Yost, E. B., & Corbishley, M. A. (1987). *Career counseling: A psychological perspective.* San Francisco: Jossey-Bass.

III

FUTURE DIRECTIONS

9

Toward a Multicultural Theory of Career Development: Prospects and Dilemmas

Samuel H. Osipow
Eugia M. Littlejohn
The Ohio State University

There is a fundamental consistency in the material presented by Arbona, Brown, Johnson, Swartz, and Martin, and Leong and Serafica (this volume) with regard to the career development of ethnic minorities. The role and importance of the history, education, and social, political, and economic experience of each of the respective ethnic groups is seen to be clearly related to their career experiences. The inclusion of these contextual perspectives must play a central role in any serious attempt toward the creation of a multicultural theory of career development.

As previously suggested in those chapters, African Americans, Asian Americans, Hispanics, and Native Americans represent four separate and distinct subgroups of the so-called "American" culture. Yet each group has a shared history of exclusion from mainstream American society. This exclusion is seen in history books, the educational system, the socioeconomic infrastructure, and the labor force, to name but a few circumstances. To varying degrees and in different ways, each group has been disenfranchised. With this knowledge, it is not surprising that (counseling) psychology has ignored ethnic minority issues and experiences in developing career theories.

The chapters on career development by Arbona on Hispanics, by Brown on African Americans, by Johnson, Swartz, and Martin on Native Americans, and by Leong and Serafica on Asian Americans each stake out an ambitious agenda, and one that is full of problems. Each chapter has reviewed an extensive literature that describes both the state of the art of empirical knowledge about the career development of populations heretofore largely ignored by career psychology researchers, and the state of theoretical wisdom for the same understudied groups. The result is a mixture of knowledge and ignorance about multicultural career development.

The state of knowledge of career theory in general (see Savickas & Lent, 1994) reveals that we continue to expand both our theoretical and empirical base while at the same time reveals a continuing lack of effort and knowledge about large segments of our population including the minority groups described in this volume as well as women (Fitzgerald & Betz, 1994).

When restricted to middle-class males, it is possible to sketch a picture of a predictable career path that hits the mark reasonably often, although we have become increasingly aware that the changes in the economy and the way the workforce is structured have impaired our ability to predict effectively even for that population. When one recognizes the increased numbers of ethnic and racial minorities of both sexes entering the labor force and seeking promising careers in the context of a sharply changing economy and workplace, the need for strong and valid career concepts and a supportive database becomes crucial. Our society may be entering a crisis in work, work values, and wealth and poverty. In other words, at the same time that we have entered a global economy and jobs are scarce and insecure for workers of all types and at all levels, pressure to obtain those good jobs and advance vocationally has increased even further by the refusal of ethnic minority men and women to accept a society and economy that relegates them to second- or third-class employment. The result is that it has become essential to develop a theoretical basis to account for the career development and behavior of all people.

What we try to accomplish in this chapter to move toward solutions is to first identify what if any of the existing theoretical concepts seem to work for all or most groups, and why. Second, we identify which concepts do not work, and why. And third, we make suggestions to identify how we might revise and/or repair our current approaches to make them work better with the diverse population in our increasingly multicultural society, or to at least identify problems for others to try to solve.

Career Assumptions

One of our problems lies in our assumptions about culture and career. It is likely that in recent 20th-century experience, immigrants to the United States strived to share the "American Experience" and the good life that was seen to result from it. If not in the first generation, at least in the second, new Americans strived to speak English and integrate, at least publicly, into the "mainstream" society. They sought to be upwardly mobile via education and employment and either discarded their diverse ethnic heritages or suppressed them from public view in order to assimilate. Thus, the view of America as the great "melting pot" emerged. This view would apply to the large number of eastern and southern Europeans who came to the United States in the late 19th century and early 20th century, as well as to many of the Spanish speakers and Asians who came to the United States somewhat more recently.

Two glaring exceptions to these groups are African Americans, who came here against their will and, although here for many generations, have never been invited wholeheartedly into what others view as the upwardly mobile American experience, and Native Americans, who were subjugated over several centuries.

The goals of many ethnic and racial group members have recently changed so that instead of valueing a melting pot that emphasizes the similarities and minimizes our differences, multiculturality has emerged as a value. The multicultural emphasis of ethnic and racial minorities points up their increasing reluctance to surrender their roots, language, and culture. At the same time, full access to the workplace is impaired for many minorities because particular cultural values and practices are either incompatible or conflict with standard work practices and schedules. For example, various religious groups cannot easily engage in required daily prayer schedules or observe religious holidays within the usual workplace daily attendance and vacation policies.

Even more difficult to resolve are the problems inherent in integrating Native-American culture into the urban workplace. In many Native-American cultures the value of unity with nature is clearly incompatible with Western industrial culture that strives to reshape nature to conform to the wishes of the human race.

In the face of such conflicts, our dilemma is how to accomplish total access and integration into the workplace for everyone, and at the same time maintain the desirable features of the workplace and the economy while preserving the cultural heritages of groups that may clash with those features. This objective is likely to be easier to achieve for some groups than for others, largely as a function of the extent of cultural differences. At the same time we need to guard against stereotyping groups and assuming all their members are alike.

In some ways, this situation is analogous with some efforts made to modify the workplace to make it more compatible for women who are mothers, such as providing day care for children, more maternity leave, job sharing, and flexible hours. Have those efforts solved the problems of women in the workplace? Probably not, even though some individual women at work may have experienced some improvement in work and family life as a result. The difficulty is that such solutions indicate that the problem is a "women's" problem and not a workplace problem. Until that shift in thinking occurs, one cannot be optimistic about the effectiveness of parallel solutions for the workplace problems facing Hispanics, Asian Americans, African Americans, and Native Americans.

Because career development begins with career choice and entry, perhaps a good way to begin reflecting on the central issues impairing our ability to develop multicultural career theory is to start with three necessary conditions for vocational choice to occur proposed by Crites (1969) a long time ago. Crites noted that for a choice to occur an individual must possess alternative options, a motivation to choose, and the freedom to choose. Are all three conditions present in the ordinary life experience of young people in the United States, or do these conditions exist to a different degree for different groups?

To follow through, Crites (1969) pointed out that the variables usually examined with career choice are, first, cultural, social geographic, economic, and so on; second, organismic; third, hypothetical constructs; and last, response variables, such as traits, interests, and values.

With these ideas as background, we can begin our analysis of career theory by examining how individual career goals contrast with those expressed by most major career development theories. Examining the major concepts of the most influential career theories, a short list emerges:

1. There is a matching of personal attributes (which includes needs, values, interests, and abilities) with work requirements. Sometimes this matching is called correspondence (Dawis & Lofquist, 1984), sometimes congruence (Holland, 1985), sometimes self-concept implementation in work (Super, 1957), but it always presumes a self-conscious searching by the individual for a good vocational fit in the universe of jobs.

2. The assumption is made that individuals have the encouragement, ability, and resources to identify their salient work attributes. (This roughly corresponds to Crites' suggestion about alternatives, motivation, and freedom to choose.) Here again, this concept is variously called the work personality (Dawis & Lofquist, 1984), vocational calculus (Holland, 1985), or self-concept (Super, 1957).

3. A process of rational compromise is assumed, through which individuals review their attributes and opportunities/access and identify a career aspiration (see L. Gottfredson, 1982) that is consistent with their personal gender-role attitudes, their resources, occupational attractiveness (e.g., prestige) at a comfortable level of expenditure of energy and resources. In simpler terms, individuals whose access to certain careers is blocked by limitations in their abilities, limitations imposed by the job market, barriers imposed by their gender, race, or ethnicity, or limitations imposed by educational opportunities, and so forth, will move down their

list of attractive occupational prospects until they identify one that they believe they can implement.

Examining these common concepts is a good place to begin our examination of where theory may go wrong with respect to multiculturality. The concepts all assume cultures that are relatively affluent and have good opportunities for education, upward mobility, and family support and encouragement. Generally speaking, a minimal income level is probably necessary to create the environment that can lead to aspirations and skills to achieve. Although not all individuals in various cultural settings lack such attributes, nor do all affluent families engender them, it does seem likely that economically depressed families and the individuals in them lack the basic elements assumed: Children may not be well nourished, may not have quiet places to study or encouragement to do so, may not have understanding and supporting parents, and so on. Even though cultures of many kinds can produce families with good income levels, it is clear that poverty is not proportionally distributed by race and ethnicity in this country.

In the context of social and economic class differences that are significantly different for various racial and ethnic groups, career development theories nonetheless attempt to predict several behaviors and processes. Most theories attempt to estimate what developmental events occur that are related to career decision behaviors. Moreover, the theories try to identify the important familial and social variables that seem to shape decisions and decision processes as individuals develop. Finally, theories try to identify individual traits, both affective and cognitive, that are important influences on career decision and adjustment behaviors.

It may well be that the three elements identified by Crites (1969) apply appropriately to a very wide variety of cultural and racial groups, and that what must be adjusted are the details of how they apply rather than the larger concepts. Of course, this application would become inappropriate if Crites's (1969) basic assumptions of career theory are inapplicable; that is, if work is not seen as a central life variable, if options and choices are not seen to be available so that individuals do not see themselves as having some control over their work lives, or if social discrimination operates to distort the effects of the individual's characteristics, then theoretically predictable behaviors cannot apply. Because these central assumptions of career development theory are often violated in the lives of ethnic or racial minority group members, career theories often fail to predict the career behaviors and lives of racial and ethnic minority group members. In other words, life and social circumstances must permit, even encourage, people to be future oriented, have hope, perceive real options, and increase their prospects for conceptual work in contrast to manual work for career theory to be useful.

Productive Directions

Perhaps the exploration of a multicultural approach to career theory could take some cues from developments growing from efforts to organize our understanding of the career development of women. Recent theorizing and subsequent data generated by Farmer (1985), Fassinger (1990), and Astin (1984) has suggested that the process women go through in their career decision making and development is more complicated than that for men. There are more variables to be addressed for women, and, thus, these models suggest that any single variable will be less important for women than for men, because it will have less weight in the sum total of all the variables. Some reasons to believe this idea has credibility lie in some recent studies by Osipow, Temple, and Rooney (1993), and Temple and Osipow (1994). They found that career indecision was more likely to be effected by self-efficacy for men than for women, in part explaining their results in terms of this differential weighting effect.

It is possible that similar such subtle differences may be observed in the career decision process of ethnic/racial minorities, if we but change our set from looking for profound effects resulting from major variables to more subtle effects resulting from minor variables. In view of the evidence that ethnicity and race alone, with other variables such as socioeconomic status held constant, exerts a relatively minor effect on at least career choice and entry, such a paradigm shift in our thinking may be very important and ultimately productive. Perhaps it is time to create career theories that try to describe career development and choice as it *is* and not as we think it *should* be. Such a shift might produce more powerful career concepts for *all* kinds of people.

CURRENT STATUS OF CAREER THEORY FOR ETHNIC GROUPS

At present, there is no single theory of career development that solely addresses the issues pertinent to ethnic groups in the United States. It is far beyond the scope of this chapter to provide such a theory. Yet, in reviewing the literature, what emerges is a need for a multicultural theory of career development that addresses more subtle variables of career choice and development such as the individual's self-concept, racial and cultural identity development, and self-efficacy, as well as factors that underlie social learning. What follows is an attempt to delineate those components/concepts of existing theories that are essential to a multicultural perspective of career choice and development. It is possible that subtle differences may be observed in the career decision process of ethnic/racial minorities, if we but shift our focus from examining the profound effects of major variables (e.g., race, socioeconomic status) to the more subtle effects resulting from "minor" variables.

One variable, self-concept, permeates much of the psychological literature. Generally, it is referred to as the way in which one views oneself; self-concept is a function of the individual, an intrinsic factor, and the environment, an extrinsic factor. According to career theories, self-concept is an attempt to express one's individuality, uniqueness, and career interests and abilities (Super, 1964). The expression of the self-concept is due in part to the individual's personal development and to the environmental factors that shape that development. It is essential, then, to consider these internal and external factors when exploring self-concept formation of ethnic minorities.

The expression of self is a complex task of competing and often opposing forces where ethnic minorities are concerned. For ethnic individuals who uphold their cultural mores, the development and expression of a sense of self that is consistent with cultural attitudes, beliefs, and values is more likely to be affirmed within that cultural context than in the larger society. However, it is the larger society that usually determines a minority's work status. This larger society, or external environment, can either be supportive, nonencouraging and nondiscouraging (producing a neutral effect), or hostile. Whatever the case, ethnic minorities, in particular, are subject to externalities that have historically proven to be anything but conducive to their development of self.

As career theory has it, the development of self and its subsequent implementation in work is influenced by one's life stage development. Those who are younger tend to manifest a less mature sense of self than those who are older. According to other theorists (e.g., Atkinson, Morten, & Sue, 1979; Cross, 1978; Sandoval, 1990), ethnic minorities, in general, and African Americans and Hispanic Americans, specifically, progress through stages of minority identity development that are also related to and reflective of one's sense of self. The individual's identity stage will determine whether we see conformity to mainstream societal norms while rejecting cultural norms or vice versa, or find a balance between the two. The fact remains, however, that identity development in addition to the general developmental cycle poses challenges to minorities in American society. These challenges may prolong the consolidation of self and ultimately the expression of self in a career. To date, there is no theory of career choice or development that accounts for these variables.

The intricacy with which racial and cultural identity are woven into the fabric of ethnic minority development cannot be accounted for by theory alone. Yet, if we look at the collective and individual histories of African Americans, Hispanic Americans, Asian Americans, and Native Americans, there are similarities of experience that theorists have ferreted out to formulate conceptions about that development. World view and ethnic identity development are two such variables that have contributed to the understanding of ethnically and culturally different groups.

World view refers to the values, attitudes, and beliefs of certain groups, and it also refers to ways in which members of these groups perceive, interpret, and respond to various life events. Sue (1981) went further to define world view according to the individual's propensity to view life conditions as a function of personal control and responsibility (internal control and internal responsibility) or environmental control and responsibility (external control and external responsibility). Sue noted that whereas most middle-class Whites fall along the internal control–internal responsibility portion of the continuum, the majority of minority-status individuals lie somewhere along the internal control–external responsibility end of the continuum. Essentially, this means that minorities view their disadvantaged status not as their personal lack of capability but as the responsibility of a larger, external "system." Extending this to career issues, minorities, then, would believe that inequitable, unjust, and differential treatment in employment practices, the workforce, and the work environment are not the result of their incompetencies, but the result of discrimination and prejudice of the larger society. The onus for change, however, rests in their (minorities') hands. For instance, if a working class Hispanic-American male who identifies very strongly with his cultural background believes that prejudicial practices are exercised in certain work settings, he may be more likely to avoid those settings or confront the unfair practices directly. Although it is obvious that avoidance of the situation could limit his job choices, confrontation could have more far-reaching deleterious effects.

Like world view, minority identity development offers insight into factors that effect career choice and development of minorities. Many theories of ethnic identity development (e.g., Atkinson et al., 1979; Cross, 1978; Parham & Helms, 1985; Sandoval, 1990) suggest that minority individuals fluctuate through a series of stages that are characterized by either rejecting their own cultural identity in favor of the majority culture, totally rejecting the majority culture in favor of their minority culture, or finding a sense of value and balance between ethnicity and mainstream society. Parham and Helms (1985), for example, found that those African Americans who reject their own culture in favor of the majority or reject the majority culture in favor of their own show an inverse correlation between these attitudes and self-concept. If self-concept, as has been postulated, is crucial in the expression of self in a vocation, it is reasonable to surmise that an individual who has a low self-concept will likely choose an occupation that is inconsistent with and does not adequately represent personal abilities and interests.

As with concepts and questions regarding world view, relationships between ethnic identity development and career development are more inferential because theory has failed to include these variables in the equation. Furthermore, only speculations can be made about the influence of these variables on ethnic minority career choice. Until empirical research is conducted, questions such as "What is the relationship between minority identity development and career choice?" "Are there correlations between world view or ethnic identity and career achievement?" and "How does level of acculturation influence career development?" remain unanswered.

Where theory is concerned, the social learning perspective of career development tends to raise many of the issues that are faced by ethnic minorities within the vocational context. According to this theory, career decisions are the result of both person and environmental determinants, including race and socioeconomic status. The reciprocal nature of the person–environment interaction serves as a basis for the individual to make career choices and evaluate career-related decisions.

Environmental factors such as the job market and job selection procedures are variables in the dyadic person–environment relationship. For instance, the job market today is saturated, particularly in vocational and technical jobs. Although this effects the American populous as a whole, it uniquely effects ethnic minority participation in the labor force, because African Americans, Asian Americans, Native Americans, and Hispanic Americans are overrepresented in these lower level positions.

It is well known that many minorities lack the educational opportunities and achievements of their White counterparts. As alluded to in the preceding chapters, the history of most minorities in America is one of disadvantage and disenfranchisement in social, political, economic, and educational realms. If minorities have historically lagged behind the "norm" in terms of educational attainment, and according to present-day statistics figures have changed only minimally, it would only logically follow that their potential for upward mobility in the job market is limited. Needless to say, this constrains career options.

In addition to lack of educational opportunities, differential selection procedures have negatively impacted the career potential of many ethnic minorities. The unwritten rules of the "old boy" network have subtlety but no less poignantly excluded minorities. For many minorities the adage, "last hired, first fired," is a reality. Unfortunately, discriminatory practices have not been accounted for in theories of vocational development.

The theory of social learning purports that individuals receive reinforcement or punishment from the environment that either increases or decreases the likelihood of subsequent behaviors. Where career-related behaviors are concerned, reinforcers and punishers are important variables that determine success or failure. The unique experience of ethnic minorities is that they, collectively and as distinct groups, have been punished by the environment. This punishment has been instituted not only in terms of their differential experience and treatment in the labor force but also in their exclusion from consideration in theories that attempt to explain the events that precipitate entering the labor force, namely, career development theories. The result is often ineffective career implementation and with no explanation of why.

A final variable to consider is self-efficacy. Bandura (1977) defined self-efficacy as an individual's confidence in the ability to successfully complete a task. One's perceived efficacy is shaped by opportunities that allow for attempts at accomplishing a task (performance accomplishments); observations of others successfully performing a task (vicarious learning); encouragement or persuasion from others with regard to the task at hand (verbal persuasion); and an appropriate amount of anxiety (emotional arousal) so as not to be debilitating.

The opportunity for minorities to "try their hand" at certain occupations often comes in the form of "special" programs with specified criteria for inclusion (e.g., low-income family, first-generation college student, etc.). The opportunity for actually attempting to gain access to information about a career prior to entering into it often evades minorities. This is in part the result of our inadequate and uneven dispersion of information as well as too few role models in positions of assistance. Moreover, minority persons, particularly students, are often not discouraged but at the same time not encouraged to pursue diverse career options, creating what Freeman (1979) referred to as the null environment.

The underlying concept of self-efficacy is the premise that people are able to define their own reality. Myers stated (1988): "Power . . . is the ability to define reality" (p. 12). It goes without saying that African Americans, Hispanic Americans, Asian Americans, and Native Americans have been on the periphery of the power distribution.

Are these variables viable considerations for a theory that explains career choice and development of ethnic minorities? Although not an exhaustive list, these variables, as defined by existing theories, do not deal with relevant aspects of minority existence. What is needed is a tailoring of concepts to include references to the historical and present-day status of minority groups. In addition, the specific value orientations of the four major minority groups discussed in this section should be the guideposts for theory building. And finally, attempts should be made both theoretically and empirically to explain within-group and between-group variance on these variables.

REFERENCES

Astin, H. S. (1984). The meaning of work in women's lives: A sociopsychological model of career choice and work behavior. *The Counseling Psychologist, 12*(4), 117–126.

Atkinson, D. R., Morten, G., & Sue, D. D. (1979). *Counseling American minorities: A cross-cultural perspective.* Dubuque, IA: Brown.

Bandura, A. (1977). Self-efficacy: Toward a unifying theory of behavioral change. *Psychological Review, 84*, 191–215.

Crites, J. O. (1969). *Vocational psychology.* New York: McGraw-Hill.

Cross, W. E. (1978). The Thomas and Cross models of psychological nigrescence: A review. *Journal of Black Psychology, 5*, 13–31.

Dawis, R., & Lofquist, L. (1984). *A psychological theory of work adjustment.* Minneapolis: University of Minnesota.

Farmer, H. S. (1985). Model of career and achievement motivation for women and men. *Journal of Counseling Psychology, 32*, 363–390.

Fassinger, R. E. (1990). Causal models of career choice in two samples of college women. *Journal of Vocational Behavior, 27*, 123–153.

Fitzgerald, L. F., & Betz, N. E. (1994). Career development in cultural context: The role of gender, race, class and sexual orientation. In M. Savickas & R. Lent (Eds.), *Convergence in theories of career choice and development* (pp. 103–117). Palo Alto, CA: Consulting Psychologists' Press.

Freeman, J. (1979). How to discriminate against women without really trying. In J. Freeman (Ed.), *Women: A feminist perspective* (2nd ed., pp. 194–208). Palo Alto, CA: Mayfield.

Gottfredson, L. (1982). Circumscription and compromise: A developmental theory of occupational aspirations. *Journal of Counseling Psychology, 28*, 545–579.

Holland, J. L. (1985). *Making vocational choices: A theory of careers.* Englewood Cliffs, NJ: Prentice-Hall.

Myers, L. J. (1988). *Understanding an afrocentric world view: Introduction to an optimal psychology.* Dubuque, IA: Kendall/Hunt.

Osipow, S. H., Temple, R., & Rooney, R. (1993). The short form of the Task-Specific Occupational Self-Efficacy Scale. *Journal of Career Assessment, 1*, 13–20.

Parham, T. A., & Helms, J. E. (1985). Attitudes of racial identity and self-esteem in black students: An exploratory investigation. *Journal of College Student Personnel, 26*, 143–147.

Sandoval, A. (1990). Ethnic identity: Crisis and resolution. *Journal of Multicultural Counseling and Development, 18*, 29–40.

Savickas, M., & Lent, R. (Eds.). (1994). *Convergence in theories of career choice and development.* Palo Alto, CA: Consulting Psychologists' Press.

Sue, D. W. (1981). *Counseling the culturally different: Theory and practice.* New York: Wiley.

Super, D. E. (1957). *The psychology of careers.* New York: Harper & Row.

Super, D. E. (1964). A developmental approach to vocational guidance. *Vocational Guidance Quarterly, 13*, 1–10.

Temple, R., & Osipow, S. H. (1994). The relationship between task-specific self-efficacy, egalitarianism and career indecision for females. *Journal of Career Assessment, 2*, 83–91.

Career Assessment and Intervention With Racial and Ethnic Minorities

Nancy E. Betz
The Ohio State University

Louise F. Fitzgerald
University of Illinois

We were pleased with the opportunity to read and react to the chapters in this volume concerning career assessment and intervention with racial and ethnic minorities, namely, Bowman's "Career Intervention Strategies for African Americans," Fouad's "Career Behavior of Hispanics: Assessment and Career Intervention," Leong and Gim's "Career Assessment and Intervention for Asian Americans," and Martin's "Career Development Assessment and Intervention Strategies with Native Americans." In this chapter we begin by reviewing five major conclusions that can be gleaned from these chapters. Second, based on these major conclusions we present our views regarding needed steps in assessment, intervention, and research.

SUMMARY OF MAJOR POINTS

Career Counseling in a Cultural Context

The first, and probably overarching, conclusion from a reading of these four chapters is, to quote Fouad, "Career counseling must take place within a cultural context," which includes not only knowledge of and respect for the values of other cultures, but comfort with and knowledge of one's *own* values and ethnicity. A cultural context is essential to effective career intervention because important variables in counseling may covary with ethnicity, and because a cultural context encourages the examination of variables heretofore not considered in such counseling.

An example of a variable that differs across cultures is values, for example, the greater emphasis on family and community orientation and the preference for cooperation among many racial and ethnic minority groups, versus the typical European-American orientations toward individualism and competition (Sue & Sue, 1990). Fouad writes, for example, about the contrast between Hispanic and White middle-class U.S. values. In contrast to the latter group's belief in mastery over nature, future time orientation, emphasis on doing, and emphasis on the individual is Hispanics' emphasis (as a group) on living in harmony with nature, living in the present, emphasis on being rather than doing, and subordination of individual to group goals. Martin notes that, among Native Americans, the home, family, and community are often more highly valued than jobs, career, or occupation. Leong and Gim summarize research suggesting that Asian Americans may be more likely to prefer extrinsic (e.g., security) to intrinsic (e.g., self-realization) work values and that they may be more conforming, externally oriented, and more socially anxious. They discuss the Chinese values of respect for authority and submergence of individuality.

Other important variables that covary with ethnicity are educational aspirations and attainments, where Hispanics, African Americans, and Native Americans are at a serious disadvantage, and Asian Americans, other than recent immigrants to this country, have done comparatively well. Given much lower rates of completion of high school among the former three groups than among Whites and Asian Americans, outreach programs into the elementary and secondary schools (like Fouad's Career Linking Program) are essential if the educational level, and thus the career options, of minority group members is to be increased. Interventions designed to stem the high rates of attrition of minorities from college degree programs are also needed (see Betz, 1991, for a fuller description of intervention and support programs within higher education).

Leong and Gim, Fouad, and Martin discuss what is (and is not) known about cultural variations in such traditional variables as career maturity and vocational interests. For example, Leong and Gim suggest that Asian Americans may more often prefer "dependent" decision-making styles than do Anglo Americans, but what our Eurocentric world view calls "dependent" decision-making styles could be reconceptualized as a "collectivist orientation" in decision making. It should be noted that our labeling of scales or variables *themselves* is a cultural construction in which the extent to which a group is described in more versus less favorable terms (e.g., collectivist orientation versus dependent) is essentially arbitrary and, therefore, influenced by researchers' biases.

Unless the counselor has knowledge of other cultures, he or she may erroneously assume that all individuals share Western, Eurocentric values. A useful term coined by Bem and Bem (1976) was that of *nonconscious ideology*, which refers to belief systems that are ingrained so deeply and subconsciously that we are not even aware that there are alternatives. The Bems' example is a fish who does not know that it lives in water. We believe that the Western value system has been a nonconscious ideology that is finally being challenged by the emergence of a cultural context in psychology.

Avoidance of Uniformity Assumptions

Although a general knowledge of other cultures is necessary, it is also important to avoid uniformity assumptions, that is, the assumption that all individuals of a given culture have the same values, goals, and experiences. The concept of individual differences is just as important when considering members of racial/ethnic minorities as with European-American clientele. Differences occur not only with one specific ethnic group, but across groups generally lumped under one "ethnicity." For example, Fouad distinguishes an "ethnic group" from a "racial group," noting that the term *Hispanic* connotes an ethnic group whose members can be of many different races (White, African American, and indigenous Native Americans). Country of origin varies from Mexico to countries in the Caribbean and Central and South America. Martin offers the striking statistic that among Native Americans there are some 509 nations, tribes, and Alakasan villages, each with its own traditions and, often, language (DeAngelis, 1992; cf. Martin, this volume). And yet another striking example is Leong and Gim's statement that the term *Asian-American* can be applied to persons from over half the globe, stretching from the Pacific Islands to the Middle East. Leong and Gim note the great variety even within members of one ethnic group—Chinese Americans have countries of origin ranging from the People's Republic of China to Taiwan to Malaysia and Singapore.

Martin (1991) provided what we believe is a useful integration of the need for a cultural context without homogenizing: "Career counselors cannot approach Indian clients as a homogeneous group but must be keenly aware of individual differences while at the same time giving consideration to potential cultural influences" (p. 280).

New Variables in Cultural Context

In addition to cultural covariations in variables traditionally included in career assessment and intervention are new variables that must be considered if the client is to be understood and effectively assisted.

One important new variable that emerges when career counseling is considered within a cultural context is that of *racial identity development*, as discussed in Bowman's chapter. Racial identity development includes the concept of client preferences regarding counselor ethnicity, perceptions of the openness of the occupational structure, and client responsiveness to counselor suggestions (Bowman, this volume). In turn, *counselor* racial identity affects the responses of counselors to African-American clients—Bowman paraphrases Helms (1991) as follows: "In *Autonomy* [the highest stage of identity development], Caucasians resonate to racial issues on an emotional and intellectual level.... A person in this stage seeks diversity, and understands that norms differ across cultures" (p. 46). A career counselor in this stage of racial identity development should be comfortable in addressing and discussing racial issues and factors with clients. A special issue of the *Journal of Vocational Behavior* (April 1994) is devoted to the topic of racial identity and vocational behavior.

Leong and Kim and Martin also introduce level of acculturation as an important variable in career counseling. Acculturation refers to acceptance/integration into self of the values of the dominant culture (White European in this case), and for those foreign born or whose recent ancestors were foreign born, generational status and degree of fluency in English are possible indicators of level of acculturation. Martin cites a model of acculturation originally proposed by LaFromboise, Trimble, and Mohatt (1990). Leong and Gim reported, for example, that high-acculturation Chinese-American children valued self-realization more than did low-acculturation Chinese-American children.

Another variable that must be introduced if a cultural context is to be adopted is *language usage*. For example, Martin notes that the extent to which an Indian person uses his or her native language, of which there are between 206 to 250, versus English will greatly influence decisions made in the career assessment and intervention process. Similarly, many Asian Americans and Hispanics are bilingual, and English may be a second rather than a first language. And some African Americans, too, may have come most recently from the Caribbean. Thus, a cultural context requires the inclusion of several *new* variables.

Race and Gender

A fourth major conclusion is that race and ethnicity must be, but often are *not*, considered in interaction with gender. Bowman discusses how research and writing throughout the years have focused on women or minorities as two separate "oppressed" groups, overlooking the fact that some people are both women *and* racial/ethnic minorities. Bowman cites Hull, Scott, and Smith's (1982) book title that poignantly conveys the feelings of invisibility of African-American women: *All the women are White, all the Blacks are men, but some of us are brave.* In this same vein, a few years ago the first author wrote a paper concerning the lack of women and non-Asian minorities in science and engineering (Betz, 1991), and although there were data for women versus men and across racial/ethnic groups, race and gender were never disaggregated, meaning that it was impossible to assess the representation of African-American or Asian-American women, for example, in science and engineering. Minority women are, in this sense, invisible.

The reality of the situation of ethnic minority women is one of double disadvantage economically and socially, because they are the victims of both racism and sexism. Also called *double jeopardy* (e.g., Beale, 1970), one result of this double "minority" status is that minority women have the lowest incomes of any group; not only do they earn less than Anglo men, but also minority men and Anglo women. Fouad cites research showing that Chicanas are severely underrepresented in institutions of higher education and are at the lowest levels of occupational attainment and income. In an important recent article, Reid (1993) noted the almost total ignorance of poor women in psychological research, women who are disproportionately African American and Latina. Her subtitle, "Shut up and shut out," refers to the silencing and invisibility of poor women.

One particularly important feature of the gender by ethnicity interaction is the differences in gender-role socialization and expectations for women's adult roles across groups. For example, most African-American women have always expected to work outside the home as adults (Bingham & Ward, 1994; Bowman, this volume), never having the Anglo woman's "luxury" of being a nonearner. And African-American women have been encouraged toward independence, self-sufficiency, and personal strength (Collins, 1991) rather than the traditional Anglo socialization of female dependency and lack of self-sufficiency. In contrast, Hispanic-American and Asian-American women have generally been subject to more traditional gender-role expectations. Fouad discusses the traditions of "machismo" and "machisma" in Hispanic cultures, noting the expectation that women will be passive, submissive, and dependent. Yang (1991) discussed the dilemmas of Chinese-American women caught between the Chinese emphasis on traditional female roles and the more common valuing of career roles for women in the United States. Counselors need to be aware of and respect cultural differences in gender-role expectations and help clients to integrate the sometimes contradictory forces of cultural values and personal beliefs and goals.

In addition to consideration of the race by gender interaction, Bowman suggests that Gainor and Forrest's (1991) model of African-American women's self-concept development may help women integrate rather than separate their gender and racial identities. This model that includes knowledge of oneself as a woman, as an African American, and as a unique individual, could be adapted as well for women of other ethnicities.

It is also useful to emphasize, as implied by Bowman, that some of the understandings gained from the study of women's career development more generally are also useful in counseling minority women. For example, the valuing of family as well as career, the perception of occupations closed to women, the perniciousness of the so-called Old Boy's System (more likely to include minority men than women of any race), the difficulty of finding quality child care, and the susceptibility of all women to sex discrimination, sexual harassment, and violence require those interested in counseling minority women to be conversant in both the women's and minority career development literature.

Inadequacy of Current Knowledge

Despite the recent upsurge of interest, it is clear in the area of career intervention and assessment with racial and ethnic minoritiesis that what we do not know far exceeds what we know. Fitzgerald and Betz (1992) compared representation of various groups (e.g., racial and ethnic minorities) in the labor force to the corresponding representation of those groups in career research. One of their striking findings was that, although the percentage of minorities in the labor force is now about 20% and is expected to reach one third early next century, only a very small fraction of research published in such journals as the *Journal of Vocational Behavior* and *Journal of Counseling Psychology* has addressed or included racial minority individuals. Compounding this relative invisibility in the literature is the relative invisibility of the non-college-educated, of whom racial and ethnic minorities comprise a disproportionate number (cf. Reid, 1993). As analyzed by Fitzgerald and Betz (1992), less than 25% of the work force possesses a college degree, but over 75% of the research database is comprised of college students and college-educated individuals. When the *joint* effects of racial and non-college-educated invisibility are considered, the lack of attention to members of racial/ethnic minority groups becomes even more striking.

Although these chapters, and (a few) other books and articles, are beginning to build a knowledge base in this area, the authors of these four chapters also note how little we actually know about using career assessment devices with minority clients or about effective career interventions. Based on the gaps they have pointed out, we proceed to make recommendations for future work in this area.

RECOMMENDATIONS FOR CAREER ASSESSMENT AND INTERVENTION

Next Steps in Career Assessment

There is both tremendous need and tremendous opportunity in the area of career assessment with members of racial and ethnic minority groups. The need results from the inadequate and spotty information base regarding the use of particular tests or inventories with particular minority groups—the most obvious kinds of information needed are relevant norms and evidence for reliability and validity. As discussed by Fouad (1993) and Leong and Gim (this volume), we know little, for example, about the utility of interest inventories with clients of different racial and ethnic groups. Work values measures (e.g., Minnesota Importance Questionnare, Work Values Inventory) do not necessarily incorporate the value systems of various important cultural groups and may therefore be inadequate for use with populations other than White European Americans. For example, values such as the uplifting of one's people, unity, and collective work and responsibility, stressed within some groups, may play a role in educational and career decisions and, therefore, should be included in measures of work values.

We suggest that a significant research program could result from the investigation of the utility of a particular assessment device (e.g., the Strong Interest Inventory) or one *class* of assessment devices (e.g., measures of career indecision) with a particular racial or ethnic minority group. Such specificity holds the greatest promise for systematic increases of knowledge in this area. Another possible strategy is cross-cultural comparisons of the utility of both specific measures and the theory underlying them. For example, Fouad's summary of evidence suggesting the validity of both Holland's theory and the Strong Interest Inventory for U.S. and Mexican engineers and lawyers provides a model of this kind of research.

In addition to research evaluating the applicability of various measures or classes of measures for minority groups, Leong and Gim note the need for research on Asians' attitudes toward and comfort with psychological testing, and this suggestion may be useful as well with other racial/ethnic groups. For example, they note that Asian Americans are more likely to live within authoritarian family and social systems and may thus be less likely to challenge the counselor's "authority" when he or she assigns and/or interprets a test. Thus, not only the test itself but the whole process of test administration and interpretation needs to be considered within a cultural context.

In addition to the examination of traditional assessment measures is the interview, which Hackett and Lonborg (1993) suggested be used to develop a "contextually-sensitive picture" (p. 200) of the client and her or his career-related concerns; although their article is addressed to the issue of career assessment with women, the importance of context, including race, ethnicity, gender, SES, and so on, applies to career counseling with *any* client. In this volume, for example, Martin proposes a "cultural and contextual guide for planning differential assessment and intervention with American Indians." This checklist includes questions about language usage, cultural orientation, home community, family system, and communication styles.

Of possibly more general use are materials suggested by Ward and Bingham (1993), who proposed the use of a Decision Tree designed to help the counselor decide when to consider racial or ethnic material. In the first step in assessment is the determination of whether a woman is seeking career or personal counseling. If the client's questions have to do with career issues, the counselor needs to assess the impact of culture (ethnicity), family influences, and finances. Ward and Bingham suggested that in some cases the examination of racial/ethnic issues may resolve the career issues, for example, by having the counselor challenge the client's beliefs that African-American women cannot be scientists or engineers.

A systematic method of inquiring about factors influencing the client's decisions, and also the counselor's readiness to incorporate a multicultural perspective in her or his counseling, is Bingham and Ward's Multicultural Career Counseling Checklist. The Multicultural Career Counseling Checklist contains 48 questions the counselor asks in the process of working a client of a different ethnicity than him- or herself. This assessment begins with self-assessment involving multicultural knowledge (e.g., the minimum cross-cultural competencies as outlined by Sue, Arrendondo, & McDavis, 1992), attitudes, and experiences. These questions contribute to an assessment of whether one has the background preparation and attitudes necessary to work effectively and proactively with minority clients.

The second set of questions ("Exploration and Assessment") taps family, cultural, financial, and self-concept influences on the client's current situation. The third section (Negotiation and Working Consensus) involves counselor–client discussion of and agreement on working goals of counseling, and knowledge of the appropriateness and utility of traditional versus nontraditional assessment instruments for use with this client.

Finally, Ward and Bingham (1993) offered a "career checklist" designed to provide a self-assessment for clients of beliefs about the process of making decisions, and the impact of such factors as race, gender, and age on career decisions. Most of these items resemble those found in existing measures of career indecision and career maturity. The checklist is currently a stimulus for counselor–client exploration and discussion rather than a scale of any kind.

Ward and Bingham suggested that the combined use of the Decision Tree, the Multicultural Career Counseling Checklist, and the Client Career Checklist will ensure a more complete assessment of ethnic minority women, but it is applicable to minority men as well. Further refinement of these potentially useful checklists is currently underway (Bingham, personal communication, August 1993).

Next Steps in Intervention Research and Development

Three themes are important in this area. These themes are: (a) the applicability of current approaches/theories to career counseling with racial/ethnic minority groups; (b) the need for the development and evaluation of interventions specifically designed for a particular minority group; and (c) the need for culturally sensitive counseling process.

Applicability of Current Approaches. Although the usefulness of vocational theory with racial and ethnic minority group members is reviewed in the first four chapters of this volume (Brown, Arbona, Leong and Serafica, and LaFromboise) and in Osipow's commentary, recommendations for career assessment and intervention cannot be made independent of the major theories that have guided counseling practice.

Models such as those of Holland, Super, Krumboltz, and Lofquist and Dawis have a rich tradition in career psychology. Fitzgerald and Rounds (1994) noted that more than 250 studies of the Theory of Work Adjustment confirm that the theory does have important implications for career counseling. Similarly, a voluminous literature exists supporting the general utility of Holland's theory (see Hackett & Lent, 1992, for a recent review), and there appears to be continuing strong interest in Super's developmental and Krumboltz's social learning theories (Hackett & Lent, 1992). It is premature to assume that such robust and rich models as Holland's theory do *not* work for minorities, but, on the other hand, we cannot assume without research evidence that they *do* work.

Therefore, we recommend more research attention to the usefulness of vocational theories within and across racial and ethnic groups and, in addition, studies comparing the utility of several theories for one racial or ethnic group. Illustrative programs of research along these lines were the studies of Walsh and his colleagues investigating the comparative validity of Holland's theory for African-American and White employed men and women (e.g., Greenlee, Damarin, & Walsh, 1988; Sheffey, Bingham, & Walsh, 1986; Walsh, Bingham, Horton, & Spokane, 1979). More recently, a series of articles in a special issue of the *Journal of Vocational Behavior* addressed the cross-cultural utility of Holland's postulates regarding the structure of interests (Fouad & Dancer, 1992; Swanson, 1992), suggesting that hexagonal order, although not necessarily shape, is invariant across different populations, including African Americans and Mexicans. However, further supporting our contention that the non-college-bound are largely ignored, even these studies of minorities focused on only college students and professionals. Thus, studies of applicability should not overlook SES, educational level, and gender as possible influential variables. As we have suggested elsewhere (Fitzgerald & Betz, 1992), relevance of career theory to large segments of the population is an open question.

We also suggest that each career theory be subject to a careful and detailed analysis of the roles of structural and cultural factors in both the conceptualization and measurement of its important variables, both dependent and independent. As defined and discussed by Fitzgerald and Betz (1992), structural factors are characteristics of the society or organization (including its people) that limit access to or opportunities in the occupational and/or organizational environment. Discrimination, poverty, and inadequate educational opportunities are examples. Cultural factors are beliefs and attitudes often found among group members—often these are socialized by society (i.e., occupational racial stereotypes), but after internalization they serve as self-perpetuating barriers to the individual.

More specifically, lack of educational opportunities often reduces the extent to which minority individuals are able to fully develop their abilities and talents, and the effects of discrimination have substantial adverse effects on minority career development (Hotchkiss & Borrow, 1990). As with occupational sex stereotypes, racial stereotypes lead to prejudice and, often, discrimination from others, but also may lead to self-selection into or out of occupations based on beliefs of racial appropriateness. For example, many young African-American women grew up believing that the only professional occupation open to them was teaching, and many Asian Americans have been expected to pursue careers in science and engineering regardless of suitability for them as individuals. Another important aspect of racial stereotyping as noted by Leong (1985) is the myth of Asians as the "model minority," the idea that they have "made it" in society and experience no prejudice nor discrimination and, thus, need no special attention from career educators or counselors.

The concept of structural and cultural factors in career choice has much in common with related ideas of barriers to career development, as proposed by Crites (1976) and as applied especially to the understanding of women's career development by Farmer (1976), Harmon (1977), and later Betz and Fitzgerald (1987). Related to the notion of barriers is Gottfredson's (1986) concept "risk factors" in career choice as especially useful in understanding problems faced by members of special groups, which include gender, racial/ethnic minorities, and handicapping conditions. Gottfredson presented a diagnostic framework that might be used for assessment and intervention in career counseling with racial/ethnic minorities as well as with other groups. And Osipow (1990) suggested that *all* career theories should be modified to include consideration of barriers to the implementation of desirable career choices. We believe that the framework of structural and cultural factors may be most useful because it does not assume that all *differences* are *harmful* (as do "barriers" and "risk factors" by definition) but, rather, that many groups differ from the "White male model" in important ways that require consideration and validation from career theorists and counselors.

In addition to the examination of existing theories of career development and counseling, we need evaluation of the effectiveness of existing interventions with members of racial/ethnic groups, for example, computer-assisted methods such as SIGI and Discover, the Vocational Card Sort, and career groups. As with assessment, important programs of research would result from the intersection of one theory or intervention and one racial or ethnic group.

Specially Focused Interventions. All four chapters discuss both special *needs* of clients of their ethnic group and possible unique or special interventions deriving from those needs. For example, Bowman's discussion of intervention needs is extensive and focuses on the importance (and lack) of same-race role models, especially within the technological fields, for African and Native Americans and Hispanics, and the lack of same-race mentors. Again, attention to the gender–race interaction is important, as minority women may benefit from (the few) models and mentors who are both female and minority.

Bowman also distinguishes and illustrates possible individual, self-directed, and group interventions for use with African-American clients. She suggests that although general models of career counseling (e.g., that of Yost & Corbishley, 1987) are useful with minority clients, special efforts to examine both internal (e.g., low self-esteem, anxiety) and external (e.g., discrimination, perceptions of occupations closed to certain minority groups, etc.) constraints and barriers are necessary. Bowman's recommendation that self-directed career decision-making programs be used with clients who have adequate levels of career maturity and vocational identity and are not chronically undecided applies equally well to racial "majority" clients as well, and, in both cases, a counselor needs to be available if unforeseen problems arise. Fouad and Martin both emphasize the potential utility for minorities of social learning theory models—Martin emphasizes Krumboltz's theory and Fouad suggests the utility of self-efficacy theory (Bandura, 1977; Betz, 1992; Hackett & Betz, 1981). Because these models provide means of learning new skills and behaviors, especially beliefs of one's own competence, they may be especially useful for minority youth.

We believe that Bowman's most important emphasis is that on the usefulness of group interventions with African-American clients. Bowman suggests that African Americans may be more group centered and find group counseling more comfortable and less threatening, especially in racially homogeneous groups. We would add that, for minority women, women's groups may also provide a forum for the discussion of gender issues in career development. Martin cites LaFromboise et al.'s (1990) "network therapy," which is a contextual model more similar to traditional Indian community-oriented guidance systems. With Asians, groups may *not* be advisable given the great emphasis on privacy of the family. However, outreach and inclusion of parents in interventions may be useful.

Both Bowman and Fouad emphasize the need for math and science awareness interventions. Fouad's Career Linking program, used with inner-city middle school students, provides a model for such program development and may be particularly helpful in being directed at younger individuals. Bowman describes a career intervention (Dunn & Veltman, 1989) focusing on science, math, and engineering careers for minority high school juniors and a program (Rea-Poteat & Martin, 1991) to encourage girls to explore technologically based occupations.

Bowman also describes additional special programs directed at minority youth. One special focus may be in assisting in school-to-work transitions. Fitzgerald and Betz (1992) noted the lack of attention to non-college-degreed individuals in career psychology. Fortunately, this group, many if not most of whom are minorities, is the focus of a major new research and intervention effort of the Grant Foundation (1988) and the American Counseling Association (Herr, 1992). Calling these young people "work-bound youth" rather than the more often used terms of "non-college-bound" or "the forgotten half" (Grant Foundation, 1988) highlights the need for job training and programs for facilitating the school-to-job transition. The structural and cultural barriers faced by these young people (e.g., see Hotchkiss & Borrow, 1990) warrant theoretical consideration as well as extensive and appropriate intervention.

A very basic point that Bowman makes concerns the necessity of simply *identifying* research participants' racial or ethnic group membership, so that readers may evaluate the representativeness of the findings and their potential relevance (or lack thereof) to a group in which they are interested. Unfortunately, many researchers (and editors) have failed to follow this guideline—Fitzgerald and Betz (1992) noted that, in a typical volume of the *Journal of Vocational Behavior* published in the 1980s, fewer than 20% of the articles reported participant ethnicity.

Culturally Sensitive Counseling Process. Leong's (1993) application of Sue's model of cross-cultural counseling to career counseling may be very helpful if the concepts of appropriate versus inappropriate process and goals are applied to other racial and ethnic groups. Leong's (1993) examples of inappropriate process and goals are from the Asian-American culture, but the ways of being a "good-hearted bumbler" are probably infinite if one considers the many extant cultural groups. We will almost certainly violate the personal goals and cultural values of our clients if we do not learn more about other cultures.

To avoid such bumbling, Leong suggests that counselors increase their awareness of Asian styles of communication, values regarding the importance of the family, impact of fluency in language, and expectations of counseling, among other dimensions. As mentioned earlier, the importance of such values differences as the collective versus individualistic orientation, which translates into strong parental influence to pursue certain majors and/or careers, cannot be overemphasized. As so well stated by Leong and Gim, telling an Asian client that "It's your life, do what you want to do, don't let them make your decisions for you" illustrates "Missed by a Mile" counseling technique. Rather, the counselor needs to help the client evaluate the functional versus dysfunctional (in *this* culture) aspects of traditional values and beliefs and to make decisions that include elements of both self-valuing and respect for traditional beliefs.

We especially liked Leong's point that, although the counselor should be aware of and *respect* other cultural values, such values need to be discussed in the context of the realities of the educational and occupational world. His example of the possible need for assertiveness training when the traditional Asian style of communication is nonassertive is a good one—the counselor helps the client to acquire a needed skill but helps the client to understand that he or she can choose when and where to use it. Leong also discusses the findings that Asian Americans may be particularly likely to seek career counseling as less stigmatizing than personal counseling, therefore often attempting to mask a need for the latter, and that they may prefer more directive, structured counseling approaches to less structured ones.

As Bowman remarks, it is impossible for a career counselor to know everything about every culture. One can, however, be aware that one does *not* know everything, to acknowledge that fact, and to be open to continued learning. In sum, what is necessary is an attitude—an attitude not only respectful of, but valueing diversity as enhancing the richness of one's life.

SUMMARY

We conclude by noting that, although a multicultural focus and emphasis within career psychology primarily enhance the quality of services to members of previously neglected groups, the entire field of career psychology will gain from the integration of the values and strategies of other cultures. Our knowledge of strategies of multiple role management—currently a "hot topic" in the study of women's career development—could have been enhanced years ago by systematically including African-American women in our studies. Similarly, there is evidence that African-American women have long been encouraged toward independence, self-sufficiency, and personal strength (Collins, 1991), aspects traditionally associated with masculinity, as well as traditionally feminine qualities such as nurturance and emotional expressiveness. In other words, African-American women were modeling psychological androgyny long before it became fashionable in the literature. Thus, learning about other cultures cannot help but enrich our own theoretical perspectives, as well as improve our counseling and research.

It is gratifying to see increased attention in the last few years to career counseling and assessment with members of racial and ethnic minority groups. This book represents a landmark volume on this topic, but we should also highlight several special issues of journals focused on this issue. The September/October (1991) issue of the *Journal of Counseling and Development* focused on "Multiculturalism as a Fourth Force in Counseling" (Pedersen, 1991a); the March 1991 issue of *Career Development Quarterly* concerned racial/ethnic minorities. The September 1993 special issue of the *Career Development Quarterly* (Savickas, 1993) was entitled "Multicultural Career Counseling," the Summer/Fall 1993 issue of the *Journal of Career Assessment* focusing on career assessment with women contained an important article on ethnic minority women by Ward and Bingham (1993), the April 1994 issue of the *Journal of Vocational Behavior* contained a special issue on the topic of racial identity and vocational behavior, and an issue of Volume 2 (1994) of the *Journal of Career Assessment* is devoted to career assessment with racial and ethnic minorities. Articles relevant to a multicultural focus in counseling more generally include Betancourt and Lopez (1993) and Pedersen (1991b).

With all this attention, we look forward to the publication of the second edition of this volume, which we hope will appear sometime early in the next century. We expect that what we know 10 years from now about career assessment and counseling with racial/ethnic minorities will have expanded greatly from our present inadequate knowledge base—this expansion of knowledge represents a crucial yet exciting challenge for counseling, vocational, and multicultural psychology.

ACKNOWLEDGMENTS

We would like to thank Rosie P. Bingham and Connie M. Ward for their helpful comments and suggestions regarding this chapter.

REFERENCES

Bandura, A. (1977). Self-efficacy: Toward a unifying theory of behavioral change. *Psychological Review, 84*, 191–215.

Beale, F. (1970). Double jeopardy: To be black and female. In T. Cade (Ed.), *The black woman: An anthology* (pp. 90–100). New York: New American Library.

Bem, S. L., & Bem, D. J. (1976). Case study of a nonconscious ideology: Training the woman to know her place. In S. Cox (Ed.), *Female psychology* (pp. 180–191). Chicago: Science Research Associates.

Betancourt, H., & Lopez, S. R. (1993). The study of culture, race, and ethnicity in American psychology. *American Psychologist, 48*, 629–637.

Betz, N. E. (1991). *What stops women and minorities from choosing and completing majors in science and engineering.* Washington, DC: Federation of Behavioral, Psychological, and Cognitive Sciences.

Betz, N. E. (1992). Counseling uses of career self-efficacy theory. *Career Development Quarterly, 41*, 22–26.

Betz, N. E., & Fitzgerald, L. F. (1987). *The career psychology of women.* New York: Academic Press.

Bingham, R. P., & Ward, C. M. (1994). Career counseling with ethnic minority women. In W. B. Walsh & S. H. Osipow (Eds.), *Career counseling for women* (pp. 165–196). Hillsdale, NJ: Lawrence Erlbaum Associates.

Collins, P. H. (1991). *Black feminist thought.* New York: Routledge.

Crites, J. O. (1976). A comprehensive model of career development in early adulthood. *Journal of Vocational Behavior, 9*, 105–118.

DeAngelis, T. (1992). Division 38 conference explores ethnic-minority health issues. *APA Monitor*, pp. 32–33.

Dunn, C. W., & Veltman, G. C. (1989). Addressing the restrictive career maturity patterns of minority youth: A program evaluation. *Journal of Multicultural Counseling and Development, 17*, 156–164.

Farmer, H. S. (1976). What inhibits achievement and career motivation in women? *The Counseling Psychologist, 6*, 12–14.

Fitzgerald, L., & Betz, N. (1992, April). *Career development in cultural context: The role of gender, race, class, and sexual orientation.* Paper presented at the conference on Theories Convergence in Vocational Psychology, East Lansing, MI.

Fitzgerald, L. F., & Rounds, J. B. (1994). Women and work: Theory encounters reality. In W. B. Walsh & S. H. Osipow (Eds.), *Career counseling for women.* Hillsdale, NJ: Lawrence Erlbaum Associates.

Fouad, N. (1993). Cross-cultural vocational assessment. *Career Development Quarterly, 42,* 4–13.

Fouad, N. A., & Dancer, L. S. (1992). Cross-cultural structure of interests: Mexico and the United States. *Journal of Vocational Behavior, 40,* 129–143.

Gainor, K. A., & Forrest, L. (1991). African American women's self-concept: Implications for career decisions and career counseling. *Career Development Quarterly, 39,* 261–272.

Gottfredson, L. S. (1986). Special groups and the beneficial use of vocational interest inventories. In W. B. Walsh & S. Osipow (Eds.), *Advances in vocational psychology: Vol. 1. The assessment of interests* (pp. 127–198). Hillsdale, NJ: Lawrence Erlbaum Associates.

Grant Foundation. (1988). *The forgotten half: Non-college bound youth in America.* Washington, DC: William T. Grant Foundation Commission on Work, Family, and Citizenship.

Greenlee, S. D., Damarin, F. L., & Walsh, W. B. (1988). Congruence and differentiation among black and white males in two non-college degree occupations. *Journal of Vocational Behavior, 32,* 298–306.

Hackett, G., & Betz, N. E. (1981). A self-efficacy approach to the career development of women. *Journal of Vocational Behavior, 18,* 326–339.

Hackett, G., & Lent, R. W. (1992). Theoretical advances and current inquiry in career psychology. In S. D. Brown & R. W. Lent (Eds.), *Handbook of counseling psychology* (2nd ed., pp. 419–452). New York: Wiley.

Hackett, G., & Lonborg, S. D. (1993). Career assessment for women: Trends and issues. *Journal of Career Assessment, 1,* 197–216.

Harmon, L. W. (1977). Career counseling for women. In E. Rawlings & D. Carter (Eds.), *Psychotherapy for women* (pp. 197–206). Springfield, IL: Thomas.

Helms, J. A. (1991). *Black and White racial identity: Theory, research, and practice.* Westport, CT: Greenwood.

Herr, E. (1992). *The school counselor and comprehensive programs for work-bound youth.* Alexandria, VA: American Counseling Association.

Hotchkiss, L., & Borrow, H. (1990). Sociological perspectives on work and career development. In D. Brown & Brooks (Eds.), *Career choice and development* (2nd ed., pp. 262–307). San Francisco: Jossey-Bass.

Hull, G. T., Scott, P. B., & Smith, B. (1982). *All the women are White, All the Blacks are men, but some of us are brave.* New York: The Feminist Press.

LaFromboise, T. D., Trimble, J. E., & Mohatt, G. V. (1990). Counseling intervention and American Indian tradition: An integrative approach. *The Counseling Psychologist, 18,* 628–654.

Leong, F. T. (1985). Career development of Asian Americans. *Journal of College Student Personnel, 26,* 539–546.

Leong, F. T. L. (1993). The career counseling process with racial-ethnic minorities: The case of Asian-Americans. *Career Development Quarterly, 42,* 26–40.

Martin, W. E., Jr. (1991). Career development and American Indians living on reservations: Cross cultural factors to consider. *Career Development Quarterly, 39,* 273–283.

Osipow, S. H. (1990). Convergence in theories of career choice and development: Review and prospect. *Journal of Vocational Behavior, 36,* 122–131.

Pedersen, P. B. (Ed.). (1991a). Multiculturalism as a fourth force in counseling [Special issue]. *Journal of Counseling and Development, 70*(1).

Pedersen, P. B. (1991b). Multiculturalism as a generic approach to counseling. *Journal of Counseling and Development, 70,* 6–12.

Rea-Poteat, M. B., & Martin, P. F. (1991). Taking your place: A summer program to encourage nontraditional career choices for adolescent girls. *Career Development Quarterly, 40*(2), 182–188.

Reid, P. T. (1993). Poor women in psychological research: Shut up and shut out. *Psychology of Women Quarterly, 17,* 133–150.

Savickas, M. L. (Ed.). (1993). A symposium on multicultural career counseling [Special issue]. *Career Development Quarterly, 42*(1).

Sheffey, M. A., Bingham, R. P., & Walsh, W. B. (1986). Concurrent validity of Holland's theory for college educated Black men. *Journal of Multicultural Counseling and Development, 14,* 149–159.

Sue, D. W., Arredondo, P., & McDavis, R. J. (1992). Multicultural counseling competencies and standards: A call to the profession. *Journal of Multicultural Counseling and Development, 20,* 64–88.

Sue, D. W., & Sue, D. (1990). *Counseling the culturally different: Theory and practice.* New York: Wiley.

Swanson, J. L. (1992). The structure of vocational interests for African-American college students. *Journal of Vocational Behavior, 40,* 144–157.

Walsh, W. B., Bingham, R., Horton, J. A., & Spokane, A. (1979). Holland's theory and college-degreed working black and white women. *Journal of Vocational Behavior, 15,* 217–223.

Ward, C. M., & Bingham, R. P. (1993). Career assessment of ethnic minority women. *Journal of Career Assessment, 1,* 246–257.

Yang, J. (1991). Career counseling of Chinese American women: Are they in limbo? *The Career Development Quarterly, 39,* 350–359.

Yost, E. B., & Corbishley, M. A. (1987). *Career counseling: A psychological approach.* San Francisco: Jossey-Bass.

The Editor and Contributors

EDITOR

Frederick T. L. Leong, PhD

Dr. Frederick Leong is an Associate Professor of Psychology at The Ohio State University. He obtained his PhD from the University of Maryland with a double specialty in Counseling and Industrial/Organizational Psychology. He completed a 2-year internship in psychodynamic psychotherapy in the Department of Psychiatry at Dartmouth Medical School. Currently he serves as a faculty member in both the Counseling and Industrial and Organizational Psychology programs at The Ohio State University. Dr. Leong is the recipient of the 1993 Division of Counseling Psychology Early Career Scientist-Practitioner Award and a Fellow of the American Psychological Association. His current and past service on editorial boards has included the *Journal of Vocational Behavior, Career Development Quarterly, Journal of College Student Development,* and the *Journal of Counseling Psychology.* He has over 40 publications in various counseling and psychology journals and 12 book chapters. He was the Guest Editor for the recent special issue of the *Career Development Quarterly* (March 1991) on the career development of racial and ethnic minorities. He is also the co-editor of the recently published *Womanpower: Managing in Times of Demographic Turbulence* (1992) (with Uma Sekaran) from Sage and the APA Bibliography entitled, *Asians in the United States: Abstracts of the Psychological and Behavioral Literature, 1967–1991* (1992) (with James

Whitfield). He has given invited presentations and conducted workshops for the Amos Tuck Business School, AT&T Bell Labs, Sandia National Laboratories, Procter & Gamble, and various universities and national conventions. His major research interests are in vocational psychology, cross-cultural psychology (particularly culture and mental health), organizational behavior, and personality and adjustment.

CONTRIBUTORS

Consuelo Arbona, PhD

Dr. Consuelo Arbona specializes in cross-cultural psychology and career and vocational counseling with an emphasis on Hispanic populations. In her research she has examined issues related to the career development of Hispanic and other minority college students including career aspirations, factors associated with college achievement and persistence, and the measurement of acculturation and ethnic identity. Her published work includes an extensive literature review of the career counseling literature with Hispanics, and a chapter about Hispanic Americans in a recently published book titled *Encyclopedia of Career and Work Issues*. In this work she has examined the applicability of career-related theories and instruments for Hispanic populations. She received a BA degree from the College of New Rochelle, MEd from the University of Puerto Rico, and a PhD in counseling psychology from the University of Wisconsin–Madison. Prior to joining the University of Houston's faculty, she taught in school and community-based programs in Puerto Rico and in the United States and worked as a counselor in a community-based youth leadership development program in Puerto Rico.

Nancy E. Betz, PhD

Dr. Betz is a Professor of Psychology at The Ohio State University. She received a PhD in psychology from the University of Minnesota in 1976. Since joining the faculty at Ohio State in 1976, her research and teaching interests have focused in the areas of psychological testing, barriers to women's and minorities' pursuit of many career fields, and the applications of self-efficacy theory to career choice and adjustment. She has delivered presentations to national congressional groups on the underrepresentation of women and minorities in the sciences and engineering and is a past recipient of the John Holland Award for Research in Career and Personality Psychology. She served as Editor of the *Journal of Vocational Behavior* from 1984 to 1990 and has also served on the Editorial

Boards of the *Journal of Counseling Psychology, Journal of Vocational Behavior, Journal of Career Assessment,* and *Psychology of Women Quarterly.* She is a Fellow of the American Psychological Association and American Psychological Society. During the 1985–1986 academic year, Professor Betz was a Visiting Scholar at Stanford University and the University of California at Santa Barbara.

Sharon L. Bowman, PhD

Dr. Bowman, a 1989 graduate of Southern Illinois University–Carbondale, is a certified counseling psychologist. She is currently an Assistant Professor in the Department of Counseling Psychology and Guidance Services at Ball State University in Muncie, Indiana. Dr. Bowman's teaching load includes graduate courses on career theory and development, multicultural counseling and development, and theories of supervision. She supervises an undergraduate course in cross-cultural issues. She has also taught courses in human development (undergraduate) and research methods (master's level). Dr. Bowman's research interests are in the areas of multicultural psychology and career development. She has six publications on various topics (including career development of Black college students and college knowledge of first-generation college students) published in the *Journal of Counseling Psychology, Journal of College Student Development, Guidance and Counseling, Career Development Quarterly,* and *Educational and Psychological Measurement.* Dr. Bowman has also presented over 25 times at various local, regional, and national conventions, including the conventions of the American Psychological Association, Association of Black Psychologists, and American College Personnel Association. She is presently the Chair of the American College Personnel Association's Commission IX (Assessment for Student Development).

Michael T. Brown, PhD

Dr. Brown is a psychologist and an Associate Professor of Counseling Psychology at The University of California at Santa Barbara. Previously he was a psychologist and assistant professor at Wayne State University in Detroit, Michigan and at Ball State University in Muncie, Indiana. Dr. Brown holds PhD and MA degrees in Counseling Psychology from Southern Illinois University at Carbondale. He also earned a BA degree in Psychology from The University of California at Irvine. He is on the editorial boards of the *Journal of Counseling Psychology* and the *Journal of Vocational Behavior* and has published numerous articles focusing primarily on career behavior.

Louise F. Fitzgerald, PhD

Dr. Fitzgerald received her PhD in Psychology from the Ohio State University in 1979. She has held faculty positions at Kent State University, the University of California at Santa Barbara, and is currently an Associate Professor in the Psychology Department at the University of Illinois. She is an internationally known scholar in the field of women's career development, especially in the area of sexual harassment. Her research in this area has been the basis of the prosecution of numerous sexual harassment court cases, including the recent Supreme Court review of *Harris v. U.S. Forklift*. She has delivered invited addresses for such audiences as the American Association for the Advancement of Science and the Federation of Cognitive, Behavioral, and Psychological Sciences. In addition, she has recently turned her attention as well to the role of race, ethnicity, and social class factors in career development. She co-authored the book *The Career Psychology of Women* with Nancy Betz and has agreed to serve as coauthor for the current revision of Samuel H. Osipow's classic text *Theories of Career Development*. Dr. Fitzgerald has served on several Editorial Boards, including the *Journal of Vocational Behavior* and has received several awards and honors, including Fellowship in the American Psychological Association and American Psychological Society and the John Holland Award for Research in Career and Personality Psychology. During the 1994 academic year she was on sabbatical at the University of Liden, The Netherlands.

Nadya A. Fouad, PhD

Dr. Fouad is an associate professor in the Department of Educational Psychology at the University of Wisconsin–Milwaukee. She has done extensive research on the impact of culture on vocational assessment across both national and ethnic boundaries, focusing on interest, values, and career maturity assessment. For the past 3 years, she has been intensively involved in researching and implementing career development interventions in urban high schools. Most recently, she is the director of a project focusing on math and science career awareness for minority youths funded by the National Science Foundation. She was the 1991 recipient of the AACD Ralph Berdie Award for Research. She is on three editorial boards, including *Journal of Vocational Behavior* and *Career Development Quarterly*, and is actively involved in American Psychological Association and American Association of Counseling and Development.

Ruth H. Gim-Chung, PhD

Dr. Gim-Chung received her PhD in counseling psychology from University of California, Santa Barbara and is currently an assistant professor in the psychology department at Pomona College and the director of the

Asian American Resource Center. Gim's dissertation was a comparative study of values and career choice among African, Asian, Chicano/Latino, and European Americans.

Marilyn J. Johnson, PhD

Dr. Johnson is a member of the Acoma tribe in New Mexico. She holds a doctorate in Special Education from Arizona State University. She is the former director of the American Indian Rehabilitation Research and Training Center at Northern Arizona University. During a 2-year stint, she worked in the Office of Indian Education Programs for the Bureau of Indian Affairs in Washington, DC. Currently, she is engaged in community development efforts focused on training and employment opportunities for people with disabilities.

Eugia Littlejohn, MA

Dr. Littlejohn is a doctoral candidate in Counseling Psychology in the Department of Psychology at The Ohio State University. Her interests include ethnic minorities' and women's issues, particularly pertaining to identity development. In addition to the present chapter, Eugia also co-authored a chapter on African-American communication styles, which appears in *Valuing Diversity and Similarities* edited by P. J. Wittmer. Presently Eugia is a member of the Association of Black Psychologists in which she serves as the Midwestern Region Representative of the Student Division. She is also the immediate past president of the Black Graduate Students in Psychology of The Ohio State University.

William E. Martin Jr., EdD

Dr. Martin is currently Associate Professor and Chair of the Educational Psychology Area in the Center for Excellence in Education at Northern Arizona University (NAU). Prior to this appointment he was the Assistant Director for Adult Programs and the Research Director for the American Indian Rehabilitation Research and Training Center (AIRRTC) at NAU. Dr. Martin's research activities relate to ecological psychology, differential psychology, and rehabilitation psychology. In recent years his research activities have focused on community-based research relative to the rehabilitation and vocational concerns of American Indians.

Samuel H. Osipow, PhD

Dr. Osipow is Professor and past Chair of the Department of Psychology at The Ohio State University. He is the author of *Theories of Career Development*, now in its third edition, founding editor of the *Journal of Vocational*

Behavior, past editor of the *Journal of Counseling Psychology*, and current editor of *Applied and Preventive Psychology*. He is also the codeveloper of the *Career Decision Scale*, the *Occupational Stress Inventory*, and the *Task Specific Scale of Occupational Self Efficacy*. He served as President of the Division of Counseling Psychology of the American Psychological Association in 1977–1978 and as Chair of the Board of Directors of the Council of the National Register of Health Service Providers in Psychology from 1986 to 1989.

Felicisima C. Serafica, PhD

Dr. Serafica, Associate Professor of Psychology at The Ohio State University, received her PhD degree from Clark University. Her specialty fields are clinical child psychology and developmental psychology. Research interests include social development, adolescent career development, developmental psychopathology, and ethnic/minority mental health. Drawing from contemporary theories and research on development of the self-system, her current work attempts to validate and extend Super's career development theory to special populations such as parochial high school students and adolescents with specific learning disabilities. She is co-author of *Psychodynamics in a Philippine Setting*, editor of *Social Cognitive Development in Context*, and co-editor of *Ethnic Minority Mental Health*. Her professional activities include service on federal research grant review panels and journal editorial boards.

Jody L. Swartz, MA

Dr. Swartz is currently a doctoral student in Educational Psychology with an emphasis in Counseling Psychology at Northern Arizona University. She received her Master of Arts in Counseling from the same institution and completed 1-year postmasters training at New Mexico State University. Her research interests include prevention and treatment of substance abuse, ecological psychology, and counseling process and theory with ethnically and racially diverse individuals.

Author Index

Subject Index

A

Abilities, 254
Ability Test, 1, 25
Academic performance, 205–206
Acculturation, 43–48, 51, 61, 63–64, 142, 168, 170, 172, 183, 186, 194–195, 198, 206–209, 210–211, 216, 217, 221, 234–235, 238
Acculturation continuum, 107–108
Achievement
  academic/educational/school, 38, 41, 50, 55, 58–62
  career, 58
  of ethnic identity, 53
  need for, 51
  of a sense of self, 52
Action, 119
African-American life, 7, 8
Alaska natives, 103
American experience, 252
Applicability
  of current approaches, 271, 272, 273
  to Native Americans, 126–129
Aspirations, 20, 21
  career/vocational, 145, 146–148, 152, 156
  educational, 146–148, 160–161

Assessment, 109, 126, 127, 166, 175 176, 181, 182
  of career interests, 69–70, 195–198
    and assimilation, 196
    and aesthetic–cultural fields, 195
    technical applied fields, 195
    methodological issues, 89–90, 92–93
Assimilation, 234, 237
Associative, 117
Assumptions underlying, 110
Attending skills, 240, 243
Attitudes, 24, 28
Average family income, 7
Avoidance
  of discrimination, 22, 23
  of uniformity assumptions, 265

B

Bandura's Social Learning Theory, 115–116
Barker's Theory of Ecological Psychology, 122
Barriers to attainment, 146, 147, 155, 160, 161
Biculturality, 44, 46, 63, 234, 237, 207–208
Bracero program, 39

297

tasks, 50, 53
testing, 203–204
theory, 252
 developmental–contextual, 48, 56, 59
Cheatham's Africentric model, 17
Chicana, 177, 188
Class differences, 255
Cognitive processes, 116
College Self-Efficacy Instrument, 61
Colorism, 18, 19, 27
Communication
 disorders, 232
 style, 230, 239–240, 243–244
Congruence, 14, 16, 114
Consistency, 16, 114
Contemporaneity, 122
Correspondence, 114
Cultural and contextual guide, Indians, 228
Cultural attitudes, 18
Cultural environmental context, 240, 244
Cultural heritage, 104
Cultural infusion, 235
Cultural orientation, 230, 234–235, 239, 240, 242
Cultural pluralism, 177
Cultural values, 165, 166, 170, 174, 180, 183, 186, 188, 253
Cultural variables
 acculturation, 266
 decision tree, 270
 gender, 266–268
 language usage, 266
 and racial identity, 266
 values, 264, 276
 uniformity assumptions, 265

D

Developmental tasks, 238
Differentiation, 16, 114
Discrimination, 43–44, 47–48, 62, 271, 272
 race, 73, 145
 women, 144, 145
Double jeopardy, 267
Drop out, 174
Dual-career families, 144, 145

E

Eco-map, 123–124
Ecological environment, 122

Ecological perspective, 227, 229–230
Ecological psychology theory, 103, 120–126
Ecological structures, 123–124
Ecological transition, 124
Economic development, 106–107
Education, 105–106, 165, 173, 175, 177, 180–182, 184, 186, 188, 190–191
 attainment gender, 165, 167, 174, 176, 184, 190
 choices, 60
 versus occupational attainment, parental influences, 73
Employment, 106–107
Environmental conditions, 116–117
Eskimo, 236
Ethnic differences, 19
Ethnic-specific role models, 221–222
Existence, 122
Expectations, 20, 21, 27
 and athletic activities, 20
 and socioeconomic status, 19, 21
 versus aspirations, 21
External pressures, 109

F

Face, 74, 86
Family network map, 123
Family occupational patterns, 74
Family system, 230, 239–239, 243, 248
Focusing skills, 240, 241, 243

G

Gender, 43, 55–56, 60–61
 and race, 266–268
 differences, 19, 21, 24, 26, 27, 28, 41, 51, 60
 and aspirations, 21
 and geographic origin, 21
 and occupational barriers, 21
 and occupational choices, 21
 and self-efficacy, 21
 and vocational self-concepts, 21
 and work-related expectations, 21
 dominated or consistent occupations, 60
 education attainment, 208, 209–210
 effects, 60
 identity, 55

Metacognition, 233
Methodological issues
  acculturation, 91
  assessment, 89–90, 92
  ethnic identity, 91
  instrumentation, 35
  perceived minority status, 91–92
Microskills, 240
Middle class, 39, 44, 51, 57, 62
  males, careers of, 252
Migration, 39, 62
  history of, 43–45
  status, 43
Minority
  adolescents, 52, 59
  and ethnic psychology, 38
  ethnic, 38, 50
  group members or population, 43, 47,
    50, 52, 55, 62
  individual, 52–53
  status, 61–62
Model minority myth, 85–86, 87
Molar activities, 125, 126

N

National Career Development Association,
  144
Native Americans, 103
Navajo, 230, 234, 239, 241
Needs, 254
Network therapy, 229
Nonconscious ideology, 265

O

Occupational aspirations, 51, 56, 59
Occupational attainment, 38, 42, 47, 56, 166,
  174, 177–178, 186–187, 202, 203, 208
Occupational behavior, 44
Occupation commitment, 53
Occupational discrimination
  model minority, 85
  university setting, 87–89
Occupational distribution, 7
  within Hispanic subgroups, 41–42
Occupational history, 43–45
Occupational identity, 52
Occupational interests, 19
Occupational mobility, 62
Occupational options, 198, 219 ,220

Occupational segregation
  and career choice, 82–83
  representation index, 81–82
Occupational self-efficacy, 60–62
Occupational sex typing, 23
Occupational socialization, 57
Occupational status, 44–45
Occupational stereotypes, 80, 82, 272
  and career interests, 85
  definition, 85
  relevant research, 78–80
Occupational values
  assessment, 198,199
  awareness of work value alternatives, 198
  nonculture specific sex differences, 198
  object orientation, 198
  work value orientations, 198
On reservation/off reservation, 104
On-the-job-training (OJT), 245

P

Parent–child relations, 13, 22
Parental influence
  and occupational aspirations, 22
  and racial/ethnic differences, 22, 27
Pequis, 237
Perceived minority status, 91–92
Performance accomplishments, 62
Performance incentives, 61
Person–environment theory, 103, 110
Personality
  assessment, 199, 200
  externally orientated, 200
  field dependent cognitive style, 201
  intolerance of ambiguity, 199, 202
  locus of control, 199
  orientation, 15
  structure hypothesis, 201
  social anxiety, 199, 200, 201
  submergence of individual, 200
  types, 111
Political and economic enclaves, 40
Political consequences, 62
Process, 19–20, 110, 115, 119, 120, 125–126

R

Race, 44–45, 51–52
  characteristics, 48,51
  differences, 19, 22, 23, 24, 26